Warren Johansson, MA
William A. Percy, PhD

D0209212

Outing: Shattering the Conspiracy of Silence

More pre-publication
REVIEWS, COMMENTARIES, EVALUATIONS . . .

"Warren Johansson and William A. Percy have written A SYMPATHETIC, COMPASSIONATE HISTORY OF OUTING, VOLUNTARY OR ENFORCED, WHICH AT THE SAME TIME SHOULD PROVE BOTH USEFUL AND CONTROVERSIAL. Although they identify literally a thousand or so individuals as gay or lesbian, it is not a book of lists, but a serious discussion of the causes and consequences of outing. They are particularly cautious in identifying historical personages as gay or lesbian, but they also mention individuals identified by others who do not meet their standards and indicate why they would not label them as gay or lesbian.

Ultimately, they conclude that outing has a historic mission, a necessary part of the emancipation of homosexuals and lesbians to overcome the deception and hypocrisy so rampant in society . . . . In short, what Johansson and Percy have done is give us a much better understanding of what it has meant to be gay or lesbian in the past and the various tentative steps that gays and lesbians have taken to remove the stigma from their beings, of which outing is the latest. The result is a significant and fascinating easy-to-read discussion of what being different has meant to gays and lesbians, and one from which both heterosexuals and homosexuals can benefit. I would strongly recommend it to both groups."

Vern L. Bullough, PhD, RN
SUNY Distinguished Professor,
SUNY College, Buffalo

Harrington Park Press
An Imprint of The Haworth Press, Inc.

Outing
Shattering the Conspiracy of Silence

HAWORTH Gay and Lesbian Studies
John P. De Cecco, PhD
Editor in Chief

Outing
Shattering the Conspiracy of Silence

Warren Johansson, MA
William A. Percy, PhD

Harrington Park Press
An Imprint of The Haworth Press, Inc.
New York • London • Norwood (Australia)

Published by

Harrington Park Press, an imprint of The Haworth Press, Inc., 10 Alice Street, Binghamton, NY
13904-1580

Library of Congress Cataloging-in-Publication Data

Johansson, Warren.
    Outing : shattering the conspiracy of silence / Warren Johansson, William A. Percy.
       p.   cm.
    Includes bibliographical references and index.
    ISBN 1-56023-041-X (acid-free paper).
    1. Gay liberation movement–United States. 2. Outing (Sexual orientation)–United States.
I. Percy, William A. II. Title.
HQ76.8.U5J64 1993
305.9′0664–dc20   93-17368
                                                           CIP

CONTENTS

ABOUT THE AUTHORS

Warren Johansson, MA, is Senior Research Fellow of the Gay Academic Union in New York City. A member of ACT UP/New York and Queer Nation/New York, he is also a member of the Gay Academic Union and the Columbia University Seminar on Homosexualities (CUSH).

William A. Percy, PhD, is Professor of History at the University of Massachusetts at Boston and formerly chaired the Lesbian and Gay Caucus of the American Historical Association. He is a member of the American Historical Association, the Medieval Academy of America and the Society for the Scientific Study of Sex.

Johansson and Percy are associate editors of the two-volume *Encyclopedia of Homosexuality* (1990), the largest work on the subject in any language, and coauthors of "Homosexuals in Nazi Germany," *Simon Wiesenthal Center Annual 7* (1990).

Preface

The theories and conclusions about the advisability and the rationale for Queer Nation in this book are entirely our own. We are indebted to Michael Petrelis, who spent weeks here discussing the book, and who generously opened up to us his extensive files which we used to great profit. The other main outer, whom we wish to thank for his relevant columns in *OutWeek* and the *Advocate*, is Michelangelo Signorile. Frank Kameny, the first to organize demonstrations, waxed most eloquent over the telephone. Wayne R. Dynes, Eugene F. Rice, Arthur Warner, James Kepner, and Ed Boyce have advised us, though they, like the others, have not always agreed with our conclusions and recommendations. Seth Weine provided us with particularly valuable copies of *The Homosexual Handbook* and *Hollywood Star News*. No one, of course, could hope to undertake such a survey without consulting Magnus Hirschfeld's still unsurpassed *Die Homosexualität des Mannes und des Weibes*, Vern Bullough's *Sexual Variance in Society and History*, David Greenberg's *Construction of Homosexuality*, and Dynes' *Homosexuality: A Research Guide*.

Some of our material, particularly that of the most recent period, has been primary: the actual leaflets and press releases distributed by activists engaged in outing. Richard Mohr's work *Gay Ideas: Outing and Other Controversies* (1992) includes an essay on the subject. We understand that Larry Gross is editing a work titled *The Contested Closet*, to be published by University of Minnesota Press, and that Michelangelo Signorile has also contracted with Random House for one with the title *Queer in America* that will cover Los Angeles, New York, and Washington.

Boston
1994

REFERENCES

Bullough, Vern L. 1976. *Sexual Variance in Society and History*. New York: John Wiley.

Dynes, Wayne R. 1987. *Homosexuality: A Research Guide*. New York and London: Garland Publishing.

Dynes, Wayne R., ed. 1990. *Encyclopedia of Homosexuality*, 2 vols. New York and London: Garland Publishing.

Greenberg, David. 1988. *The Construction of Homosexuality*. Chicago: University of Chicago Press.

Gross, Larry. 1991. "The Contested Closet: The Ethics and Politics of Outing." *Critical Studies in Mass Communication* 8: 352-388.

Hirschfeld, Magnus. 1914. *Die Homosexualität des Mannes und des Weibes*. Berlin: Louis Marcus Verlagsbuchhandlung.

Mohr, Richard D. 1992. "The Outing Controversy: Privacy and Dignity in Gay Ethics." In *Gay Ideas: Outing and Other Controversies*. Boston: Beacon Press, pp. 11-48.

Chapter I

Outing: What It Means and How It Came to Mean It

Outing may become the great debate of the 1990s. It raises the question of whether we are a nation, strong and united–a Queer Nation–or merely a gay community or a homosexual culture or subculture. It counterposes group interests, patriotic loyalty to the Queer Nation, against the right of the individual to privacy. It vitalizes disputes about the ethics of the press in reporting or refusing to report gossip and facts about homosexual conduct, which has normally been taboo. Cutting across all previous alignments, outing realigns Marxists and conservatives, even the religious right and the gay avant-garde, for and against it. It threatens heterosexuals by destroying their pretense that all important and worthwhile human beings share their own sexual persuasion–obligatory heterosexuality–and by shattering negative stereotypes of the homosexual.

Heretofore heterosexuals ("breeders" in our slang) outed homosexuals to destroy us. Now we are seizing the initiative to help our cause–our nation! Only the increasing integration of overt homosexuals into society and our increasing, albeit still noteworthy, acceptance by society has finally made outing by gay activists feasible. AIDS had already outed certain screen and sports idols–more prominent than any that had ever come out on their own–as well as hundreds of thousands of ordinary gay men. The epidemic, long neglected by authorities, also had made activists (increasingly queer nationalists, often themselves HIV positive) much more impatient and bolder. Looking further into the past, without the massive coming out in public of hundreds of thousands of gay people during the 1970s–one of the greatest achievements of the post-Stonewall decade–pro-gay outings would not have been imagined. But none of the truly rich and famous came out on their own even then.

In the 1950s the intrepid pioneers of the American homophile movement prepared the way, although because of the extreme hostility and danger even many of them hid behind pseudonyms. Hostile authorities then outed many more than had come out under fire during or between the wars. Previously, far fewer had dared to come out. The unprecedented expansion of higher education after the Second World War contributed to their resolve. American homosexuals had been virtually invisible before then, leaving the "sleep of reason" free to "engender monsters."

Pagan Greeks had institutionalized pederasty under decorous and socially beneficial guidelines, and Romans had never outlawed it. During the Middle Ages and the Reformation, Christians sporadically persecuted sodomites brutally, if selectively, to terrify the others. The Enlightenment and the Revolutionary and Romantic periods, which ended the reign of Christianity, began the abolition of sodomy laws but left social opprobrium intact. Inspired by the trial of Oscar Wilde, homosexual emancipation began in fin-de-siècle Germany and grew into a mass movement under the Weimar Republic; but not even 1,000 came out in public before Hitler crushed it. Not enough of us were visible to undermine the negative stereotypes propagated by clerics, lawyers, and psychiatrists.

Although for almost a century now activists have from time to time advocated that everyone come out, no one has yet seriously advocated outing everyone. Pedophiles who prefer prepubescent children of the same sex, sadomasochists who prefer partners of the same sex, and members of other categories who might incur social and legal attacks if they were outed (see the last chapter) are, for the purpose of this book, not "queer nationals." They form communities as distinct as zoerasts who prefer animals of their own sex or necrophiliacs who prefer corpses of their own sex. Pederasts, those who prefer adolescents between the ages of 12 and 17, are a marginal group because their sexual conduct, even in private, remains illegal and strongly tabooed.

To what *extent* should an individual be outed? Should the bare fact of his (or her) being homosexual or bisexual be the limit, and if so, what would that prove? When one comes out, of course, one need not specify the details of one's sexual life. But for someone outed involuntarily, would the press demand the minute details of the subject's private sexual behavior as proof and then broadcast them to the world? The latter revelation would probably subject most outees to scorn and ridicule, which the curtain of decency drawn over their sexual lives would largely spare them. In measuring how much to reveal, should one distinguish those in sedate, monogamous gay marriages from those who pursue only one-night stands with any casual partner they may pick up? So the definition of outing must be formulated in a manner that takes into account the extent to which the subject's privacy need be violated to satisfy the demands of the media before they publicize the outing.

For two decades, an increasing number of activists have been urging the closeted to come out. In contrast, scarcely any homophiles, no matter how vociferously they recommended coming out, urged outing before 1989. Until then the unwritten law of silence vis-à-vis lovers of the opposite sex was tacitly accepted by everyone involved in the gay subculture, even if gay activists and barflies freely touted the names of closeted celebrities to other homosexuals. Outing *within the gay community* was a customary, commonplace event, but we did not normally relay the gossip to heterosexuals. That was *verboten.* The new practice thus signals the abandonment of a long-standing principle that participants in the homosexual subculture or the gay community do not reveal one another's orientation to a hostile and vindictive world. In the new concept of a Queer Nation, however, disloyalty through hypocritical perjury of one's identity seems to merit outing, even if the closeted are in no other way harming fellow queer nationals. The need for collective visibility overrules the right of privacy.

Few are as yet preoccupied with these issues. The vast majority, and they are a happy lot indeed, still innocently understand "outing" to mean going out for a ride or a picnic in the countryside. To "out," as verb, dates from at least the late fourteenth century, when it was used to mean putting (someone) out of a house or parish. With its new derivatives "outer" and "outee," "to out" revived at the beginning of the 1990s with a new meaning. Current usage derives from the recent homosexual slang contrast between "being in the closet" and "being out," i.e., admitting to being gay. One can be out to family, friends, or fellow workers, or to the public in general. Retrospectively we can say that inquisitors and police as well as spiteful gossips outed sodomites over the centuries. But outing in the new sense means militant activists dragging the cowardly and disloyal out of the closet by trumpeting their proclivities to all and sundry, ostensibly in the political interest of the Queer Nation. Although we do not know who first used it in the current sense, an article in *Harper's* of October 1982 predicted that "outage" would become a political tactic in which the closeted would find themselves trapped in their own crossfire. Then, in its issue of January 29, 1990, *Time* introduced "outing" to the great American public. This raised the curtain on the debates, conflicts, and revelations of the decade just beginning.

It should be mentioned that after the seventeenth century "to out" ceded to the form "to oust" the meaning that it had in earlier usage, of forcing or driving (someone) out of a house or parish. Consequently, "to out" has made itself available for redefinition in the new sense popularized by *Time*. On March 23, 1990 the *Atlanta Constitution* wrote: "Mr. Forbes has become the latest target of 'outing,' a growing practice in which undeclared gay men, lesbians or bisexuals are involuntarily yanked from the sexual closet, typically by activists in the gay community." William Safire appropriately commented on the *Time* article in his column On Language in the *New York Times Magazine* of May 6, 1990: "The language is dexterous in giving sinister meanings to familiar words. *Outing* comes from 'coming out of the closet,' which has meant the public assertion of previously secret homosexuality." He added: "Lexies take note: we are witnessing the birth of new meaning to a gerund." John Algeo and Adele Algeo promptly recorded the coinage in "Among the New Words"(*American Speech* 65, 1990, pp. 256-257). The rapidity with which the new meaning spread is shown by the fact that on August 29, 1991, *outing* was used in French in the biweekly *Gai Pied,* so that in exactly 19 months it had made the crossing from New York to Le Havre and boarded the express for Paris.

Vociferously condemned as it may be by the majority of heterosexuals and perhaps even of us, outing is here to stay. It will not end until the tradition of secrecy and hypocrisy in regard to the subject ends. Like homosexuality itself (a term first coined in 1869), the practice of outing existed long before today's term for it came into use. Previously it was nearly always heterosexuals who did the outing (without coining a special term), using this potent weapon against homosexual or bisexual foes. Now a handful of gay journalists and activists, or as we term ourselves, queer nationals, have seized the initiative.

The idea of "coming out," which predominated among gay activists in the 1970s and 1980s and was advocated by some German homosexual emancipationists even in the pre-Hitler period, preceded the notion of "outing" one's own, which is aimed particularly at celebrities and power brokers who have obstinately refused to come out of the closet. By analogy, outing might imply forcing others to come out by threatening to out them, as some now recommend–giving them the chance under compulsion to come out of their own free will. The threat can of course come from ordinary blackmailers, police or other investigators, rivals, or–in the newest phase that began in 1989–from gay activists and journalists. Properly handled, it can be a precise and perhaps indispensable weapon in our arsenal, and we must deploy every one at our disposal now that the AIDS epidemic has made our war against homophobia more urgent than ever. But it must be used with discretion, and the establishment media, however reluctant they be, must be dexterously pressed into service.

THE CLOSET

Homosexuals who hide their orientation from a hostile entourage are said to be "in the closet." All the senses of "closet" derive from house construction: The American usage, denoting a windowless and airless alcove for storing clothes, sealed off by a door, differs from the older English meaning of any private room or chamber. Through a merging of these meanings, "to closet oneself" came to connote privacy and remoteness on the one hand and narrow confinement on the other. The aspect of secrecy and the suspect character of whatever was hidden appears in the old expression "a skeleton in the closet." Literary historians also speak of a "closet drama," one never intended for public performance. The adjectival use has a long history. During the reign of James I of England an ecclesiastic coined the phrase "closet sins." Gay speakers often hark back to the architectural origins of the metaphor, as when they refer to the "stifling closet" or say "his closet is nailed shut."

Introduced only in the mid-1960s and restricted until the late 1970s to gay jargon, to be "in the closet" means to conceal one's homosexuality. Donald Webster Cory (pseudonym of Edward Sagarin) did not know the term when he wrote *The Homosexual in America* (1951), nor did the English writer Douglas Plummer use it in *Queer People* (1963). One of the earliest to join the Mattachine Society, Jim Kepner of the International Gay and Lesbian Archives, remembers that when he employed the expression in a speech at a movement conference in 1966, most of the hearers did not know the new meaning. In the specifically homosexual sense it first appears in print in Wainwright Churchill's *Homosexual Behavior Among Males* (1967). In point of fact, the idea of a "closet homosexual" would have had no meaning when, apart from a few individuals on the outer margin of society, *everyone* gay was in the closet. The phrase originally meant hiding even from oneself, i.e., not admitting one's homosexuality even to oneself, or else being aware of one's tendencies but hating and repressing them–keeping *them*, as it were, inside the closet. At times such people were even understood as persecuting other homosexuals in revenge for their own frustration and misery or to bolster their heterosexual image. In any case the state of mind imputed to the subject was defined by recourse to the Freudian notions of "latent" and "repressed" homosexual tendencies.

By the end of the 1960s, individuals maintaining a heterosexual façade, or at least hoping to do so, were said to be "in the closet" with respect to outsiders or even at times to others of their ilk. Chastised for their illusions, they were labeled "closet queens," implying that they remained what they were no matter how skillful their public heterosexual impersonation might seem. Others emerged from the closet, i.e., "came out," to one extent or another. They might come out only to themselves, to a few select acquaintances, or to other homosexuals in general. By the 1970s mainstream journalists had learned and amplified the usage; they now could speak of "closet conservatives" and "closet gourmets" with no sexual connotation.

Quite different is the contemporary meaning in queer national circles. There it commonly refers to someone leading a homosexual life *in private* but maintaining a homophobic political stance *in public*. Such a character is hypocritical in a way that the "closet case" of the 1960s, however wretched he or she may have been, was not. Hence "the closet" in its present meaning and implications for queer nationals is a product of the 1970s, and "outing" an expression of the political impasse of the late 1980s and early 1990s.

The long-time Philadelphia activist Barbara Gittings, a participant in some of the first demonstrations, has dubbed assisting the process of coming out "oiling the hinges of the closet door." "Returning to the closet" designates the retreat of those who have come to feel ill at ease with their open homosexuality or to sense that it is unwise to continue to advertise their sexual orientation. Only a small minority of African-Americans, Jews, Native Americans, Hispanics, and other members of stigmatized groups have even tried to pass as WASPs. In contrast, even the most obvious homosexuals until recently tried to pose as straight. Arrest, accident, or the spite of their enemies outed many unfortunates, but practically no one dared to come out to the general public before Stonewall.

Sociologists, above all Erving Goffman, have written of ways of life among other persecuted groups, such as ex-prisoners and former mental patients, who learn to "manage spoiled identity" by editing their presentation of self. Most closet cases, however, do not think of themselves in quite the same way. Unencumbered as most are–unlike members of ethnic communities–by the stigma of official records of ancestry and birth, and convinced, often in the face of common sense and weighty evidence to the contrary, that their cover has not been blown, they rarely ponder the problems involved in their own self-concealment. When pressed as to why they remain closeted, they appeal to the English-speaking world's tradition of the separation of public business from private lives. And many heterosexuals would concur that sexuality is a private matter.

For a variety of reasons, which they themselves do not clearly understand, the overwhelming majority of homosexual men and women can and do even today remain in the closet. This is so despite fervent appeals by movement leaders to come out. Such coyness makes it hard for those in the vanguard to estimate the true number of their potential followers, to collect valid samples for research, and most important of all, to organize them for political struggle. In fact, because of this unwillingness there has been increasing discussion of the ethics of "forced de-closeting" or outing.

The pressure to remain in the closet comes not only from heterosexuals, but from others hiding in the same closet, as it were on the principle "the more the merrier." The gay novelist Armistead Maupin observed that "one of the unwritten laws of gay life is where you reach a certain level of fame, you shut up about your homosexuality. You're not told this by straight people, you're told it by other famous homosexuals who are ushering you into the pantheon of the right" (Warren 1989).

The closet protects not merely the living. Even corpses are often left to rest in peace in their underground closets. Many newspaper obituaries still refuse to mention that a lover has survived, or allude to other aspects of gayness, presumably in order to protect the privacy of relatives and the reputation of the deceased. Today this reticence seems out of place. And the restriction on information has made it difficult to ascertain the true sexual orientation of figures of the past who very likely had homosexual feelings, whether they acted on them or not. Homophobic scholars have been as busy fabricating heterosexual scenarios for historical figures as press agents have been for their show business clients. Outing the dead is no easy matter.

The biographer who must sift the evidence for the sexual proclivities of a historic personality faces a challenging task. The subjects themselves almost always took great precautions to destroy or have their heirs and executors destroy any "incriminating" evidence. Then their biographers bent over backwards to shield them from accusations of homosexuality. The painter Théodore Géricault and First Lady Eleanor Roosevelt, in whom we have good reason to believe that there were strong elements of a homoerotic sensibility, cannot be proven to everyone's satisfaction to have done anything. Even such twentieth-century figures as New York's Francis Cardinal Spellman and FBI Director J. Edgar Hoover–despite repeated signals from the grapevine during their lifetimes–continue to resist any final pigeonholing. As knowledge advances, many historical question marks will remain. A great many, perhaps the majority, burrowed so deeply into the closet while they were alive that no one will ever be able to out them convincingly. Apropos of matters of sexual orientation, as the Rabbinic saying goes, "The confession of one's own mouth is worth a hundred witnesses." But to prove that another person is homosexual or bisexual may demand the testimony of more than a hundred witnesses, especially if none claims carnal intimacy with the subject. Thus gay historians, especially of countries with a meta-Latin or meta-Byzantine tradition, face often impermeable closet walls. Some, like Wayne R. Dynes, favor a minimalist approach, while others such as Noel I. Garde (pseud.) claim the dead uncritically.

Almost immediately after the Roman emperor Constantine the Great converted, ecclesiastical excommunication, state persecution, and social ostracism proved the lot of those who loved their own sex. Constantine's own sons decreed death by the sword, and Justinian, excruciating tortures and the avenging flames. Virtual death sentences continued sporadically until and through the regimes of Hitler and Stalin, and executions still occur under Islamic law. Consequently lovers of their own sex have historically taken great pains to hide their true nature and predilections from a hostile world. Even today scarcely any prominent members of the queer nation have come out.

Scholars have gone to unbelievable lengths to deny that the famous were homosexual or bisexual. The resulting invisibility allowed our enemies to invent the most bizarre and terrifying fantasies. Not only were we lustful and depraved, but the sodomy delusion allied us like witches with the demonic powers of another world. Thus we were invested with diabolical urges and powers. We threatened other individuals with eternal damnation by corrupting them, and menaced society itself with divinely sent famines, plagues and earthquakes if it did not ferret us out and punish us. In the Enlightenment, the sodomy delusion waned, but was replaced in the late nineteenth century by caricatures almost as ghoulish propounded as empirical findings of physicians and psychologists.

Our need to refute and dispel such damaging characterizations remains great. Even historians still adamantly deny that it can be proven that there have been any Catholic or Orthodox saints or presidents of the United States who were sexually active with other males. Much less can it be claimed that there were any overt lesbian saints. No one has been able to establish beyond doubt the homosexuality (or bisexuality) of some of the most famous Renaissance intellectuals and artists: Pius II (Aeneas Silvius de' Piccolomini), Desiderius Erasmus, Montaigne, or Newton, however much probable cause exists for suspicion. Not one of them had an article in the *Encyclopedia of Homosexuality*, however much probable cause we had and have for suspicion if not conviction. The Freudian doctrine that creative minds sublimated their instinctual drives has been used not just for them, but even for Walt Whitman until recently, when Charley Shively's detective work brought the truth to light: at some periods of his life the poet almost nightly cruised the streets of large cities in search of male partners from 12 to 24. A play performed not long ago in Cambridge raised the age of one of his youthful lovers from 14 to 25–a truly Orwellian falsification.

Denied our claim to such genius, we have been thrown back on lesser mortals and of course, on the aristocratic Greeks of antiquity, most of whom were pederasts and had played the passive role as boys, from the age of 12 or 14 to 18 or 20, before becoming active lovers during their twenties, most of them marrying at 30. Social Constructionists, followers of a now fading French intellectual of the 1960s, deny the Greeks' "homosexuality." They argue that homosexuals–as reciprocal couples of the same age–evolved in Western Europe circa 1700 or 1800 (they are not very precise), or even as late as 1892 (Halperin 1990). Thus they exclude pederasty, the almost universal form before modern times, from the definition of homosexuality as now understood.

FROM SODOMITE TO QUEER

The term by which medieval theology and law stigmatized homosexual activity is *sodomy,* which first appears in Latin about 1175. It is derived from *sodomite,* the word used in Genesis 19 for an inhabitant of Sodom. It came to signify anyone who practiced the vice for which God allegedly rained brimstone and fire on the city. Because the "crime against the law of nature," as Philo Judaeus dubbed it, acquired a wider meaning in Christian usage, *sodomy* in the broadest sense can signify any of various forms of nonreproductive sexual activity: with the wrong species, with the wrong sex, or in the wrong orifice, as St. Thomas Aquinas pontificated in the *Summa Theologica*. In the late Middle Ages the mytho-poetic Christian imagination even spawned the notion that the sister city of Gomorrah had been a hotbed of lesbianism, so that as late as Marcel Proust *gomorrhéenne* could mean "lesbian."

A term preserved by British legal usage, dating from the 1533 statute of Henry VIII which was the first English law against sodomy, was *bugger,* from Latin *Bulgarus,* originally a designation of the Cathars of southern France whose heresy was traced to the Bogomils of Bulgaria. This interface between the meanings of *heretic* and *sodomite* suggests how the two notions overlapped in medieval theology. After all, Leviticus, which had prescribed death for "males who lay with males as with womankind," also ordained the death penalty for apostasy from Judaism. Just as New Testament stories of demonic possession reinforced the fear of witches, the Pauline condemnation of those who dishonor their persons "contrary to nature" ratified the death penalty ordained in Leviticus for sodomites. These assumptions created the "sodomy delusion" alongside the "witchcraft delusion" of late medieval and early modern Europe. In everyday British speech *bugger* became an exceedingly obscene and abusive word, but contrary to popular belief *faggot* (in British dialect usage, "fat, slovenly woman) in this sense is found no earlier than a slang dictionary of 1914 from the northwestern United States. Tenacious myths to the contrary, it has no semantic tie to the "faggots" used to burn witches and sodomites in the Middle Ages; in fact in England the act of 1533 ordained hanging as the penalty for buggery.

The Church invented and inculcated the "sodomy delusion," a complex of paranoid beliefs that prevails throughout Christendom to this day: Nonprocreative sexuality in general, and sexual acts between males in particular, are contrary to the law of Nature, to the exercise of right reason, and to the will of God. Sodomy is practiced by individuals whose wills have been enslaved by demonic powers. Everyone is heterosexually oriented, but susceptible of the demonic temptation to commit sodomy, and potentially guilty of the crime. Everyone hates and condemns sodomy, but the practice is ubiquitously threatening and infinitely contagious. Everyone regards the practice with loathing and disgust, but whoever has experienced sodomitic pleasure retains a lifelong craving for it. It is a crime committed by the merest handful of abandoned sinners, but if not checked by the harshest penalties it would become so rampant as to lead to the suicide of the human race. It is a source of eternal damnation for the individual sinner, it impairs and undermines the moral character of those who practice it, and it is so hateful as to provoke God's retribution in the form of catastrophes befalling an entire community for the crime of a single individual left unpunished in its midst. For its own self-preservation every Christian community must be eternally vigilant against its occurrence and spread. The parties guilty of such abominable practices should be punished with the utmost severity and, if not put to death in accordance with Biblical precept, then totally excluded from Christian society.

Partly to avoid the theological associations of *sodomy,* the secular-minded eighteenth-century writers adopted for homosexuals in general such classical terms as *pederast,* which in Ancient Greek had meant only "boy-lover," or paraphrased it as "devotee of *Greek love*" or of "*amour socratique,*" an expression revived in the twentieth century. Other expressions figure from time to time: *bardache* (the Persian word for slave that came to mean the passive homosexual and then the quasi-hermaphroditic possessor of shamanistic powers), *catamite* (the Etruscan, then Latin corruption of Zeus' beloved Ganymede), and the like, while the Anglo-Saxon word *bædling* survived only in certain British dialects and in the adjective *bad.* German writers distinguished between *Knabenliebe* (boy-love) and *Männerliebe* (love between adult males).

In the late nineteenth century, homophile apologists and psychiatrists under their influence invented a new set of terms. The earliest of these was the pioneer advocate of homosexual rights, the Hanoverian lawyer Karl Heinrich Ulrichs (1825-95) who, inspired by Kabbalistic lore on metempsychosis, coined the word *Urning* (feminine *Urninde,* from Plato's *Aphroditē Uranios*) to designate an individual who had "a female soul trapped in a male body," that is, a male attracted to other members of his own sex and vice versa. This term never gained favor and was displaced by a word introduced five years after Ulrichs published (under the pseudonym of Numa Numantius, which he later dropped) the first pamphlet in a series on *The Enigma of Male Love* in 1864.

This new and ultimately successful coinage was *homosexual,* modeled on the French botanical terms *bisexuel* and *unisexuel*. American gay activists eventually scorned the term because it sounded medical and opprobrious. This rejection was grounded in ignorance of the truth of the term's origin. It was first used in an anonymous pamphlet of 1869 with the unobtrusive title *§143 of the Prussian Penal Code and its Maintenance as §152 of the Draft of a Penal Code for the North German Confederation*. This was a denunciation of the planned extension of the Prussian law to jurisdictions that had earlier adopted the Code Napoléon.

In *Homosexuality in Men and Women* (1914), Magnus Hirschfeld, the leader of the German homophile movement, confirmed what Ulrichs had attested–that the word *homosexual* was invented by Karl Maria Benkert (1824-82), whose name in Hungarian was Károly Mária Kertbeny. In 1884 Ulrichs revealed to Karl Egells that Kertbeny, whom he came to know in 1864 or 1865 as one of the first "comrades," was the author of *§143,* and that "out of jealousy" he did not want to use Ulrichs' terms but invented his own. Kertbeny first opted for anonymity, then in Gustav Jaeger's publications of 1880 and 1900 he was designated only as "Dr. M.," which gave rise to the erroneous but interminably repeated belief that he was "a Hungarian doctor." In fact a dissertation written at the University of Szeged in 1936 showed that Kertbeny never received a doctorate in any subject and never wrote on medicine or the natural sciences. Kertbeny had in the meantime supplied Jaeger with the material included in the second edition of *Discovery of the Soul* (1880), which introduced the terms *homosexual* and *heterosexual* to a wider public. To boot, Kertbeny wrote a panoramic description of Europe's homosexual subculture that Jaeger published only in 1900 in the second volume of Hirschfeld's journal, the *Jahrbuch für sexuelle Zwischenstufen*. Presumably sometime between 1900 and 1905 Hirschfeld learned Kertbeny's identity from Egells, and announced it in the preface to the reprint of the first pamphlet in the seventh volume of the *Jahrbuch* in 1905. So the inventor of the word *homosexual* never came out, and was outed only 23 years after his death and 36 years after the first use of the word in print.

Urged by Ulrichs to investigate the subject more closely, the Prussian psychiatrist Karl Friedrich Otto Westphal (1833-90) published an article in *Archiv für Psychiatrie* in 1869 in which he designated the condition as *die konträre Sexualempfindung*, "contrary sexual feeling." This term also failed to gain favor and was replaced by the translation invented by Arrigo Tamassia (1849-1917), who had succeeded the homophobic Sephardic Jew Cesare Lombroso in the chair of legal medicine at the University of Pavia. This coinage, which Tamassia first used in a paper published in the fourth volume of *Rivista sperimentale di freniatria e medicina legale* in 1878, was *inversione dell'istinto sessuale*, "inversion of the sexual instinct." In the concise form *sexual inversion*, it quickly became the *medical* term in the other Romance languages and in English.

The new term *homosexual* designated us as persons oriented solely toward others with the genitalia of the same sex, and thus reflected but negated the older view of the sodomite who committed a sin but was not necessarily different in mind or body from any other human being. The sin may indeed have been graver than any other, but anyone might be tempted to it. Some medieval theologians held that sodomy was worse than murder, but like any other sin one could atone for it. In his statute criminalizing buggery, Henry VIII provided that wives and children of such a felon could inherit his goods–a notable privilege given that those convicted of other felonies forfeited their property to the crown. Sodomites were not thought to have innate or exclusive tendencies; they were frequently married fathers. Likewise, before the second half of the nineteenth century, unalterable traits were not usually ascribed to any minority community or nationality. Then Kertbeny and Jaeger introduced the concept and the term *homosexual* with its antonym *heterosexual*. And the wake of the interest in sexuality generated by the debate on evolution, the Freudian school made sexual orientation central to its analyses of individual psychodynamics.

The emergence during the late nineteenth century of the medical concept of sexual inversion–supposedly more scientific and objective than the clerical notion of sodomy–meant only that instead of prison, courts and families could have homosexuals subjected to indefinite confinement in asylums, with electroshock, prefrontal lobotomy, castration, and other forms of "treatment" recommended by physicians or psychoanalysts. Supposedly all this was not only for the good of the patients but also to keep them from infecting society with their degeneracy. Although Freud's views were equivocal, if demeaning, in regarding homosexuals as imperfectly developed human beings, his American disciples unequivocally classified homosexuality as a mental illness. The American Psychiatric Association in 1973 and the American Psychological Association in 1974 finally removed homosexuality from their Diagnostic Manuals. Yet some courts and practitioners still impose "therapeutic measures" upon patients whom–as experience has long since amply proved–there is really no hope of "curing." "Converting" would probably be a better word; the difference is in the last analysis purely semantic. It would probably be easier, as some have flatly asserted for so long, to turn a heterosexual into a homosexual than to do the reverse. Think of the fees these quacks extorted from their unfortunate patients whom in reality they crucified more than cured.

Because of the stigma which they felt attached to the term *homosexual* as it was used by psychiatrists in the United States, American activists from 1969 onward preferred the word *gay*. A Middle English borrowing from Anglo-Norman French, which had in turn obtained it from Old Provençal, it meant "fond of sexual pleasures and available for erotic liaisons." In British English *gay girls* meant "prostitutes." There is some evidence that *gay* was used in Walt Whitman's circle, and later, in a narrower sense, in Gertrude Stein's, but it became a password of the American homosexual subculture only in the 1920s. Familiar enough to the cognoscenti by the 1960s to be the usual word, it was blazoned on the banners of the gay liberation movement in the following decade. In the minds of many activists, this political context has narrowed the applicability of the word: *gay* can mean only someone who consciously identifies with an aggrieved minority or community fighting for its rights–a criterion that leftists of the 1960s often preferred.

This is but one aspect of the increasingly difficult problem of defining whether an individual is "gay" or homosexual. From the legal standpoint, until the recent past a single homosexual act sufficed to convict of sodomy or buggery. Such a proceeding destroyed a man's reputation and social existence, if it did not deprive him of life through mob violence at the pillory or by execution. Orientation is quite another matter. Is someone "gay" who has homosexual impulses but never acts on them because he regards them as "unnatural" and sinful–as is probably true of a large number of celibate clergy (perhaps no longer the majority in the United States) and of most if not all saints? Is a married man gay who occasionally indulges in furtive sex with other males? What about married women who fail to reach climax with each other?

The Kinsey report of 1948 blurred the line: it posited a scale from 0 to 6, indicating that his subjects graded continuously from exclusive homosexuality to exclusive heterosexuality, with 3 indicating equal attraction to or experience with both sexes. It claimed that 37 percent of American males had climaxed with another male since puberty, that 10 percent practiced homosexuality predominantly at any one time, and that 4 percent were exclusives. Its findings seem to have been confirmed for industrialized Western societies by the study of Michel Bon and Antoine d'Arc, *Rapport sur l'homosexualité de l'homme* (1974), which used a scale of 1 to 10. The same findings, however, have been called into question by David Forman of Oxford University (*British Medical Journal* 298, 1989, pp. 1137-42). Based on a survey made in England and Wales, he concluded that a mere 1.7 percent of the respondents had had homosexual intercourse. Another survey, *Adult Sexual Behavior in 1989: Number of Partners Frequency and Risk*, conducted by the sociologist Tom Smith of the University of Chicago for the National Opinion Research Center, found that fewer than 1 percent of those sampled were "exclusively homosexual."

The latest to reject such cumbersome triptychs as "lesbian, bisexual, and gay" is the group that broke off from AIDS Coalition To Unleash Power (ACT UP) in March 1990 and styled itself Queer Nation. *Queer,* which began as a rather derogatory term for homosexual in American criminal slang in the early years of the century, became common in British English of the 1950s and 1960s. Those who adopted it in 1990 felt it to be a liberating word. The concept of a Queer Nation may in the long run prove more inspirational than descriptive. Aspiring to nationhood represents a new stage in the political consciousness of the movement.

Some activists strongly resist *queer* because they dislike the other meanings and associations–"odd," "eccentric," "counterfeit," and the like–as well as the insulting colloquial use of the term, equivalent to the English bugger. Conservatives and legal and medical professionals cling to "homosexual" and speak of a minority. Most movement writers use "gay and lesbian," (sticklers say "gay men and lesbians"), and refer to a community. Young radicals increasingly prefer "queer" and "nation." Only a few retrograde theologians still refer to "sodomites." "Pederast" has regained its specificity, referring to those who prefer adolescents, while "pedophiles" seek prepubescent children. "Homosexual" connoted a plea for toleration and legal reform, "gay" was a term of liberation demanding respect, and "queer" expresses defiance and patriotic nationalism.

One of the reasons many are queasy about the appropriation of the word "queer" is that those who hate us, including fag-bashers, will feel that it is again acceptable for them to use such epithets–to our detriment. A biographer of the Norwegian collaborationist Vidkun Quisling noted how many words beginning with the cluster *qu-* convey a sense of unease and doubt: question, queasy, quibble, quixotic, quiz, quizzical, quagmire, qualm, quandary . . . *queer.* It is therefore understandable that a mere two days after Quisling's name was blazoned in headlines in the British press, it was degraded to a common noun: *quisling*, a collaborationist, traitor, defector, would-be collaborator with the enemy. The names of his French contemporary Pierre Laval and of his Croatian equivalent Ante Pavelic underwent no such semantic debasement.

There may be an analogous problem with outing. This book abundantly documents how widespread hostile outing has been, and indeed continues to be. How can we be certain that our own growing custom of outing the quick as well as the dead will not find a dismal parallel as straight enemies–from the highest of motives, of course–start to out us viciously once again? What is sauce for the (gay) goose may be sauce for the (straight) gander. On the other hand, it may be argued, some breeders will doubtless continue to out queers no matter what we do.

FROM BEING FERRETED OUT TO CLAIMING OUR OWN

Outing, though not by that name, was originally the act of a society that ferreted out the individual guilty of sodomy and expelled him from its midst, if it did not execute him. This hostility reflects a prohibition that in Western society has prevailed since the fourth century, when Christian persecution replaced Greco-Roman tolerance with the death penalty. Intolerance peaked in the late thirteenth century, when the High Scholastics declared sodomy second in heinousness only to murder. A South Italian jurist of the mid-fourteenth century, Luca da Penne, even reasoned that it was worse than murder because it aimed at the death of the entire human race. The paranoid loathing and detestation that such beliefs inspired forced homosexuals into a closet of social invisibility.

The individual outed in a wave of persecution or chance discovery could expect to be prosecuted and imprisoned, banished, or executed. Even in more recent times, outing to society–to one's family, friends, associates, employer, and the like–meant ostracism, disinheritance, loss of employment and career–a civil death, as the phrase has it, leaving the victim no option but exile or suicide, or else to suffer ostracism, assault, battery, or murder. It is true that legal records for the entire period before the French Revolution show that only in exceptional cases did the state inflict the drastic penalties sanctioned by criminal law. On the other hand, the clergy succeeded in making the sodomite infamous in the eyes of all Christian society. That infamy survived the Reformation and the Enlightenment to flourish under liberal and totalitarian regimes alike (indeed, it persists in attenuated form even in the last decade of the twentieth century). In such dire situations crypto-homosexuals came out only to others who shared their proclivities and secret lore.

Individuals who have decided of their own free will to come out have realized that there are degrees of being out: to oneself, to sex partners, friends, family, roommates, colleagues, coworkers, neighbors, teammates, bosses, and the like. Besides degrees of being out, there are also various depths of concealment. Some are deeper inside the closet than others. In societies which account homosexual behavior but a minor peccadillo–as in some parts of the Third World not yet too impacted by Judeo-Christian morality–the closet is a very shallow space, for one needs no great depths into which to retreat; whereas Christianity, because of its implacable condemnation and frequently severe persecution of homosexual activity, has bequeathed a very different situation to a supposedly enlightened Western world. Thus outing needs to be seen in its historical relationship to coming out.

"The closet," said one member of the Scholarship Committee of the Gay Academic Union, "is a Chinese box." Perhaps the most forlorn are those who cannot come out *even to themselves,* so fearful or ashamed are they of their innermost feelings and responses. On becoming aware of one's orientation one may choose to tell relatives or close friends, then workmates, and finally larger circles, or be outed to them, in whatever order, by others. Unless one is as famous as Boy George or John Lennon, it is almost impossible to attain the blessed state of being completely "out," because there are always some people who will simply assume that the person they encounter is heterosexual. There are even those who opt to disbelieve when one admits to being gay; after all, it is impossible truly to know what another human being *feels.* The older habit of "dropping pins"–outlandish behavior and dress or letting down one's hair to friends or in closed groups–was a form of coming out mainly used by "queens." Of course, there are buttons or T-shirts that enable the wearer to announce "How Dare You Assume I'm Heterosexual!" but they are often donned only in gay resorts or bars, not at race tracks or in Baptist churches. Nevertheless, before the coming of gay liberation this kind of self-advertisement could have occurred only in a nightmare.

Some may be out to others whom they encounter at the work place, in their leisure hours, and in their political activity on behalf of the movement, but not to their families and neighbors in the town where they grew up. This pattern is particularly true of gay men who have moved to New York or San Francisco to escape the repressive atmosphere of their midwestern or southern birthplaces. A scale indicating the extent to which a subject is open about his or her identity would therefore not be a continuum, but rather a series of points of social contact each of which would be positive or negative. In any case, only a small proportion of those who engage in sexual activity with members of their own sex join organizations furthering the ideology and aims of gay liberation, much less join chapters of Queer Nation. But as such organizations become a feature of the political landscape, more and more young people are first contacting the community of their peers by attending meetings and rallies.

By a cultural and psychological process, individuals internalize a "gay" or "lesbian" identity in accordance with a particular one of

many possible models. An animal, even if it were exclusively attracted to others of its own sex, could never have the consciousness
of being "homosexual." This consciousness entails both a self-def-
inition–which may be termed "coming out to oneself"–and the
recognition that other human beings are "bisexual" or "heterosexual," and that their orientation in turn limits their availability as
sexual partners. The bisexual has to accept that exclusive homosexuals of the opposite sex and exclusive heterosexuals of the same
sex will always be unresponsive to his or her advances. All these
things must be learned through social contact and acculturation.
Because different cultures have different identity models of homosexuality (or none at all), the coming out process, even to oneself,
also shows wide variation, as do the stages of progressively coming
out to others.

A homosexual identity, although it may be formed during childhood or even infancy, is not part of one's upbringing by adults. It
differs radically from acculturation into a religious or ethnic minority. If you are descended from a religious or ethnic group that has
suffered persecution or oppression in the past–Protestants in a Catholic country, or Christians under Islamic rule–no matter how
shunned, despised and humiliated your ilk may have been, within
the circle of your family and friends you are accepted and loved for
what you are. The life histories of your parents and more distant
relatives furnish object lessons in how to survive in a hostile milieu.
Your very existence is proof that the community or nation has
surmounted all the tragic vicissitudes of its past–legal inferiority
and exclusion, humiliation and persecution, famine and slaughter,
forced migration and exile.

But membership in the gay subculture comes only with self-
awareness–and, far from bonding you with your family and friends,
carries the seeds of complete and irrevocable alienation from them.
You are, even if by no choice of your own, setting out on a path in
life that is dark and unfamiliar, even forbidding and terrifying, to
those closest to you. On your own you must internalize the symbolic systems of the gay subculture, or queer nation, and learn to
negotiate its hidden paths and perilous byways. Your task is not
only to manage your self-image, but to maintain the persona necessary for a *modus vivendi* with a still largely hostile environment.

This dilemma of self-image and identity brings you face to face with the long tradition of suppressing and falsifying the existence of homosexuality in public discourse. And in turn, it may fill you with an intense desire to know more about those who were or are like you–their lives, their accomplishments, their legacy to you as a child of the late twentieth century. In the case of other minorities or nationalities this search often means unearthing obscure, virtually forgotten figures whose sole claim to attention was their accidental origin in the outsider group. But some of the most famous men and women of all time were actively, even proudly, homosexual or bisexual–a fact which the standard histories and biographies painstakingly ignore. It is the dominant Christian culture that has made past and present lovers of their own sex invisible–and that in not so subtle a manner tells us to remain unseen. We need to out the quick and the dead: visibility is our best hope for acceptance by ourselves and by society.

In the industrialized societies of North America and Western Europe, anyone with a sufficient erotic interest in others of the same sex can come out as a "homosexual" or a "lesbian." In other societies, however, the process of gender reidentification primarily affects the sexually passive, receptive male, rather than the active one who plays the insertive role. An example is the quasi-female identification which Hispanics term a *maricón*. It is not clear to what extent a corresponding process exists for women (though Latinos have long recognized the "bull dyke" or *marimacho*); much less research has been done on or by them. In other cultures and at other times, and in particular where pederasty has been popular, distinct homosexual identity models are lacking and the question of "coming out" does not arise.

Theorists have generally characterized coming out as a series of crucial steps. The subject moves from virtual, almost complete unawareness or total concealment to self-recognition or even to proclamation of a homosexual identity to the whole world. Political shifts have led to considerable dispute over where "coming out" ends. The older, minimalist view held it to be a state of internal acceptance of a homosexual self-identity (which could be wholly private). Then gay liberationists redefined it as a state in which one's homosexuality is made known to virtually anyone with whom one has socially meaningful contact, or even more daringly, is revealed to the public through open involvement in gay organizations whose leaders are named and quoted in the media. At that point one may become a "professional gay activist." Various moderates take intermediate positions.

Wide media exposure of the homosexual subculture makes coming out in these days primarily a matter for youth from puberty through the mid-twenties. Before the taboos on public mention of homosexuality were broken, however, the process was not uncommon at much older ages, sometimes prompted by a chance encounter. Coming out is, it seems, occurring earlier and more quickly with each new age cohort, especially in cities and on campuses. Now coming out often begins shortly after puberty, and is completed by the end of adolescence. The recent visibility of our distinctive subculture accelerated the process. Today even early adolescents commonly know what it means to be "gay" or "queer." A few of them, especially in the United States, proudly identify with what they consider their special category of society.

Stages of coming out often dramatically affect the individual. Many recall, and some even celebrate, the anniversary of their coming out. Stories and plays reflect and articulate the fear, vacillation, isolation, alienation, and sometimes also the violence and pain that often accompany it. For many, however, the evolution is not very memorable or painful. Some become aware of their future orientation at of four, five, or six, and cannot even remember not being out, at least to themselves, though they may only gradually come out to others.

Coming out as infants, or very young children, they never imagine that they are straight but at once perceive that they have different sexual interests. The present coauthor Percy, for example, like André Gide, feels that he came out to himself at the age of four or five when he realized that while other boys were interested in girls, he was interested only in boys. He never felt any shame but only fear that he might be discovered and unjustly punished. By the age of 12 he realized that famous Greeks and Romans as well as some of his own successful relatives had loved others of their own sex. So he never felt guilty but merely took measures not to be caught or exposed to a hostile society. Coming as he did from a prominent family of the South, where ancestry defined status, he never let his homosexuality damage his sense of self-worth.

As prosecution and blackmail receded into the past during the 1960s, coming out became paramount. Gay liberation gave coming out a new meaning: the defiant revelation of one's identity to an intolerant society. Last of all, only at the very end of the 1980s, activists and journalists undertook to out closeted members of their presumed community, at least who were maliciously and hypocritically acting against its interests. Hence gay-initiated outing breaks a well established code of silence, a rule enforced until now almost as rigorously as that of a secret society or of the Mafia. Now some queer nationals believe that they have a right to out passive as well as active traitors and collaborationists.

Coming out and outing are two sides of the same coin. While the triggering mechanism–others' denunciation versus one's own choice–is different, the two phenomena still offer striking similarities. The very process of coming out is usually attributed to a homophobic environment in which one must take a stance against the majority in order to assert one's own orientation or personality with its preferences, attractions, feelings, and inclinations. The slogan "We are the people our parents warned us against" epitomizes this mind-set. In this view, full social acceptance of homosexuality as a natural and universal variation would end most of the emotional difficulties as well as the fateful significance of what is otherwise described as coming out. Now, of course, the retarding and favoring aspects of voluntary coming out are joined by outing, for some an ominous prospect, for others a satisfactory development.

Christianity has over the centuries pursued an undeviating policy in regard to homosexual behavior: either defamation or silence. If "the sleep of reason engenders monsters" (as Goya, the painter of the grotesque, entitled one of his etchings), Christian unreason imagined the sodomite as a monster addicted to unutterably loathsome forms of depravity and bringing down the vengeance of the Creator upon himself and all around him. On the other hand, the positive achievements of those who loved their own sex, both in pagan antiquity and in more recent times, were blotted from the annals of history. The result was that those attracted to their own sex were forced underground, into an invisible, pariah community. The invisibility that resulted from the hypocrisy and deception which Christian intolerance had imposed on homosexuals and bisexuals of every and all persuasions allowed the most absurd and fantastic notions and stereotypes to flourish. But paradoxically enough, some of the most prestigious figures in Christendom were at the same time covert members of this secret society.

From the very beginning, homophile apologists recognized that visibility was a prerequisite for converting this invisible, pariah caste into a community with prestige commensurate with the objective merits and achievements of its members. Ulrichs, who emphasized the role of great homosexuals (who we know today were rather bisexuals and pederasts than exclusive androphiles) in ancient Greece and Rome, where alone in Western history they were visible, had already asserted that "Urnings must come out as Urnings." He realized when he began his campaign in 1864 that invisibility was a major obstacle in the way of changing public opinion. And 128 years later, the challenge remains the same: If we can out the rich and the famous, the geniuses and heroes, the saints and the self-sacrificers and benefactors of mankind, whether quick or dead, we can discredit the derogatory stereotypes and regain our rightful place in the sun.

The demand for outing results from the knowledge on the part of the newly visible members of the largely still pariah community that prestigious individuals are secret members of our nation, together with ressentiment at the prestige which they reap from invisibility. Conversely the closeted celebrities in our pariah community resent the freedom from the burden of hypocrisy which the open members have gained, and fear that their own status may be jeopardized by activists' demands and by the public attention focused on their own secretive conduct.

During the early years of the twentieth century, other German pioneers followed Ulrichs with similar proposals. In *The Sexual Life of Our Time in its Relation to Modern Civilization* (1907), the German-Jewish physician Iwan Bloch urged that elderly homosexuals reveal their identity to those in their milieu, that is, come out even to their heterosexual family members and acquaintances. Magnus Hirschfeld's major work of 1914, *Homosexuality in Men and Women,* mentions a proposal by his friend, the political theorist

Kurt Hiller (1885-1972). In his article of 1913, "Ethical Tasks of Homosexuals," Hiller called for a mass "self-denunciation" of homosexuals to the police (what we would today style "coming out") in order to influence legislators and public opinion. Hirschfeld, even though he claimed homosexuals to be a third sex identifiable by marked inversion of the secondary and tertiary sexual characters, admitted that it would certainly be an effective weapon if several thousand men and women of rank and standing would make such a self-sacrificing confession. But the proposal overlooked one vital factor: the psyche of the homosexual; "it is this," wrote Hirschfeld, "that makes the whole idea utopian and illusory." Hirschfeld correctly asserted that the external and internal inhibitions were then much too strong for a significant number of socially prominent homosexuals to find the courage for a voluntary and open acknowledgement of their orientation. Indeed, one of those who had most zealously championed this early coming-out proposal, when the press ascribed homosexual tendencies to him, nevertheless urgently sent the newspapers a message denying the allegation (Hirschfeld 1914, pp. 1003-4).

For this reason, said Hirschfeld, Otto de Joux, the author of *Disinherited from the Happiness of Love,* was probably right when in 1893–four years before the Scientific-Humanitarian Committee was founded–he wrote:

> Given the case that the hour struck when by international agreement a general Uranide [homosexual] amnesty was suddenly proclaimed and everyone of them was urged to enter his name unabashedly on the open Urning census lists, in order to clarify the question once and for all whether the percentage of humanity that is homosexual does in point of fact demand a comprehensive reform of all the laws of social life–then quite certainly out of a hundred Uranians barely three would summon up the courage suddenly to drop the mask that has all but fused with their inner selves. [Joux 1893, p. 244]

How things have changed since then, and especially since Stonewall! The ethics of outing varies according to the overall political climate. Those who had come out before 1933 in Germany, seem-

ingly the most tolerant country, faced sanctions or even extermina-
tion after the National Socialist seizure of power. Outing is obviously more acceptable to other gay people and considerably less
hazardous to the outee in today's relatively favorable climate than it
would have been, say, at the time of the mass trials of the Knights
Templar in the fourteenth century, or in the Third Reich.

In 1951 when the American movement was just beginning, and
independent of the Mattachine Society in Los Angeles, the New
Yorker Donald Webster Cory (pseudonym of Edward Sagarin)
wrote in *The Homosexual in America* that until considerable numbers of homosexuals revealed their identity to the world, or as we
would say today, came out, there was not likely to be any significant
change in public attitudes. But in the 18 years that followed, only
the fewest and bravest did "come out" completely, mainly those
like the government astronomer Frank Kameny and others who had
involuntarily been exposed and stigmatized. The majority, including every single crypto-homosexual celebrity in America, still
lurked behind the scenes, as did Sagarin himself who like many
activists felt that he had to use a pseudonym so as not to jeopardize
his livelihood or very existence. The organizations themselves can
be said to have been in the closet, preferring to act by proxy or
double proxy rather than to speak, let alone act, up openly for their
cause. And when they did humbly approach official bodies and
public institutions, they were often refused elementary courtesy, let
alone a serious hearing. Steady if erratic progress was achieved,
however, in identifying and publicizing figures from history and
literature who were safely in the past, so as to compile a lengthening
list of reputable homosexuals, but traditionalists contested and still
contest many of the most heroic and brilliant. The battle to out the
dead is far from over.

Not surprisingly, activists after Stonewall took as their slogans
"Come out!" and "Out of the closets and into the streets!" Inspired
by Third World liberation fronts and emulating their guerrilla ethos
and élan, they renounced their predecessors' reticence. Immediately
rather than gradually, confrontation rather than education, demands
rather than petitions, youth rather than experience were their watch-
words.

The tactical shift from "passing" to coming out and from petitioning to demanding can be formulated as a change from *crypsis*–hiding behind a façade of "normality"–to *mimicry*–imitating the political tactics of ethnic minorities seeking to better their status within American society. From adopting measures that would make them invisible to the straight world, gay liberationists went over to imitating the vocal tactics used before them by racial minorities and by women, neither of whom, with rare exceptions, could disguise their identity. Of course, we were neither a religious nor an ethnic community; in fact, we were too diverse and too scattered (in spite of burgeoning gay ghettos) to constitute a community at all. We nonetheless had common interests beyond ending persecution, and these helped galvanize us out of passivity. Many of us, including most activists, found the courage to come out to heterosexuals during the 1970s. Even so, John Alan Lee estimated (1977, p. 58) that of the 100 male leaders in Toronto's gay organizations, a mere half had allowed their real names to appear in print identifying them as gay. Activists who only cautiously came out had no motive for outing others until they saw that wielders of power and other celebrities were refusing to come out. To boot, AIDS had begun to out hitherto closeted celebrities during the 1980s with startling results. Outing was reinforced by the painful discovery that closeted individuals, dreading visibility and potential stigmatization, would refuse to associate any longer with, and would offer no support or encouragement to, anyone known to be gay. The definition of the gay community with its leftist connotation, or better still aspirations for a Queer Nation without such connotation yet portending greater militancy, are central to the issue of outing. Michelangelo Signorile, himself one of the leading outers as well as a theoretician, has written that the analogy with other outsider groups motivates "the accountability by gays in high places to their own community, much the way that Blacks, Jews and women in high places are accountable to their respective communities" (Hartman 1990).

Outsider groups whose members are not highly visible face a choice between assimilation and separatism. This produces an ideological bifurcation: what the assimilationist denies, the separatist proudly affirms. It has been said that by and large, those who can assimilate do, while those who stand out by virtue of physical

appearance and mannerisms, others' discovery of their identity, or
their own compulsive, even involuntary revelation of it, tend to
make a virtue of necessity and espouse the separatist cause. The
assimilationist may reject and hate the separatist for serving as a
constant reminder of his (or her) own "otherness," while the separatist may envy and hate the assimilationist who almost effortlessly
crosses the barriers that for the other remain invisible but impenetrable. This clash of personalities and identities fuels the tension
that leads to our outing "invisible" celebrities.

The historical situation of the homosexual minority in America
obliges us to adopt a separatist position, because we are subject to
*forced assimilation by and into the heterosexual majority and to
their imposition of a cloak of invisibility on us.* The ideological
difference is between the minimalist, who prefers a conventional
life in all areas except the sexual, and the maximalist, who opts for a
totally gay "lifestyle." The former's view amounts to acceptance of
minority status and survival by the majority's leave; the latter's
sense of "community" unduly stresses likenesses within the group.
Queer nationalism is an open rejection of both forms of compromise; it stresses our right to be as different, as flamboyant as we
wish without deferring to the feelings and prejudices of "breeders."
Class and occupation make the choice less than voluntary: even
today one cannot be openly "gay," much less "queer," in certain
professions because formal and informal sanctions would be too
severe. Until quite recently overt homosexuals were prohibited
from practicing psychiatry and still cannot serve in the military or
be ordained as Roman Catholic or Orthodox priests or as ministers
in many Protestant denominations. These include the largest in
America, the Southern Baptists, as that organization has recently
affirmed by expelling two congregations in spite of its old principle
of letting each church go its own way.

What Karl Heinrich Ulrichs once wrote of Urnings like himself is
interesting in this context: "We only play the male, as the German
born in Paris plays the Frenchman, as the Jew reared in Germany
plays the German." This is true, to be sure, only of the feminine-
identified male homosexual to whom the male persona is profoundly alien. In *The Cities of the Plain* (1921) Marcel Proust wrote that
"inverts" were a "race upon which a curse weighs and which must

live amid falsehood and perjury, because it knows the world to regard as a punishable and a scandalous, as an inadmissible thing, its desire, that which constitutes for every human creature the greatest happiness in life . . . but also brought into the company of their own kind by the ostracism that strikes them, the opprobrium under which they have fallen, having finally been invested, by a persecution similar to that of Israel, with the physical and moral characteristics of a race." Richard Bernstein described the lot of the assimilated Jew in Weimar Germany, who "trembles at the revelation of his real origin; he keeps a constant watch on himself lest he betray himself by a word, a gesture, a look; his life has no aim and purpose save one: successful camouflage" (Gross 1991, p. 375).

These considerations enable us to summarize the stages in the development of homosexual visibility: (1) outing by the Church and its accomplices or by the public authorities and police; (2) coming out privately or in a coded language to other crypto-homosexuals; (3) coming out publicly to an intolerant Christian society; 4) outing by movement activists.

This book mainly treats those who have been brought out or made to come out unwillingly. They contrast with those who, as far as the United States is concerned, beginning in the second half of the twentieth century, have chosen to come out of their own accord. But an absolute separation between "coming out" and "outing" is not possible. In fact, the two processes interact in a twofold dialectic. Outing in late medieval and early modern society meant exposing a sodomite or bugger to the penalties which the law and the infamy which society attached to "unnatural vice." Then homosexuals would come out–but only in private or in a discreet, coded language to others who shared the burden of outlawry and infamy. In the next phase, the pioneer homophile activists in late nineteenth- and early twentieth-century Germany and their successors in late twentieth-century America called upon their followers to come out voluntarily–to defy an intolerant society as a political move toward achieving our rights. The final innovation, which began only in the 1980s, saw queer nationalists outing closet cases who, by refusing to come out of their own volition and even professing indifference or hostility to the movement, are hypocritically perpetuating an intolerance from which we who are visible suffer continuously.

We quote various commentators and then address the various points of view about the advisability of outing. This debate will seem far more significant, however, once we have examined some of the many cases unearthed from the annals. Those who do not learn from the past are condemned to repeat its mistakes! Outing of closeted celebrities is needed for the good of the cause. We insist upon our right to claim them as our brothers and sisters. This may seem appalling, but–before reaching a conclusion, read the following chapters.

REFERENCES

Bloch, Iwan. 1907. *Das Sexualleben unserer Zeit in seinen Beziehungen zur modernen Kultur.* Berlin: Marcus.

Churchill, Wainwright. 1967. *Homosexual Behavior Among Males: A Cross-Cultural and Cross-Species Investigation.* New York: Hawthorne Books.

Cory, Donald Webster (pseudonym of Edward Sagarin). 1951. *The Homosexual in America: A Subjective Approach.* New York: Greenberg.

Goffman, Erving. 1963. *Stigma: Notes on the Management of Spoiled Identity.* Englewood Cliffs, NJ: Prentice-Hall.

Halperin, David M. 1990. *One Hundred Years of Homosexuality, and Other Essays on Greek Love.* New York: Routledge.

Hiller, Kurt. 1991. "Ethical Tasks of Homosexuals." *The James White Review* 9/1 (Fall), pp. 13-15.

Hirschfeld, Magnus. 1914. *Die Homosexualität des Mannes und des Weibes.* Berlin: Louis Marcus Verlagsbuchhandlung.

Jaeger, Gustav. 1880. *Entdeckung der Seele,* second edition. Leipzig: E. Guenther.

Joux, Otto de. 1893. *Die Enterbten des Liebesglückes. Ein Beitrag zur Seelenkunde.* Leipzig: Max Spohr.

[Kertbeny, Károly Mária]. 1869. *§143 des Preußischen Strafgesetzbuches von 14. April 1851 und seine Aufrechterhaltung als §152 im Entwurfe eines Strafgesetzbuches für den Norddeutschen Bund.* Leipzig: Serbe.

Lee, John Alan. 1977. "Going Public: A Study in the Sociology of Homosexual Liberation." *Journal of Homosexuality* 3: 49-78.

Plummer, Douglas. 1963. *Queer People: The Truth about Homosexuals.* London: W. H. Allen.

Proust, Marcel. *1927. Cities of the Plain,* 2 volumes. Translated by C. K. Scott Moncrieff. New York: Boni.

Warren, S. 1989. "Telling 'Tales' about Celebrity Closets." *Au Courant* (Philadelphia), October 23, pp. 12, 20.

Chapter II

Why Outing Came About

Outing is as old as Christian intolerance. Many continue to fear it as a fate almost worse than death. There are three historical stages in the technique of outing, all of which may come into play nowadays. First, gossip and innuendo circulate in any community. Ancient Greek and Roman politicians learned to denigrate their opponents with not too subtle allegations of sexual misconduct, as it was then defined. This included adolescent homosexual prostitution, adult male passivity, effeminacy in dress, gait and speech, and orgiastic excesses of all sorts. Today, as in ancient Greece and Rome, gossip of this sort is often ephemerally recorded in graffiti. The second stage of outing, not present in pagan civilization, was the Judeo-Christian taboo against and condemnation of any and all forms of homosexual activity. This persists today, often in secular guise. The third stage is the deliberate exposure of "closeted" homosexuals by movement activists weary of their hypocrisy and treason to the cause.

In contrast to the visibility of a handicap or physical illness, visibility here means primarily others' knowledge that the subject is homosexual (or bisexual) or has engaged in homosexual activity. The negative reactions of others (physical avoidance, difficulty in obtaining or holding a job, inability to make close friends) result from perception of the homosexual subject as "immoral" or "mentally ill." For the individual visibility spawns social and economic problems that can be avoided by the simple expedient of remaining–invisible. But for the movement the collective invisibility of its constituents creates political problems that can be resolved only by their becoming–visible. Secondarily, visibility means public awareness of the phenomenon of love for one's own sex and of its role in history and in society. For many centuries, Christian civilization opted to deny the very existence of homosexuality as orientation and sought in every way to blot homosexual behavior out of consciousness.

Until the 1970s, most lovers of their own sex preferred to remain invisible, and allowed others to do likewise for fear of the penalties that society would not hesitate to inflict on them. Outing meant being apprehended by the authorities of church or state and exposed as a "bugger" or "sodomite." Such a revelation made the accused infamous: it was tantamount to a civil death. Often the only recourse was exile or suicide.

The church, the state, and Christian society committed countless atrocities against queer nationals. But perhaps their worst, their ignoblest crime against us was a crime against the truth: to force every individual with homoerotic feelings to become a lifelong hypocrite. Even if one shunned overt physical contact, one had to lie and deceive, to live in constant fear and anxiety lest one's inner nature and desires be discovered. One might be disowned by family and friends, expelled from school, church, or military, ruined socially and boycotted economically, and driven into exile or even to suicide.

Those publicly labeled "sodomites" were exposed to all the cruelty and vindictiveness of an intolerant society. Not just criminal prosecution, but merciless, unrelenting ostracism–the end of their civil existence–were the almost inevitable consequences (Gruter and Master 1986). Loss of employment, expulsion from school, eviction from apartment, loss of custody of children, denial of visiting rights in hospital or prison, and rejection by kith and kin were commonplace as recently as 20 years ago for known "perverts."

The basic questions that have been debated from Homeric times to the present day are: (1) the morality of sexual acts, (2) the motives for sexual acts, and (3) the moral responsibility of those who perform sexual acts (Cantarella 1980). The medical and biological disputes over "homosexuality" are all secondary, if not an evasion of the issue of the *morality of pleasure derived from erotic contact with one's own sex.* The vicissitudes of society's judgment on this subject have in turn motivated the arguments over the ethics of outing.

PAGAN GREEK AND ROMAN TOLERANCE AND VISIBILITY

Outing, in the sense that it has now acquired, had no meaning in the pagan world because Greeks and Romans were fully aware of homosexual conduct, but neither outlawed it nor ostracized those so inclined. Exclusive homosexuality was a personal idiosyncrasy, mentioned in passing and without reproach. As a rule the Greeks, from the late seventh century onwards, encouraged upper-class men in their early twenties to take a boy of 12 or so to love and train until the man married at 30 and the boy, now grown and bearded, in turn took a boy of his own. Thus by sanctioning pederasty and encouraging late marriage for males, the Greeks hoped to curb overpopulation and refine the initiation and instruction of the young. In Sparta a boy who failed to attract a lover by the end of his twelfth year was considered a failure, but in turn, enormous pressure, amounting almost to social ostracism, was applied to bachelors who failed to marry by 30. All the famous Spartans, about whom we have sufficient biographical information, engaged in pederasty, and roughly half of the great Athenians did likewise. Plato averred that what distinguished Greeks from barbarians was nude gymnastics, philosophy, and pederasty. The Romans, who often gave lip service to the stern, family-centered, patriarchal *mos maiorum* (ancestral customs), never institutionalized pederasty in this way. They did, however, tolerate male prostitution and homosexual relations between masters and slaves, both of which became very common. Occasionally upper-class males had affairs with one another, usually pederastic.

In his earlier works such as the *Phaedrus,* Plato, who matured late and never married, argued the view that pederastic attachments encouraged the soul to sprout wings and the intellect to become active. Maintaining that abstinence between lovers was best, he recognized that even good lovers might occasionally lapse into physical intimacy. Another student of Socrates, the puritanical Xenophon, insisted that Spartans, whom he so admired, avoided physical intimacy with their beloved boys. Their lawgiver Lycurgus, he asserted, had forbidden it. The well-educated, skeptical Cicero was not deceived by such claims, and Spartans were generally thought to be virile boy-lovers. Holding that some passive-effeminate types were born that way and that others acquired the habit, Aristotle felt that the purer form of friendship would not lead to homosexual activity. But these few philosophers, appealing as they did solely to an ideal of "self-restraint" or "civic virtue," went unheeded. Myriads of poets and artists celebrated pederastic love and the beauty of the adolescent male in song and sculpture, and historians faithfully reported the love affairs of prominent statesmen and military leaders.

Nevertheless, forms of male homosexuality (as well as of heterosexuality) that involved force, intimidation, or the selling of the body of a free youth, were penalized or outlawed. Oral-genital relations were so frowned upon in Greece, as well as in Rome, that a reputation for indulging in them brought social ostracism if not worse. Those who actually or reputedly engaged in these stigmatized forms of homosexual activity could be and were outed in this sense and at times even convicted. Orators regularly accused their opponents of violating these taboos. The Athenian orator Aeschines vilified Timarchus for having been a hustler in a male brothel in the port of Piraeus. Cicero even accused Mark Anthony of having lived, as a boy, in the house and served as the "wife" of a tough gang leader Curio.

JUDEO-CHRISTIAN INTOLERANCE AND INVISIBILITY

While the Greeks cultivated *paiderasteia* as a fundamental institution of male society and attribute of gods and heroes, in two centuries, under Persian rule (538-332 B.C.), Biblical Judaism came to reject and penalize male homosexuality in all forms. Jewish religious consciousness deeply internalized this taboo, which became a distinctive feature of Judaic sexual morality, setting the worshippers of the god of Israel apart from the gentiles whose idols they despised. This divergence set the stage for the confrontation between Judaism and Hellenism. The age-asymmetrical homosexuality of the Greeks must have particularly exacerbated the abhorrence of incest that forms the unconscious infrastructure of Judaic morality. Following the onset of the Hellenistic period with the conquests of Alexander the Great, this antagonism grew marked and bitter, and hardened into the latter implacable condemnation and persecution by the Christian Church.

The underlying paradox of sexual psychology is the simple fact that it is impossible to know what another human being feels. One may observe the sexual behavior of others directly or indirectly through narratives, jokes and the like, but one can never experience either the sexual urge that compels others to behave as they do, or the sexual pleasure that they derive from actions that strike the observer as ridiculous, demeaning, and degrading. This incomprehension, joined with the proximity of the sexual organs to the urinary system and the end of the gastro-intestinal tract, makes for oscillation between ridicule and disgust. The Greeks seem to have experienced disgust only minimally and therefore relished the humorous aspect maximally, while the Judaic mentality found every aspect of homosexuality too disgusting for public mention even in a humorous or satiric context. The invisible wall separating the two cultures generated the intense, paranoid homophobia that accompanied the Judean resistance to Hellenization in the Maccabean period and was bequeathed to Christianity when it broke from Judaism to become an independent world religion.

A feature of Plato's thinking in regard to homosexuality that has not been noticed until now is its incorporation of non-Greek elements. The myth of Aristophanes in the *Symposium*, as shown almost eighty years ago by Ziegler (1913, pp. 571-572), derives from a Babylonian myth preserved by Eusebius of Caesarea in a quotation from Berossus. Ziegler equally argued that the myth of the creation of Adam and Eve in Genesis was a Judaic, monotheistic–and heterosexualizing–version of the same. Greek pederasty rather assumed that bisexuality was the potential if not the norm, that an adult male could be both boy-lover and husband with no inner conflict or social ambiguity. The myth in the *Symposium* (189d-e, 191e-192c) instead implies three "exclusive" types, (1) the heterosexual male-and-female, (2) the male homosexual, and (3) the lesbian. It is noteworthy that the male homosexual and the lesbian are distinct sexes, not a variant of one "third sex."

But in the *Laws* (ca. 346 B.C.) Plato adopted the Persian (and Judaic, though he could scarcely have known this) attitude toward pederasty and homosexuality in general. In fact, the definition in the *Laws* (636c) anticipates, albeit clumsily, the modern notion of homosexuality as *behavior*: sexual intercourse with an individual having the genitalia of the same sex. The more abstract thinking of the Greeks thus equated male homosexuality and lesbianism, as the meta-Babylonian etiology of homosexuality as *orientation* had *not* done. One might ask what had alienated Plato, in his old age, so much from Athenian (and Hellenic) mores that he could urge the complete suppression of sexual contact between members of the same sex. Disappointment in love and growing resentment toward those younger and more attractive than himself may have motivated him. It is true that Plato did not so much urge penal sanctions against homosexual activity of either sex, as think that universal condemnation could banish it from consciousness, much as it does incestuous wishes and urges, and so create an exclusively heterosexual citizenry.

By and large, although Plato made concessions to the Greek ideal of *paiderasteia* as a psychological component of education and male bonding and echoed the contempt which his countrymen felt for the *kinaidos* (passive-effeminate male), he never felt comfortable with the practice of boy-love. His own approach to the phenomenon was Oriental and not Greek. The same is true of Xenophon, who had spent much time in Persia. It is thus doubly incorrect to represent the Platonic ideas as characteristic of Greek mores of his own time; they are rather an intrusion of Semitic and Iranian elements that in no way mirrored the distinctive beliefs and practices which the Hellenes had developed in the preceding three centuries. No one in Plato's time could have anticipated that the non-Hellenic attitude was to prevail in later centuries.

At the heart of the "sodomy delusion" lies the Judaic rejection of Hellenism and *paiderasteia*, one of the distinctive features of the culture brought by the Greek conquerors of Asia Minor. It is a fundamental, ineluctable clash of values within what was destined to become Western civilization. Only in the Maccabean era did the opposition to Hellenization and everything Hellenic lead to the intense, virtually paranoid hatred and condemnation of male homosexuality, a hatred that Judaism bequeathed to the nascent Christian Church, accompanied by fantasies of divine retribution on the sinners in this world and in the next. In this instance, it was the conquered race whose morality prevailed over that of the conqueror. This circumstance also explains why "liberation theology" in its historic context is useless to queer nation: the revolt against Syrian rule–which succeeded only because Rome was already extending its hegemony to the Eastern Mediterranean–was accompanied by a paroxysm of homophobia, not to speak of the outlawing of all sexual intimacy with non-Jews. "Liberation" from Hellenism plunged lovers of their own sex into a starless, unending night of oppression. Within Western man two souls struggle for hegemony: the Hellenic and the Judaic, and their duel mirrors a cultural schizophrenia in regard to homoeroticism.

The transformation was the work of Hellenistic Judaism, which blended the Mosaic and Platonic definitions to arrive at the more abstract concept of homosexual *behavior* as blameworthy in pseudo-Phocylides 192 and Romans 1:26-27. Christian moral theology subsequently condemned *sodomia ratione sexus* as a "crime against nature," where it does not matter which sex it is, but rejected and suppressed the notion of homosexuality as *orientation*. In other words, homosexuality as an exclusive attraction to one's own sex was invisible and unknown to the Christian mind from the late Middle Ages onward. It disappeared from the intellectual repertory of Western civilization, and had to be rediscovered in the nineteenth century thanks to Karl Heinrich Ulrichs and Károly Mária Kertbeny. Some modern historians–the Social Constructionists–argue unconvincingly that before Kertbeny coined the term in 1869, "homosexuals" did not even exist.

Pagans viewed non-reproductive eroticism, as long as it did not involve force against a citizen or undue pressure on a subordinate, as a matter of taste. Whether one preferred boys or women made as little difference as whether one preferred fish or fowl. In contrast, at the very moment when Christianity was emerging from Hellenistic Judaism, the latter had already formulated a moral code that limited sexual expression to heterosexual marriage solely for the purpose of procreation, and forbade abortion and infanticide. There was nothing left for St. Paul, St. Augustine or St. Thomas Aquinas to invent. They could, it is true, add their own motivations and morbid fantasies, but the fundamental belief system was adopted from Hellenistic Judaism without change, even while many other provisions of the Mosaic Law were discarded forever. The distinctive feature of Christian sexual morality–the one it does not share with Judaism–

was its asceticism, but this, by its very nature, could be no more favorable to homosexual expression than the Judaic code, although in due time it furnished a convenient pretext to those wishing to evade marriage and the burdens of heterosexual life. Judaism with its positive attitude toward heterosexuality had never offered an alternative to it. Gnosticism bequeathed a fundamental rejection of Eros to Christianity that made even heterosexual intercourse for procreation little more than a necessary evil and homosexual activity a wholly unnecessary and unjustifiable one.

As edited by the Jewish priests in the fifth pre-Christian century, the Mosaic Law (Leviticus 18:22 and 20:13) prescribed death for lying with another male "an abomination." It stipulated that "their blood is upon them," which meant that the perpetrators were to die unavenged: executing them entailed no guilt or pollution. Later the Talmud (b.Sanhedrin 73a) went so far as to ordain that one had the right to kill another individual to prevent his committing the crime. In the New Testament (Romans 1:26-27), St. Paul, employing a Platonic concept that had already penetrated Hellenistic Judaism, condemned the inversion of sexual roles by males and also by females, who had escaped censure by the Jewish scriptures, as "contrary to nature."

No sooner had they converted the Roman emperors than the triumphant Christians introduced the Levitical death penalty for sexual acts between males. Although the punishment was seldom enforced during the anarchy of the Dark Ages, it was reimposed toward the end of the thirteenth century and became normative for Christian society–Orthodox, Catholic and Protestant. This crucial shift from toleration and visibility to intolerance and invisibility underlies the conflict that remains unresolved to this day. From this dual heritage stems our current dilemma–the irreconcilable clash between the Greco-Roman humanism of antiquity and the Judeo-Christian condemnation that prevailed in after ages. It is and remains one of the fundamental contradictions within Western civilization.

CHRISTIAN MIDDLE AGES

Ever since its triumph under Constantine the Great in 323, institutionalized Christianity has uncompromisingly condemned homosexual activity. Constantine's sons first ordained death by the sword. In the sixth century, Byzantine emperor Justinian prescribed in his summary of Roman law the more excruciating penalty of burning at the stake to keep God from inflicting "famines, earthquakes, and pestilences" on a society that neglected to punish sodomites. After an interval of neglect, Roman law, in the form of Justinian's *Corpus*, was revived in Western Europe during the eleventh century. No church father ever defended, much less commended any form of eroticism with one's own sex. In the entire *Patrologia Graeca* and *Patrologia Latina*, collections of the writings of the Church Fathers from the sub-apostolic age to 1453 and 1215 respectively, there is not one sentence on the subject of homosexuality that is even slightly positive. All that gay Christian apologists of the late twentieth century can cherish is the pathetic wish that it had been otherwise. Sanctions in canon law inspired secular authorities to impose ever more severe penalties. These ranged from penances to fines and banishment and from flogging and exposure in the pillory to castration, drowning, stoning, hanging, and burning at the stake.

Too disorganized to persecute sexual misconduct vigorously during the Dark Ages, the Western church lost no opportunity once it gained the moral and political strength in the thirteenth century. Then Western society, which had fully recovered and reorganized its institutions, reached the all-time high-water mark for intolerance: its unrelenting sanctions forced everyone involved in homosexual activity not just to hide his "sinful" behavior, but to perjure his sexual identity–to become a lifelong prevaricator and hypocrite. In composing the *Summa Theologica* St. Thomas Aquinas incorporated (I-II, q. 31, 7) a passage from Aristotle's *Nicomachean Ethics* (VII v 3-4, 1148b) which recognized that some individuals are naturally attracted to their own sex, but altered it to insist that the inclination was always secondarily acquired (Thomas Aquinas 1953, vol. 2, pp., 885b-886a). Thus he precluded any understanding of homosexuality as an exclusive *orientation*, and stigmatized such individuals as sinners against nature.

Christian intolerance bred the cruelest and most absurd fantasies about homosexual *behavior*. Toward 1360 a South Italian jurist,

Luca da Penne, wrote in his *Commentaria in Tres Libros Codicis,* Book XII, 60 (61), 3:

> If a sodomite had been executed, and subsequently several times brought back to life, each time he should be punished even more severely if this were possible: hence those who practice this vice are seen to be enemies of God and nature, because in the sight of God such a sin is deemed graver than murder, for the reason that the murderer is seen as destroying only one human being, but the sodomite as destroying the whole human race. . . .

Homosexuality became invisible to the Christian mind, yet the object of a thousand obscene fantasies. It was nowhere, yet everywhere threatened society with destruction. It was blotted out of the annals of the past, unrecorded in the present, forbidden to exist in the future. Records of trials were burned along with the culprit, so that no trace of the crime should remain. Yet enveloped in the impenetrable darkness of ignorance and superstition, it existed silent and unseen, a phantom eluding the clutches of an intolerant world.

From the end of the thirteenth century onward, conforming to the asceticism of Latin Christendom, church and state fanatically persecuted and society remorselessly ostracized those whom they labeled sodomites. Branded as infamous, shunned and detested, like witches and heretics we were thought to be in league with the demonic powers of another world. In the eyes of the church we were not just sinners, but criminals and outcasts with no rights or feelings that Christian society needed to respect in any way. The very subject of love for one's own sex was banished from Christian consciousness; it was deemed a "crime so abominable that it is not fit to be discussed, named, or even obliquely mentioned in any country where the Christian religion is practiced." Even in the 1990s, publishers issue classical history textbooks that do not say a word about the homosexuality (or bisexuality) of the Greeks and Romans.

While it was always against the law to rob stagecoaches and trains, the highwayman or train robber gained an almost romantic image in life and literature, but the sodomite earned universal hatred and execration. The crime of sodomy was never idealized or romanticized, it inspired only loathing and disgust.

Not all outings resulted in death, but public humiliations, tortures, and executions sufficed to terrorize the population so that no one came out except perhaps indirectly to intimates worthy of trust. From the thirteenth century through the eighteenth the Inquisitors' highly publicized show trials "relaxed" (delivered) sodomites to the secular arm for execution, usually by hanging or burning at the stake. If only some two or three thousand refugees from Sodom suffered its auto-da-fés ("acts of faith"–trials and burnings of heretics), the executions attracted myriads of spectators. Tribunals doomed legions of other victims to exile, galleys, flogging, and other lesser penalties and humiliations. Operating on their own but inspired by Christian moral theology, secular courts, Protestant as well as Roman Catholic, sent several thousand more to the stake, to the gallows, or (in England) to the pillory. Although a handful had felt safe enough to write homoerotic verse as late as the twelfth century, by the late Middle Ages the only refuge for lovers of their own sex was the darkest, most impenetrable corner of the closet.

Crucial to understanding the attitude toward homosexual behavior and those who engaged in it is the concept of *infamy of fact* (Franklin 1954). This was the stigma attached to those who violated specific canons and ordinances of the Church, and in the case of the sodomite it entailed perpetual infamy, which is to say lifelong exclusion from the sacral community of Christian belief. The persistence of medieval infamy into modern times, not some "instinctive aversion" to homosexual activity, fully explains the ostracism and persecution that lovers of their own sex have endured down to the end of the twentieth century.

No question is more intriguing than that of saints who were "heretics in the flesh." If Christianity had been but one of several competing faiths in the Middle Ages, those enamored of their own sex would have had scant motive for adopting it. But because it became the religion of the state, the only one (other than Judaism) tolerated at all, many whose nature destined them for a spiritual vocation had to profess a faith that defamed and denied their innermost longings. Although Wayne R. Dynes holds that evidence is insufficient to out even one saint, John Boswell (1980), the Yale historian, suggests that there were a good many and searches for proof. The greatest Latin father, St. Augustine, confessed to a homosexual phase before his conversion, but that adolescent phase hardly counts. Boswell argues passionately that the Orthodox patron saints of the Byzantine military, Sergius and Bacchus, the commander of a military academy in Syria and his subordinate, who were martyred in 303 when they refused the emperor's command to worship pagan gods, were lovers after converting. Boswell even claims to have the text of Orthodox rites from the eighth and ninth centuries in which the clergy blessed the union, if not the marriage, of male couples—what in Serbian is called *pobratimstvo*, "blood brotherhood." Even Dynes (1990, vol. 2, pp. 1133-34) admits that the eleventh century St. Moses, the Hungarian, is an example of an early Russian Orthodox saint who had homosexual impulses but who may never have acted on them. Sold as a slave by the prince of Kiev to a Polish noblewoman, Moses adamantly resisted her sexual advances. The exasperated master ordered him flogged and castrated, and a triumphant Moses, who very nearly expired during his ordeals, ended his days as a monk in the Kievan Crypt Monastery.

As Bennett Hill pointed out in the only entry on homosexuality in Joseph R. Strayer's 12-volume *Dictionary of the Middle Ages* (1989), the monk Aelred, abbot of Rievaulx (ca. 1110-1167) epitomized homoeroticism in his writings, although as Dynes insists, there is no proof that he yielded to his cravings. Dante placed his detested enemy, Pope Boniface VIII, as well as his cherished teacher Brunetto Latini in hell for sodomy. Edward Gibbon commented wryly on the accusations hurled at the trial of the anti-pope John XXIII, who reigned from 1410 to 1415: "The most scandalous charges were suppressed; the vicar of Christ was only accused of piracy, murder, rape, sodomy, and incest." Evidence to convict any of these clerics beyond a reasonable doubt is lacking, as indeed it is for certain Renaissance popes like Pius II. But there is more than enough probable cause to believe that some saints were guilty of the crime of Sodom. An eleventh-century pope and St. Amselm, a twelfth-century Archbishop of Canterbury, counseled against hunting down clerical sodomites as certain fanatics were already urging—a task relinquished to inquisitors in the thirteenth century.

RENAISSANCE AND REFORMATION

The Renaissance was permeated with homophilia of the classical culture that it revived. The civilization-building élan of the Greeks and Romans in their Golden Ages gave the West a powerful, nay incomparable cultural impetus. Protected by powerful patrons, a few revered Italian artists managed, like certain of the social elite, to flourish in spite of their reputation for sodomy. The new era brought little relief for the mass of less privileged sodomites, though sometimes a de facto tolerance prevailed briefly in certain clandestine "bohemian" urban circles. From time to time the Inquisitors actually ferreted out a number in Italy and Spain so that all remained in dread.

The Renaissance–especially in Italy, then the most influential country in art and learning–saw the passage of new laws against sodomy. The city-states developed efficient methods of surveillance and record keeping, though the apparent increase of outings and trials may reflect, in part, only better documentation. Keeping records meant that recidivists were more likely to be stigmatized for the rest of their lives, even when gossip eventually died down. One alternative was to flee, if possible before the trial began, and indeed, the number of homosexual exiles and émigrés mounted. As in most previous societies, pederasty was the prevalent form of homosexuality in Italy, though not the sole one.

Even in periods of the worst intolerance, those who defended or at least excused their homosexual contemporaries could point to the roster of great men and women who loved their own sex. In his tragedy *Edward II,* published posthumously in 1594, Christopher Marlowe, who quipped that St. John was Jesus' boy, already voiced such a defense:

Great Alexander loved Ephestion,
The conquering Hercules for Hilas wept,
And for Patroclus sterne Achilles droopt:
And not kings onelie, but the wisest men,
The Romaine Tullie loved Octavius,
Grave Socrates, wilde Alcibiades.

A character in the *Aloisia Sigea* of Nicolas Chorier (circa 1660) cited no fewer than 30 such examples. In the satirical *Alcibiade fanciullo a scola*, written in 1630 and published in 1652, the pedant Philotimus, a thinly disguised Socrates, deploys all the arguments for pederasty to convince his pupil, the handsome youth Alcibiades, to yield to his amorous advances.

As one can read even in the hypercritical *Encyclopedia of Homosexuality* (1990), whose chief editor cautiously refused to include any characters who were not clearly homosexual, four Italian Renaissance artists and one poet were clearly outed in their own lifetimes. One even came out on his own. Leonardo da Vinci, the best exemplar of the universal man (*uomo universale*), perhaps the greatest genius of all time, was anonymously accused. The *Uffiziali di Notte*, the officials, as in other Italian states, appointed by the commune of Florence to oversee morals, claimed that he had sexual relations with four males, including one from the princely family of the Medici and a 17-year-old model. The unmarried Botticelli, one of the most distinguished of the pre-Raphaelite painters, was, like Leonardo, denounced to the *Uffiziali di Notte* for having sexual relations with one of his young assistants, but his age and artistic reputation saved him from prosecution. A lesser-known but more ebullient painter, Giovanni Antonio Bazzi, when asked what name should be announced when his horse won the race at Florence, shouted "Sodoma, Sodoma!" in an apparent disregard for public opinion or perhaps misplaced confidence that he would be tolerated because of his artistic talent. Although the authorities did not move against him, the mob fagbashed him. The celebrated goldsmith Benvenuto Cellini was outed by a rival artist exclaiming before Grandduke Cosimo of Florence, "Oh keep quiet, you filthy sodomite!" He was eventually placed under house arrest for sodomy, which gave him the occasion to compose his famous *Autobiography*. The historian and poet Varchi did not even take the trouble to conceal his homosexuality, composing openly homoerotic sonnets, some addressed to the young aristocrat Giulio della Stufa, whose parents forbade him to see Varchi.

In the sixteenth century, Copernicus' daring heliocentric speculations were published thanks only to the efforts of a sodomitical disciple, Georg Joachim von Lauchen, surnamed Rheticus after his homeland in the Rhaetian Alps. Outed more than once, he died at Kosice in Slovakia, which was safely under Ottoman rule (Voss 1931; Zinner 1943, pp. 231-232, 244, 259, 262). Although the lives of scientists are frequently more obscure than those of writers and artists, there is evidence that Sir Isaac Newton, who completed the Scientific Revolution with his laws of gravitation, was attracted to his own sex.

By elevating marriage above celibacy, and making all single males suspect, the Protestants in some respects outdid their Catholic antagonists. Harkening back to Biblical Judaism, where marriage and fatherhood were the norm for the religious elite, they rejected clerical celibacy. Moreover, they rhetorically flagellated the Catholic clergy, including inmates of nunneries, for indulging in perverse sexual acts among themselves and with the laity. All mainstream reformers also condemned simple fornication more than had the medieval church, which had ordained mitigation with confession and penance. In the reformers' polemics, a principal advantage of abolishing monasticism and allowing marriage of priests and bishops was preventing clerical sodomy. Reformers also tried to abolish prostitution which the unreformed Church had condoned as a lesser evil than adultery or the "crime against nature." But in making that option less available, they probably did increase the likelihood of homosexual sodomy. Protestant churches and states perpetuated the Catholic policy of publicly executing sodomites whom they too detested as enemies of God and man.

ANCIEN RÉGIME, FRENCH REVOLUTION, AND ROMANTICISM

Triumphing as the disastrous religious wars ended in 1648, the Scientific Revolution had created a new faith in human reason. Enlightened Europeans began to view the human body and its sexuality more positively. The Christian rejection of this world, the flesh, and its pleasures yielded to a belief in progress and even in mankind's perfectibility. But if *philosophes* disowned the entire Judeo-Christian tradition as irrelevant if not abominable, they did not for that reason eschew the deeply ingrained homophobia that stemmed from it. On the threshold of the eighteenth century Pierre

Bayle, the skeptical French philosopher, began to discredit the belief in miracles, witches, demons, and comets as harbingers of misfortune. Among the skeptical or the enlightened, the dogma that sexuality, save when directed toward procreation within the holy bonds of matrimony, was an evil certain to provoke the wrath of the deity yielded to a positive evaluation of pleasure. A positive legacy of the Age of Exploration was that comparisons with non-European cultures, discovered and described by seafarers and travelers, left no custom or convention unqueried and so undermined the belief in the uniquely "revealed truth" of Christianity.

Although the learned and privileged often carried on affairs in the lax atmosphere of the Old Regime's royal entourages, the mass of the population remained oppressed. The Paris police kept lists of known sodomites, a ledger that by 1783 under Louis XVI, grew to 40,000 names. Yet the individuals recorded on the list were rarely if ever prosecuted. Some, including members of the nobility, were exposed to the public in two Revolutionary pamphlets of 1791. As Louis Crompton showed in *Byron and Greek Love* (1985), down to 1816 the bugger unfortunate enough to be apprehended by the British authorities was usually not hanged, but had to face an ordeal perhaps worse than the gallows–the pillory. Scenes of mob violence against the ill-fated perpetrator undoubtedly moved Jeremy Bentham to propose decriminalization of sodomy, but even this intrepid legal reformer and philosopher dared not publish his extensive writings on the subject.

One of the most promising developments of the Enlightenment was its critique of the penal practice of the Old Regime: cruel and unusual punishments and the use of torture during interrogations. Sodomites endured more than their share of both practices. A new conception of rights to "life, liberty and property" (which the thinkers of the Enlightenment set in opposition to the suppposedly revealed laws of the Old Testament) sanctioned individual freedom: the state should not hinder the pursuit of pleasure so long as it infringed the rights of no third party.

Nevertheless, even among those *philosophes* who professed to endorse free love, few dared to advocate homosexual relations. Notable exceptions were the materialist Julien Offray de la Mettrie; the uncertain author of the novel *Thérèse philosophe*; Mirabeau somewhat ambivalently in the *Erotika Biblion*; and the Marquis de Sade in *La philosophie dans le boudoir*. Jeremy Bentham (1748-1832) did so obliquely in his bitter denunciation of asceticism in the second chapter of *Introduction to Principles of Morals and Legislation*, but his major defense of what he styled pederasty remained in manuscript, unpublished and unread. A year after his death, however, a book (now apparently lost) advocating repeal of the British statutes against buggery was printed on the Continent, and its arguments in turn inspired the still to be identified author of the poem *Don Leon* (1836), which celebrated in verse not only pagans but also "Christians of the highest stamp" who were impassioned of their own sex. At this time Western society still knew homosexuality only as behavior–disgusting, immoral, and unnatural. The *philosophes* advocated repeal of the laws punishing homosexual conduct for the simple reason that such activity in private harmed no one, and the sanctions themselves were motivated by the superstition and fanaticism of the Old Regime. Accordingly the new Penal Code, adopted by the Constituent Assembly in France in September and October of 1791, omitted the offense of sodomy.

Enamored of liberty and hating the Church, revolutionaries struck down the penalties for sodomy when they swept away the ancient laws. Attacking the clergy as well as the nobility, they demolished the Old Regime and repealed codes with cruelty, superstition and fanaticism. Their attempts to establish a "Religion of Reason" failed disastrously, but the Church never recovered from the abolition of tithes and the confiscation of its estates. Girondins and Jacobins alike denounced and persecuted it. As the victorious French armies liberated Belgium and Northern Italy, they implemented the revolutionary reforms and rescinded laws against sodomy.

Promulgating a new penal code, that made no mention of sodomy as part of the complex of laws enacted for his empire in 1810, Napoleon extended it to Holland, western Germany (which he reorganized as the Confederation of the Rhine) and Spain, in fact to virtually the whole of western Europe. But in spite of the abolition of legal sanctions, the social ones–the infamy that attached to the bugger or *pédéraste*, as the enlightened called those whom the clerics had dubbed sodomites–remained. In consequence those erotically involved with their own sex created a "freemasonry of love," joining an underground network of connoisseurs of forbidden pleasure, clandestine and invisible to respectable society. This underworld was invisible to the mass of the citizenry, but visible to those "in the know"–the participants themselves and the police, in particular the morals squad, which kept a watchful eye on all unconventional sexual activity.

Social historians have failed to explain, indeed have often neglected even to ask, why attitudes toward homosexuality changed little throughout this whole dynamic age. Raging since the thirteenth century in Western civilization, homophobia had survived the Protestant Reformation and the Enlightenment intact. The death penalty for buggery, as English law termed it, remained on the books in Russia until 1769, in France until 1791, in Holland until 1811, in England itself until 1861, in South Carolina until 1870, in Scotland until 1887. A key element in this system lay in punishing a few "notorious examples" to terrify millions of others. Even before the mass persecutions of the twentieth-century totalitarian states, legal inertia and conservatism made the punishment relatively even more severe than it had been under the Old Regime. To crown the edifice of illogic, earlier penalties were replaced by long sentences in a prison inhabited solely by others of the same sex. As penal codes were revised, they came to impose a longer term of confinement for consensual sodomy than for armed robbery, theft of funds from a charitable institution, or beating and neglecting a small child.

So far from abating this legacy of intolerance, Victorian morality and bourgeois respectability exacerbated it. The transition from an agrarian Christian society to an industrialized, secular one entailed a psychological transformation of the first magnitude. The *philosophes'* successful campaign against religious intolerance had led after the French Revolution to abolition of the right of the state to impose its religion upon its subjects. At the same time, however, it left an enormous residue of hostility that had previously been vented on adherents of other faiths with no better object than the sexually depraved. Such outcasts became convenient scapegoats for moral indignation. Furthermore, guilt must have burdened the bourgeois mind for having violated the theological prohibition of greed and avarice. Ideologists of capitalism had tried to rationalize these vices as "enlightened self-interest" and then to sanctify them as the "profit motive." Taking over the concern of enlightened despots for man-power, nationalists echoed theological condemnations of birth control to stigmatize those who did not produce children as unpatriotic and brand them as effeminate, weak, and cowardly.

The secular asceticism introduced by the Calvinists and propagated by the Methodists also played a role in the outlawing of erotic pleasures. The ideal victim upon whom the middle classes could unleash their repressed guilt, frustration, hatred, and envy was the sexual non-conformist. The Abrahamic religions had all inherited the Judaic taboo on homosexuality, reinforced in the case of Christianity–as it was not in Islam–by a pronounced ascetic tendency. This now revived with a vengeance given the increasing sacralization of sexual life.

This mélange of guilt, self-interest and the need for a psychological scapegoat best explains "Victorian morality." It was powerfully reinforced by women's unconscious fears of male sexual aggression. The "moral purity" leagues (Fout 1992) could in the name of Christian asceticism seek to prohibit all sexual expression outside of "lifelong monogamous heterosexual marriage." True, they sometimes condoned sexual intimacy between husband and wife intended to express tenderness rather than to spawn offspring. Certain teleological interpretations of Darwin's *Origin of Species* (1859) made procreation the sole "purpose" of sexuality and every non-procreative form of sexual gratification "perverse" and "un-natural." These gave a scientific cast to the traditional Christian belief that reproduction alone morally legitimated sexual pleasure.

Ironically, the wealth and privileges of the haute bourgeoisie demanded a psychological compensation in the form of a revived and heightened sexual asceticism. Single women and male homosexuals became the chief victims bearing the full brunt of medieval intolerance. Bourgeois morality doomed both groups to lifelong abstinence–the fate of a medieval monk, nun or a prisoner in solitary confinement. The psychological valve, that vented society's uncompromising scorn and rejection on them if they lapsed from this ideal, allowed industrialists and speculators to enjoy their fortunes, and all the pleasure and power that money could buy, in psychological and political safety.

Lovers of their own sex were, in fact, the last of those defamed and persecuted by the medieval Church: infidels, heretics, Jews, witches, lepers, to demand–much less receive–the rights promised them by the ideology of the Enlightenment. Even when an organized movement in their favor began, the bourgeois and clerical parties ignored or opposed its demands. After 30 years of patient lobbying, Magnus Hirschfeld, the founder of the German movement, concluded that the bourgeois parties were unable or unwilling to reform the penal laws in accord with the findings of modern biology and psychology.

THE HOMOPHILE MOVEMENT

In opposition to the norms of bourgeois society, German Romanticism brought a new intellectual current–one that left behind the narrow rationalism of the eighteenth century. Thinkers such as Carl Gustav Carus and Eduard von Hartmann introduced the concept of the unconscious, preparing the way for depth psychology and for the introspectiveness that led to the recognition of homosexuality as an *orientation*–a spontaneous, involuntary, erotic attraction to members of one's own sex. The first to write on this hitherto forbidden subject was an obscure Swiss milliner, Heinrich Hoessli, whose two-volume work *Eros* fielded a concept not before defended or celebrated, a harbinger of modern androphilia: *Männerliebe* "male love." It was this mental state that his successor analyzed by looking inward into their own emotions and outward at the clandestine subculture of those with whom they interacted, socially and sexually, and then differentiated from others whose sensuality was directed elsewhere.

The end of the nineteenth century and the Edwardian age saw powerful international countercurrents to conformity in politics and the arts. Forces long fermenting beneath the surface challenged society's whole approach to sexual mores. New, tolerant attitudes toward sexual and particularly homosexual expression gained ground in enlightened quarters, so that the homophile movement joined a growing front of advocates of sexual reform. The historical preconditions for the founding of an organized movement for the rights of homosexuals were:

1. The new approach "in depth" to the human psyche initiated by German Romanticism.
2. The biological debate over human evolution begun by Darwin's *Origin of Species.*
3. The emergence of the Social Democracy as an organized political force opposed to the interests of the haute bourgeoisie and of the state power which the latter controlled.

Together, all these created a climate of opinion that legitimated an organization that, for the first time in modern history, openly rejected asceticism as the basis of sexual morality, challenged the Christian condemnation of homosexual activity, and sought understanding and toleration for lovers of their own sex.

The Hanoverian jurist Karl Heinrich Ulrichs began the homophile movement in Germany in 1864 (Hirschfeld 1914, pp. 952-967; Kennedy 1988, pp. 56-63), but remained alone because no one else was willing to speak out publicly for such an unpopular cause. He invented the word *Urningtum* to describe the aggregate of those attracted by their psychic nature solely to their own sex (which he explained by the Kabbalistic notion of "a female soul trapped in a male body" and vice versa), but with no further predicate and under the assumption that they amounted to a few thousand in the whole of Germany. His corollary was that such individuals were not culpable and should not be punished as male homosexuals were under Prussian law and were soon to be throughout the German Empire when it received a uniform penal code in 1871.

Not until 1897 did a few brave pioneers take the next step, to organize publicly for education and lobbying. Ulrichs' successor, the Jewish physician Magnus Hirschfeld, founded the Scientific-Humanitarian Committee in the suburb of Berlin. It became the homosexual wing of the sexual reform movement. This movement grew slowly at first, then flourished under the Weimar Republic until Hitler assumed power in 1933 and crushed it. This unprecedented step marked a new phase in the struggle for the emancipation of a minority from the hatred, intolerance, and invisibility in which medieval ignorance and fanaticism had tenaciously enshrouded it into the twentieth century.

But the arguments of movement spokesmen were not received at once, in fact the past 128 years have witnessed a still unfinished conflict between the old and the new in sexual psychology and sexual politics. The major problem–of which Foucault never had the slightest inkling–has been the *non-reception* of the new apologetic concepts created by defenders of love for one's own sex. This negative outcome stemmed directly from the fact that for Western society homosexual orientation was an incomprehensible *anomaly*–a phenomenon with which official science could not deal (Westrum et al. 1982) and which could only call into question one of the fundamental taboos of Western civilization. In this taboo, Christianity has invested so much of its moral credit that if it were ever forced to renounce its claims in this sphere, it would be well advised to file a petition in bankruptcy.

The infamy, which the medieval Church imposed on those guilty of "crimes against nature," was what the homophile movement had to discredit in the eyes of the public. Our defenders, it is true, often preferred to evade the challenge by posing the issue in medical or biological terms–or as one of "civil rights for a minority that had been the object of discrimination." But in the final analysis there is no alternative to challenging the religious dogmas underlying that stigma, and the fundamental notion of the "sinfulness" of homosexual acts. To maintain that what is "sinful" should not be criminal is no solution, because it leaves the social sanctions and penalties unchanged–the ostracism, the economic boycott, the random violence inflicted precisely because the perpetrators feel that society is failing to punish the culprits in a deserved manner.

As he gained more knowledge through interviews and questionnaires, Hirschfeld (1914) raised his estimate of the homosexual population step by step from 0.2 percent to 2.2 percent of the whole, making it a not insignificant segment of society. The movement that he headed had a centralized leadership unknown to its later American counterpart. Like his predecessor Ulrichs, Hirschfeld firmly believed homosexuality to be innate. He adamantly argued that it could not be an acquired condition. His remained the position of the German movement to the bitter end.

The Scientific-Humanitarian Committee championed Ulrichs' theory that homosexuality was inborn and unmodifiable. It even

added the notion of an evolutionary "third sex" intermediate between the male and the female. These views, which derived homosexuality from intersexuality, were increasingly challenged by the
insight which depth psychology brought to the dynamics of sexual
orientation. No one, however, could, in the last analysis, explain
why particular individuals become exclusively homosexual or exclusively heterosexual while others oscillated along a bisexual continuum. On the other hand, authorities like Richard von Krafft-Ebing who adhered to the not yet discredited Lamarckian theories of
the heritability of acquired characteristics interpreted homosexuality as the outcome of "degeneration of the central nervous system."
This untenable construct was adopted only gradually and with a
homophobic gloss by theologizing psychiatrists and other retrograde segments of the population.

The homosexual rights movement had its own dialectic. On the
one hand, the survival of medieval infamy profoundly contradicted
the official ideology of the Enlightenment that on the other hand,
called for universal human rights, freedom of conscience, and separation of state and church. The politicization of the homosexual
subculture was thus an absolutely new phenomenon. Abundantly
documented though the subculture itself is for mid-nineteenth century Europe and the United States, the political consciousness
awakened by Ulrichs (who founded the movement) and Kertbeny
(who invented the word) spread very slowly from Germany to the
rest of the world. The older consensus, which surfaced in the *Don
Leon* poems (1823-36) and elsewhere, that lovers of their own sex
belonged to a "freemasonry of pleasure" which should never
betray its secrets to a hostile world clashed with the new public
stance. The contemporary demand for outing stems from the irrec-
oncilability of the two positions: the older one, which sanctioned
clandestinity and invisibility, and the newer, which calls for a public, visible presence for the queer nation.

The German pioneers launched the struggle for homosexual visibility—a subject that merits an article if not a book. Theirs was not
just a campaign for repeal of the sodomy laws, cornerstone of
intolerance that these were and are. It was a concerted effort to end
the taboo on the public discussion of love for one's own sex and the
monumental distortion and falsification of history, biography, litera-

ture and art that ensued from this prohibition. The Scientific-Humanitarian Committee entertained proposals that urgently called for a
mass self-outing, or as we would say voluntary coming out, on the
part of homosexuals, initiatives mentioned in the *Monatsbericht des
Wissenschaftlich-humanitären Komitees* for November and December of 1905 (Hirschfeld 1914, p. 1003). However, from that time 85
years passed–with few concrete results. Even in Germany, few
acceded to the appeal of movement activists to come out, simply
because the person engaging in overt activity could be prosecuted if
revealed to the police. The social risk was too great and the immediate political return too slight. Consequently, all who could remained
invisible, except for a handful of daring poets and artists whom
prestige and eminent patrons shielded from a vindictive society.

In its 36 years the German homophile movement never held a
single public demonstration, parade, or rally. The Scientific-Humanitarian Committee's conferences were sedate. Even attendees did not
necessarily identify as homosexual. In turn-of-the-century Berlin, the
police kept a list of homosexuals similar to that long maintained by
the Paris police. This time, however, the keeper "was one" himself,
Leopold von Meerscheidt-Hüllessem. A secret collaborator of
Hirschfeld's, he even intended to publish the dossier in order to
reveal to the world once and for all the absurdity of §175 of the
Reich Penal Code. In effect the first "would-be" outer, he was
prevented only by the intervention of higher powers, many of
whom were implicated themselves. Elsewhere, only in Austria and
the Netherlands did the Scientific-Humanitarian Committee find
imitators. When attempts were made in democratic France and the
United States to found such groups, they were promptly suppressed
by the police.

Furthermore, when open-minded psychiatrists had the opportunity to meet homosexual subjects in their homes and places of work,
they quickly realized that these were sane, functional human beings
who had nothing in common with the catatonics and schizophrenics
whom the physicians had, since their days in medical school, observed in clinics and insane asylums. But in deference to Victorian
morality, from the early 1890s onward the psychiatric profession
simply turned its back on the plight of those snared in the net of an
ascetic morality. They tacitly sanctioned continued prosecution and

punishment by the bourgeois-liberal state, now increasingly conservative and defensive as social democratic parties gained ground. From the second decade of the twentieth century, legislatures imposed new disabilities on us in civil and administrative law, supplementing the old criminal sanctions, on the grounds that we were mentally ill–in addition to being sinners, criminals and outcasts. This analysis of the relationship among the churches, the psychiatric profession, and the state power should be the essence of a scientific interpretation of the tenacity of Christian homophobia in modern times, the non-reception of the arguments of the homophile movement, and the perpetuation of the criminality and social infamy against which the queer nation is struggling to this day.

RECEPTION AND NON-RECEPTION OF THE MOVEMENT

The medicalization of sodomy had begun with Paolo Zacchia and his *Quaestiones medico-legales* (1621-50), but in a different sense from the one in which the Social Constructionists understand it. Zacchia, the chief physician at the papal court, and his successors were concerned with applying their art to uncovering the telltale evidence of the guilt of the accused, that is to say they placed forensic medicine at the service of the sodomy delusion. Between 1630 and 1880 casuistic writings were published–first in Latin, then in the vernacular–that anticipate Krafft-Ebing in all details except in seeking to exculpate the subject on the grounds of his abnormal mental state. Casper's *Handbuch der gerichtlichen Medizin* (1857) and Tardieu's *Étude médico-légale sur les attentats aux moeurs* (7th edition 1878) were the last major writings in the older tradition. But from the time that Ulrichs began to nudge them in the other direction, enlightened forensic experts worked to undermine and overthrow the delusion. Westphal, Krafft-Ebing and their epigones shifted the focus of attention to the mental state that impelled the accused to commit the crime–which the Church in its infinite wisdom had been unable to detect in all of the preceding 600 years. In other words, instead of testifying for the prosecution, the forensic psychiatrist now came forward as an expert witness for the defense, arguing that the sexual orientation of the defendant absolved him from moral responsibility for his action.

The authority independent of the churches that medical science enjoyed in the public mind, and the privilege accorded the medical expert to treat matters otherwise banned from public mention, were crucial in undermining the taboo that had kept the whole subject out of consciousness for six centuries. Krafft-Ebing's *Psychopathia sexualis* (first edition 1886) reached a readership far beyond the audience of "jurists and forensic psychiatrists" for whom it was ostensibly destined, and made the educated classes aware of the phenomena of abnormal sexuality, even if in a one-sided and not always insightful manner.

This new, quite unexpected role of the psychiatrist heightens the significance of the debate that took place at the session of the Berlin Society for Psychiatry and Nervous Diseases on June 8, 1891. There Friedrich Jolly (1844-1904), Westphal's successor at the psychiatric division of the Charité, and the other leading Prussian experts on forensic psychiatry debated the question of whether homosexuality was a mental illness and decided unanimously in the negative; they concluded correctly that it did not constitute grounds for relieving the defendant from responsibility for violations of §175 of the Reich Penal Code (Kronthal 1891).

They based this judgment on four reasons:

1. There is no failure of cognition or clouding of the conscious mind.
2. There is no irresistible impulse.
3. The subject has no delusion as to the character of his own or the partner's sexual organs.
4. The subject is aware that his sexual orientation differs from that of the majority of the population.

Common as it is to all healthy, adult human beings, the periodic recurrence of the sexual drive entails no element of pathology. The notion that homosexual acts are "contrary to nature" is a legacy of polytheistic belief in a mother goddess of fertility whose will is contravened by sterile modes of sexual congress. Modern science has abandoned this concept along with all other residues of teleological thinking. It operates instead with a model of the universe that is absolutely indifferent to man, his actions and purposes.

The outcome of the discussion in Berlin and psychiatric articles in the same vein did not prevent the "new homophobia" from emerging in the 1890s. It found its fullest expression at the Fifth International Congress of Criminal Anthropology at Amsterdam in 1901. There Arnold Aletrino, who spoke in defense of the "uranist," was roundly abused by Cesare Lombroso and the psychiatrists who not only insisted that homosexuality was "always a disease," but urged that police take measures to silence propaganda in favor of toleration and lock up homosexuals when they put their theories into action. This conference marked the beginning of the pseudo-medical and pseudo-scientific defamation of homosexuality that little by little supplanted the old theological one.

Characteristically enough, theologians almost entirely ignored the writings of the homosexual emancipation movement and of psychiatrists and psychoanalysts sympathetic to it, which they conveniently dismissed as "perverted filth." Practitioners of the occult and the supernatural are, however, exceedingly brazen, and their technique of deception entails reformulating their archaic, discredited notions in scientific terms superficially plausible to the modern mind. By the 1940s the clergy and others came to appreciate that the psychoanalysts, after borrowing so much from the homophile advocates, had turned their backs on the sexual reform movement. Now they could furnish a weapon that would allow the defenders of tradition to modernize their opprobrium. So the belief that sodomy was "an unnatural and disgusting vice" yielded to clerical insistence that homosexuality was "a loathsome and contagious disease."

NEW OUTINGS AND THEIR CONSEQUENCES

The last decade of the nineteenth century and the first of the twentieth saw the most spectacular outings yet–sensationalized by the yellow press. The invention of printing had made the issuing of broadsheets possible–single printed leaves, sometimes containing crude illustrations–that conveyed scandalous or marvelous doings to a credulous public. Early in the eighteenth century this function shifted to periodicals, and towards its end to regular newspapers. The so-called "penny press" reached millions by the end of the nineteenth century. To be sure, Victorian prudery restrained explicit discussion of sexual matters, and the victims sometimes had the option of libel suits. Nevertheless, the "lords of the press," who sought to drive circulation figures up, became expert in the suggestive innuendo. They remained within the law–if only just–if not within the bounds of propriety, while conveying spicy tidbits to readers versed in the not-so-subtle code. Such scandals, potentially ruinous for politicians and businessmen, titillated respectable bourgeois. Today this legacy of the "yellow press" survives in the tabloids sold in supermarkets and in programs on late-night television.

In what was perhaps the most famous outing of all history, and certainly of the fin de siècle, Oscar Wilde, the Irish wit, poet, dramatist, novelist, and writer of fairy tales was destroyed when outed by a not very intelligent Scottish aristocrat, the Marquess of Queensberry. At the height of his popularity, Wilde fell madly in love with the very handsome but morally flawed Lord Alfred Douglas ("Bosie"). In 1895 Queensberry, Bosie's father, who in 1867 had formulated the standard rules for boxing, left a card at their club addressed "To Oscar Wilde posing as a somdomite [sic]." Douglas pushed Wilde into a suit for libel. Under cross-examination Wilde was maneuvered into confessing that he was sexually attracted to males. He was convicted of gross indecency with several hustlers whom Queensberry had managed to dredge up from London's sexual underworld. He was sentenced to two years' hard labor–the maximum penalty under the Criminal Law Amendment Act of 1885, which had first criminalized gross indecency. His marriage collapsed, and his possessions were auctioned to defray the costs of his defense. His plays could no longer be performed on the London stage. Most of his friends abandoned him. The ear infection that he contracted in Reading Gaol killed him three years after his release.

The scandal reverberated throughout the Western world. In North America it abetted intolerance, while in France Wilde's treatment drew merited comment on British hypocrisy and intolerance. A great artist, it was felt, should not have been subjected to such indignities. The trial also made lovers of their own sex, throughout the civilized world, conscious for the first time that they were an oppressed group. It catalyzed the resistance that led, two years after Wilde's conviction, to the founding in 1897 in Germany of the Scientific-Humanitarian Committee, the world's first homosexual rights organization. Thus Wilde's outing awakened gay political consciousness in the twentieth century, as the almost contemporary Dreyfus affair sparked Zionism in reaction to anti-Semitism.

In Imperial Germany Alfred Krupp, the multi-millionaire industrialist and friend of the Kaiser, whose case in some ways resembled that of our own Malcolm Forbes, was driven to suicide. Then in the Harden-Eulenburg affair of 1907-09, a Jewish journalist exposed the Kaiser's powerful intimate as the center of a clique that had been infiltrated by a French diplomat relaying information to the Quai d'Orsay. The American author Edward Irenaeus Prime-Stevenson and the German critic and littérateur Alfred Kerr dared to intimate in print during the scandal that Wilhelm II himself was homosexual; as it were the queen bee in the hive.

THE WORLD WARS

The mass slaughter of the two world wars eroded Victorian confidence in liberal values and traditional ethics more than the criticisms of Edwardian philosophers and historians. The precariousness of life persuaded many, especially soldiers facing death daily, to live for the here and now. Enforced deprivation of every kind, on the home front as much as on the battlefield, stripped "abstinence" of its moral grandeur. Colonial peoples saw the conflicts as a civil war within the white race, while Marxists hailed them as the inevitable prelude to the fall of capitalism.

Released from caution and tradition by the extraordinary danger and carnage in the trenches and liberated by their own heroism, a great many men came out to one another (Bérubé 1990). The booming 1920s saw a greater disregard for traditional morals than the depressed 1930s, when fascist and Communist attacks on sexual promiscuity and bourgeois decadence pushed even the democratic societies to greater conformity. In contrast to the witchhunts conducted by the American services in the Second World War, during the First World War the intelligence services of the belligerents made no concerted effort to hunt down and expose individuals with a homosexual orientation. In 1914 the very concept of "homosexuality" was still too new and unfamiliar, except perhaps in Germany and Austria, to serve as the basis for any state policy. Given the mass slaughter, all men, of whatever sexual predisposition, were, in any case, desperately needed if only as cannon fodder.

The Fourteen Points, President Wilson's formulation of Allied war aims, promised self-determination to the emerging nationalities long submerged in the Austro-Hungarian, Russian, and Ottoman Empires. It was on the basis of this new Central European concept of ethnic "minorities," as opposed to the old British parliamentary usage, that Hirschfeld's ally Kurt Hiller (1885-1972), writing in the spring of 1918, defined homosexuals as a biological minority within every population, equally deserving of legal toleration and protection.

In the aftermath of the First World War, a few intellectuals such as Radclyffe Hall in England and André Gide in France came out. Even so, most others, such as Thomas Mann and A. E. Housman, revealed their inner selves only to initiates in the "freemasonry of pleasure" or at least to the educated and sophisticated few through subtle or not so subtle poetic and artistic intimations. Like those who had come out in Germany during the homophile emancipation movement from 1897 to 1933, they were mostly professionals or intellectuals. In France, Proust and Gide set the pace in 1921 and 1924. But perhaps in all of Western history since the fall of Rome, not more than two or three thousand came out before the 1970s. Invisibility perpetuated hostile stereotypes and grossly distorted caricatures, but enabled all those who avoided this image to pass as "straight."

The half-Jew Marcel Proust realized that like diaspora Jewry we constituted a hated and persecuted race. The first American to come out fully to the public was the poet Robert Duncan, who startled America by his bravery in using his own name in an article he published in the anarchist magazine *Politics* in 1944. He argued that like Negroes and Jews, homosexuals were an oppressed minority. To be sure, the risks of everyday life and the oases of refuge could vary from one generation and one locality to the next.

Unlike Central Europe, the Western democracies rejected such departures from convention as homosexual rights and veered toward prewar normalcy. The totalitarian regimes that gained power in the Soviet Union and Germany between the wars instituted a new wave of repression of homosexuals. National Socialists and Communists imprisoned thousands who did not escape their clutches by flight, by hiding even more deeply, or by suicide. Hitler crushed the German homosexual movement in 1933, and enacted even more punitive laws in 1935. Of all categories of prisoners in the Nazi concentration camps male homosexuals–the men with the pink triangle–had the lowest survival rate (Johansson and Percy 1990; Consoli 1991). Reversing the toleration of the post-revolutionary regime, Stalin clamped down on Russian homosexuals in 1933-34 (branding them "fascists") as brutally as Hitler persecuted the German ones (Lauritsen and Thorstad 1974). All totalitarian states instituted methods of surveillance and control exceeding the rigor of the most intolerant pre-modern regimes. The final chapter in this tale was written by the Stalinists and pseudo-Maoists of the 1970s who castigated homosexuality as "bourgeois decadence"–as if Victorian morality represented a lost ideal which a future socialist order should revive.

The psychoanalysts who fled from Central Europe to America themselves, after the National Socialist seizure or power, imbibed the homophobia of their new homeland. Their patients were ideologically disarmed because the United States had no movement that could have given them a positive identity and esprit de corps. During the Second World War, psychiatrists encouraged the American military to exclude and stigmatize homosexuals. When theologians saw an alliance offered them by the reactionaries in the psychoanalytic camp, who gained ascendancy in the United States after Hitler's suppression of the sexual reform movement and Freud's death, they welcomed the new ideas as pseudomedical rationalizations of their long-cherished religious antipathy to homosexuals. From then onward, writers on "pastoral psychology" confidently quoted psychoanalytic authorities to insist that "homosexuality is always a serious disease," that "homosexual love is hate," and similar nonsense.

In sum, while a few more individuals felt liberated enough to come out in public during the "Roaring Twenties," than during the "Nightmare Years" of the 1930s, on the whole the turmoil and catastrophes after 1914, and far more during the National Socialist and Stalinist reaction between 1933 and 1945, inflicted more setbacks than gains. The homosexual emancipation movement collapsed, the "new homophobia" gained ground among the half-educated, and despite endless pronunciamentos that the war was being fought to guarantee human rights and freedoms, queer nationals in the English-speaking world remained a pariah community, invisible and defenseless.

But the "new homophobia" was not confined to theory; it soon learned to put its barely masked intolerance into practice. The Italian inventors of electroshock therapy, Ugo Cerletti and Lucio Bini, as one may see from the collection of articles that announced it to the world in *Rivista sperimentale di freniatria* in 1940, never employed it on patients suffering from psychosexual disorders. This tactic was innovated by American psychiatrists who used the new procedure to torment their homosexual patients, often those forcibly subjected to their custody. This difference shows that in order to establish precisely where the Americans went beyond their European mentors, the historian must track ideas and practices from their point of origin to the very moment at which the ship carrying them docked in New York harbor. The inability of American "gay historians" to do so precludes their ever understanding what happened and keeps their approach provincial and naive.

The 1940-60 period saw the full reception of the "new homophobia" by the American political and religious establishment. The complex of moves cannot have stemmed from oversight or from a layman's misunderstanding of psychiatric concepts; it went wholly unopposed by the medical profession. In fact, as late as 1956 a committee of psychiatrists reviewing a military code penalizing even those who merely "associated with homosexuals" would not suggest that the regulations be changed, but only expressed apprehension that "some innocent persons might be punished."

HOMOSEXUALS IN THE MILITARY

Like the celibate clergy, the military has always attracted those disinclined to settled family life, of whom many preferred their own sex. They experience an all-male environment remote from civilian life and intense male bonding in the face of danger, which seems to accentuate homoeroticism. A British career officer writes from personal recollection:

> Where officers are concerned the officers' mess has often been the preferred and almost the only real home of unmarried men.

This was especially obvious in my early days in the Army, when early marriage was actively discouraged, made difficult in some regiments, virtually forbidden until what would now be regarded as much too great an age. . . . Elderly bachelors, as they seemed to me, warming their behinds as they monopolized the fire, booming away about old campaigns, were a familiar feature of the military landscape (Richardson 1981, p. 33).

The Romans did not allow troops on active duty to marry, and until the late nineteenth century the British forbade their officer corps to marry.

The list of celebrated commanders who loved their own sex, from nearly all the Greeks and Macedonians through Julius Caesar and Mark Anthony down to modern times, is too long to be recited here (see Rowse 1977). At Marathon, at Thermopylae, at Salamis the pederastic spirit faithfully guarded the cradle of Western civilization from Persian despotism. The Sacred Band, composed of pairs of lovers united by fidelity in combat, liberated Greece from Spartan tyranny and died to the last man fighting for Greek liberty at Chaeronea. It found imitators outside the Hellenic world, in Semitic Carthage with its African warriors.

Even in the Christian Middle Ages Richard the Lion-Hearted had to do public penance for sodomy twice, and the Knights Templar were formally accused of it, though the question remains moot. Louis XIV's brother "Monsieur" and another of his best generals, the Prince de Condé, were homosexual, as was his most formidable opponent Prince Eugene of Savoy. Not so was the British general who fought beside Eugene, John Churchill, first Duke of Marlborough, but his wife supposedly had a long affair with their sovereign Queen Anne. In the great struggle of the mid-eighteenth century, the Seven Years War (for us the French and Indian War), which determined that the English rather than the French would rule both North America and India, England's chief ally and one of the greatest generals and statesmen of all time, Frederick the Great of Prussia, was bisexual and his brother Henry exclusively homosexual. Prince Henry was even considered by a monarchist circle around George Washington for king of the newly independent nation, and Charley Shively maintains that Washington himself, who was ably

aided by another Prussian homosexual, Baron von Steuben, may
have been compromised with his own sex. Washington's favorite
aide, Alexander Hamilton, is also suspect at the very least of having
exploited the Commander in Chief's infatuation with him, as Paul
Hardman argues in *Homoaffectionalism: A Study of Male Bonding
from Gilgamesh to the Present* (1993). Of course, situational homosexuality was even more rife among sailors and crews of pirate
ships who in those days were often at sea for many months, even
years at a time. Even if the ancient Greek tradition that lovers
fought more bravely as warrior pairs than did woman-lovers was
dead, the military never lacked homoerotic heroes. Many loved
overseas adventures, the most famous modern British hero of that
ilk being General "Chinese" Gordon, who died a hero's death at
Khartoum. The hero of Mafeking, Lieutenant-General Sir Robert
Baden-Powell, founded the Boy Scouts in Great Britain in 1908, an
organization that quickly spread to almost every civilized country.
A recent biography has outed him as a pederast, rather amusingly
just before the current quarrel over the exclusionary policy of the
American branch. General Lyautey, who conquered Morocco for
France in the early twentieth century, undoubtedly, however, expressed a minority position when he declared that he could effectively command only officers with whom he had slept. Viscount
Montgomery of Alamein, the British general who drove the Axis
armies out of North Africa, has been exposed as a self-hating "closet case" in the original meaning of the term (see p. 6).

The coming of the theological-forensic concept of homosexuality
influenced the military, but in a negative direction. It was precisely
in those countries where the law still penalized "crimes against
nature," rather than in ones that had adopted the Code Napoléon
which did not, that the military authorities were preoccupied with
the supposed problem. But remarkably enough, at the outbreak of
the First World War an unusual number of homosexual men
streamed into the German army and volunteered for service, including many who had been living virtually in exile for fear of §175, the
article of the penal code that proscribed male homosexuality.
"Many of them must have been attracted by the possibility of living
for a long time in an exclusively masculine environment which
even without any coarse, sensual activity, exercises upon the major-

ity of the homosexuals the satisfying and releasing influence of erotic satisfaction" (Hirschfeld 1934). Others were motivated by the tragic wish or hope to end their lives gloriously on the battle-field rather than disgrace and dishonor themselves and their families if their sexual orientation became known, or even worse, if they were prosecuted for infractions of the penal code.

German officers who had run afoul of blackmailers or been convicted of "lewd and unnatural conduct" were mercilessly expelled from the service, a practice retained even during the war. Some hoped to regain their former military positions, but had to file a special request to the throne, which in nearly every case Wilhelm II, himself homosexual and surrounded by courtiers of the same stripe, hypocritically rejected. Some persevered in submitting their applications, but the most that they ever achieved was to be inducted as volunteers without an officer's rank, and they could never hope for promotion. The German military authorities adhered to the standpoint that a homosexual predisposition or homosexual activity were grounds for court-marital. Such cases multiplied during the war. Officers were immediately sent home to be tried by a military court; and unless the accused was able to dispel every last trace of doubt, he was certain to be discharged. Despite the fact that officers were usually punished rather mildly for most other misdemeanors, homosexuality was more severely penalized among them than among non-commissioned officers and private soldiers, in order to maintain strict discipline. The belief was commonly held that a homosexual officer could not preserve the proper distance from his subordinates and might therefore provoke insubordination. Officers attracted to their own sex, however, were very popular because they did not conform to the authoritarian norm of masochism toward one's superiors but merciless sadism toward one's inferiors. Non-commissioned officers usually were let off with a disciplinary pen-alty—two weeks in the brig—and then returned to the front owing to the chronic scarcity of cannon fodder in the German army as the Marne, the Somme and then Verdun cut a bloody swath through its ranks (Hirschfeld 1934, pp. 125, 128, 133).

In the First World War, the American, like the other Allied armies, made no attempt to screen out recruits with homosexual inclinations or predilections. A sexual offense could make the individual "unfit" for military service and result in his incarceration, but merely *being* a homosexual had as yet no meaning. The Navy did, however, employ decoys to entrap personnel in Newport, Rhode Island–an episode that almost proved politically ruinous for Assistant Secretary of the Navy Franklin Delano Roosevelt. However, by the late 1930s the "new homophobia" was arriving in America with the exodus of Jewish psychiatrists and psychoanalysts from Central Europe. Their advice was welcomed by military professionals and adopted to justify exclusionary or punitive measures. Medical science thus served perfectly to rationalize existing prejudices that could no longer be formulated and justified exclusively in Biblical or theological terms.

The systematic psychiatric screening of inductees began in 1941 at the instigation of Harry Stack Sullivan, an influential thinker in the field who was also a closeted homosexual who lived with his lover. It involved a concerted effort to ferret out "sodomists," as they were termed by the military, while the run-of-mill psychiatric examiners who ran the programs tended to favor aggressive detection of "perverts." There were two main rationales for screening out "sodomists," whom the newer terminology styled variously as "sex deviates," "habitual homosexuals," "pathics," "sexual perverts," "confirmed perverts," and "moral perverts." First was the claim that the psychiatrically unfit of 1917-18 (when inductees had been screened only for physical defects) furnished a large share of inmates of Veterans Administration hospitals. This burden on the taxpayer should not be repeated by admitting such misfits into the uniformed services. Second, it was held that homosexual recruits would have a bad effect on the morale of "normal" soldiers, a claim that the American armed services are still voicing today. The result of these measures was to make the homosexual excludable as a personality type, for one needed only to be "prone" to engage in the tabooed behavior to fall under the ban.'

After the United States entered the war in December 1941, with an urgent need to draft every available man, the psychiatric interviews tended to become negligent and perfunctory. When manpower was scarce in the initial phase of mobilization, the services made no great effort to screen out either male homosexuals or lesbians. Widespread naïveté on the subject of sexual inversion further undercut the enforcement of such policies of exclusion. Only 5,000 were rejected at induction centers.

By the beginning of 1943, however, the Navy (followed by the Army), adhering to psychiatrists' recommendations, established policies to eliminate such individuals from the service, provided that they were not deemed essential. As the tide of battle turned the bureaucracy that had been created to rid the armed services of sexual deviates geared up to deal with the "problem." It was recognized that a great many homosexuals had slipped through the earlier screening. A concerted effort was begun to identify them, to concentrate them in hospitals, and eventually to drum them out of the service with an undesirable or dishonorable discharge. By 1944, Army and Navy administrators, replacing the archaic label "sodomists" with the modern "homosexuals," enjoined officers to turn them all over, including even so-called "latent" ones, to psychiatrists for observation and diagnosis. Military authorities, however, retained the last word in the disposal of the cases. Those caught in homosexual acts or admitting to them were pressured to name their previous sexual partners. In this way an atmosphere resembling that of the Spanish Inquisition developed. It was noticed that many women in the armed forces had a noticeably "mannish" appearance, and they too were subject to surveillance and ultimately separation from the service in greater proportion than males (Bérubé 1990).

Ominously for the future, these policies foreshadowed the dismissal of homosexuals even from civilian government employment under the "loyalty-security program" from 1947 onwards, the Report of the Senate subcommittee of 1950, and the ban which the armed forces has maintained for the last fifty years. Even men and women with exemplary records have been discharged from the services, and appeals to the courts have largely brought adverse decisions.

On taking office in 1993 President Clinton had to face the problem, aggravated as it was by the homophobic stance of his two predecessors and of virtually the whole professional officer corps. The military, in league with the obscurantist clergy and the right wing of the Republican Party, have become the bedrock of opposition to gay rights. Even the Vatican, in a document released in June

1992, counseled secular states to persist in excluding homosexuals from the military, a clear admission that such a policy is grounded in the rationalization of religious intolerance. Homophobia portends to be a cause unifying the right in the coming decades–like anti-Semitism in Europe between 1880 and 1945. Yet even our foes have been pressed to concede that lovers of their own sex can perform loyally and competently–so long as they remain in the closet. Their motto would seem to be: only the hypocritical may serve.

At the same time the negative labeling of so many who yearned to serve their country drove some into an adversary stance. An inadvertent result of the persecution of homosexuals in the Second World War and its perpetuation in the "loyalty-security program" of the Cold War was the emergence of a new political consciousness in the gay underworld–animated by the sentiment "we're fed up and we're not going to take it any more."

THE ENDURING CONFLICT

In the last analysis two moralities stand opposed: a Christian one and a pagan one. The Christian one derives from ancient Judaism and its abreaction to Zoroastrianism and Hellenism, the antithesis from Greco-Roman paganism and its legacy to the Renaissance and the Enlightenment. The medical and biological discussion of the past hundred and twenty-eight years is a classic instance of intellectual shadow-boxing; what has always been debated is the morality and legitimacy of homosexual acts.

Mid-twentieth century Western society had still not received the ideas of the homophile movement, but lingered in the grip of medieval hatred and obscurantism that precluded any rational state policy. We, the invisible, the persecuted, the rightless, had to found our movement anew and make it visible and influential, this time in another country, a colony of the Old World, but one that in three hundred years had evolved its own political structure and cultural setting. The story of that movement, and of how its struggle for visibility has led to the current demand for outing, will be told in the following chapters.

REFERENCES

Bérubé, Allan. 1990. *Coming Out Under Fire: The History of Gay Men and Women in World War Two.* New York: Free Press.

Boswell, John. 1980. *Christianity, Social Tolerance, and Homosexuality: Gay People in Western Europe from the Beginning of the Christian Era to the Fourteenth Century.* Chicago: University of Chicago Press.

Cantarella, Eva. 1980. "Aítios. Archeologia di un concetto." In: *Studi in onore di Cesare Grassetti.* Milan: Giuffrè vol. 1, pp. 209-240.

Casper, Johann Ludwig. 1857. *Handbuch der gerichtlichen Medicin.* Berlin: Hirschwald.

Chorier, Nicolas, 1885. *Aloisiae Sigeae Toletanae Satyra sotadica de arcanis amoris et Veneris. Aloisia hispanice scripsit, latinitate donavit Joannes Meursius.* Paris: Isidore Liseux.

Consoli, Massimo. 1991. *Homocaust*, second edition. Rome: Rome Gay News.

Crompton, Louis. 1985. *Byron and Greek Love: Homophobia in 19th-Century England.* Berkeley: University of California Press.

Fout, John. 1992. "Sexual Politics in Wilhelmine Germany: The Male Gender Crisis, Moral Purity, and Homophobia." *Journal of the History of Sexuality* 2: 388-421.

Franklin, Mitchell. 1954. "Infamy and Constitutional Civil Liberties." *Lawyers Guild Review* 14: 1-10.

Gruter, Margaret and Roger D. Masters (eds.). 1986. *Ostracism: A Social and Biological Phenomenon.* New York: Elsevier Science Publishing.

Hirschfeld, Magnus. 1934. *The Sexual History of the World War.* New York: The Panurge Press.

_____. 1914. *Die Homosexualität des Mannes und des Weibes.* Berlin: Louis Marcus Verlagsbuchhandlung.

Hoessli, Heinrich. 1836-38. *Eros: Die Männerliebe der Griechen, ihre Beziehungen zur Geschichte, Erziehung, Literatur und Gesetzgebung aller Zeiten.* Glarus: By the author.

Johansson, Warren and William A. Percy. 1990. "Homosexuals in Nazi Germany." *Simon Wiesenthal Center Annual* 7: 225-263.

Kennedy, Hubert. 1988. *Ulrichs: The Life and Works of Karl Heinrich Ulrichs, Pioneer of the Modern Gay Movement.* Boston: Alyson.

Krafft-Ebing, Richard von. 1886. *Psychopathia sexualis.* Stuttgart: Ferdinand Enke.

Kronthal, Paul. 1891. Discussion of Lewin, "Ueber perverse und conträre Sexualempfindungen." *Neurologisches Centralblatt* 10: 378-379.

Lauritsen, John and David Thorstad. 1974. *The Early Homosexual Rights Movement.* New York: Times Change Press.

Luca da Penne. 1538. *Lectura Domini Luce de Penna . . . Super tribus libris Codicis, x. videlicet, xi. xii. nunc luculentius edita.* Lyon: Jacob Myt.

Richardson, Frank M. 1981. *Mars without Venus: A Study of Some Homosexual Generals.* Edinburgh: William Blackwood.

Rocco, Antonio. 1988. *L'Alcibiade fanciullo a scola*. Rome: Salerno.
Rowse, A. L. 1977. *Homosexuals in History: A Study of Ambivalence in Society, Literature and the Arts*. New York: Dorset Press.
Strayer, Joseph R. (ed.). 1982. *Dictionary of the Middle Ages*. 12 volumes. New York: Scribner.
Tardieu, Ambroise. 1878. *Etude médico-légale sur les attentats aux moeurs*, seventh edition. Paris: J. B. Baillière et fils.
Thomas Aquinas, Saint. 1953. *Summa Theologiae, cura et studio Instituti Studiorum Medievalium Ottaviensis ad textum S. Pii Pp. V iussu confectum recognita*, second, revised edition. 5 volumes. Ottawa: Commissio Piana.
Voss, Wilhelm. 1931. "Handschriftliche Bemerkungen in alten Büchern." *Die Sterne* 11: 182-183.
Westrum, Ron, Roy P. Mackal, Robert Rosenthal, Hans J. Eysenck, Patrick Grim, Henry H. Bauer, Susan Smith-Cunnien and Gary Alan Fine, Andrew Neher, Daniel Cohen, Sonja Grover, William R. Corliss, Norman Dixon, Piet Hein Hoebens, C. L. Hardin, Stanley Krippner, Trevor Pinch, Gerd H. Hövelmann, Brian Inglis, Roy Wallis, Willis W. Harman, J. Richard Greenwell, Morris Goran, Gerald L. Eberlein, and Roger W. Wescott. 1982. "Crypto-Science and Social Intelligence about Anomalies." *Zetetic Scholar* 10: 89-142.
Zacchia, Paolo. 1621-50. *Quaestiones medico-legales*. Rome.
Ziegler, Konrat. 1913. "Menschen- und Weltenwerden. Ein Beitrag zur Geschichte der Mikrokosmosidee." *Neue Jahrbücher für das klassische Altertum* 31: 529-573.
Zinner, Ernst. 1943. *Entstehung und Ausbreitung der Coppernicanischen Lehre [Sitzungsberichte der Physikalisch-medizinischen Sozietät zu Erlangen 74]*. Erlangen: Kommissionsverlag von Max Mencke.

Chapter III

Behind the Mask–The American Homophile Movement (1945-1969)

The postwar years saw American homosexuals coming out to one another for political self-defense for the first time. Victorious over the Axis powers, the United States emerged from the war by far the strongest and richest country in the world. While in subsequent decades other nations, above all the two defeated foes, made successful efforts to catch up economically, American popular culture permeated everywhere, even its Communist rivals. Our scholarship and science, reinforced by émigrés, most of whom remained after the war's end, also reached the front rank for the first time. Foreigners began to send their children to our universities in large numbers, and baby boomers flocked there too. Film and television liberated them and their counterparts throughout the free world from traditional restraints and religious scruples. In the 1960s, protected by penicillin against venereal disease and by the pill against unwanted pregnancies, the educated, secularized, upwardly and geographically mobile youth brought about a sexual revolution.

Having survived the dangers and enjoyed the relative sexual freedom of the war, homosexual veterans of both sexes and their counterparts who had worked in factories and offices were less willing to endure the repression that middle-class mores and small towns imposed. Many flocked to large cities where, coming out to one another, they built gay ghettos and a subculture. Try as it might, the establishment found it impossible to put the genie back in the bottle. The effort to restore the status quo ante inflicted much suffering. Because of the hysterical McCarthyite campaign fomenting a new type of inquisition against "security risks" and "sex perverts" in government, hostile outings and official prying reached new heights in the United States and Canada. Projective psychological tests were used to screen out "undesirable" applicants for employment, of whom "sex perverts" were a prime category. The military continued as it had done since 1942 to screen out and discharge us. Even in teaching and in private businesses "undesirables" were hounded.

Before 1969 progress toward toleration had been slow and irregular. Denmark, taking over from Switzerland (where a splinter group of the German movement had survived the war, publishing a monthly titled *Der Kreis/Le Cercle),* then temporarily led the way. In the late 1950s Dutch Protestants and Catholics formed study groups to discuss homosexuality and religion. Dutch Catholic bishops in Holland even defied a papal order to remove a priest who had married two men. The English-speaking countries, now independent of German tutelage, took their first strides forward. Beginning in 1939 the zoologist and taxonomist Alfred C. Kinsey and his associates applied nonjudgmental and statistical methods to sexual behavior. In *Sexual Behavior in the Human Male* (1948) and *Sexual Behavior in the Human Female* (1953) they adopted a scientific approach that treated homosexual activity with deadpan neutrality, as if they were examining the sexual life of insects, and discovered it to be far more widespread than anyone had imagined. Pundits were outraged but hard put to refute the Kinsey findings. In the 1950s the Mattachine Society and ONE Incorporated, and in the 1960s SIR, all in California, and from 1957 onward the Homosexual Law Reform Society in England created a new movement with no significant continuity with the organizations that Hitler had destroyed in 1933. Having lost the earlier tradition begun in Wilhelmine Germany, they tended to cite Kinsey and even more recent Anglo-Saxon authors. Open-minded, Kinsey addressed the problem afresh from the standpoint of an evolutionary biologist trained in the second decade of the century, with no more use for the kabbalistic fantasy of the "female soul trapped in a male body" than for psychoanalytic explanations of the patient's life history.

The American Bar Association Model Penal Code (1955) recommended decriminalizing sodomy, but only one state, Illinois, adopted it (1961) before Stonewall. Canon Derrick Sherwin Bailey of the Church of England also argued in 1955 that the Sodom story, the most frequently cited biblical text, was not originally homophobic, but rather a condemnation of inhospitality and that Christians could therefore accept us as brethren rather than condemn us as sinners.

In 1956 the UCLA clinical psychologist Evelyn Hooker, who worked closely with the ONE Institute, presented a study to the American Psychological Association demonstrating that homosexual men were as well adjusted as heterosexual ones. The two groups could not be distinguished on standard psychological tests, contrary to prevailing theories derived from studies of arrestees and analysands (Hooker 1956; Marcus 1992, pp. 16-25). She rediscovered what the pupils of Griesinger and Westphal at the Charité had concluded in 1891–that homosexuality was not mental illness. In 1957 the British parliamentary committee named for its chairman, Baron Wolfenden, found no good reason to prosecute homosexual behavior between consenting adults in private and no social benefits accruing from such prosecution, which only furnished opportunities for blackmail or other crimes. In short, our defenders, growing in numbers little by little, and publishing their own periodicals, beginning in the United States in 1953, found increasing evidence from within the professions themselves to question the old prescriptions that jointly and severally condemned us as sinners, criminals, and mentally ill.

Nevertheless, the establishment in all industrialized countries continued to oppress us. Émigré psychoanalysts voiced their hostility toward homosexuality more loudly on American soil than Freud and his disciples had in Europe, where until 1933 they had a strong homophile movement to monitor their publications and "keep them honest." Widely perceived as flagrantly effeminate, "homos" were confused with transvestites, child molesters, and sissies. Authorities branded us as immature, unstable, weak-minded, self-damaging, narcissistic, superficial, unreliable, cowardly, frivolous, worthless, inclined to drug addiction and crime, or even prepsychotic. In short, the professions and society at large confused homosexuals in general with the obvious, even flamboyant minority that could not escape the clutches of the law or of involuntary psychiatric treatment.

With everyone respectable in hiding, no one visibly contradicted the stereotype or offered role models for distraught young homosexuals who had trouble identifying with the unsavory caricatures which both psychiatric writers and the popular press displayed. Consequently some of us could not even recognize that we were homosexual at all. Anyone who was discovered or exposed was promptly ostracized, fired, or worse, prosecuted. Historians perpetuated the tradition of suppressing the truth about great figures of the past. As Greek and then Latin dropped out of the curriculum, the classics were increasingly encountered only in censored or bowdlerized English renderings. Homoerotic novels and poetry were not included in syllabi, or were falsely interpreted as heterosexual. Biographers even turned Walt Whitman into a woman-lover. Ignorance of the past reinforced the prejudices of religion, law, and medicine.

Donald Webster Cory, the pseudonym (from *Cory-don,* the title of Gide's book defending homosexuality, and from Daniel *Webster)* of Edward Sagarin, an expert in the chemistry of perfumes who dared not sign his own name, wrote in *The Homosexual in America* (1951), the vade mecum of every politically conscious member of our subculture of the 1950s: "Society has handed me a mask to wear, a ukase that it shall never be lifted except in the presence of those who hide with me behind its protective shadows. Everywhere I go, at all times and before all sections of society, I pretend. As my being rebels against the hypocrisy that is forced upon me, I realize that its greatest repercussion has been the wave of self-doubt that I must harbor" (Cory 1951, p.11). Cory was one of the first Americans to describe his ilk as a minority:

> We who are homosexual are a minority, not only numerically, but also as a result of a caste-like status in society. . . . Our minority status is similar, in a variety of respects, to that of national, religious and other ethnic groups: in the denial of civil liberties; in the legal, extra-legal and quasi-legal discrimination; in the assignment of an inferior social position; in the exclusion from the mainstream of life and culture. (Cory 1951, p. 13-14)

Persecutors targeted us as a defenseless prey. Because of the unchallenged moral condemnation and cold war paranoia over "security risks," the police made us their special target, often out of indignation that society was not punishing us sufficiently for our depravity. Practices begun in France under the Old Regime and modernized at the outset of the Third Republic were by the 1940s common among metropolitan police squads in the United States and Canada as well as in Europe. Plainclothes men entrapped us in cruising areas, posing as potential partners until they flashed a badge and made an arrest. Uniformed police frequently raided our bars and restaurants–even when their owners regularly paid them off–and would haul everyone off to a precinct house. Often they released the names of all who chanced to be netted in such raids to the newspapers or made them known to their families and employers. Editors did not hesitate to print the names, addresses, and employers of those unfortunate enough to be arrested and identified.

This harassment fell chiefly on males, as the police regarded heterosexual prostitution as the chief sexual offense of women, although they did occasionally raid lesbian bars. In 1953 the New Orleans vice squad carted off 64 lesbians from a French Quarter club. In other words, every one of us who stepped out in the evening in search of a partner for casual sex could end the night with our lives in ruins. The few criminal lawyers who would touch such cases were often little more than blackmailers in their own right, extorting enormous sums from a client for having the case quietly settled with no arrest record. Even the honest judges who heard the charges in these cases could at times be incredibly ignorant and naive. Some even imagined that if a defendant whose only crime was to have propositioned a 45-year-old plainclothesman were not "put away," the very next day he would be raping defenseless old women and children! In such a legal and social morass the shadow of blackmail, arrest, exposure, and ruin hung over every active homosexual, whatever his (or her) social position.

The regular operation of the vice squads produced a constant stream of arrests. According to John D'Emilio, in the District of Columbia they amounted to more than 1,000 a year in the early 1950s. Washington police often resorted to entrapment in Lafayette Park and in downtown movie theaters. In Philadelphia misdemeanor charges against homosexuals numbered 100 a month. Arrests could fluctuate enormously in response to political situations such as the eve of an election in which a police chief or district attorney wanted to convince the voters that he was "cracking down on vice" in his bailiwick. Bar raids could result in arrests in scores or even hundreds and spread panic through the gay community of a large city. A single police raid in 1955 in a Baltimore club bagged 162. Ann Arbor, Baltimore, Boise, Dallas, Memphis, Seattle, and Wichita saw unprecedented bursts of police harassment throughout the 1950s.

A survey by the Institute for Sex Research found that officers of the law had victimized one male homosexual in five. Before the District Attorney's office took the sound advice of the Kinsey Institute, arrests in Manhattan in the 1940s had numbered as many as 15,000 a year. Like prostitutes, homosexuals were "sex offenders" subject to verbal and sometimes physical abuse and to humiliating forced examinations for venereal disease, followed, if they were found positive, by brutal interrogations to trace their sexual partners. In the eyes of the law, and even of the national American Civil Liberties Union until 1966, we were simply criminals against whom the police legitimately and routinely took repressive measures. We deserved no protection when, on top of police harassment, we suffered random violence by robbers posing as hustlers or simply by homophobic men out to "prove their virility." While tens of thousands of us were thus outed after the end of the war and the discharge of most of the veterans, the armed services also continued to screen out inductees and discharge under less than honorable conditions those whom they labeled "perverts." These unceasing outrages implanted a sense of being an oppressed group, and motivated the creation of the first homosexual rights organizations in 1950-51, when a few bold leaders emerged to voice our grievances and struggle for our rights.

To come out publicly or be outed of course still meant ostracism and ruin, sometimes leading to suicide. If an outee lived in a small town, he or she virtually had to flee and attempt to begin life again elsewhere, often in a new occupation and under an assumed name. Even in the largest cities victims were normally fired, unless they worked in one of the "gay professions." Every form of business, from banks, insurance companies, and brokerage houses to car dealerships, construction companies, and engineering firms joined the learned professions and academia in denouncing, excluding, persecuting, and firing us.

Homophobes, police, security watchdogs, and gossip columnists sporadically outed even the rich, famous, and privileged while neighbors, schoolmates, fellow workers, and even relatives often disowned kith and kin when they discovered "the awful truth." No one was safe from gay bashing even in the few gay ghettos that had sprung up in such places as New York's Greenwich Village and Upper West Side (which jointly had perhaps 50 gay bars and restaurants) and similar neighborhoods in other large cities from Washington and Chicago to Los Angeles and San Francisco. Cities such as Houston, Philadelphia, Boston, and New Orleans had also spawned small enclaves; but outside them, at work and even at play, one had to "pass" to avoid trouble with employers, gangs, police, and other predators. Virtually no one came out to the general public rather than merely to friends or relations. Outing almost invariably entailed ruin, at least of one's career, and homosexuals (except for psychopaths like Roy Cohn) did not, as a point of honor, out one another. Hence only a very few had dared to come out to heterosexuals, even those closest to them, and probably not even a hundred in the whole country had come out to the general public.

It was less the brave but discreet pioneers who often hid behind pseudonyms than the self-proclaimed student radicals of the late 1960s who, by their raucous, even violent demonstrations, prepared the way for Stonewall. Inspired by the counterculture to defy what they dubbed the Establishment and to scorn conventions openly and even rudely, the young, with hippies in the vanguard, set about building a new, more open, and fairer society. When the sexual revolution came in the 1960s and 1970s, it was often anarchic, undisciplined, and sometimes motivated by irresponsible hedonism. But swept along by the mood of the times, it made a breach in the hitherto impregnable wall of puritanical morality and hypocrisy.

AMERICAN CONTRADICTIONS

American attitudes towards sexuality in the immediate postwar period were contradictory. On the one hand, millions–both abroad and at home–had proved themselves in battle and tasted sexual freedom. Just as they naturally sought ways of continuing their altered lifestyles in peacetime, they confronted powerful efforts to restore the old arrangements, to reimpose "normalcy." As Betty Friedan in *The Feminine Mystique* (1963) has shown, these pressures particularly affected women. They were urged to give up their jobs and independence and return to subservience in the home. But only in the late 1960s did the refusal by many to do so, perhaps particularly by lesbians, inspire a new phase of the women's rights movement.

Psychoanalysis gained influence as the Jewish émigrés driven out of Germany and Austria found a new clientele in the American upper and upper-middle class, particularly among those most alienated from traditional religion. The urban elites turned to the analyst not so much for therapy as for secular confession and moral guidance. As a result, many homosexuals were induced or even compelled to embark on futile and expensive "cures" to become "normal." Howard Brown (1976) and Martin Duberman (1991) deftly described their own failed attempts in their autobiographies. As Alfred Kinsey commented in 1948, among all their clientele the psychiatrists encountered only the most disturbed and maladjusted personalities–those shipwrecked on the reefs of an intolerant society and without a map to guide them through perilous waters. Moreover, the émigrés from Central Europe arrived in a country that had never had an organized homosexual rights movement, but where even ministers and rabbis became a major source of referrals. Consequently the psychoanalysts drifted rightward into the ingrained prejudices of the Judeo-Christian tradition. From them we received not sympathy, but condescension, ridicule, and disdain.

The Viennese psychoanalyst Edmund Bergler (1899-1962) became the coryphaeus, the leading voice, of this regressive tendency. In 1937 he had written a benign and tolerant article on homosexuality, but as the years passed in New York, where he had found refuge from Hitler, he grew more hostile and embittered against his homosexual patients. He concocted an elaborate theory of "psychic masochism" that depicted us as foes of the social order who earned the suffering inflicted upon us. These "injustice collectors," he insisted, constantly blamed others for misfortunes which they had unconsciously brought upon themselves. In *Fashion and the Unconscious* (1953) he pilloried gay fashion designers as "women's worst enemies" who did their best to make them *un*attractive to men. In *Homosexuality: Disease or Way of Life?* (1956) he excoriated Kinsey, who had taken him to task in *Sexual Behavior in the*

Human Female (1953), for "making propaganda for homosexuals." In *One Thousand Homosexuals* (1959) he reached the all-time high-water mark in medical literature for the undisguised hatred and contempt which he heaped upon his unfortunate analysands. He went so far as to urge that influential homosexuals in the arts be outed by such snide innuendos as "He is a man among men but not among women." His blatant prejudices assured his works a welcome reception among the clergy, and they even became *Pastoral Psychology* book-of-the-month club selections, while *Time* magazine cited him as the "final authority."

Bergler died before the post-Stonewall gay liberation movement could drive him to new heights of frenzied vituperation. However, his antipathy was widely shared by his colleagues, who inclined to denigrate Kinsey. The other most virulent psychiatric homophobes–all widely acclaimed in both professional and popular media–were Irving Bieber, Abram Kardiner, and Charles Socarides. Bergler, and then Bieber in *Homosexuality: A Psychoanalytic Study* (1962), insisted that homosexuality is an acquired illness and therefore curable. They were followed by the New York Academy of Medicine's report in 1964.

Psychiatrists–and psychologists, who in those days often trailed in their wake–could express only an ill-concealed rage at the recommendations of the Wolfenden committee. In contrast, they had never objected to any policy, even of Hitler's or of Stalin's, or to any decision that deprived us of rights or subjected us to legal sanctions. Evidently they believed that ostracism and punishment were the best–if not the only–therapy. Hence they explicitly favored the notion that only the fear of legal penalties would pressure homosexuals to "seek help." Nevertheless, the Mattachine Society of New York and other homosexual rights groups often invited such oracles–as well as members of the clergy–to address their meetings. The audience listened demurely while they bitterly reproached the "homosexual personality" or harped on the "sinfulness" of homosexual acts. After all, they represented the establishment whose "understanding" we desperately needed. In California homophile groups began to reject this absurd and self-demeaning tactic as early as 1955.

As chance would have it, the one leader of the German sexual reform movement who gained influence and a personal following in the United States was Wilhelm Reich (1897-1957). In his early years he had sought to fuse the emerging psychoanalytic doctrines of the 1920s and the political radicalism of the Communist Party into a unified program for the revolutionary transformation of society–a consummation still devoutly wished by part of what remains of the American left. Although his name became a near-synonym of "sexual freedom" among his admirers, who number some gay activists, he did not make a single positive comment about homosexuality in any of his writings. Proving that his preexilic homophobia had not abated, Reich wrote to the educator A. S. Neill in 1948 that while his doctrine of sex economy treated the problems of "natural genitality," Hirschfeld's World League for Sexual Reform had promoted a sexology that concentrated on lingams (the Sanskrit word for phallus), condoms, and perversions. His curious dictum that homosexuality was a fascist disease destined to "wither away" under socialism is still parroted by the dwindling gaggle of American adherents to leftist orthodoxy. So with his imprimatur the belief that homosexuality is a disease took hold, even among political radicals, only in this case it was the late capitalist environment rather than genetic predisposition or childhood experiences that bore the hideous responsibility.

As this regressive atmosphere was enveloping the country, a momentous event occurred: the publication of the Kinsey Reports (1948 and 1953), as they came to be known. These volumes of statistics plotted sexual orientation on a continuum from heterosexual to homosexual. "Perverts" could no longer simply be relegated to some alien sphere light years removed from the rest of the human race. Most controversially, the Male report, which was based on interviews with 10,000 subjects, still by far the largest sample ever made, showed that 37 percent of the male population had had at least one homosexual experience resulting in orgasm sometime after adolescence.

It showed that those predominantly or exclusively homosexual at a given moment might constitute 10 percent of the male population (4 percent lifelong exclusives). An immediate best seller, the Report on males was followed in 1953 by one on females, showing that a much smaller but still significant percentage of women (2 to 6 percent of the unmarried and less than 1 percent of the married) were almost exclusively homosexual. These figures, flatly refuting the notion that homosexuality was a rare disorder of "the insane and half-insane not in institutions" (Gershon Legman) but in our midst, excited disbelief and furious denunciation.

Gradually, despite the redoubtable opposition of the clergy and even of most of the medical profession, the import of the Kinsey findings sank in. As his colleague C. A. Tripp wrote in the *Encyclopedia of Homosexuality* (1, 662-666), "its great value was the establishment of reliable baseline data . . . the realization that masturbation is practiced by at least 95% of males . . . [and] the occurrence of homosexuality in over a third (37 percent) of males." But many individuals had to suffer before more enlightened attitudes took hold.

McCARTHYISM

A new pretext for persecuting us arose as the implications of the Kinsey Report percolated through society. As the spirit of wartime collaboration faded and the Soviet Union extended its control over East Central Europe, tensions with the Communist bloc increased. The outbreak of the cold war not only inspired a virtual obsession with "the Communist menace" but offered some right-wing demagogues a golden opportunity to link the Stalinist left, even though it had not promoted–indeed, had resisted–sexual reform for a decade and a half, with other "subversive" phenomena, including modern art and homosexuality.

Those right-wingers who strove to tar the left with homosexuality remarkably ignored the Communist regimes' official repression. Beginning just 15 months after Truman's stunning election upset of November 1948, Senator Joseph R. McCarthy made ill-founded but skillfully publicized charges against civil servants whom he sensationally accused from his privileged position on the floor of the U.S. Senate. He denounced the Truman administration for harboring Communists and lesser security risks. Finding fewer Communists than anticipated, the Wisconsin senator turned his attention to "sex perverts in government." Thus McCarthyism made homosexuality an issue in American politics which it had never before been. In his Lincoln's Birthday speech in Wheeling, West Virginia in February 1950, he captured the headlines by claiming that he had "in his hand a list of 205" active Communist Party members, along with the names of those in a spy ring in the State Department. Discussing "security risks," Undersecretary John Peurifoy testified that most of 91 employees discharged from the State Department for "moral turpitude" were homosexual. Their names, however, were not published, so that they were not outed to the general public, but the government did keep secret blacklists of them and of others. In March the senator brought the alleged case of a convicted homosexual who, though he had quit the State Department in 1948, was now holding a "top-salaried, important position" with the CIA. McCarthy demanded the immediate firing of the man whose name he disclosed only in executive session: "It seems unusual to me, in that we have so many normal people . . . that we must employ so many very, very unusual men in Washington." In June 1950 the Senate, caving in to mounting pressure, authorized a subcommittee to probe into the allegations of "homosexuals and other sex perverts" working for the government and to report in December, after the elections.

Consisting of four Democrats and three Republicans, the subcommittee was headed by Senator Clyde Hoey of North Carolina. Hoey, a southerner generally conservative on economic issues, had until that time resisted the right-wingers' assaults on civil liberties. Moreover, an earlier body headed by the Democratic senator Millard Tydings of Maryland had concluded that McCarthy "had perpetrated a monstrous fraud and a hoax on the Senate" because he "had in his hand" only documents in the public domain which were readily accessible to any congressman or journalist. But this time McCarthy won a bloodless victory because the subcommittee did not denounce him. Absent a gay rights organization, or even visible homosexuals in public life, no one at any point on the political spectrum would come to the defense of the loathsome "sex perverts" polluting the capital. Now the prohibition of homosexuals in the military was extended to civilian employees, not only those in sensitive positions but even ones in the Library of Congress and the Department of Agriculture.

The subcommittee held that those engaging in homosexual activities were "social outcasts" who feared exposure and thus became subject to blackmail by foreign agents. The best case that it could use to bolster this assertion was that of an Austrian counterintelligence officer, Alfred Redl, who committed suicide in 1913 after a letter was intercepted with payment for information that he furnished to the Russians. The report falsely averred that the Russians had taken advantage of the officer's homosexual proclivities to blackmail him, and that his treason was discovered only after the outbreak of the First World War; it even misspelled his name. Never mentioned was the far more interesting Harden-Eulenburg affair that had occurred a few years earlier in Wilhelmine Germany, perhaps because even into the 1970s this scandal was a lingering embarrassment to German historians and to the right-wing Christian Democratic regime which the Western powers had helped to install in the Federal Republic of Germany. Only recently did a conservative Soviet monthly, *Nash sovremennik,* publish an article by Valentin Pikul' (1988) which confirmed that Redl acted on financial motives, not because the Russians coerced him by threatening to out him to his Austrian superiors.

The subcommittee opined that the District of Columbia's laws against "sexual perverts" were *inadequate.* Private homosexual acts were *not* then a crime there, and those arrested by the vice squad– often entrapped by agents provocateurs–commonly slipped back into the shadows after posting derisory sums of money as surety. It is just possible that an earlier body which drafted the penal code for the District counted at least one member who persuaded the others to follow Enlightenment principles and omit the offense in question. The subcommittee recommended correcting these shortcomings in the law and its enforcement so that no one guilty of "perverted sexual acts" would escape identification and punishment.

The unchallenged traditional attitudes toward homosexuality precluded any but a punitive approach; a vicious circle of reasoning underlay such a policy. The threat of blackmail with which the Scientific-Humanitarian Committee had cried to high heaven to urge the repeal of §175 and which law reform protagonists were to invoke in England against the "blackmailers' charter" was now cited to deny homosexuals employment in order to protect "national security." To this day no American secret has ever, so far as is known, been betrayed by a homosexual out of fear of disclosure or for gain, much less for sexual favors.

This new situation made our plight even worse: now not only guilty of "moral turpitude," we were even a threat to the security of any organization to whose secrets we had access. Even law firms, banks, and other corporations feared that their secrets were unsafe in our hands. Given the absence of any organized gay movement and the defensive on which media coverage of McCarthy's repeated accusations had put the Democratic administration, homosexuals were the most helpless of his targets.

Other factors such as the escalating cold war worked in McCarthy's favor. Despite bitter opposition, he became a hero of the Right. Reelected in the Eisenhower landslide of 1952 that gave the White House back to Republicans after 20 years, McCarthy basked in his glory. And in 1953 a Republican majority in Congress did finally amend the criminal code of the District of Columbia to make private homosexual conduct illegal.

With Republicans in control of both Congress and the White House, McCarthy's accusations against the executive branch and the army began to embarrass them. In 1954 a campaign against him in the Senate featured the accusation, which was accurate, that a young graduate from the University of Wisconsin employed to handle veterans' affairs in his office had been arrested as a homosexual–and then summarily fired. Senator Ralph Flanders of Vermont added the humiliating charge that McCarthy himself was a homosexual. Hank Greenspun, publisher of the *Las Vegas Sun,* openly and repeatedly charged not only McCarthy but most of his staff with being homosexual, and challenged the senator to sue. McCarthy failed as completely in this instance to pick up the glove as in almost every other where he was called a liar and a slanderer. The need to squelch the rumors of his own sexual deviation may have motivated the senator's sudden marriage in 1953 at the age of 45. The childless couple adopted a little girl. In those days marriage counted as proof positive of an individual's normality. Censured by the Senate in 1954, McCarthy thereafter faded from the political scene. His death in 1957 seemed anticlimactic and provoked no great wave of emotion among either friends or foes.

The young New York attorney who along with G. David Schine served as one of McCarthy's chief aides during his heyday, Roy Cohn, was undeniably a classic hypocritical, self-hating homosexual. He gave lavish gay parties while publicly denouncing perversion at every opportunity. Those who currently favor outing have cited his case as an egregious one that truly deserved it. Although the rumor mills constantly ground about him and his friend and ally Cardinal Spellman, Cohn's homosexuality was not publicly confirmed until his death of AIDS in 1986. Panels not exactly respectful of his memory figured in the AIDS Memorial Quilt from 1987 onward.

McCarthyism is a complex historical phenomenon. It goes far beyond the victimization of an unorganized, defenseless minority– which is what homosexuals were in the America of 1950. During the whole of the 1940s the conservative bloc in Congress–most northern and western Republicans and certain southern Democrats– had steadily opposed defense appropriations, compulsory military service, and foreign aid to America's allies; McCarthy himself had done so as late as 1949 in spite of Truman's efforts to establish a bipartisan anti-Communist foreign policy. After the McCarthy era, which peaked with Eisenhower's victory over Taft at the Republican Convention in 1952, the isolationist (noninterventionist) stance of the Right was dramatically reversed. Even arch-conservatives could not vote enough money for the military establishment; they unanimously renewed the draft (which in the summer of 1941 had passed the House by a majority of one), and cheerfully granted billions of dollars to shore up right-wing regimes threatened by "the international Communist conspiracy."

THE BUREAU WAS A CLOSET

That this turnabout did not have exclusively patriotic motives was clear to insiders such as J. Edgar Hoover (1895-1972), the immensely powerful director of the Federal Bureau of Investigation from 1924 until his death. Persistent rumors identified this Argus-eyed guardian of America's internal security as an exclusive homosexual, but confirmation had to wait until two decades after his death. Hoover never married, had no apparent interest in the opposite sex, and never allowed a female agent in the Bureau. In addition, he had a very close lifelong relationship with his chief subordinate Clyde Tolson. In the late 1950s a pseudonymous article in *ONE* magazine named them as lovers, whereupon FBI agents descended upon *ONE*'s office, but found the editor, Dorr Legg, adamantly uncooperative. Other articles on Hoover faintly echoed this assertion. Johansson later approached the author of a piece in *The Nation* at a meeting of the New York Mattachine Society and received explicit confirmation. About 1967, when the manuscript of a volume of fiction by Casimir Dukahz (pseud.) titled *Vice Versa* included a chapter in which J. Edgar H. writes a letter to his friend Francis C. S. on "how to become a boy-lover," the printers refused to set type for it for fear that the FBI would persecute them for the rest of their lives. When in the mid-1960s Angelo d'Arcangelo's *Homosexual Handbook* indiscreetly outed Hoover, the FBI did pressure the publisher to remove the embarrassing mention, but obligingly provided some 30 or 40 additional names for the last chapter of the second edition (1969).

That a national idol, the head of the Federal Bureau of Investigation for 48 years, could have been a lover of his own sex must come as an astonishing revelation to many Americans. Magnus Hirschfeld, however, had written: "Like the judges, the first Uranian police officials whom I met struck me as a contradiction in themselves. More than once policemen who had fallen into the hands of blackmailers came to me for advice, even police captains and high police officials" (1914, p. 515). Hoover's psychological vantage point may have given him penetrating insight into the murky depths of the clandestine and illegal. As a homosexual in the America of the 1920s and later, he understood perfectly how the artfully maintained façade of the social order conceals a reality that in many directions departs from its norms. He also fully appreciated the imperative to project at all times a personal and institutional public image that need correspond to no objective truth. His power over official Washington rested less upon his knowledge of who was a drug addict or a "sex pervert" (and even during the McCarthy era, it seems, he held the persecution of homosexuals to a minimum) than upon his scrutiny of how large a share of the countless billions of dollars voted for military supply contracts and foreign aid was finding its way back into the pockets of those who cast the votes. Conveniently enough for the beneficiaries in this cabal, Hoover magnified the "Communist threat" out of all proportion to its internal dimensions by the late 1940s, although privately he believed that the activists of the American left belonged less in prison than in an insane asylum. It is even alleged that the information which magnified Watergate into a political crisis and led to the resignation of Richard M. Nixon from the presidency came from his personal files. On the other hand, his reluctance to prosecute organized crime–which had received its initial impetus from the ill-fated Prohibition experiment and was about to regroup around clandestine traffic in drugs–with the requisite vigor has been acsribed to the mobster Meyer Lansky's having procured photographs of him in sexual intimacy with Tolson. Well-informed insiders, however, flatly reject this explanation as apocryphal–in all likelihood another fantasy inspired by the meretricious Senate subcommittee report of 1950.

During Hoover's lifetime, and even the following decade, the establishment media either never explicitly mentioned the truth about his sexual proclivities or else vigorously denied them. For example, Merle Miller, who himself achieved a certain notoriety by coming out in the book *On Being Different: What It Means to Be a Homosexual* (1971), asked President Truman: "What did you think of J. Edgar Hoover?" The reply was: "One time they brought me a lot of stuff about his personal life, and I told them I didn't give a damn about that. That wasn't my business. It was what he did *while* he was at work that was my business" (Miller 1973, p. 389). General Harry Vaughan, who as Truman's top military aide had worked with Hoover, was asked by Ovid Demaris: "Do you think Hoover and Tolson were homosexuals?" He answered: "Oh, no!" Demaris continued: "What makes you so positive?" Vaughan explained: "Well, because he was a red-blooded, virile individual. I can imagine that I might be in a job like that, having an old college classmate of mine associated with me, and we'd be living together" (Demaris 1975, pp. 109-110). But as the years passed and dread of the Director's vengeance waned, the truth seeped out, and on Tuesday February 9, 1993 the Public Broadcasting System aired an hour-long program based on a forthcoming book by the British journalist Anthony Summers, *Official and Confidential: The Secret Life of J. Edgar Hoover* (1993), which reveals all about Hoover's private life.

For all his personal idiosyncrasies, Hoover earned a lasting place in history. He not only "began professional police training in America" but brought American law enforcement into the twentieth century, thanks to a "fascination with scientific police work and record-keeping" which "accords almost perfectly with the American love of science and technology." "His career represents a record of organizational design and control with enormous ramifications for the political culture of the United States. His activities in overcoming the built-in divisions of federalism, while simultaneously (and successfully) denying that a national secret police was under construction, are but one unique aspect of a career" that reshaped the structure of the government without overtly violating America's received political values. "His pioneering entrepreneurship into public relations of a scale and quality to water the mouths of the best politicians of the century led the way for contemporary bureaucratic actors" (Lewis 1980, pp. 139, 154, 155). His managerial ethos reflected the skill of a lover of his own sex who, forever aware of the discrepancy between image and reality, knew how to control and manipulate the one and the other with consummate finesse.

THE UNFORESEEN CONSEQUENCES OF McCARTHYISM

It remains for the future historians to uncover the morass of corruption, waste, and theft of public funds into which McCarthyism plunged the nation for the ensuing four decades–and bled it white so that now, in the 1990s, almost every public institution finds itself in fiscal crisis. McCarthy engineered the greatest gay witchhunt in American history, but the names of those dismissed from government service, as it seems mostly minor officials and employees, were not made public. Many more, including both of the present authors, who had thought of a career in the Foreign Service, were deterred from entering any branch of the Federal Government–as were many other homosexuals.

The refusal to employ homosexuals on moral grounds and because we were deemed to be security risks lingered long after McCarthy himself faded away. Even private employers and universities scrutinized their employees' sexual lives more carefully. Journalistic exposés such as Laird and Mortimer's *Confidential* series smeared political opponents with lurid accusations of homosexuality. Also, new devices such as lie detectors probed ever more deeply into the past actions and into the inclinations and orientations of applicants for "sensitive" positions. The "homofiles" that police kept in major cities as far back as the early modern era could now be maintained on a national scale, instantaneously updated by data communicated electronically to a central index. The apparatus of the modern state was capable of a surveillance that far exceeded the powers of the Inquisition or the post-Reformation heresy hunters. It was only in the 1970s that the gay rights movement gained the strength to combat the exclusionary measures that had cost many hundreds of "outed" homosexuals and lesbians their jobs in the Federal Government–often in positions where no conceivable security issue was involved. Until then both radicals and liberals had shunned such an outcast minority, which found its first open and brave spokesman in Franklin Kameny.

Given its blanket rejection of sexual reform, the Stalinist left has on occasion resorted to its own brand of McCarthyism. Whittaker Chambers clandestinely joined the Communist Party in the 1930s. With others he spied for the Soviet Union. By the 1950s he had lost his earlier faith and turned conservative. Soon he denounced his former companions. His testimony proved crucial in convicting the diplomat Alger Hiss of perjury, as he had maintained close relations with both Hiss and his wife. His former friends began a word-of-mouth campaign based on the allegation that his evidence was tainted because as a homosexual he was untrustworthy. Chambers was indeed homosexual, but his opponents used the information in a way tantamount to a homophobic smear campaign. On the other hand, defenders of Alger Hiss noted that Chambers gave far more proof of intimacy with Mrs. Hiss than with the convicted former State Department official.

The lovers of their own sex who had fought to "make the world safe for democracy" were no longer willing to endure such injustice and persecution in their own country. McCarthyism proved the stimulus for founding the homophile movement. But it was in England that homosexuals and their allies in the establishment repealed the laws against buggery and gross indecency and, most important of all, set in motion a wave of legal reform that reached the farthest corners of the English-speaking world.

PERSECUTION IN BRITAIN

American experience interfaced with that of other English-speaking countries. Like the Americans, the British believed that the war had caused an increase in homosexual activities and that they should take vigorous measures to reverse the trend. Eventually their rampant homophobia abated, but not before considerable harm had been done there too. Postwar austerity and reaction to wartime laxity may have aggravated puritanism and intolerance. Toward the end of the 1950s economic conditions began to improve and a less severe attitude towards "morals" set in, heralding the changes of the 1960s.

One notable espionage case resonated with McCarthyism. The flight of two ultra-elite British diplomats, Guy Burgess and Donald Maclean, to the Soviet Union in March 1951 caused a considerable uproar. Both were on the verge of exposure as spies. Though not lovers as widely reported at the time, the pair, of whom only Burgess was really homosexual, were manipulated by the heterosexual master spy Kim Philby and–as only came out many years later–also by Anthony Blunt. Curator of the Queen's art collection, Blunt also directed the Courtauld Institute in London, the leading British institution for art history. All of the four spies issued from a homosexual coterie of which they had been undergraduate members while at Cambridge. Regarded as above suspicion, Maclean had worked his way into the British Embassy in Washington with top secret clearance, so that he had access to American as well as British intelligence. The affair occasioned much hostile comment in America about our ally's lax security measures.

MOVIE STARS: IDOLS OF THE MASSES

In America, where there are no lords and no established church, reform had to wait until the opinion of the masses changed. In this, popular culture, especially Hollywood movies, was particularly influential in the early-postwar period. True, film stars' homosexuality did not become evident until long after their deaths, usually because the hints were too subtle or too obscure for the average moviegoer to catch. The gay underground, however, knew its *Who's Who in the Closet,* and in the mid-1950s scurrilous publications like *Hush-Hush* and *Confidential* ventured to out several. As Michael Bronski pointed out in his perceptive study, *Culture Clash* (1984), Sal Mineo's first prominent role, in *Rebel Without a Cause* (1955), was a juvenile who kept a photograph of Alan Ladd, upon whom he had a crush, in his locker at school, and died so that James Dean, the star, could pursue his romance with Natalie Wood. Dean played a self-conscious, insecure teenager seeking any way at all of proving his manhood. After participating in a hot-rod race in which his rival was killed, he suffered acute anguish: "What can you do when you have to be a man? It was a matter of honor. They called me a chicken. You know, chicken? I had to go." Dean realized his mistake in acquiescing in the image. "You can't keep pretending you're tough, you know?" He later accepted Sal Mineo's love. Throughout the production, the homoerotic context predominated, although the obligatory heterosexual finale capped it off. In 1976 Mineo–by now a rotund, middle-aged retiree–was murdered under circumstances that suggested, as the tabloids gloated, a homosexual motive. Two years later police arrested a large black man, a holdup man, as the assailant. Eyewitnesses had seen a slender man with long blond hair. Many suspect that the police had simply found a convenient fall guy.

Although many homosexuals, deeply aroused by actors' sex appeal, often identified with the actresses on the screen so that they could imagine the male stars making love to them, they never received the slightest encouragement of their emotions from such stars as Douglas Fairbanks and Rudolph Valentino.

Hollywood is forever accused of producing shallow, nonideological films, mere escapist entertainment. But in fact the characters are stereotypical, the plots improbable, and the endings contrived precisely because these films are works of pure ideology that subtly, almost subliminally propagate a set of beliefs and values with which reality is never allowed to interfere. Because sex role stereotypes framed the plots, the male film stars, as Bronski observed, "often projected lifeless, wooden images."

A sensational 1968 case lifted the curtain briefly: the murder of Ramón Novarro. The Mexican-born actor had starred in romantic leads in silent films, such as *The Prisoner of Zenda* (1922) and *Ben Hur* (1925). After advent of the talkies he reemerged as a character actor. Apparently he would have a servant bring hustlers to his home in Hollywood. One night he invited a pair of brothers, and, tempted by the aging actor's wealth, the younger of the hustlers murdered him. The protracted trial in Los Angeles in 1969-1970–in which the older brother was convicted–revealed all the sordid details of Novarro's proclivities and activities. Whereupon the curtain promptly fell again on homosexuality in Hollywood.

Berating the film industry for blacking out the subject, Vito Russo (1981) analyzed the contrast between the he-man and the sissy. The chief burden of his book is Hollywood's imagery and its shaping of popular notions of gender identity, rather than homosexuality proper. Instead of any honest portrayal of homosexuality on celluloid, moguls and agents in collusion fabricated heterosexual romances even for their most active homosexual stars. Because outing ended careers in acting as abruptly as in sports, no one dared to come out.

HOMOPHILE ORGANIZATIONS: MATTACHINE AND DAUGHTERS OF BILITIS

The American movement, an immediate byproduct of McCarthyism, which doomed a number of individuals to outing, induced a few to come out to all and sundry. The pioneer activist Harry Hay, who had worked in the movies, founded the Mattachine Society in Los Angeles in 1950-51. James Gruber, a veteran studying at Occidental College, suggested the name, taken from the French Renaissance *Société Mattachine*, a shadowy group that performed musical masques about which Hay had read while preparing lectures on the evolution of popular music for a course in a worker's education project. The word Mattachine itself derived from *mutawajjihīn*, which in the Arabic of Moorish Spain meant "masqueraders." It symbolized the fact that the Society's members were a masked people, unknown and anonymous, and implied that they were still, so to speak, wearing masks (D'Emilio 1983, pp. 66-67). And indeed, many felt obliged to use pseudonyms so that no one who knew them in everyday life would suspect their activism on behalf of such outcasts. During the following two decades this tradition of anonymity and secrecy was faithfully observed.

McCarthyism shaped the political situation in which the Society grew. Hay and his associates modeled it rather on Freemasonry than on the Communist Party which he had long devotedly served. Both enjoined secrecy, had hierarchical structures and, as D'Emilio explained, practiced "democratic centralism." Imitating the orders of freemasonry, the founders envisaged a pyramid with five "orders." Members gained responsibility as they rose within the structure. Each order was to have one or two representatives from a higher level. As the Society expanded its membership, the orders would subdivide. Thus separate divisions in each layer of the pyramid could extend horizontally. Consequently, members of the same order in different divisions would not know one another. The fifth order, made up of the founders, would centralize leadership. Their decisions would pass down to the lower orders. The membership groups were called "guilds" until May 1953 and "chapters" thereafter. The structure was designed to create obstacles for infiltrators such as FBI agents. It offered the members, who were not expected to come out publicly, a modicum of security.

Mattachine was formed at a moment when the organized left was rapidly shrinking under an incessant barrage of vilification. After Henry Wallace lost his third-party bid for the presidency, which Hay had supported, the Mattachine leaders, most of whom had Marxist-Leninist leanings, decided they had to express their concepts in language intelligible to ordinary laymen. In April 1951 they set out their goals and their ideas about homosexuals as a minority in a one-page document.

Initial discussions in the fall of 1950 led to the formation of the Society, which adopted its official title in July 1951. The founders believed that "relations of production" had created the injustice and oppression which they endured. The structure of society produced these relationships, which they analyzed by treating homosexuals as an oppressed cultural minority that accepted a "mechanically . . . superimposed heterosexual ethic." Their existence therefore became fraught with "self-deceit, hypocrisy, and charlatanism" and a "disturbed, inadequate, and undesirable . . . sense of value." Collectively we thus constituted a "social minority." Unaware of its oppression, this minority needed to develop a group consciousness. That, and recognition of its status, would give it pride in its own identity. By promoting such a positive self-image, the founders intended to forge a unified national movement with other minorities and those whom they deemed "progressive." A small number of homosexuals had become ready, willing, and able to resist. With this maximalist ideology, and with the help of a stirring initiation ceremony, the organization aimed to instill pride in our distinctive values and traditions. Still trying to keep from being outed themselves, its members certainly never thought of exposing others. Outing was utterly foreign to the mentality of a day when everyone "wore the mask."

The semipublic meetings that the organization sponsored suddenly became popular. Many war veterans, unwilling after they had fought for their country to be oppressed by it, joined Mattachine. Its chapters proliferated, first in southern California and then in a few large cities across the nation. Aware of the onus of loathing and disgust that his leadership of a band of homosexuals was certain to earn, Hay himself felt obliged to sever all his ties with the Communist Party. Moreover, such an involvement had become anomalous: in the wake of Stalin's repudiation of the sexual reform movement between 1933 and 1936, any interest that the American Communists had ever taken in radical sexual politics had long since evaporated. In the Soviet Union and other Communist countries male homosexuals were branded as "enemies of the working class" and sent to concentration camps for "reeducation."

In February 1952 the members of Mattachine faced their first crisis when plainclothes men entrapped one of their founders, Dale Jennings, in a Los Angeles park. When let out on bail, he phoned Harry Hay, who quickly convened a meeting of the fifth order. Because the Society was still operating clandestinely, it set up a front, a Citizens Committee to Outlaw Entrapment, to publicize the incident. Failing to get any response from the media, it distributed leaflets in gay bars and on beaches. This may have been the first use ever in the United States of such broadsides to raise gay political consciousness. When the trial opened in June, Jennings forthrightly acknowledged that he was a homosexual but denied the accusations leveled against him. When the jury deadlocked after lengthy debate, the district attorney dropped the charges. The contrast with the usual self-demeaning hypocrisy in such cases was such that the Citizens Committee justifiably exulted that the event was a "great victory for the homosexual minority." A victory it was, but in a certain sense a Pyrrhic one because it had made Jennings' homosexuality public knowledge. He remained bitter for years about having thus been outed and had great trouble getting jobs for a long time afterwards.

After this initial triumph the Society grew rapidly. It extended its network across southern and central California, with groups in Berkeley, Oakland, and San Francisco. The membership also diversified, attracting more conservatives. By May 1953 the fifth order estimated that there were nine guilds with a membership of 200, with about 2,000 attending discussion groups with some regularity.

Encouraged by their success, the leaders moved to incorporate the Society as a nonprofit educational institution. The Mattachine Foundation was established as an acceptable front for dealing with society at large, especially with heterosexual experts from the professions and with bureaucrats, and with the hope of conducting research and using the findings to enlighten the public. The Foundation's very existence might persuade potential members that they would not run afoul of the law in such an organization. Professional support, however, materialized but slowly. Although the research psychologist Evelyn Hooker of UCLA declined an invitation to sit on the board of directors, she maintained close ties with Mattachine and *ONE*, from whom she secured the pool of homosexual subjects for her groundbreaking investigations.

Hay's and the other founders' political careers provided them with the skills to construct a movement within an intensely homophobic society, but also compromised them in most Americans' eyes. A Los Angeles newspaperman, Paul Coates, attacked the Mattachine Society in March 1953. He linked "sexual deviates" with "security risks," asserting that they were conspiring to gain "tremendous political power." To quiet the ensuing uproar, the fifth order convened a two-day-long meeting in Los Angeles in April to reorganize Mattachine as an open organization. They exhorted members to defend everybody's First Amendment rights, whatever political views they had espoused. Any of them might be interrogated by the dreaded Un-American Activities Committee. Kenneth Burns, Marilyn Rieger, and Hal Call allied against the leftists and partially drafted the society's constitution.

Paradoxically, despite the McCarthyite offensive, the leftist founders prevailed on every issue. Nevertheless, because anti-Communism had become so strident, the fifth order agreed not to run for office in the restructured Society. With a minimalist ideology, the new leaders denied all significant differences, except sexual orientation, between homosexuals and the rest of the population. Now in control, these quasi-assimilationists rejected the concept of a "homosexual minority." Under their leadership, the convention approved an organization with open membership. The bitter infighting, and his own resignation, made Harry Hay despondent. For a long time he played but a slight political role. In the late 1970s, in the autumn of his life, after brief participation in the Council on Religion and the Homosexual and later the Gay Liberation Front of Los Angeles, he was to reemerge as the godfather of the Radical Faery movement.

The 1950s also witnessed the rise of the first lesbian organization in the United States. In October 1955 four couples in San Francisco formed the Daughters of Bilitis, named for the heroine in Pierre Louÿs' *Les Chansons de Bilitis* (1894), which purported to be a translation of ancient texts recounting the adventures of a half-Greek, half-Phoenician woman who settled in Mytilene and became a member of the poetess Sappho's circle. The group's founders and moving spirits were Del Martin and Phyllis Lyon, lovers who had migrated to the Bay Area two years earlier. Martin and Lyon widened and transformed what began as a social club into a movement to educate the public. Though created independently, Daughters of Bilitis allied with Mattachine and sponsored discussion sessions. Its monthly magazine *The Ladder* published stories, verse, biographies, and history as well as columns discussing problems of concern to lesbians. But DOB remained a tiny group. It attracted white collar semiprofessional women but not professionals or workers. After 1960 much friction developed between DOB and the far larger Mattachine Society and ONE Incorporated. Daughters of Bilitis was the most cautious, apologetic, and conformist of the three groups; it in no way anticipated the élan of the later feminist movement.

A figure characteristic of that period was Arthur C. Warner (b. 1918), a graduate of Princeton and Harvard Law School, whose sexuality had compromised him with the authorities while he was serving in the Navy during the war, and again in 1957 when he was entrapped in Lafayette Park in Washington. Based in Princeton, but

Chairman of the Legal Committee of New York Mattachine throughout its existence, he cultivated a wholly unobtrusive style of seeking legal reform. Posing as a disinterested expert, he attended dull committee meetings, where he waited for the opportune moment to suggest a change in the law so minor (or so unimportant to the others present) that it would escape public notice and debate. Warner opposed not just the sodomy laws, under which few men and almost no women were actually prosecuted, but also loitering and solicitation statutes under which large numbers of gay men were entrapped. The pretext ratified by the courts was that such an affront to masculinity would so outrage the party propositioned that he would assault the other on the very spot. Entrapment thus protected "law and order." Warner's activism persisted well after Stonewall. He succeeded in having the solicitation clause removed from the New Jersey Criminal Code, and with other legal activists, after all pleading with conservative-dominated legislatures had failed, won decisions from state supreme courts that declared the sodomy statutes unconstitutional. In the long run, however, such oblique tactics had severe limitations, not the least of which was to leave public opinion unchanged. In the illogic which then prevailed, we, who had to endure insult and defamation in total silence, were mentally ill, while those who could not hear "unnatural vice" mentioned without falling into hysterical abuse were paragons of right reason.

FRANK KAMENY–THE FIRST VISIBLE GAY ACTIVIST

Franklin Kameny (b. 1925) emerged as a new leader with a far more visible and public style. A middle-class Jew from New York City, he entered college at the age of 15. Following military service, he completed his undergraduate education and enrolled in Harvard's Ph.D. program in astronomy. While conducting research in Arizona in 1954, Kameny came out. He acquired an undergraduate lover, and was initiated into the homosexual society of Tucson. After finishing his doctorate, Kameny joined the army map service. In December of 1957 he lost his job because the government learned of his arrest in 1956 for lewd conduct. Thus outed and ousted, he appealed without success to the Supreme Court (it denied *certiorari,* a request for review of the case). By 1959 he was broke, living on Salvation Army handouts. Even as his unpaid bills mounted and his health deteriorated from malnutrition, he never lost his resolve. A letter of his from 1960 conveys the strength of his character:

> I am not a belligerent person, nor do I seek wars, but having been forced into a battle, I am determined that this thing will be fought thru to a successful conclusion, come what may. . . . I will not be deprived of my proper rights, freedoms, and liberties, as I see them, or of career, profession, and livelihood, or of my right to live my life as I choose. . . .
>
> The past 2 [and] 3/4 years have not been easy ones. . . . The mills of justice in this country grind slow and exceedingly expensive, and unless the Government decides to surrender, there will be much time and money needed before victory is ours.

Kameny fought back to become, from his base in Washington, a leading gay activist of the 1960s. He was the first American to insist repeatedly on naming his sexual orientation and stubbornly to demand media visibility for it. Kameny frequently spoke out against "security clearances" as a weapon to intimidate government employees. Sometimes he represented the victims as a lay advocate at official hearings. He argued quite pointedly that "In this society, rightly or wrongly, those called mentally ill simply do not get all their rights. The entire homophile movement is going to stand or fall on the question of whether or not homosexuality is a sickness." Under his guidance, the new policy of the Washington chapter of Mattachine affirmed that "homosexuality *per se* cannot properly be considered a sickness, illness, disturbance, disorder or pathology of any kind, nor a symptom of any of these, but must be considered as a preference, orientation, or propensity, not different in kind from heterosexuality and fully on par with it" (Lee 1977, pp. 50-51). On the Fourth of July in 1964 he and Barbara Gittings of DOB led the first public demonstration for gay rights ever–symbolically outside of the cradle of American liberty, Independence Hall in Philadelphia. Not once in its 36-year history had the earlier German movement found the courage to stage such an action. As Lee remarked, only a very strong character who throve on notoriety was likely to survive a highly visible public homosexuality.

CONTINUING REPRESSION AND DEFAMATION

In June 1954, a conservative Democratic senator elected from Wyoming in the 1948 Democratic landslide, Lester C. Hunt, took his own life. The press could only hint at the truth. As it turned out, the Washington police had arrested Hunt's son in a raid on a homosexual party. Two Republican senators–one of whom might have been McCarthy himself–warned Hunt that every voter in the state would receive mail about his son's disgrace if he ran again. After claiming that a kidney ailment prevented him from running for a second term, Hunt killed himself in his room at the Senate Office Building.

In his novel *Advise and Consent,* which became a play and a film, Allen Drury hypocritically turned the story into a tale of leftist intrigue. In it, a former Communist is on the verge of being named Secretary of State. To conceal his Communist affiliations, the villain threatens to reveal a compromising wartime episode from the past of the closeted chairman of the Senate Foreign Relations Committee. The novel thus indicted the Left as subverting national policy by blackmailing patriotic Americans with threats to expose their homosexual proclivities or activities. The film trivialized the wartime homosexual encounter, picturing it as a half-forgotten episode. It even contained a scene with the senator, in search of his old partner in his lapse from heterosexuality, entering a gay bar full of "obvious" types but fleeing in horror from the scene of abnormality as his erstwhile accomplice, who had sold the compromising story to blackmailers, falls headlong into the gutter. Outed by leftist opponents as "morally unfit" for office, the senator ultimately commits suicide.

A local witchhunt got out of hand in Boise, Idaho. Towards the end of 1955, the police arrested three men and charged them with having sex with adolescents. The New Left journalist John Gerassi, who wrote *The Boys of Boise* about the events, believed that an elite group in the Idaho capital was eager to embarrass opponents who controlled the city government. Whatever the merits of this conspiracy theory about driving their enemies from power, the police entrapped and arrested many. For over a year Boise's gay underworld was subjected to an investigation so intense that, as D'Emilio observed, scores fled the city and many lives were ruined. With growing local and then national media publicity, the affair escalated. Gossip about the "boys of Boise" made the city a laughingstock. This donnybrook probably signaled the end of the most acute phase of McCarthyite persecution.

Experts at the Kinsey Institute explained, in a conversation with coauthor Warren Johansson in 1962, that in a big city the vice squad is cognizant of the extent of "perversion" and of the crucial fact that such tabooed activities involve wealthy and powerful members of society. Consequently it never pursues the investigation of a "ring" too far, but is content to entrap and arrest the friendless and powerless–the street hustler, the procurer, the naive out-of-towner. But in Boise it was not the local police but the private Dice detective agency, brought in by an angry father, that intensified the search to the point of compromising the prominent and influential. Probably Boise's "homosexual underworld" was no more extensive or threatening than that of any other medium-sized city of the Rocky Mountain states, but the number and prominence of those outed was unparalleled, at least proportionately to its population.

In the 1930s Newton Arvin won recognition as a socially conscious literary critic. He analyzed major works by homosexuals such as Whitman and Melville, in a leftist, albeit nondoctrinaire manner. While denouncing social injustices throughout his life, to the extent that William Buckley's sister accused him of Communist sympathies, he prudently concealed his homosexuality not only from society in general but from his left-wing colleagues as well. In 1960 Arvin was teaching at Smith College, then the socially most elite women's school. On September 2, the police arrested him and another instructor, Edward Spofford, in their homes. They were charged with possessing obscene photographs and literature and outed in a barrage of local newspaper stories which accused them of being members of a "smut ring." In addition, Arvin was identified as "being a lewd and lascivious person in speech and behavior." Almost without delay the college fired Arvin. Depressed and frequently hospitalized, he died of cancer three years later (Katz 1989).

There were many less well-known cases at other colleges and universities, in England as well as America. The medievalist Ernst Kantorowicz, who went undetected in his lifetime, was outed post-humously by coauthor William A. Percy in the *Encyclopedia of Homosexuality* (1, 657-658), based on a private letter from Kanto-rowicz's successor at the Institute for Advanced Study, Felix Gil-bert. Norman F. Cantor raised the subject in his book *Inventing the Middle Ages,* in a chapter titled "The Nazi Twins." Surprisingly, Kantorowicz's students and relatives contest the assertion, claiming that he was bisexual if not heterosexual.

Most academic outings lacked any angle other than that of uni-versity politics; the exposure of a professor meant instant dismissal that would conveniently make a tenured position vacant for others who coveted it. Mostly the outings resulted from accidental de-nunciation, often by persons the professor approached, or by an outraged bystander, or from entrapment by the police. No one was safe, tenured or untenured, administrator or student, at any level. All lived in dread, because being outed meant being ousted from their profession, just as in most others: law, medicine, the clergy and the military.

SCANDAL AND LAW REFORM IN BRITAIN

The case of the 27-year-old Lord Edward Montague made head-lines on both sides of the Atlantic. The wealthy peer liked to give bohemian parties at his historic Hampshire home, Beaulieu. On these occasions, he and some friends, including the journalist Peter Wildeblood, were in the habit of taking young men to a hut on the seashore. In August 1953 someone complained. With a peer of the realm under suspicion, the police decided to make a major inves-tigation. Eventually two gay airmen were pressured to testify against Wildeblood and Montague. After an eight-day trial, Wilde-blood and another man were sentenced to 18 months, Montague to 12 (Hyde 1970). But in 1957, Wildeblood had the last word in his hardhitting book about the affair and his experience in prison, *Against the Law,* which was widely read in Britain and played a beneficial role in shifting public opinion in favor of law reform.

The case of the noted actor John Gielgud had less grave consequences. From his debut in the 1920s Sir John had been noted for his elegant style and expressive clarity of voice. He excelled as Hamlet, performing the role more than 500 times. After the war he championed the work of modern playwrights, including the homosexual Terence Rattigan. At a Chelsea party in 1953 Sir John had a bit too much to drink and later in a public place asked a young man to go to bed with him. He refused to take no for an answer and, as the British say, there was a bit of a row. On the young man's complaint Gielgud was arraigned and fined ten pounds upon conviction for "persistently importuning for immoral purposes." The negative effects were short-lived, however, and at his next appearance Gielgud received an ovation (Hyde 1970).

Instead of reinforcing the campaign against "perversion," these British outings caused the political elite to question policies about sexual conduct. Until then the Christian churches had turned a deaf ear to pleas for toleration. But in February 1954 the Moral Welfare Council of the Church of England published a report which professed to "take the initiative" in conceding some justification to the demands of those who sympathized with "the invert's plight." It admitted that criminal law reform was long overdue.

The following year the Secretary of the Moral Welfare Council, Derrick Sherwin Bailey (1910-84), published *Homosexuality and the Western Christian Tradition*. Canon Bailey knew only a few books on the topic written in English earlier in the century–by Edward Carpenter, Havelock Ellis, Edward Westermarck–whom he bitterly excoriated for "casting slurs on the Church." He attempted to rewrite history so as to shield the church from reproaches by "prejudiced defenders of the homosexual." The most novel thesis of his work was that the destruction of Sodom and Gomorrah–which he believed historical–was motivated by divine wrath not at the homosexual depravity of the inhabitants, but only at their inhospitality.

Against all evidence, he claimed that the verb "to know" in Genesis 19:5 had been falsely interpreted to mean that the Sodomites desired carnal knowledge of the (male) angels (though clear from the whole of 19:5-8, where Lot offers his daughters "which have not known man"–a quotation from the text of the Code of

Hammurabi, which even used the Akkadian cognate of the Hebrew word–instead of the angels, that this is indeed a legal euphemism of sexual import). Bailey argued that the myth of Sodom as a hotbed of unnatural vice was invented only later and by Hellenistic Judaism.

These interventions set the stage, however, for a Conservative government to appoint a committee under Sir John Wolfenden. In testimony to that committee, the Moral Welfare Council, joined by the Roman Catholic Church and the Society of Friends, urged repeal of the statute of 1861 which abolished the death penalty for buggery but replaced it with life imprisonment, and that of 1885 which penalized as "gross indecency" all other male homosexual acts even when committed in private. Meanwhile, on the other side of the Atlantic, present coauthor Warren Johansson, independent of Franklin Kameny but anticipating his stand against the label of "mental illness," had obtained from the Austrian National Library in Vienna a photostat of Freud's statement in the newspaper *Die Zeit* of October 27, 1905 in which he flatly denied that homosexuality was a disease: "Should we not then have to classify as sick men many great thinkers and scholars of all ages, whose sound minds it is exactly that we admire?" On December 1, 1955 Johansson sent this text together with a translation and commentary to the Wolfenden committee–and effectively pulled out the rug from under the British psychiatric-psychoanalytic establishment.

In August 1957 the committee by a vote of 12 to 1 recommended decriminalizing homosexual conduct among consenting adult males, endorsing after two centuries Enlightenment ideas on the irrelevance of sexual behavior to the criminal law. It carefully skirted the history of the law (terming its biblical and theological sources "obscure") and the efforts to reform it, but stigmatized the Criminal Law Amendment Act of 1885 as "the blackmailer's charter" because of the opportunity it gave the criminal underworld to prey upon otherwise respectable, law-abiding citizens. Rejecting the claim that homosexuality was an illness, it even incorporated a segment of Johansson's paper–to the rage and dismay of psychiatric reviewers who could not figure out what hit them! A British commentator in the fall of 1957 concluded that the liberal wing of the establishment was solidly behind the reform, whose adoption was only a matter of time. Ten years later, on a private member's bill, after several lame-duck votes for reform, a Parliament with a Labour majority enacted this recommendation into law in England and Wales. Scotland, where the law of 1887 was still in force, did not follow until the 1980s, and the Republic of Ireland's antisodomy law fell only in 1991 when the European Court of Human Rights in Strasbourg held that homosexual behavior fell within the scope of the right of privacy.

THE REBELLIOUS 1960s

In the 1960s our society and culture changed rapidly. Restrictions on premarital sex went largely by the wayside thanks to penicillin and the pill. Sexual experiments became fashionable: "If it feels good, do it," "If it moves, kiss it." Increasing prosperity fostered hedonism and luxury. An ethos of freedom and libertinism replaced one of duty and bourgeois morality (the so-called "Protestant ethic") that Cold Warriors had reimposed during the previous decade, as James Levin wrote in the *Encyclopedia of Homosexuality*. Successful agitation for civil rights for African-Americans and (later) for equal opportunity for women created a climate for change. The cultural blackout diminished; fiction, drama, and even, finally, film occasionally portrayed homosexual characters or relationships. After 1963, Andy Warhol and other underground artists began to treat the subject with few if any inhibitions.

Some of the old patterns of queer-baiting persisted. The 1963 assassination of President Kennedy was wrapped in mysteries that have not yet been resolved to everyone's satisfaction, and assassination buffs have composed a vast literature around its puzzling aspects. The official report held Lee Harvey Oswald to be the lone assassin, although later tests have purportedly shown that the Mannlicher-Carcano rifle he allegedly used was incapable of such a performance. In the welter of speculation and conspiracy allegations, it was almost inevitable that a homosexual connection would be forged. The dubious honor of proposing it lies at the doorstep of then New Orleans District Attorney Jim Garrison, who charged that Clay Shaw, a prominent, though closeted Louisiana businessman and covert CIA operative, had been involved. In the judgment of most observers, Garrison's machinations, which were exposed in full (Kirkwood, 1970), failed to produce the alleged link. Shaw's homosexuality now exposed as part of a conspiracy theory *manqué*, he lived only a few more years after the trial. As so often occurs in conspiracy theories, a minority was made the scapegoat in this version. In the years immediately preceding the tragedy, coauthor William Percy was on several occasions present at cocktail parties given by the Laurie brothers, two New Orleans socialites, in the French Quarter and frequented by gay and straight guests alike, at one of which he even met Jim Garrison. At these social gatherings the desirability of assassinating Kennedy was advocated. In 1991 the film *JFK* made Garrison the hero, reviving some of the homophobic stereotypes.

On October 7, 1964 police arrested President Johnson's confidant, Walter W. Jenkins, in the men's room of the YMCA (according to others, of the Hay-Adams Hotel frequented by J. Edgar Hoover). According to police blotters, the charge was "Disorderly conduct (indecent gestures)," as we learn from an article in *U.S. News & World Report* (October 26, 1964). The $50 collateral Jenkins posted was forfeited. Andy Choka, 61, a resident of the Washington U.S. Soldiers Home, was also arrested and forfeited his $50 collateral. Reporters followed a tip that led to the disclosure of Jenkins' arrest on October 14, just three weeks before the Presidential election. Jenkins, it was further revealed, had been arrested at the same YMCA five years earlier, when Senator Johnson's administrative assistant was also charged with "disorderly conduct (pervert)," forfeiting the $25 collateral.

As a result of his outing Jenkins was obliged to resign as the chief special assistant to the president. He was then hospitalized with "nervous exhaustion and high blood pressure." Bill Moyers, another longtime associate of the president's, replaced him as the number one aide. Thus the outing moved him into position to play a fateful role during that administration. On October 15 the President ordered the FBI, still firmly in the grip of J. Edgar Hoover, to hold a "full and complete" inquiry into the affair. Jenkins, then 46 years old, the father of no fewer than six children, had served Johnson as a highly trusted aide since 1939 while his fellow Texan rose through the ranks: representative, senator, vice president, and then president.

Officials in Washington had been concerned about the presence of homosexuals in important positions involving national security because of the belief, as the 1950 Senate subcommittee report had put it, that "Soviet Russia preys upon such persons, threatening them with exposure to force them into espionage." No specific instance of such pressure had, however, come to light in October of 1964 when the Jenkins scandal broke, yet the Senate subcommittee assertion of 1950 was repeated interminably in the media. No evidence, as Congressman Barney Frank has often reiterated, was produced–then or subsequently–that Jenkins or any other homosexual in America had voluntarily or involuntarily betrayed confidential or "sensitive" information to the Soviet Union or any other Communist country, though such individuals, it must be admitted, have betrayed many European governments.

It was anticipated that the outing of Jenkins would harm Johnson's prospects of winning the White House in his own right, but the Republican candidate barely managed to carry his own Arizona and the core of the historic Confederacy, alienated from the Democratic party by Johnson's opportunistic support for civil rights for "Negroes." So the Jenkins affair was soon forgotten, even if it inspired jokes such as one about the sign on the White House lawn: "Trespassers will be violated."

Despite occasional throwbacks to homophobia and the incessant blacking out of homosexuals, the 1960s were generally positive. Gay bars and other haunts proliferated. Nevertheless, police harassment never relented. In 1964, on the occasion of the New York World's Fair, Mayor Robert Wagner closed down all the gay bars–heedless of the tourist business which they might have attracted. Some establishments had clienteles differentiated by age, class, style of dress, and in rare cases by sadomasochistic preferences and other fetishes. Bath houses with abundant opportunities for hedonistic self-indulgence and raw sex flourished as never before. No longer stunted by the inhospitable climate of the 1950s, gay organizations revived on both coasts. While San Francisco began its rise as the "gay capital," the gay lifestyle expanded into new areas in the interior.

Sponsored by East Coast homophile groups, where Barbara Gittings and Franklin Kameny broke with the conservative old guard, the first public demonstrations were held in Philadelphia and Washington–a harbinger of the role that the East Coast was to play after 1969. As D'Emilio wrote:

> Kameny argued relentlessly for gay activists to embrace an aggressive direct action strategy modeled on the civil rights movement. . . . [The movement's three options were:] social service, information and education, and civil rights-direct action. The first two, he stated, must take a back seat to the third. "No LASTING good can be accomplished by administration of social services alone," he wrote. . . . The prejudiced mind, he asserted, "is NOT penetrated by information, and is not educable." . . . Kameny's civil rights orientation led him to break decisively with the East Coast homophile movement's lingering respect for experts. "We cannot ask for our rights," he told an audience of New York activists, "from a position of inferiority, or from a position, shall I say, as less than WHOLE human beings." Kameny condemned the movement's receptivity to medical theories about the causes of homosexuality and to the belief that gay men and women were susceptible to cures . . . [He declared] "I take the stand that not only is homosexuality . . . not immoral, but that homosexual acts engaged in by consenting adults are moral, in a positive and real sense, and are right, good, and desirable, both for the individual participants and for the society in which they live." (D'Emilio 1983, pp. 163-64)

Under Kameny's influence, members of Washington Mattachine wrote every representative, senator, Supreme Court justice, the president and his cabinet, as well as numerous federal bureaucrats, to arrange meetings to air their grievances. In May 1963 they protested to the head of the Selective Service, Lewis Hershey, against the policy of disclosing data about sexual preference to state and federal agencies, a sort of indirect outing. They countered Hershey's refusal with a visit to the Secretary of the Army's office, but he proved equally adamant. That very month the Democratic representative John Dowdy from Texas introduced a bill to revoke the Society's permit to raise money, and despite the joint efforts of Kameny and other liberal groups the House approved an amended measure.

Nevertheless, Washington Mattachine survived with its prestige at a new high. It contested police harassment with vigorous legal action rather than weak editorials. For example, Kameny took up the case of several men who had been arrested at a restaurant. One of the defendants had been hauled away merely for "winking at my friend." The police called him a "queer" and a "cocksucker" and then beat him badly. Kameny tracked down the victims, assembled affidavits, and complained to the Washington police department and to the city's board of commissioners. Washington Mattachine won the support of the local ACLU, which in August 1964 condemned the ban on homosexuals as "discriminatory" and appealed to the United States government to "end its policy of rejection of all homosexuals." (D'Emilio 1983, p. 157)

Inspired by Kameny, in the fall of 1966 Robert A. Martin formed the first student group, the Student Homophile League, at Columbia University in New York City, which officially recognized it in April 1967. However, during the uprising and student strike that began on April 23 of the following year the group could obtain no support at all from Columbia SDS (Students for a Democratic Society), which lingered under the spell of the party line emanating from Havana and Peking that castigated homosexuality as bourgeois decadence and gay people as enemies of the revolution. Half a dozen student groups formed, but for most, coming out in public was still too traumatic.

Annual meetings were held by the North American Conference of Homophile Organizations (NACHO, 1966-70), a growing American and Canadian coalition of almost all the homosexual organizations, which frequently feuded bitterly with one another. Only a few people attended and their activity received scant notice in the media, but their debates anticipated the burgeoning movement of the following decade. Their achievements, like those of the even older West Coast groups, are often slighted by those who imagine that the struggle for gay rights began only in New York City in June 1969.

However, it must be acknowledged that as late as the spring of 1969 the homophile movement was still a tiny, semiclandestine affair. It had yet to make more than a small dent on prevailing public opinion. In all the States there were perhaps two score organizations, with 150 committed activists doggedly fighting the society's massive indifference and obloquy. They remained politically invisible to the leaders of the radical wave that had swept over the campuses. Most would have been afraid even to testify before the closed hearing of a legislative body, much less hold a public demonstration or just participate in an antiwar action under their own colors, although several hundred marchers had in fact done so. The strategy of these groups was still to seek law reform as obliquely and unobtrusively as possible lest any publicity on the subject activate the "sodomy delusion" and so unleash an avalanche of hate and abuse that would preclude a rational move on the part of legislatures and executives. When two Toronto homosexuals appeared on a Canadian Broadcasting Corporation television interview in 1968, their faces were shrouded in shadow to prevent recognition. A David Susskind program from New York in 1969 showed homosexuals being interviewed with bags over their heads. *Mattachine Review* had ceased publishing about 1963, although Dorr Legg's *ONE* was still appearing in 1968; four final issues came out in 1972. The *Advocate* was a local sheet published in Los Angeles. Jim Kepner heroically and at great expense continued to build up what was destined to become the IGLA (International Gay and Lesbian Archives) in Hollywood. The chapters of the recently founded Student Homophile League were dwindling on account of losses from graduation and the hostility of university administrations. Our movement needed a shot in the arm!

REFERENCES

Bailey, Derrick Sherwin. 1955. *Homosexuality and the Western Christian Tradition*. London and New York: Longmans, Green.

Bronski, Michael. 1984. *Culture Clash: The Making of Gay Sensibility*. Boston: South End Press.

Brown, Howard. 1976. *Familiar Faces, Hidden Lives: The Story of Homosexual Men in America Today*. New York: Harcourt Brace Jovanovich.

Cantor, Norman F. 1991. *Inventing the Middle Ages: The Lives, Works, and Ideas of the Great Medievalists of the Twentieth Century*. New York: Morrow.

Cory, Donald Webster (pseudonym. of Edward Sagarin). 1951. *The Homosexual in America: A Subjective Approach*. New York: Greenberg.

d'Arcangelo, Angelo. 1969. *The Homosexual Handbook*. New York: Ophelia Press.

Demaris, Ovid. 1975. *The Director: An Oral Biography of J. Edgar Hoover*. New York: Harper's Magazine Press.

D'Emilio, John. 1983. *Sexual Politics, Sexual Communities: The Making of a Homosexual Minority in the United States, 1940-1970.* Chicago: University of Chicago Press.

Duberman, Martin. 1991. *Cures: A Gay Man's Odyssey.* New York: Dutton.

Friedan, Betty. 1963. *The Feminine Mystique.* New York: Norton.

Gerassi, John. 1966. *The Boys of Boise: Furor, Vice and Folly in an American City.* New York: Macmillan.

Gide, André. 1950. *Corydon.* New York: Farrar, Straus and Giroux.

Hirschfeld, Magnus. 1914. *Die Homosexualität des Mannes und des Weibes.* Berlin: Louis Marcus Verlagsbuchhandlung.

Hooker, Evelyn. 1957. "The Adjustment of the Male Overt Homosexual." *Journal of Projective Techniques* 21: 18-31.

Hyde, H. Montgomery. 1970. *The Love that Dared Not Speak Its Name: A Candid History of Homosexuality in Britain.* Boston: Little, Brown.

Katz, Jonathan Ned. 1989. "Hunting Witches in Massachusetts, 1960." *The Advocate*, August 15.

Kinsey, Alfred C., Wardell B. Pomeroy, and Clyde E. Martin. 1948. *Sexual Behavior in the Human Male.* Philadelphia: W. B. Saunders.

Kinsey, Alfred C., Wardell B. Pomeroy, Clyde E. Martin, and Paul Gebhard. 1953. *Sexual Behavior in the Human Female.* Philadelphia: W. B. Saunders.

Kirkwood, James. 1970. *American Grotesque: An Account of the Clay Shaw-Jim Garrison Affair in the City of New Orleans.* New York: Simon & Schuster.

Lee, John Alan. 1977. "Going Public: A Study in the Sociology of Homosexual Liberation." *Journal of Homosexuality* 3: 49-78.

Lewis, Eugene. 1980. *Public Entrepreneurship: Toward a Theory of Bureaucratic Political Power.* Bloomington: Indiana University Press.

Marcus, Eric. 1992. *Making History: The Struggle for Gay and Lesbian Equal Rights, 1945-1990.* New York: HarperCollins.

Miller, Merle. 1973. *Plain Speaking: An Oral Biography of Harry S. Truman.* New York: Berkley Publishing Corporation.

————. 1971. *On Being Different: What It Means to Be a Homosexual.* New York: Random House.

Pikul', Valentin. 1988. "Chest' imeiu. Ispoved' ofitsera rossiiskogo genshtaba" [I Have the Honor. Confessions of an Officer of the Russian General Staff]. *Nash sovremennik*, September, pp. 74-76.

Russo, Vito. 1981. *The Celluloid Closet: Homosexuality in the Movies.* New York: Harper & Row.

Summers, Anthony. 1993. *Official and Confidential: The Secret Life of J. Edgar Hoover.* New York: The Putnam Publishing Group.

Timmons, Stuart. 1990. *The Trouble with Harry Hay.* Boston: Alyson.

Tripp, C. A. 1975. *The Homosexual Matrix.* New York: McGraw-Hill.

Wildeblood, Peter. 1957. *Against the Law.* Harmondsworth, Middlesex: Penguin Books.

Wolfenden, Sir John et al. 1957. *Report of the Committee on Homosexual Offences and Prostitution.* London: H. M. S. O.

Chapter IV

Gay Pride–Out of the Closets and into the Streets! (1969-1980)

As the 1960s drew to a close, the American political establishment found it increasingly difficult to conduct business as usual. Passionate opposition to the Vietnam War inspired even more militant tactics than had the civil rights movement. This conflict led to Lyndon Johnson's surprise announcement in March 1968 that he would not seek another term in the White House. The assassination of Martin Luther King in April, which provoked riots in Washington and in other cities, suppressed by the National Guard, and of Robert Kennedy in June of 1968, added to the violent and confrontational atmosphere. In August what some have called a "police riot" occurred outside the Democratic National Convention in Chicago, when officers overreacted and assaulted hundreds of unruly, chanting demonstrators. To many, this incident was proof that the norms of liberal democracy were breaking down. Students, first at Columbia on April 23, 1968 and then on many other campuses, revolted, occupying buildings and paralyzing the educational process. It was in this climate, both dire (after Nixon defeated Humphrey) and hopeful, that a new and vigorous phase of the struggle for gay rights began.

As early as January 1967 and August 1968 incidents occurred in the Los Angeles area that intensified the radical mood of the movement. Before long, mobs of angry demonstrators were shouting slogans of liberation, threatening revolution, and dubbing themselves the spearhead of what they named the "gay community," whose members they exhorted to "come out!" with pride.

STONEWALL

Scholars as well as activists agree that the key moment of the revolution was "Stonewall." On the early morning of June 28, 1969, the police–following a familiar pattern–raided a bar in Greenwich Village that many deemed seedy: the Stonewall Inn. Some patrons, joined by numerous "street people," resisted. Three days of disorder and rioting followed (*Village Voice,* July 3, 1969).

This quasi-legendary event, often called the Uprising, is today hailed as the beginning of a new and incomparably more visible phase, in which gay liberation replaced homosexual emancipation. Each June marches and rallies in ever more cities across the nation commemorate the anniversary. "Come out!" now emerged as one of the major slogans of the new movement, carrying multiple meanings–a call for defiant activism, for proud self-affirmation, and for a loud and angry gay presence in politics. Instead of hiding in subterranean darkness, members of the pariah community now revealed their identity–and more importantly, their political commitment–in a multitude of ways. Public protests, demonstrations, and parades became the order of the day, first in the United States, then in England and other English-speaking countries, and finally in non-Communist Europe. From the outburst of gay liberation in the summer of 1969 a direct line runs to the slogan of Queer Nation, the radical group founded in 1990: "We're here, we're queer, get used to it!" No longer would we endure in silent humiliation the insults and wrongs that Christian society had inflicted and was inflicting upon us.

The Gay Liberation Front that formed in July 1969, shortly after the Uprising, took as its theoretical model the liberation fronts (particularly the Vietnamese FLN, or National Liberation Front) that were fighting–usually under Communist leadership–for national independence and freedom from imperialist domination in many countries of the Third World. It mimicked the rhetoric and the mass demonstrations of those more violent organizations, without actually resorting to killing, bombing, or even much destruction of property. It also found inspiration closer to home, in the movements for equal rights for African-Americans, for women, for ethnic minorities.

The short-lived, Marxist-inspired Gay Liberation Front (1969-73), even more than the gay liberation movement in general, was guilty of profound self-deception. With no memory of earlier phases of homosexual emancipation, it fielded no coherent program of its own, only a set of ideological hand-me-downs from the aforementioned models–which seldom if ever reciprocated the support that the gay activists tendered to what they believed was a common cause. The economic grievances of the Communist-led peasantry in the Third World simply did not parallel the pariah status of the gay underworld in the United States, even if the latter leaned towards, though did not yet join, what came to be called the "rainbow coalition." In fact, the mass of the population in Third World cultures either has no conception of what Americans mean by "homosexuality," or harbors toward those who invert gender roles a loathing that no words in any human language could ever fully express.

This irony reflects one of the contradictions of the American left (*pace* Adam 1978). For the last three-quarters of a century it has largely adopted the terminology, the rhetoric, often the specific demands of Marxist-Leninist parties around the world. Yet these are in essence collectivist, authoritarian organizations with highly centralized leadership and control aiming at a planned society, while the Americans' political credo reflects a native tradition of anarcho-individualism. In other words, the ideologies of the two movements are antithetical, and ever diverging. A hundred years from now historians will wonder how anyone could ever have imagined that they had anything in common. Moreover, Marxist theory centered on conflict between classes, that is, groups sharing common economic interests. From a gay perspective, to make matters worse, in the writings of Marx, Engels, Lenin, Trotsky, Stalin, and Mao Tse-tung, just as in the works of the church fathers, there is not one sentence on the subject of homosexuality that is even slightly positive–not one. The mirror image of the gay Christians, the gay Marxists could only cherish the pathetic wish that it had been otherwise. The Marxist-Leninist tradition rejected homosexuality, which throughout the 1970s remained a crime in all major Communist countries. Some even imprisoned homosexuals in concentration camps for "reeducation," or, as in Cuba, stigmatized us as mentally ill and subjected us to various exclusionary policies–lines which were dutifully mimicked by Stalinists and by pseudo-Maoist *groupuscules* in the United States itself. All of them formally rejected gay liberation. Even in the East

Central European satellite states which, in the lingering aftermath of
the pre-1935 sexual reform movement, repealed the laws against
sodomy, no gay organizations, no gay media, no active campaign of
enlightenment were allowed. The uninhibited, hedonistic lifestyle
flaunted by the Western counterculture not only remained anathema
to the Communists to the bitter end, but was clearly identified with
the bourgeois way of life which the revolution had forever abolished.
Drugs of every sort, combined with Marxism vulgarized to the nth
power, blurred and distorted even what little perception the activists
of the Gay Liberation Front had of reality. If they had carried their
campaign to the streets of Havana or Moscow, they would quickly
have been thrown into a prison or an insane asylum–there is little
difference–as "enemies of the people."

As a result of being integrated into a consumer society, the proletari-
at of classical Marxism had in the United States long since lost interest
in socialism. In the advanced countries Marxist thinkers could look
only to students, women, homosexuals, and sundry alienated or marginalized elements for the cadres of the future revolution. Such an
alignment bore as little resemblance to the revolutionary vanguard of
industrial workers that Marx himself envisioned as did the peasant-
based liberation movements of the Third World, but rather amounted
to what some observers styled "comic book Marxism."

Not surprisingly, the leftist trend faded in favor of the single-issue
Gay Activists Alliance, which at the close of the Vietnam War splin-
tered into a broad and ever-expanding spectrum of organizations
committed solely to bettering our lot within the framework of established American institutions. From the two score that existed on the
eve of Stonewall, the gay rights movement has in 23 years blossomed into a myriad of groups as diverse in their origins, as complex
in their identities, as multifaceted in their aspirations as America
itself.

THE 1970s IN THE UNITED STATES

From 1969 onward "gay" replaced "homophile" or "homosexual" as the code word of choice, and "community," with its left-wing
popular associations, replaced "minority," the legalistic concept of
the old gradualist elite. Some of the "old fogies," often Mattachine

members who had never fully come out, resisted this change of nomenclature–but to no avail. Asserting their representation of the gay community, brash young militants demanding acceptance took to the streets in hundreds, in contrast to the cautious handful of older intellectuals petitioning for toleration. One of the organizers of the first Gay Pride march in New York City (June 1970) stated: "We're probably the most harassed, persecuted minority group in history, but we'll never have the freedom and civil rights we deserve as human beings unless we stop hiding in closets and in the shelter of anonymity." In a rash of enthusiasm, many optimistically supposed that droves of prominent closeted gay men and women would come out. They would then serve as role models for gay youth and give the lie to religious homophobes and to those who psittacinely denigrated us as morally depraved or mentally ill. The world would have to admit that those attracted to their own sex included prestigious members of every elite. Sadly, self-interest prevailed: very few celebrities–and no really prominent ones–came out, even before a backlash gathered steam in the second half of the decade.

How central the idea of coming out was emerges from the title of one of the first gay liberation periodicals, *Come Out!,* which produced some seven issues during its brief existence. Another gay periodical was named *Out.* As yet, however, the word *out* and its derivatives carried only a voluntary connotation.

Before Stonewall only a handful of American notables had come out as homosexual: Gertrude Stein and her circle of lesbians in Paris; Maxwell Bodenheim in the Greenwich Village of the 1930s; Robert Duncan, a poet (some would say not of the first rank), in 1944–perhaps the first to come out in America under his own name rather than a pseudonym. Barbara Gittings and Frank Kameny had both courageously gone public in the late 1950s. Suddenly, people of some prominence surprised the public by coming out. The scientist Dr. Bruce Voeller, a founder of the National Gay Task Force, and the novelist Merle Miller both came out in 1971. Martin Duberman, Distinguished Professor at Lehman College of the City University of New York, and the Minnesota state senator Allan H. Spear came out in 1972. As for real celebrities, no ranking politicians or administrators, financiers or industrialists, clerics or military leaders came out. With the exception perhaps of the Italian film directors Luchino

Visconti and Pier Paolo Pasolini, the few film and television personalities and professional athletes who did come out, such as the British
actor Dirk Bogarde and the American athlete David Kopay, were not
the top names. Perhaps it was utopian to expect better at the highest
echelons. When at Stonewall the oppressed finally fought back, it
was not the middle or the upper class but rather street people, transvestites, naive youths, hustlers, and ribbon clerks. Such denizens of
the submerged counterculture had little–or nothing–to lose, since
society had already–short of mass murder–inflicted as full a retribution upon them as it could. The open, politically conscious, publicity-
seeking gay liberationists threatened those who by tacitly agreeing to
remain in the closet had reached a psychological and social *modus
vivendi* with a hostile society.

In the early 1970s gay liberation scored victory after victory,
despite the reticence and even the resistance to new tactics and
leaders by old-time activists and established gay professionals. Suddenly, with so many lending their support to the cause, conditions
began to change with unexpected rapidity. In 1973, after Frank
Kameny had staged a zap action at its convention, the American
Psychiatric Association removed homosexuality from its official list
of psychiatric disorders, but left as a compromise in its resolution the
clause "sexual orientation disturbance." The APA panel, which included the implacable homophobes Charles W. Socarides and Irving
Bieber (1908-91), for the first time confronted an openly gay member, Ronald Gold, the public relations director of the Gay Activists
Alliance. Instrumental, like Kameny, in removing the sickness label
from homosexuality, Gold swayed his audience partly by ridiculing
the caricatures of the homosexual touted by his opponents:

> If you were an employer, a landlord, or a judge, would I get a job
> or an apartment or the custody of a child if you thought I had
> "wild self-damaging tendencies" and "onslaughts of paranoid
> ideation" [Socarides] or "grossly defective peer-group related-
> ness" and "rage reactions disproportionate to the provocation."

In 1973 the New York Court of Appeals mandated that the bar
admit an openly gay member. The following year the City of New
York witnessed hearings on a proposed gay rights bill, which was
openly supported by politicians as well as by intellectuals, legal

experts, public health officials, and labor leaders but opposed with all their political might by the Catholic hierarchy and the Orthodox Jewish leadership. Despite the never-flagging opposition of religious conservatives spearheaded by the Roman Catholic Archdiocese, and thanks to the tireless campaign by the Coalition for Lesbian and Gay Rights under the leadership of Andy Humm, the ultimate passage of the antidiscrimination ordinance in March 1986 made the city the 50th American jurisdiction to have such a law. The United States Civil Service Commission changed its policy and admitted homosexuals. The ramparts were tumbling down one after another.

Gay ghettos, to which refugees had been fleeing rural and small town America since the nineteenth century, burgeoned in every major city. Famed as a bohemian quarter since the 1920s, Greenwich Village was already established as the major East Coast center by the time Hollywood and San Francisco's Castro began to blossom as gay enclaves in the aftermath of the Second World War. By the 1970s, even Boston, St. Louis, New Orleans, Chicago, Seattle, Houston, Orlando, Philadelphia, Dallas, Miami, and other lesser cities had expanding gay ghettos. By 1992 nearly 30 cities held their own Gay Pride parades. These visibly and publicly celebrated the new ethos of coming out collectively. With America in the lead, more people showed their true selves in the 1970s than in all previous history.

Thus in that decade the United States gained a dominant position in the international movement with an impressive series of gay organizations and triumphs. In spite of Nixon's election the civil rights movement, much more visible than the gay movement, advanced more rapidly and boldly than ever. Its repeated successes in courts, street demonstrations, and government directives fired up other minorities. Latinos, Asians, and even Native Americans backed up demands for justice and redress of past wrongs with threats of riots. The women's movement, adopting less violent means but benefitting from greater numbers, surpassed the movements of ethnic minorities. Although gay activists continued to deem us a minority to be recognized and protected by antidiscrimination laws, their widening demands included not just formal, legal tolerance but social and institutional acceptance of the community's values and lifestyles. In both the number of its active members and in progress achieved, the organized gay movement lagged behind the other groups, even though we made more gains than ever before (or since). We received no benefits from affirmative action and little legal protection against discrimination. In these respects, sexual orientation was not yet included with religion, race, color, sex, national origin, and other criteria. The sodomy laws were by 1990 repealed or declared unconstitutional in half the states, but remained on the books in the others. Even in the 1990s homophobic legislators in New York and other states echoed obscurantist religious groups in rearguard actions against the inclusion of sexual orientation in antidiscrimination bills.

> From its beginning, gay liberation transformed the meaning of "coming out." Previously coming out had signified the private decision to accept one's homosexual desires and to acknowledge one's sexual identity to other gay men and women. Throughout the 1950s and 1960s, leaders of the homophile cause had in effect extended their coming out to the public sphere through their work in the movement. But only rarely did they counsel lesbians and homosexuals at large to follow their example, and when they did, homophile activists presented it as a selfless step taken for the benefit of others. Gay liberationists, on the other hand, recast coming out as a profoundly political act that could offer enormous personal benefits to an individual. The open avowal of one's sexual identity, whether at work, at school, at home, or before television cameras, symbolized the shedding of the self-hatred that gay men and women internalized, and consequently it promised an immediate improvement in one's life. To come out of the "closet" quintessentially expressed the fusion of the personal and the political that the radicalism of the late 1960s exalted. (D'Emilio 1983)

Coming out–and even more, going public–became a crucial strategy in forging the movement. It often proved cathartic. The anger and exhilaration that individuals felt when relieved of the gnawing fear of discovery made them politically militant. Those who came out took a decisive step. Their public visibility exposed them to all the recriminations of which an intolerant society was capable, and thus conferred a vital stake in the movement's success. Such visible activists also acted as magnets that enticed others to come out. Once out, they could not easily resume the mask. Coming out, as D'Emilio observed, created "an army of permanent enlistees."

For the ideologists of gay liberation, coming out in the new style was entirely novel. None but a very few had the faintest inkling of their predecessors, Ulrichs in the Germany of the 1860s or even Hiller in the Wilhelmine era. They did not even remember what Cory (whom a resurgence of religious guilt drove to desert the movement completely at the end of the 1960s and to turn its embittered foe in the 1970s) had written in 1951 in *The Homosexual in America*. They understood coming out as a break with the ingrained tradition of secrecy and deception–and a perilous one at that.

In this mixed climate of liberation and continuing repression, thousands nevertheless came out to one degree or another. We joined organizations that held public meetings, wrote letters to officials, testified in great numbers and without using pseudonyms before legislative committees, and demonstrated, marched, and rallied on a scale that exceeded the wildest dreams of ten years earlier. Now visible in droves, we flocked to ghettos where our sense of collective identity was continually reinforced, not least by businesses catering to our special interests, places of recreation of all sorts, and periodicals that replaced the grapevine of yore. As a result, overt homophobia became unfashionable among sophisticated, avant-garde heterosexuals. Police harassment greatly relented, if it did not virtually disappear. In 1972 New York's Mayor Lindsay forbade police entrapments, which had run to over 100 a week in 1966. Blackmail, our bane since the eighteenth century, also abated, as evidenced by the fact that even within the gay subculture stories of blackmail and extortion were no longer heard, and the topic was scarcely mentioned at Gay Liberation Front and Gay Activists Alliance meetings. Even gay-bashing may have waned, although statistics are complicated by the problem of the willingness of the victims to come forward and of the readiness of the authorities to lend a sympathetic ear. The traditional code of silence about others' orientation still allowed those who so opted to stay in the closet. No one of prominence was outed by fellow homosexuals against his wishes in the 1970s, or until the very end of the 1980s–only a few obscure people by vindictive rivals, and none at all in the name of gay liberation. Myriads came out of the closet on their own–but not one truly famous or powerful person.

The lack of visible celebrities hindered the drive for public acceptance. One of the most highly placed who did come out was Dr. Howard Brown, Mayor Lindsay's Health Commissioner, but only after he suffered a nearly fatal heart attack, which led him to abandon his political apathy. As he lay recovering, acutely conscious of his mortality, he reaffirmed his homosexuality: "I found that I was not afraid to die. And I saw that if I could overcome the greatest of all fears, I should also be able to overcome the fear of standing up to declare and defend my identity as a homosexual" (Brown 1976). The epitome of staid respectability, Brown could not have presented a more striking contrast to the long-haired, wild-eyed militants that the public found so appalling. After consulting with Martin Duberman and some other prominent open homosexuals, Brown came out on October 3, 1973 to a gathering of New Jersey physicians and a phalanx of reporters. The chairman of the conference, Richard Cross, had urged him to discuss homosexuality in order that "physicians would stop thinking of homosexuals as just hairdressers, interior decorators, and male nurses." Brown dwelt on this theme:

> I have met far more homosexual physicians than I have homosexual nurses, more homosexual politicians than homosexual hairdressers, more homosexual lawyers than homosexual interior decorators. One of my best friends, for example, is a former All-American football player, a Stanford graduate, and now the president of a large New York advertising firm. I have homosexual friends who would be regarded as humanitarians, just as I have homosexual friends who have narrow and limited interests. Members of the gay activist groups have been beaten up by the police and sent to jail for their activities, just as civil rights activists were in the 1960s. But I also know homosexual policemen who have been among those arresting gay demonstrators.

The most prominent open homosexual in the country, as he described himself, Brown gained front-page coverage in *The New York Times* on October 4, 1973. Soon afterwards he wrote an article for *The New York Times Magazine* which he expanded into an autobiography, published posthumously.

Brown described the brutal but useless electric shock treatment administered to him by one psychiatrist and the nine years of futile visits to another to "cure" him of his urges. Psychiatrists, he pointed out, no longer classified the homosexual as a sinner but as "a psychopathic inferior and moral defective." Before his death in 1975 from a heart attack, Brown wrote: "If there was one legacy I wanted to leave, it was to have helped in some way to free future generations of homosexuals from the agony of secrecy and the constant need to hide."

Many others then confidently hoped that congressmen, judges, athletes, and entertainers would follow in the good doctor's wake. As the San Francisco journalist Randy Shilts noted in his introduction to the 1989 reprint of Brown's book: "At that point Dr. Howard Brown was the most respectable person in America to openly acknowledge being gay." Brown helped to found the National Gay Task Force, the first of the centrist lobbying groups, and was also active in the Gay Academic Union founded in 1973. On the basis of his own experience with groups like the National Gay Task Force, Martin Duberman told the Gay Academic Union that "Anyone who has worked with any gay organization . . . will tell you that even when total anonymity is guaranteed . . . it's been possible to raise only pitiful sums from those gay men who have the most to give–doctors, lawyers, professional chiefs. Even anonymously, even indirectly, even marginally, these men have refused any identification with or any contribution to the gay movement." With the end of the radical wave in 1973, however, middle-class professionals began to displace the scruffy "hotheads" of the gay liberation movement. For mainstream homosexuals who had felt ill at ease with the confrontational style and leftist rhetoric of the post-Stonewall era, the new formations helped make gay activism acceptable and respectable.

Brown defined "to come out" as "giving up any effort to conceal your homosexuality." He analyzed the need for role models for gay youth and examples for a skeptical society. He hoped to start an avalanche of comings out, but explained that most were reluctant to follow his example because they lacked a legal shield against discrimination.

Despite his inspiring action and moving book, Brown never persuaded the rich and famous to come out, and in that decade no activists, however annoyed and envy-ridden they may have been, were ready to out them. As Brown pointed out, members of the middle class who took the risk of coming out watched distant celebrities benefit from both the movement and their privileged position inside the closet, so aggravating the crisis.

Nevertheless, for the first time local celebrities who were outed survived and even flourished in their own communities. Elaine Noble of Massachusetts and Allan H. Spear of Minnesota became the first openly gay state legislators. In those days no other prominent politicians came out of their own free will. Still, rumor incessantly shadowed some–particularly ones in the public eye. For example, before the municipal elections of 1971 a meeting of New York's Gay Liberation Front publicly discussed the homosexuality of a City Council member and the whispering campaign an opponent was trying to field against him. The candidate was later elected to the United States House of Representatives and then to the office of mayor–albeit with much malicious innuendo in the press about his sexual preferences. Even while he was in office, the gay "City Hall gang" speculated on whether: (1) he had no sexual life at all, (2) he was served by call boys who were paid $150 a night and sworn to absolute secrecy for the rest of their lives, or (3) he had a lover who was occasionally seen at municipal functions. Both as public official and even now in private life he has resolutely denied his homosexuality.

A minor celebrity who did come out of his own accord in the early 1970s, in the glow of the post-Stonewall period, was the aforementioned National Football League player David Kopay. He appeared on many television shows and cooperated in an as-told-to biography (1977). He recounted his Catholic upbringing, sports career, failed marriage, discovery and acceptance of his homosexuality, and the aftermath of coming out. He claimed that many professional athletes are gay behind their façade of masculinity.

QUEER NATIONALS AND THE MILITARY

Because of the extensive efforts to exclude homosexuals from the military, it had been assumed that very few of us would choose this career path, or if we did we would keep ourselves very hidden. One who was outed, but resisted the effort to discharge him, was Air Force Sergeant Leonard Matlovich (Hippler 1989). His sensational public statements gained him the accolade of a *Time* magazine cover in 1975. Matlovich ultimately failed and had to make a new civilian life for himself before succumbing to AIDS in 1988.

Less publicized was the case of Naval Ensign Vernon ("Copy") Berg III. As we learn from Gibson (1978), as well as from Warren Johansson, who interviewed him at a Gay Academic Union conference, Berg's affair with a civilian employee of the service came to light when he was stationed on a ship near Naples, Italy in 1975. His commanding officer became so irately homophobic that he would not even let him remain on the ship. Effectively outed by the discharge, Berg too left the service.

During the 1970s the Navy began to take cognizance of purported lesbian activity among WAVES on the U.S.S. *Norton Sound,* a missile test ship based at Long Beach, California. Some of the unhappiness with the situation seems to have arisen from male sailors annoyed by being rebuffed in their sexual advances. During the summer of 1980 the controversy came out in the open, and 16 of the 61 women aboard were implicated. As the investigation continued, the number of those accused dropped first to eight, then to four. In the end only two women, Wendy Williams and Alicia Harris, were found to have engaged in homosexual activity, but they were given honorable discharges. This witch-hunt received wide coverage in both establishment and gay presses.

There have been many cases since (and over 100,000 in all since 1942). Some veterans of the Gulf War were discharged. A disproportionate number of cases involved lesbians. In some the Department of Defense has attempted to reclaim Reserve Officer Training Corps subsidies after the recipients acknowledged their homosexuality. This issue of rights of queer nationals in our armed forces–perhaps our most homophobic secular institution–remains unresolved today, and will continue to generate further turmoil–and outings, both by authorities and by activists–until Congress or a future president acts to change the policy.

HOMOPHOBIC BACKLASH

Already in the second half of the 1970s a backlash against the new militancy and the substantial strides made by the gay movement set in. In 1977 Protestant fundamentalists who had been spear-heading the antigay crusade, Anita Bryant, Ed Davis, Jerry Falwell, and Judy-Ann Densen-Gerber, coordinated their campaign with district attorneys, police, and the press. They succeeded in having gay rights repealed in Miami, St. Paul, and Wichita, although they experienced a severe defeat in Seattle and in 1978 in California, where voters rejected the Briggs Initiative to exclude gay teachers from the classroom. As more and more came out of the closet and some were elected to public office, gay rights bills and ordinances were passing. More important, courts were deciding in favor of gay plaintiffs on grounds of privacy and equal protection of the laws.

Thus the backlash had been gathering force among conservatives and right-wing fundamentalists well before Reagan's election in 1980, even if it became most evident afterwards. One of the early stalwarts was the Reverend Billy James Hargis, who built a small empire in Tulsa around his Crusade for Christian Morality. In 1968 his organization published a bestseller, *Is the School House the Proper Place to Teach Raw Sex?* Fund-raising appeals stressed the dangers posed by the "decline of morals and decency," above all through acceptance of pornography and homosexuality. Hargis and his allies spread their message through radio and television programs and the *Christian Crusade Weekly.* In 1976, however, he was accused of some of the very sins for which he had pilloried others. Five students came forward to charge that he had been intimate with them. In 1974 he performed a wedding for two students: on their honeymoon they learned that Hargis had slept with both of them. After the groom told the story to the American Christian College president, three more male students came forward to say that Hargis had likewise sinned with them. They claimed that he had threatened to blacklist them if they talked. The trysts, they said, had occurred in the evangelist's office, at his Ozarks farm, and even during tours with the college choir, known as the All-American Kids. Hargis justified his actions by citing the friendship between David and Jonathan. After withdrawing to his farm for meditation and seeming repentance, Hargis, who was married with four children, unsuccessfully attempted a comeback.

The straight world struck, not only with virulent propaganda but with at least one witch-hunt. It was led by an octogenarian, Garrett

Byrne, who, fearful of not winning reelection in Boston as district attorney, targeted the pedophiles, a group more hated and more vulnerable in America than even male prostitutes and homosexual sadomasochists. The tactic was to discredit and stereotype gay men by outing and soundly punishing first the pedophiles, then one group after another of the "bad" homosexuals so that the "good" ones would not defend them, and eventually, when their turn came, no one would be left to defend them.

In 1974 a 15-year-old gay runaway killed himself in Boston with a gun stolen from the collection of his social worker, with whom he was living. The next year the social worker killed himself with a drug overdose. The police picked up another teenager who had lived with him and induced him to identify, through snapshots that they provided him, as many men as he could who had been his partners. It came out that the social worker had participated in a kiddie porn ring which the media sensationalized. In 1977 and 1978 almost every state passed stringent anti-child pornography laws, some mandating imprisonment for mere possession of pictures of a child engaging in sexual acts.

In this climate, Byrne began making arrests. One defendant testified that since 1964 he had been involved with as many as 200 boys, of many of whom he had taken snapshots. He announced that there was a homosexual sex ring in Revere, a working-class suburb of Boston. From pictures he identified more than 60 local boys, of whom 13, pressured by priests, psychologists, and police, agreed to cooperate. Similar dragnets were instigated in Seattle and Chicago. Although when comparable heterosexual rings were uncovered the names of the clients were not publicized, those of the alleged members of the homosexual ring in Revere were. A boy who had been sexually active before his 12th birthday became the chief witness in eight of the 24 cases.

Boston's *Gay Community News* organized a committee to seek a fair hearing for those outed. It was named the Boston Boise Committee, in reference to the scandal in Boise, Idaho where so many men were implicated in 1955. On April 5, 1978 the bisexual novelist and historian Gore Vidal, cousin of Jacqueline Kennedy, addressed a fund-raiser for the Boston Boise Committee, which Robert Bonin, whom Governor Dukakis had recently appointed

Chief Justice of Massachusetts, attended. Bonin was drummed out of office for this indiscretion. On a live television talk show in Boston, where he was conducting a reading at that time, the leading beat poet Allen Ginsberg, sidestepping a request that he confine his remarks to reminiscences about his beat days, declared, "When I was eight years old I had sex with a man in the back of my grandfather's candy store in Revere, and I turned out O.K." While being hustled off the set, he screamed "Out of the closet, onto the screens!"

Denouncing pederasts, Elaine Noble, the state representative, refused to picket the concert that arch-homophobe Anita Bryant planned in Boston, but the rally forced Bryant to cancel her appearance anyway. The old district attorney was swept from office, as John Mitzel triumphantly recounted in his book on the Boston events (1980). In all, only one man was convicted. Two cases were *noloprossed* (legal slang meaning that the charges were dropped on account of faulty police work and lack of evidence), two others were continued without a finding, with charges to be dropped if the accused had not been arrested within a year for the same offense, and another fell apart. Ten defendants avoided trial by plea bargaining. As a result of these victories, Elaine Noble's attempt to demarcate those whom the community should and should not defend suffered a severe setback.

From the crisis, two organizations emerged. The still controversial North American Man-Boy Love Association (NAMBLA) was founded in Boston on December 2, 1978. It advocates complete abolition of age-of-consent laws even though this stance would justify heterosexual pedophilia (Mitzel 1980). Boston's Gay and Lesbian Advocates and Defenders (GLAAD) has ever since fought for the rights of its constituency in New England.

Nothing like the Boise or Revere trials, the largest and most spectacular outings in court in postwar America, has recurred. They resemble the scandals and trials in eighteenth-century London and Amsterdam except that the penalty was no longer death. The gay organizations' intervention helped to halt the Revere witch-hunt in its tracks. The consequences of this victory are still with us and have probably discouraged subsequent police dragnets for adult sexual partners of teenagers. Of course, these cases, like the ones in Boise, did not involve prepubertal boys. A distinction can and should be made between pederasty and pedophilia, the latter involving prepubescent children. Opinion among gay leaders and the public is far more averse to pedophiles than to pederasts (insofar as they are distinguished at all), but *en revanche* the courts tend to punish homosexual pedophiles much more harshly than heterosexual pedophiles. In point of fact pedophiles tend to be bisexual and often married and to pursue prepubescent children of both sexes, while the pederast, if he is bisexual, is usually attracted to adult women, not to teenaged girls. This was the finding of a survey conducted by *MagPIE,* the journal of the British Paedophile Information Exchange, in the mid-1980s.

ON THE MARGINS OF POLITICS

On the afternoon of September 22, 1975 several thousand people gathered outside the St. Francis Hotel in San Francisco to see President Ford. At three-thirty he emerged and waved at the crowd before entering his limousine. At that point a deranged woman, Sara Jane Moore, pulled out a .38 revolver and shot at him. Instantly a man lunged at the gun. A second shot rang out, followed by screams and confusion. Secret Service agents hustled away the unharmed president.

The man who saved Ford's life by deflecting the shot was a 33-year-old ex-Marine. Attempted assassinations are always big news, and Oliver Sipple was lionized. Journalists in quest of information on the hero's life soon learned that he had worked in a San Francisco gay bar. He had campaigned for the nationally famed gay politician Harvey Milk and had been active in one of the "imperial courts," social service organizations revolving around drag events. The newspapers took to calling him the "gay vet" and the "gay ex-Marine." Proudly claiming Sipple as their own, San Francisco gay activists insisted that the White House failed to honor him because of his homosexuality.

Sipple's mother, a conservative Baptist living near Detroit, was hardly pleased. She secluded herself. Eventually she decided never again to speak to her son. The rest of his family followed suit. All this, the publicity and the family ruckus, dealt Sipple a severe blow. Distressed, he brought a $15 million lawsuit charging several newspapers with invasion of his privacy. In particular he alleged that in disclosing his sexual orientation, journalists had ruined his relations with his family. The press had been "unthinking, unfeeling, barbaric, and morbid."

The battle dragged on until, in 1980, a superior court dismissed the suit. The judge ruled that the plaintiff had, by his heroic action in defending the president, become a celebrity and so forfeited his right to privacy. The lesson seemed to be that if one has something to hide–and as the author of *Don Leon* wrote, "Had conscience tongues what back would go unwhipped?"–it is unwise to be a good samaritan. This incident shows how someone even halfway in the closet must shun attention as deftly as would an undercover agent or spy; such a character cannot afford to become a "limited public person," one who has been thrust into the media spotlight by an event or issue not of one's own choosing (McBride 1992). Sipple's relations with his family never improved. Suffering from pneumonia, he died alone in a Bay Area rooming house in 1989. Fred W. Friendly, Edward R. Murrow professor emeritus at the Columbia University School of Journalism, and Deni Elliott, director of the Ethics Institute at Dartmouth College, have both written essays about the outing. Friendly declared: "After thinking about Sipple's dilemma for 15 years, I have concluded that the press had a legal license, but no ethical justification, to rip away the harmless mask that protected his sexual orientation" (Gross 1991, p. 353).

Richard Nixon's Supreme Court nominee, the Floridian G. Harrold Carswell, failed confirmation by the Senate because of his mediocrity and conservatism. Later he was arrested for soliciting in a men's room in Florida. Retired General Edwin L. Walker, another conservative stalwart, suffered a similar fate in Texas. Thus even the rich and powerful continued to be ensnared. Routine outings by the police continued but now became politically insignificant in comparison with those who came out on their own.

TWO OUTINGS FROM OPPOSITE POLES

It is a commonplace that homosexuals are found at all points on the political spectrum. Accidents of personal fate determine sexual orientation wholly independent of one's political and economic beliefs. No party or faction has a monopoly of gay adherents. The truism that "politics makes strange bedfellows" was never more ironically demonstrated than in the almost simultaneous outing of two political antipodes, one an organizer of a neo-Nazi movement in the Chicago area, the other a charismatic leader of the New Left.

Frank Collin, who founded the National Socialist Party of America, a tiny Chicago-based neo-Nazi group, had a strange, disturbing career. He advocated that all African-Americans, Jews, and Latinos be forcibly deported. Seeking to draw attention to themselves, Collin and his followers appeared in the street in full Nazi regalia: brown shirts, black boots, and armbands with swastikas. During the mid-1970s his organization succeeded for a while in sowing division in the ethnically mixed Marquette Park neighborhood.

A legal maneuver in 1976 forced Collin's group out of their stomping grounds in the Chicago park. He then decided to take them to the city's environs. After rejecting several localities, he announced a particularly outrageous plan. He would march his followers through Skokie, a largely Jewish suburb where many Holocaust survivors lived. The town authorities legally blocked the march, whereupon the American Civil Liberties Union took up the neo-Nazis' case. That principled decision caused no little anguish within the liberal organization not to mention among others at large. After protracted legal maneuvering, Collin's group was authorized to demonstrate, but not in Skokie. The pathetic neo-Nazi march in Chicago that ensued betrayed his group's weakness.

However, America's National Socialist Party garnered much publicity from the controversy. The press blew it out of all proportion. The spotlight led to a highly embarrassing disclosure: Frank Collin was outed as a Jew. The FBI released information disclosing that he had been born Frank Cohn. He was reportedly a Holocaust survivor's son. If this allegation is true, he would be one of a handful of American Jews to commit the ultimate act of self-contempt–to revile one's own group by joining its most hateful enemy. Such cases demonstrate how self-hatred is not unique to gay people, but is a far more general phenomenon: some members of oppressed groups do internalize the very belief system that assails and demeans them. However anomalous, their existence reinforces the case for identifying and exposing queer nationals who consciously harm others of their ilk.

Worse was in store for Frank Collin than outing as a Jew: He was outed as a pederast. At the end of 1979 the media reported that the police–this time acting on information furnished by the American Nazi Party–had arrested him for taking indecent liberties with boys between ages 10 and 14. Collin was tried, convicted, and sentenced to prison for seven years on these charges. Not surprisingly, in this scandal's wake the remnants of his party formally expelled him.

A leftist leader during the 1970s, Allard K. Lowenstein (1924-80) became something of a celebrity as a result of his opposition to the Vietnam War. He had even served in Congress (D., NY) from 1969 to 1971, but had positioned himself too far to the left to succeed thereafter in what radicals scornfully term "electoral politics." As time went on, he also had increasing difficulty reconciling his public persona with his private longings. A friend of his pointedly commented on the character of his household (Cummings 1985):

> The more I hung around the Lowensteins' house, the more I noticed that there was an extraordinary number of incredibly good-looking young men involved with the "crusade." They had a "look" about them; preppy (or Ivy League), thick necks, broad chests, etc. Definitely country club material. Some were so perfect they could have been models. I'd never seen people who looked like that before. Often two or three would be living in the Lowenstein house. . . . Every now and then Al–this nonviolent man–would wrestle with one of these hunks. I wondered about this, but not too much.

Cummings had befriended a Californian, Doug Chandler, who told him that he had become friends with Al when the two were working in Indonesia. Doug awoke one night in the room they shared to find Al on top of him. Doug rejected the advance. After this revelation Cummings felt that he had to protect Al's reputation. When a newscaster reported that Al had been shot, Cummings thought that the hit man must have been a former lover of Lowenstein's.

A fellow antiwar activist, the Reverend William Sloane Coffin (dubbed "Sarcophagus" by certain dissident parishioners at his Riverside Church), said: "I hope the gay issue and Al will not be sensationalized. There were lots of guys from that period who had wives and kids but who turned out to be gay. It wasn't socially acceptable so they hid it." But as Cummings noted, it was more than socially unacceptable. It made one virtually unemployable, unable to obtain government security clearance, a liability to a political party or cause–a source of potential embarrassment in all directions.

Though vanity about his good looks induced him often to roll up his sleeves to show off his impressive biceps, Lowenstein's cover was the usual image of asexuality. Privately he claimed that all he wanted from other males was to hold them and be held by them. Never, his intimates later felt, was he in fact able to have a rewarding, satisfying sexual relationship with another man. In any event, hiding in the closet, he could not fight openly for gay rights.

Lowenstein talked to Bruce Voeller about his experiences. He feared that his coming out might have an adverse impact. "From the outset," said Voeller, "he said he was in the process of 'coming out' and discovering things about himself. Lowenstein said he was attracted affectionally to men." He wondered whether people could have a heterosexual affair and a family, if the spouse knew how he felt. Voeller, whose coming out had shattered his own marriage, could not assure Lowenstein. Voeller emphasized that many, including celebrities, led closeted lives, and told Lowenstein that "the grapevine" had Lowenstein as a closeted homosexual. That "grapevine," Voeller intoned, was quite accurate.

On March 14, 1980 a disturbed young man, Dennis Sweeney, assassinated Lowenstein. Sweeney instructed his attorney, Jesse Zaslov, to say that Lowenstein had approached him one night in a hotel during the civil rights struggle and made advances. Sweeney claimed that he had spurned those overtures. The court dismissed this episode as a possible mitigating excuse for the murder. The revelation nonetheless created a media quarrel which outed Lowenstein posthumously. Debating the issue of Lowenstein's sympathy for the gay cause, James Wechsler, editor of the *New York Post,* claimed that he was a disinterested advocate, while Voeller maintained that Lowenstein's hidden sexual identity (bisexual or homosexual) underlay his ideological affinity.

In the *New York Native* of July 14, 1981 gay journalist Larry Bush championed the view that Lowenstein had been a closet case:

As he struggled with his sexual identity, so also must those who chronicle his life give due respect for the many unanswered questions about sexual identity in general. . . . We would be better served by thoughtful consideration of what these issues mean as public figures reclaim their private lives, and moralistic crusaders seek to make private lives public for all citizens.

In a curious way this analysis anticipated the controversy that was to erupt when outing came to the fore.

OVERSEAS

Events in the United States after 1969 completed a transformation that had begun in the early postwar era. Efforts in West Germany to recreate the pre-Hitler sexual reform organizations in the 1950s and 1960s had ended in failure. Too much had changed since 1933 and even more since 1897. The new wave from the United States revived the movement, but with little continuity with the Weimar era. Although Communist countries such as East Germany, Poland, Czechoslovakia, and Hungary had repealed the laws enacted by the Hohenzollerns and Habsburgs, their regimes would not tolerate a gay rights movement like that of the 1920s. But in the English-speaking world, where activists were for all intents beginning entirely afresh, the movement took shape, found ideologists, leaders, novelists, poets, researchers–and when the tide of change became irresistible, emerged onto the political scene of the 1970s. By then America served as the focal point and exporter of gay liberation to the rest of the globe. Following other trends and fashions initiated in American popular culture, the new paradigm of gay life and ideology spread rapidly abroad, first to Europe and then to Japan and the third world.

The slogan "Come out!" spread beyond the limits of the English-speaking world; for example it found a Spanish equivalent in the title of the journal *Afuera!* London and Paris soon had their own periodicals, pride parades, and ghettos. The timid old guard in western European countries and in Canada and Australia was as appalled as its American counterparts had been by the new confrontational tactics and by the hedonistic abandon of the liberated new generation. Coming out of the closets and into the streets, bold, aggressive, youthful leaders shoved them aside.

THE HEYDAY OF THE GAY COMMUNITY

By the end of the 1970s the notion of the "gay community" was firmly established. The rapid victories won since Stonewall had confirmed the brash tactics of the new leftist leaders. Demonstrations, replete with "zaps" and street theater, became the order of the day. Zaps are surprise actions, quick confrontations with minimal advance notice in contrast to carefully planned, publicized, and orchestrated demonstrations. Virtually all segments participated in the Gay Pride parades which "dykes on bikes" sometimes led and where only the NAMBLA contingent was now and then excluded. A joyous, carnivalesque atmosphere often reigned.

Meanwhile, hedonism flourished, stimulated by the ubiquitousness of recreational drugs of every sort as well as penicillin. Instant gratification was to be found in bathhouses, the back room bars, certain parks, piers, and warehouse areas, even in the back of parked trucks emptied overnight and lined up to receive produce the next morning. Rampant sex in men's rooms, in movie houses, and on beaches rewarded the bold. Promiscuity among gay men exceeded even the wildest exploits of heterosexual groupies. Never anywhere in all of history had contact with one's own sex been so readily available as in the America of 1980.

Dismayed observers imagined that the reign of uninhibited sex, drugs, and pleasure of every kind had ushered in the universal depravity that is foretold to precede the Second Coming of Christ and the Last Judgment. But over all this unblushing eroticism hovered the as yet unfeared specter of disease. So far from taking precautions, most gay men allowed themselves to be infected again and again, blithely expecting a visit to the specialist and the proper injection to ready them for the next orgy. All the greater, then, was to be their horror and rage when, stricken by AIDS, they were to discover that the physicians could do nothing for them.

While America led the gay efflorescence, major European cities–London, Hamburg, Berlin, Munich, Paris, Barcelona–were not far behind American metropolises. Baths, bars, parks, motion picture theaters and the like flourished across the whole of Western Europe. Although Italy, Greece, and southern Spain remained more traditional, tourists made Taormina, Mykonos, and Ibiza resemble Fire Island and Provincetown.

While there was great diversity, with some males developing faithful unions that resembled those of straight married couples, and lesbians in general tending to more fidelity and less promiscuity, the rhetoric of a gay community predominated. A certain egalitarianism, inspired by the civil rights movement, permeated "the community." The clone look, an imitation of a construction worker, complete with boots, blue jeans, plaid shirt, and mustache, became the rage. The old fancy dress with suit and tie or effeminate mannerisms went out of style. The image projected was strength, proletarian and comradely.

THE 1970s IN RETROSPECT

In this decade most gay people, it is true, signally failed to come out to the public. One expression of the annoyance which some activists felt at this reticence was a song which they sang at the Republican nominating convention in 1980 to the tune of "Frère Jacques":

Gay Republicans, gay Republicans,
Where are you? Where are you?
Hiding in the closet, hiding in the closet,
Peek-a-boo! Peek-a-boo!

The Canadian John Alan Lee summed up the situation at the end of the 1970s in a perceptive article:

In terms of the "power elite" or whatever equivalent term one wishes to apply to those in Canadian society who have power in the major institutions–business, government, education, religion, law, and trade unions, for example–*not one* truly influential, highly placed homosexual has yet gone public. Thus the illusion is maintained that there are no homosexuals at these rarified levels of society, despite the fact that any well-informed homosexual knows such individuals who have come out at least . . . occasionally at the bars, at gay parties. . . .

The implication is that a time of crisis is ahead for those who have gone public–a time when the truly powerful homosexuals in our society will have to decide whether to throw in their lot with the gay liberation movement and come out of the closet, or to throw their weight, as assumed heterosexuals, to moral entrepreneurs instigating a backlash, hoping to destroy the public gays without being themselves destroyed in the ensuing conflict. (Lee 1977, p. 67)

Lee referred to Edgar Z. Friedenberg's analysis of the reaction of closeted individuals in high positions to those who have torn off the mask as one of ressentiment: "a disposition to fear, envy, and punish others, arising out of the bitterness of realizing one's own surrender of authenticity to those whom one allows to *use* for purposes other than one's own." Insightful and prophetic words indeed! This interpretation perfectly defined the social and psychological parameters of the impasse that at the end of the 1980s would lead to activists outing "closet cases in high places."

Who could have doubted in 1980 that complete success would soon come to the gay rights movement? Who could have imagined that a specter far more horrible than communism would soon stalk our carefree community and strike down many of our promising leaders as well as thousands of our rank and file? If only AIDS had not descended on us at the beginning of the 1980s, what might we not have achieved? But the plague years that decimated our ranks while society and government watched complacently were to transform the self-indulgent, pleasure-loving community of the 1970s into a Queer Nation at war that would no longer wait interminably for its prestigious members to come out. The suffering and death inflicted by AIDS made the homophobia of other queer nationals intolerable and led to the new phase of outing by activists.

REFERENCES

Adam, Barry D. 1978. *The Survival of Domination: Inferiorization and Everyday Life*. New York: Elsevier.

Brown, Howard. 1976. *Familiar Faces, Hidden Lives: The Story of Homosexual Men in America Today*. New York: Harcourt Brace Jovanovich.

Cummings, Richard. 1985. *The Pied Piper: Allard K. Lowenstein and the Liberal Dream*. New York: Grove Press.

D'Emilio, John. 1983. *Sexual Politics, Sexual Communities: The Making of a Homosexual Minority in the United States, 1940-1970.* Chicago: University of Chicago Press.

Gibson, E. Lawrence. 1978. *Get Off My Ship: Ensign Berg v. the U.S. Navy.* New York: Avon.

Hippler, Mike. 1989. *Matlovich: The Good Soldier.* Boston: Alyson.

Hollywood Star News, 1979.

Kopay, David (with Perry Deane Young). 1977. *The David Kopay Story: An Extraordinary Self-Revelation.* New York: Arbor House.

Lee, John Alan. 1977. "Going Public: A Study in the Sociology of Homosexual Liberation." *Journal of Homosexuality* 3: 49-78.

McBride, Donald L. 1992. "What Do You Say to Those in the Spotlight of the News Media?" *Journal of Pastoral Care* 46: 19-21.

Mitzel, John. 1980. *The Boston Sex Scandal.* Boston: Glad Day Books.

Chapter V

The 1980s: Outing by AIDS

In the 1980s Acquired Immune Deficiency Syndrome unexpectedly became the outer. The stigma attached to it reduced the coming out of American males from the feverish pace of the previous decade. AIDS, ARC, and HIV-positive status, on the other hand, outed more homosexual men than all other agents combined had in all previous history. More than 100,000 have died in the United States alone since 1981. By 1992 more than 1,000,000 Americans were infected. Globally more than 1,000,000 have died and 10 to 20 million are infected, mostly in underdeveloped countries too poor even to test, much less to treat or succor the victims. By the early years of the next century the toll will exceed that of the Black Death, the greatest scourge in history. A Hindu religious leader even warned his followers that two-thirds of the human race will die of AIDS–but unlike Catholic theologians sensibly instructed his flock to use condoms.

AIDS, long perceived even by the "responsible" media as the "gay disease," may have come from East Africa, although there it spreads mainly through heterosexual intimacy. First discovered among gay men in California and New York, the illness rapidly spread to IV-drug users, hemophiliacs, and recipients of blood transfusions. Fetuses became infected in their mothers' wombs. Both government at various levels and the health care system were crippled by Reagan's budgetary cuts, which coincided with the plague's onset. The establishment was not ready for a wholly new disease unknown even to tropical medicine. Third World countries, where at first it spread more slowly, were nonetheless quickly overwhelmed, burdened as they were at the same time by debt and falling commodity prices. The media long paid little heed–indeed, maintained a virtual blackout. Even gay leaders with few exceptions defended life as usual and the recently won sexual freedoms–helping keep baths and backrooms open while the plague relentlessly spread.

Almost alone, Larry Kramer of Gay Men's Health Crisis (GMHC), founded in 1981 in New York, argued indefatigably and at times shrilly, even obnoxiously, that the volunteer efforts of such groups would be inadequate to stem the plague. Instead of concentrating on helping the afflicted–a task beyond their meager resources–gay leaders should, he argued, become more political. They had to pressure the government, which alone could provide adequate funding. The small clusters of concerned, in fact consternated physicians in New York, San Francisco, Paris, Copenhagen, and Harvard, some of whom made contact with certain activists, could also achieve little headway against the massive ignorance, indifference, and homophobia, as the journalist Randy Shilts brilliantly analyzed in his columns in the *San Francisco Chronicle,* on which his best-selling *And the Band Played On* (1987) was based.

As time passed without adequate response, the frustrations and feelings of rejection and alienation turned to desperation and rage. Such emotions led activists to ACT UP (AIDS Coalition To Unleash Power) and its single-issue focus. ACT UP spread as far as Australia and Italy, growing exponentially with its slogan "Silence = Death." Its supporters revived the tactics, if not the ideology, of the late 1960s: confrontation, guerrilla theater, sit-ins, nonviolent civil disobedience. Above all, its grievance against the establishment for failure of leadership and want of decisive action paralleled the indictment of normative culture by the radicals of 1969. But only its heir, Queer Nation, a multi-issue group that broke off from ACT UP early in 1990, was to give a theoretical backing and an institutional basis for outing.

More people were outed in the 1980s than came out during the ebullient 1970s. But the main agent of their outing was not police action or newspaper exposés. It was the HIV virus. Just as syphilis and other venereal diseases had previously outed the sexually uninhibited (despite myths about getting the germs from toilet seats), AIDS outed even the rich and celebrated. And once infected, neither powerful connections nor access to the best therapeutic procedures could help. Never before had so many–rich and poor, anonymous and celebrated–been outed so quickly and so brutally.

There is, however, a crucial distinction. Unlike ordinary folk, many of whom came out on their own, celebrities had to be outed. Except for a handful of intellectuals and entertainment figures, not a single highly prominent, queer American has ever–even now–come out on his own. AIDS outed Rock Hudson in his final months and Liberace after his death. Tom Selleck, the television and film actor, sued those who outed him and won his case. Others in public life, including Congressmen Studds, outed by former partners, and Barney Frank, on the verge of being denounced by a hustler whom he had kept, were both reelected, breaking an old tradition. In spite of this climate of opinion which lessened the penalties imposed upon those who came out or were outed, it was not until the very end of the decade that desperate, frustrated activists, often with the HIV virus in their own bodies, decided to out our reluctant superstars.

During the 1970s, it became clear that the American gay model had arrived in all advanced industrial countries, and even to some extent in the so-called Third World. While lagging behind in fundamentalist Islamic societies as well as in hard-line Stalinist countries, gay liberation nevertheless seemed to have become self-sustaining even south of the Rio Grande (despite the Latino cult of *machismo*). This American model, it appeared, could and would adapt successfully to all manner of national cultures. Meanwhile, in the United States the movement would continue to stride happily forward. Alas, this optimistic scenario was not to be played out–at least not without our first undergoing some travail in the slough of despair. A conservative reaction that had begun in the late 1970s swept America while AIDS began to decimate our ranks. The "gay plague" bolstered the arguments of homophobes and made fundamentalist bigots rejoice at this token of God's wrath.

AIDS AND REAGAN

Two major processes acting in combination changed North America. Ronald Reagan's election victory in 1980 wrote finis to the radical wave. Far more important was the onset of AIDS, tragically identified as the gay disease. Although Reagan's ideology proved to be less damaging than had been anticipated, his budget cuts proved much more destructive because they crippled the national health machinery just when it needed to make a massive response to the plague.

The gay political community, which had placed most of its eggs in the left-liberal basket, found the neoconservative climate trying. The beginning of the crisis augmented the apprehensions raised by the rightward shift of politics. The new disease, unnamed and unknown, first received public attention in 1981. A predictably paranoid reaction ensued. Calls were heard for the quarantining (and possible deportation) of homosexuals. The Catholic conservative intellectual and talk show host William F. Buckley (one of whose closest associates, Marvin Liebman, recently came out, but did not object at the time to Buckley's proposal) recommended branding on the buttocks those carrying the virus, presumably to deter them from luring active partners into anal intercourse. Although in Africa AIDS is mainly transmitted heterosexually, it was first diagnosed in North America and Western Europe among homosexual men. Even physicians at first called it Gay Related Immune Deficiency (GRID). In this instance first impressions proved almost tragic. The media, like the government and the health establishment, largely ignored the subject, in sharp contrast to the spectacular coverage accorded the much less significant Legionnaires' disease. By 1983, however, the statistics for the toll of the dead and infected documented a major crisis that no epidemiologist foreseeing its future spread could any longer deny. By 1985 the gay male communities of San Francisco, Los Angeles, and New York were being decimated.

Half-year		Cases diagnosed	Deaths	Case-fatality rate
Before 1981		79	30	83.5
1981	Jan.-June	92	38	93.5
	July-Dec.	203	86	91.1
1982	Jan.-June	392	153	90.8
	July-Dec.	688	282	89.0
1983	Jan.-June	1,276	519	92.6
	July-Dec.	1,639	922	92.3
1984	Jan.-June	2,549	1,381	90.3
	July-Dec.	3,360	1,937	91.2

1985	JanJune	4,837	2,780	90.1
	JulyDec.	6,218	3,787	88.6
1986	JanJune	8,202	4,980	87.2
	JulyDec.	9,852	6,357	84.3
1987	JanJune	12,754	7,384	83.8
	JulyDec.	14,144	7,736	78.7
1988	JanJune	16,071	9,028	73.6
	JulyDec.	16,458	10,249	69.1
1989	JanJune	18,356	11,744	60.0
	JulyDec.	18,136	13,330	53.0
1990	JanJune	18,341	12,651	41.9
	JulyDec.	16,162	11,952	29.1
1991	JanJune	9,885	6,820	16.0
Total		**179,694**	**114,146**	**63.5**

Source: *HIV/AIDS Surveillance Report,* July 1991, p. 13.

Bigots seized upon the epidemic as a sign of God's displeasure. Some hospital staffs named it WOG (Wrath Of God), alluding to Romans 1:18. Sensationalized, often still misinformed and homophobic media coverage reached a peak in the fatal illness of Rock Hudson, who died on October 2, 1985. It led many to distrust repeated official and medical assurances that casual contact could not spread the virus. Incidents of homophobic violence and undisguised prejudice increased markedly. The earlier backlash personified by Anita Bryant now revived with new ammunition and new leadership. "Until recently," Hannah Arendt noted in *The Origins of Totalitarianism* (1951), "the inner inconsistency of the scapegoat theory was not sufficient reason to discard it as one of many theories which are motivated by escapism." Half-informed opinion blamed us all (including lesbians who were unscathed by the epidemic) for the spread of AIDS, which in the United States was only rarely or dubiously acquired by heterosexual transmission. An even more marginalized and despised category of victims were IV-drug users, whom public opinion, led by fundamentalists and Roman Catholic bigots, also found guilty.

Only gradually did we respond to the health crisis by altering our sexual behavior. We were slow to renounce the sexual freedom and promiscuity that our movement had cherished during the 1970s. At first the disease baffled the medical establishment, which had no idea what caused it or how it was transmitted. Because the bath-houses and other vested interests of the gay new order represented major investments, their owners, who had often contributed gener-ously to the movement, struggled to justify them and to keep them open. Monogamy and even quasi-marital relationships eventually returned to favor, and condoms and dental dams became *de rigueur* as part of safe sex. Heterosexual couples normally used condoms to prevent conception and not for prophylaxis (from disease), but until then homosexual men had not used condoms for prophylactic pur-poses, even though high school boys knew that every drugstore sold them under that name. Because the popular mind gave the condom a specifically contraceptive role, despite the widespread incidence of venereal disease among male homosexuals, if a gay man had even suggested using one, most of his partners would have thought he was crazy! Sexually transmitted diseases and parasites were rampant among gay men during the 1960s and 1970s. Syphilis, herpes, and gonorrhea rates soared and a wide variety of parasites transmitted by fecal matter were found by medical examiners.

But nothing prepared us for the frightful toll from AIDS. In the absence of adequate government response, community energy was increasingly allocated to meeting the emergency, from raising money for research to helping the victims. Most backrooms and baths closed (or were closed) in the mid-1980s, at least in the largest and most infected cities, where they had been busiest and most numerous. Cruising became rarer, male prostitution declined, women shunned bisexuals, who had become fashionable in the euphoric years of sexual experimentation and unconventional pleas-ures. Recreational drug use waned. And young males were less inclined to experiment sexually, while countless others scurried back into the closets from which they had only just, and often only half, emerged. If they had not come out at all, they resolutely locked themselves inside and nailed the door shut.

As noted above, Reagan's ideology turned out to be less deleteri-ous than his budget cuts. The Republican Party, which had never been "progressive," was now in the hands of those who cham-pioned a dogmatic free-market orientation. This development proved to be part of a larger world-wide trend away from neomercantilist policies–the welfare-state model that largely predominated after 1945. Like-minded, conservative regimes took power in Britain, West Germany, Canada, Italy, and (for a time) France. At the end of the decade Marxism effectively collapsed in Eastern Europe, the Soviet Union, and much of the Third World. Reagan himself, with his Hollywood background, seems to have been sophisticated in regard to sexual nonconformity, but some of his allies on the religious right were virulently homophobic. The political trend was uniformly unfavorable to socialism but not, surprisingly, to gay liberation, since the free-market approach stemmed from classical laissez-faire. It revived a doctrinaire libertarianism that sought to minimize state interference in all aspects of life, the intimate sphere as much as the economic. Hence the Republican Party was split on the issue of gay rights, with the laissez-faire faction favoring toleration and the religious conservatives fiercely opposing it. To the former all government intervention, especially social engineering, became anathema, while libertarian ideals received at least lip service. Nevertheless, the drastic budget cuts that Reagan ordered in domestic spending, including budgets for health, undermined efforts to stem the plague in the first crucial years.

The progress of the previous decade did, however, continue on other fronts. By the end of the 1980s two Democratic representatives from Massachusetts, Barney Frank and Gerry Studds, had publicly revealed their homosexuality, and unlike anyone who had come out or been outed before, kept their seats and even won reelection. Approximately 50 openly and proudly gay legislators held local and state government posts across the nation, among them a few Republicans. Gay culture in the form of novels, plays, and films flourished as never before. Bookstores, publications, and telephone sex lines proliferated. Gay and lesbian organizations, political and social as well as charitable, dramatically increased their membership. In spite of and in part because of the crisis, more were out (whether they had come out or been outed) than ever before. We were clearly here to stay as a visible and significant segment of the body politic. To their credit, opinion-makers in government and the media did their very best to prevent the hysteria that might have resulted in a worse backlash than actually occurred.

While AIDS wreaked havoc on the male half of our community, it left lesbians essentially untouched because of the anatomical differences in the manner of their lovemaking. Many lesbians nonetheless gave unstintingly in the fight to end the AIDS crisis and to alleviate the victims' suffering. The Gay and Lesbian Alliance Against Defamation in New York City sponsored events such as the Lesbian Blood Drive. Yet one net effect of the crisis was to differentiate further the situations and interests of gay men and lesbians. Men operated in an atmosphere of defensive retrenchment, a reversion to more conservative social mores, dread of the future, and nostalgia for the unspoiled pleasures of the past, while lesbians concentrated on applying feminist thought and practice to their own predicament.

Some who had considered coming out decided that the time was not ripe. In spite of occasional setbacks, gay advocates continued to win legal victories such as the Onofry case that struck down New York State's sodomy statute. In our greatest legal debacle, *Bowers v. Hardwick* (1986), the Supreme Court, citing religious teachings and biblical passages, ruled that states like Georgia could continue to outlaw sodomy, even if committed in private. Georgia had, incidentally, kept life imprisonment for that offense on the books until 1949, as neighboring South Carolina had retained the death penalty until 1870. We advanced, however, on bread-and-butter issues such as child custody, adoption, spousal rights, employment, housing, and protection against hate-mongering. Now these innovations were imitated in other countries such as Norway and Denmark.

In view of the danger that the entire community sensed, most felt reservations about outing their brothers and sisters. But some felt anger at the fact that closeted Republicans, notably Terry Dolan, were aiding and abetting the right. In two articles in New York City's *Village Voice* in April 1982, investigative reporter Larry Bush, who had interviewed Dolan, called for exposés of gay politicians and officeholders perceived as working against the common interest, in order to neutralize them. Though few rallied to his suggestion at the time, Bush anticipated the advocates of outing in the 1990s.

A passage in Taylor Branch's article "Closets of Power" on Dan Bradley, who in March 1982 became the highest federal official in

American history to declare publicly that he was a homosexual and was duly interviewed by *The New York Times,* reads (1982, p. 36): "Some gay public officials in Washington have criticized Bradley for drawing attention to them at a time when closeted politicians are menaced on several fronts. Shortly after the *Times* article on Bradley, an incipient scandal broke out in Washington over charges that several congressmen had had homosexual relations with young pages. Meanwhile, political groups affiliated with the Moral Majority have stepped up their mass solicitations for a war against the 'homosexual conspiracy' in Washington, and conservative scandal sheets have surfaced, naming the names of liberal gay congressmen."

These remarks prove that there was an earlier phase of "outage" that preceded the current one, was largely independent of the AIDS issue (which had not yet emerged into public consciousness), and inspired a conservative reaction aimed at discrediting closeted liberal congressmen while it exploited the paranoia of its financial backers on the subject of "sex perverts in government." Moreover, this development was part of the ongoing political struggle between power blocs and interest groups in the nation's capital–just as it had been in ancient Athens and Rome, and in modern Berlin. The last sentence in Branch's article must refer to such publications as *Deep Backgrounder,* an exposé magazine which began its short life in 1982 and specialized in outing left-leaning politicians. So all the possibilities of outing were anticipated by the end of 1982–more than six years before Petrelis and Signorile launched their campaigns.

ENTERTAINERS AND ARTISTS

Rumors had, of course, long circulated about celebrities, but the truth about their private lives was and is carefully hidden from the public. Several television talk show hosts, including Merv Griffin, are suspect. Tiny Tim was apparently wrongly suspected, but perhaps not Mae West. Gossip columnists and tabloids thrive on such rumors, but publicity agents and studios assiduously counterfeit heterosexual affairs and liaisons because they feel this ambience essential to keeping fans and getting new roles. Popular articles collude, where deemed prudent, by substituting evasive accounts of actors on the set, or even scenes from their films, in place of anything like real biography. Well into the 1980s no star came out: an actor or actress would sooner have admitted to alcoholism, drug abuse, and even to having been molested as a child.

Despite common stereotypes about actors' homosexuality, the belief prevails that the prejudices of the public must be respected, not flouted or antagonized, and that a homosexual identity is not a box office draw. Thus, press agents for stars whose orientation is primarily or exclusively homosexual have their work cut out for them implicating their clients in fictional romances. Even when an actor plays a homosexual, the press agent creates a piece of gossip intended to reassure the public that he (or she) is heterosexual, that the role is slightly distasteful, and that the star is merely "acting."

Few entertained suspicions about one of Hollywood's most durable sex symbols, Cary Grant (1904-86). After an early career in vaudeville in London and New York, the debonair, English-born leading man, who had at one time worked as a call boy in his native land, successfully made the transition to Hollywood in 1932, at the beginning of the talkies. Shortly after he arrived in Tinseltown, tongues wagged when he took up residence with a another newcomer, the handsome ex-football player Randolph Scott. Both of them played stereotypically masculine roles. Although gossip columnists preferred innuendo to outright assertion, those in the know generally accepted that Grant and Scott were lovers. Encouraged by his studio, Grant covered up his orientation through a series of front marriages. In 1943, however, during a tour of camps to entertain the troops, he was caught with a sailor. Money and influence worked their magic to cover up the incident. At 61 Grant managed to sire a child by his wife Dyan Cannon. Although the couple soon divorced, Cary's secret now at last seemed safe. But times were changing. As the 1960s drew to a close, and especially after Stonewall, a new frankness regarding homosexuality emerged.

Still, the icon of Cary Grant the ladies' man was not shattered until November 1980. When host Tom Snyder on NBC's *Tomorrow* show asked the unpredictable comedian Chevy Chase, his opinion of Grant, his guest replied: "He was really a great physical comic, and I understand he was a homo. What a gal!" To make matters worse, Chase lisped the remark in a high-pitched voice, gesturing with a limp wrist. The horrified Grant immediately instructed his lawyer to file a $10-million slander suit. Apart from the decloseting, Grant may also have been offended by the younger comedian's reference to him in the past tense–as an aging has-been. Friends advised the old actor to withdraw the suit because it might prove disastrous. For his part, Chase allowed that he did regret the slur. The matter was quietly dropped. But the incident did not escape the attention of Charles Higham and Roy Moseley, who included it in their frank account of the actor's troubled life (1989). Like fellow show business personality Tyrone Power and like Howard Hughes, Grant eluded full outing during his life. Once he was dead, however, no restrictions applied.

Biographers outed the classical musicians Vladimir Horowitz and Leonard Bernstein, more or less with their consent. In her scandalous 1987 life of Bernstein, Joan Peyser fingered composers David Diamond and Aaron Copeland. So many prominent figures belong here that one can refer to a "gay music mafia": Samuel Barber, Marc Blitzstein, Paul Bowles, John Cage, Henry Cowell, Gian-Carlo Menotti, Ned Rorem, and Virgil Thompson. Among popular musicians, David Bowie has been out and in, as has Elton John.

The artists Andy Warhol and Keith Haring made no secret of their orientation. Haring, who died of AIDS in 1990, donated many of his works to raise money for ACT UP. His designs representing gay sexuality have been used on posters, buttons, T-shirts, and the special postal cachet commemorating the twentieth anniversary of Stonewall conceived by coauthor Warren Johansson in 1989. Robert Mapplethorpe, too, was open about his homosexuality during his life, but became a *cause célèbre* only with the protests and trial over the posthumous exhibitions of his photographs in Washington and Cincinnati in 1990. It may be that a larger number of renowned artists than musicians remain in the closet today, reversing the historical preponderance of homoerotic artists over musicians.

As AIDS pursued its ravages, rumors about stars who ostensibly had the disease were flying. Some were false, others uncertain; but two widely publicized cases turned out to be true: Rock Hudson and Liberace. Suspected in the 1950s, their gayness was confirmed for the general public only as a result of their battles with AIDS.

Countless fans throughout the world admired Roy Scherer Fitz-
gerald (1925-85), better known as Rock Hudson. Achieving stardom
in 1954 with the release of *Magnificent Obsession,* he personified
unquestionable heterosexual masculinity for his female audiences.
Ironically, for most of his life he was in fact predominantly homosexual. Henry Willson, the agent who gave him his screen name,
shaped, burnished, and protected his image, while Hudson, who had
never received much training as an actor and also lacked flair, took
pains to cultivate an air of butchness, as his autobiography revealed
in 1986. Almost from the beginning, the gay grapevine pegged him
as "one of us." For example, when a student in Naples, coauthor
William A. Percy heard that Hudson and Peter, the ex-king of
Yugoslavia, participated in orgies at a spectacular castle on an island near Naples owned by an Austrian baron, which Oscar Wilde
had visited in earlier times. When such rumors grazed the ears of
gossip magazine editors, Rock's handlers feared that the truth about
their property would become public. As a preemptive measure,
Willson prodded Hudson into a lightning courtship of his attractive
secretary Phyllis Gates, whom he married in 1955. When the couple
divorced three years later, Phyllis was sworn to secrecy by both the
terms of the settlement and veiled threats, leaving Rock free to enter
into affairs with one male after another. His last lover was Marc
Christian, who in a palimony dispute sued his estate.

In 1984 Hudson tried to keep his diagnosis of AIDS secret. His
unsuspecting costars and sex partners alike were later horrified to
learn of it. As his health deteriorated, however, he could no longer
hide the truth. Before his death on October 2, 1985, the media had
extensively publicized both his illness and his sexual orientation.
Liz Taylor, who loyally supported him, has since played a noble
role in fund raising and in helping quell popular hysteria and homophobia.

Liberace (1919-87), born Wladziu Valentino, had long occasioned gossip by virtue of his swishiness. He began his career
performing abbreviated versions of piano classics at restaurants in
his native Wisconsin. After appearances on the vaudeville circuit,
the schmaltzy performer found his niche in television. He was (literally) suited for the new visual medium: his flamboyant costumes
and other props won him increasing popularity through the 1950s,

and he became one of the highest paid entertainers yet seen. In spite of his mincing gait and lisp, many of his most loyal fans were middle-aged women, who seem to have accepted at face value his public denial of his abnormal tendencies. Already in his West Milwaukee high school he revealed a fondness for drag. However, he seemingly remained indifferent to sex until the 1940s. Then he began to explore his homosexual feelings. "Cassandra" (pen name of William Connor), an acerbic reporter for the London *Daily Mirror,* reviewed a concert in 1956, describing Liberace as "the summit of sex–the pinnacle of masculine, feminine and neuter. Everything that he, she, and it can ever want." Then the American tabloid *Confidential* titled a cover story "Why Liberace's Theme Song Should Be 'Mad About the Boy'." Undaunted, Liberace successfully sued both publications.

Rumors continued to make the rounds. Although he professed to be dedicated only to his canine pets, a series of attractive young men visited Liberace's opulent homes. In 1982 an ex-lover, Scott Thorson, brought a palimony suit. Diagnosed with AIDS five months before his death, Liberace continually denied the illness. His persona remained artificial to the bitter end, when a mandatory coroner's autopsy finally outed the star (Thorson 1988). The pressures in Hollywood are such that, unlike Rock Hudson, Liberace did not come out until it was a matter of "out of the closet and into the morgue."

Only a handful of film directors have admitted a gay identity, despite apparently feeling less threatened than the stars, many of whom cognoscenti knew as early as the 1920s to have renounced conventional sexuality. One gay director, Luchino Visconti, made a film about homosexual cliques among the early Nazis, *The Damned.* Closer to home, Paul Bartel, director of *Eating Raoul* and *Scenes from the Class Struggle in Beverly Hills,* said that he "never encountered much homophobia in Hollywood." The problem "was within myself." In a recent interview on National Public Radio, Bartel, when asked if he was traveling with his wife, Mary Woronov, replied unruffled: "We're not married. I'm gay, and Mary's a painter." In an article for *Libération,* a French periodical, he had already recounted an early homosexual experience. The American monthly *Christopher Street* had reprinted it in English. Bartel therefore considered himself already out, but perhaps was glad that the NPR interviewer was unclear about his homosexuality.

AUTHORS

Many American authors have loved their own sex: James Fenimore Cooper, Herman Melville, Hart Crane, Bayard Taylor, George Santayana, Nathaniel Hawthorne, Emily Dickinson, Gore Vidal, Allen Ginsberg, Langston Hughes, and James Baldwin are but a few names on a roster to which others of nearly equal stature could be added, such as one model of Southern chivalry, William Alexander Percy. There is evidence as well for Henry James and T. S. Eliot. In the nineteenth and early twentieth centuries writers here as in Europe came out only to initiates, by means of code words or innuendos (Martin 1979). In his old age Whitman, who earlier had cruised for partners from the ages of 12 to 24 on the waterfront and on trams, and revealed his love cryptically in the *Calamus* poems, even slunk back into the closet out of which the premature activist and British man of letters John Addington Symonds was vainly trying to coax him (Shively 1989 and forthcoming).

Authors could always dissemble by the convenient tactic of disowning identity with their fictional characters. Their personae of a work of fiction are in a sense masks worn by their creator. Thus the gay writer has three levels of identity: the real, closeted self; the mask of conventional sexuality; and the freely unconventional personalities of the characters in the plays, novels or short stories. The interaction of all three can engender sufficient complexity and ambiguity to baffle the analytic powers of the literary critic or biographer.

Even so, no one had been fooled by Tennessee Williams, Truman Capote, or Carson McCullers. Even before the Mattachine Society was formed, homosexuality had become a recognized theme in American literature (Austen 1977; Levin 1991). And from the 1940s onward, some writers gradually let their homosexuality become transparent. Duncan boldly came out in 1944, Duberman in 1971. In the 1960s, the poets of the "beat generation," led by Allen Ginsberg, proudly announced their outlawed sexuality to their admirers.

The most influential writer on food in recent decades, Craig Claiborne, celebrated his 60th birthday by revealing on the air that he is homosexual and that those like him should come out. If any of his admirers missed that broadcast, his *Feast Made for Laughter* (1982), published soon afterward, removed any lingering doubt regarding his orientation. The food editor for *The New York Times* traced his homosexuality to surprising roots: his first erotic experience in bed with his father. Their household was so poor that most of the beds had to be rented to paying guests. His first taste of what he unashamedly calls "ecstasy" in his father's arms, he wrote, "altered my approach and outlook on life, particularly where sex is concerned."

But many leading artists, writers, and performers continue to be outed only by AIDS or by scandal. The late Jane Chambers, now best known for her plays on lesbian themes, had a secure job, grinding out tragic serials for television soap operas. Then, when her *Last Summer at Bluefish Cove* premiered on June 3, 1980 at New York City's First American Gay Arts Festival, her employers decided that they no longer required the services of a lesbian playwright. Chambers went on to create several superior lesbian dramas. In 1975, Michael Kearns, who won fame briefly as a member of the cast of *The Waltons*, imprudently "loaned" his picture–a single color photograph–to be used for the cover of *The Happy Hustler*. Thus exposed as a bisexual prostitute, he took on the persona of the hustler in the book. He toured the country in character to promote the book and titillate audiences. Kearns later said: "I had come out on a personal level. That book brought me out on a professional level."

ATHLETES

Stereotypes would have homosexuality as common among entertainers and fashion designers as it is rare or unknown among athletes. In 1981 the media sensationally exploited an outing, when Marilyn Barnett brought a "palimony" suit against tennis star Billie Jean King (b. 1943). Barnett based her case against her ex-lover upon more than 100 love letters from Billie Jean, which she and her husband had desperately tried to buy back for $125,000. Thus the suit bordered on blackmail. Barnett insisted that their seven-year affair entitled her both to the $550,000 Malibu house, where the

Kings had allowed her to live, and to half of the tennis player's earnings. In mid-December 1981 a Los Angeles superior court dismissed her financial demands and ordered her to vacate the beach house in January. The judge characterized her use of the letters, for which she had received $25,000 from the Kings before the suit, as "certainly close to extortion."

The attendant publicity humiliated the Kings, however gratified they were by the decision. Beyond the $100,000 in legal fees, their financial losses were huge. The star retained her association with Nike shoes, Yonex rackets, and NBC, but lost endorsements with six other firms–including a $1 million contract with Murjani Clothing. Major corporations also quit sponsoring her husband's Atlanta and Chicago tennis tournaments and abandoned his revived Team Tennis circuit. Billie Jean, the winner of 20 Wimbledon championships, was heckled during play in the summer of 1981. She limited herself to three major tournaments, where she played only doubles, and kept her public appearances to a minimum. Although her associates stood by her, King suffered intensely, an ordeal described by her in 1982.

Ironically, King's suffering paved the way for the coming out of Czech-born Martina Navratilova, whose lesbianism is now widely known and accepted. Born into a family of tennis champions in 1956, Martina had already displayed extraordinary talent in tennis by the age of 17, when the Czechoslovak Communists first permitted her to compete in international tournaments. Often at odds with the Czechoslovak Tennis Federation, she decided in 1975 to defect to the United States, where her career blossomed. Before long it became known that she was sharing a three-bedroom ranch house in Dallas with Sandra Haynie, a golf pro. On the eve of her departure to the Wimbledon Tournament in 1991, she learned that Judy Nelson, her former "live-in companion" of six years, was suing her, allegedly for breach of a nonmarital cohabitation and partnership agreement which they had not only signed but videotaped, giving Nelson half ownership of the property that Navratilova acquired while they were together. Nelson's lawyer, who earlier had worked for the tennis star, characterized the case as a "partnermony" suit. Calling the allegations "malicious" and "bewildering," Navratilova declared that "there is a great deal more than what the press is being told" by Nelson's attorney. Eventually Navratilova settled by giving the plaintiff a house in Aspen, Colorado and over $1,000,000 in cash.

In an interview, "The Magic of Martina" (*Advocate,* December 31, 1991), she said: "I would love to see more gay athletes speak out. Yes, I have lost endorsements, and I'm not going to get any endorsements . . . so it has cost me money, but I can still do my job; I can still play tennis. . . . I can't be blackballed out of the game. Whereas it would happen for most other professional athletes, and it probably would happen for a lot of entertainers, singers, and actors. They wouldn't be able to get a job, and that's pretty sad." The media taste for blood had seemingly been slaked by the spectacular affair.

On February 16, 1992 at the Virginia Slims of Chicago tournament, Navratilova won her 158th victory, breaking a record that she had previously shared with Chris Evert. In the entire history of tennis no other player, male or female, has gained so many championships. The most prolific winner in the history of her sport, Martina also had the strength of character to defy first the totalitarian regime in her homeland and then the prejudices of a still intolerant sporting world. Her name deserves to be celebrated in the annals of Queer Nation until the end of time. ("Martina Navratilova," *Current Biography Yearbook 1977,* pp. 309-312; Nicholas Dawidoff, "For the Record," *Sports Illustrated,* June 17, 1991, p. 98; "Pact would give Nelson a House," *The New York Times,* September 20, 1991, p. B13; Robin Finn, "Navratilova Victory Is One for the Record Book," *The New York Times,* February 17, 1992, p. C2.)

Most of the sports world remained rigidly homophobic, as umpire Dave Pallone made clear in his 1990 autobiography. Working his way up to the National League, he learned early on that extreme discretion was required. Pallone had a three-year affair with an undergraduate, who died in an automobile accident. Despite Pallone's precautions, rumors began to circulate about him. Some people whom he had offended in the baseball players' union wanted to "get" him. In 1988 he had a celebrated shoving incident with manager Pete Rose. The *New York Post* linked him to a sex scandal with teenage boys, although in fact he was not involved. But he was nevertheless asked to go on a leave of absence. "I remember that day so vividly," he recalled. "I felt like the whole world had just crumbled down upon me." Still, he sensed relief that the awful truth was at long last coming out. But worse yet was to befall him. "It didn't really hit me until I finally got back home, and I realized that my family [knew] that I'm gay." Pallone realized that his days in baseball were over. The gay major league players, of whom Pallone knew some 12, form "a sort of small club," but their situation is indeed precarious, most of all because of the media's ruthlessness.

With their macho image and teammates, male athletes still face certain ruin when outed. Even among lesbian athletes, who are much more commonly suspected than their male counterparts, none has chosen to come out. Those outed, however, have not suffered as decisively as the males.

POLITICIANS

Politicians, who play to their electorate rather than to their fans, have been as reluctant as athletes to come out, and not one major leader has yet voluntarily done so (with the qualified exception of Barney Frank–see below). But a new, younger generation has been elected, making a wholly different impact on the political scene.

According to the Kinsey estimate that 10 percent of the population has some homosexual inclinations, one might expect some 53 Congressmen to have them. At a conference in Providence, Rhode Island in the spring of 1977, a lobbyist from Washington–speaking from his own personal experience–remarked that 10 percent of the members of the Senate and 25 percent of their aides are gay. If so, most have hidden the matter fairly successfully, at least from outsiders. Barney Frank has threatened to out many Republican representatives who he claims are gay, and he should know. The intrepid Michael Petrelis, who began with ACT UP/New York and is now based in Washington, publicized a list of gay congressmen (discussed below).

The outing of conservative representative Robert E. Bauman (R., Maryland), first elected in 1972, was the result of intrigue in high places. According to his own account, he had alienated Democratic leaders by his parliamentary adroitness in thwarting their measures. Because he was relatively unfamiliar with the gay world and tended to go with hustlers only when drunk, he proved a fairly easy target. The eight-year Congressional veteran had a wife and four children. Bauman had already been in counseling for four months, trying desperately to cope with his sexual problems. He did not know that investigators from the FBI had been observing his "indiscretions" for about a year.

Bauman claimed that he was the victim of a deliberate campaign by the FBI to expose and discredit him, and that in particular Special Agent M. Glenn Tuttle pursued him relentlessly. He was in effect entrapped by a blond hustler using the name Michael at Chesapeake House. The hustler's 17-year-old lover "Steve," "through his own brand of moral indignation, jealousy and a dose of machismo," according to Bauman, informed him that he intended to tell the police what he had done and that he knew that he was a congressman. The lover was not 17 but 24 and a seasoned hustler and drug user–as well as a paid informant for the FBI. On September 3, 1980 FBI agents confronted Bauman with evidence of his homosexual offenses and charged with violation of Section 22-2701 of the District's Code, accusing him of visiting gay bars in order to solicit sexual favors from various young men (obviously hustlers), and transporting some of them within the District of Columbia for sexual purposes–a federal felony. As a result of being outed, he was one of only three Republicans to lose their House seats in November. Despite his defeat, he then entered the Republican primary in Maryland's First District in 1982, but was forced to withdraw after a well-orchestrated campaign of defamation by his opponent. Because of his conservatism and "politically incorrect" line the gay community refused to support him, while other Republicans shied away from him whatever their own sexual proclivities.

The Bauman case may be regarded as an application of the principle of punishing our "enemies" who happen to be closeted. According to Christopher Hitchens (1987), Bauman was hypocritical enough to work actively against gay interests:

> No individual in politics had fought against homosexuality–his own and other people's–as strenuously as he did. . . . Once he was caught, no conservative would take his phone calls. . . . But Terry Dolan belonged, as Channell does, to that special

group of closet homosexuals who delight in joining the gay-bashing pack. Their friends and relatives often help to keep up this unpleasing pretense. . . . Bauman tells of sabotaging a Maryland fair-housing bill *because* it prohibited discrimination against homosexuals. . . . Bigotry and denial are apparently opposing sides of an identical coin. The fear of being exposed is what spurs the witchhunter.

Hitchens concluded, almost prophetically, just five months after the founding of ACT UP, that "the way through this morass is clear. It is marked by a simple signpost reading 'Out'."

Also married and with children, Congressman Fred Richmond (D., New York), first elected to the House in 1974, had a series of scrapes, one involving a black teenager, that alienated voters from his largely African-American district in Brooklyn. However, when a hustler from Boston whom he had befriended committed suicide in his high-rise Manhattan condominium, tragedy ensued. He resigned his seat on August 25, 1982. Convicted on a financial matter, Richmond served time. Wealthy from business, he apparently has no plans to seek further elective office and has set up a charitable foundation that awards grants, some to gay organizations.

In 1976 Jon Clifton Hinson was arrested at the Iwo Jima Memorial in Arlington National Cemetery, a well-known cruising spot outside Washington (*Newsweek,* October 20, 1980). A year later he nearly lost his life in a fire at a gay movie theater in Washington. Yet in 1978 he won a congressional seat as a Republican from Mississippi. At first fundamentalist voters did not seem to care about his peccadillos, even when a local paper wrote them up. He managed to be reelected in 1980. However, on April 13, 1981, barely into his second term, Hinson was forced to resign after two toilet arrests. One took place in the men's room of the Longworth House Office Building, where he was caught behaving indecently with a Library of Congress employee.

In the 1980s a series of sex scandals in the House began with obscure charges. In 1983 Gerry Studds (D., Massachusetts), first elected in 1972, was subjected to a reprimand for sexual intimacy with a 17-year-old Congressional page ten years previously. Refusing to capitulate, he proudly affirmed his orientation. Reelected several times since, he has lent significant support to gay causes in the House–more perhaps than he could or would have if he had remained closeted as in his earlier years–and is now a leading opponent of the Pentagon's ban on homosexuals.

Studds' colleague Barney Frank (D., Massachusetts), who won his seat in 1980, has undergone a longer siege. The unruly bisexual hustler Steve Gobie, named as a user of narcotics, publicly alleged not only to have served the congressman sexually but to have operated as a male prostitute from Frank's own apartment. Gobie has also sold stories to the tabloids. Many gay activists feared that with what we may dub this "secondary outing," (because Frank came out only shortly before the scandal broke, perhaps to be in a better position to withstand its effects), his political usefulness had come to an end; but events proved them wrong. In July 1990 the House committee on ethics found that he merited "personal censure" but not expulsion, and since then the Congressman has recouped his position as one of the most articulate representatives. Like Studds working to end discrimination in the military, he has successfully combatted homophobic policies of the Immigration and Naturalization Service.

Rumors that have circulated about Democratic Speaker Thomas Foley (who is not gay, according to Frank) and Republican ex-representative Jack Kemp are unsubstantiated and may reflect innuendos by their opponents. Senator Mark Hatfield and Congressman Steven Gunderson seem more likely. Thus far no senators (except for the murky case of David Walsh in 1942) and no lesbians in Congress have been successfully outed, though rumors abound, even if the "respectable" movement press hesitates to print them. Few attempts by activists to out political figures have been successful. This point is illustrated by the 1982 primary campaign for the Democratic nomination for governor of New York State. Some supporters of Mario Cuomo, apparently without the candidate's knowledge, spread the rumor that his opponent, then mayor of New York City, was gay. They did this through such tactics as word-of-mouth slogans like "Vote for Cuomo, not the homo" and "Don't be a Koch-sucker." Even the usually reticent *New York Times* maliciously alluded to the innuendos. In the event, Cuomo won the nomination by an upset, and then the governorship. Most observers doubt that the smear campaign, such as it was, much affected the outcome of the election. And Edward Koch, the target of the slogans, went on to be reelected in 1985 and to sign the city's gay rights bill into law the following spring–the crowning accomplishment of New York's Coalition for Lesbian and Gay Rights.

In 1987 a gay reporter at National Public Radio, Frank Browning, broke the story that the network of right-wing Americans raising funds for the contras in Nicaragua was largely homosexual and that Carl "Spitz" Channell's lover was on the payroll of a tax-exempt foundation as a "consultant." When certain parties objected to the exposé, Browning retorted that there would have been no qualms if the beneficiary had been Channell's wife. Since the Reagan Administration had been unsympathetic to the gay cause, this indignation at the exposé was interpreted as another instance of hypocrisy (Gup 1988).

PROFESSORS AND PREACHERS

Homosexuality has been called the disease of professors, and homosexuals have traditionally been drawn to teaching youth. We can therefore reasonably surmise that some professors at least made their career choice primarily for this reason, just as some queer nationals were drawn into the Roman Catholic clergy precisely (if paradoxically) because of its celibacy. When Princeton was an all-male school and the chairman of the English Department was criticized at a cocktail party for retaining gay instructors, he rejoined that they make the finest teachers because they are more *interested* in their students. In any case, college administrators and professors, like priests and pastors, not infrequently use their positions of authority, trust, and respect to initiate affairs with their charges, and (if they are of the opposite sex, and excepting the Catholic clergy) sometimes even marry them.

So far no college chief administrators and surprisingly few professors have come out. Princeton, for example, continues to lag, having not a single openly homosexual tenured male full professor. Nor have many religious officials at any level come out–not one bishop or cardinal in the Roman Catholic Church, not a single Episcopal, Methodist, or Orthodox bishop. Few clerics at the lower levels have come out and no Orthodox or Conservative rabbis. Yet the numbers that have been outed reflect how numerous crypto-homosexuals are in those institutions.

In the fall of 1991 Harvard University witnessed a conflict provoked by an issue of a right-wing student magazine, *Peninsula,* whose pages were wholly devoted to attacking the homosexual rights movement. At a rally protesting the publication, Peter J. Gomes, Plummer Professor of Christian Morals and minister of Memorial Church, publicly announced: "I have all the authority in the world [to speak on the religious case against gay people] as the Plummer Professor of Christian Morals and because I am a Christian who happens as well to be gay." In February 1992 five undergraduates formed the organization Concerned Christians at Harvard to demand that Gomes resign as minister because he preached that homosexuality is not a sin. Its chair, Sumner E. Anderson, said that he expected between 80 and 100 members to join the new group. The President of Harvard, Neil L. Rudenstine, defended Gomes on the grounds that it is not the University's task to dictate theological doctrine. Meanwhile Harvard's Puritan founders must have been spinning in their graves. (*Harvard Gay & Lesbian Newsletter,* Winter 1992, p. 4; *Harvard Crimson,* February 20, 1992, p. 1; February 21, 1992, p. 1.)

A church that imposes celibacy upon its clergy faces a considerable problem: Almost inevitably its ministerial candidates will include a sizable number who for whatever reasons feel unattracted to marital bliss, but may not choose to abstain when their own abnormal proclivities can be discreetly gratified. The Latin maxim *si non castē, tamen cautē* (if not chastely, then cautiously) perfectly epitomizes such clerics' policy. Such covert behavior is not limited to the Roman Catholic clergy. To be sure, it is less common among Protestant ministers and Jewish rabbis, who are encouraged to marry and hence less likely to pursue homosexual partners. Appearances, however, can be deceiving.

During the 1980s the Dominican priest Bruce Ritter won many admirers for providing shelter and counseling for runaway teenagers in New York City's West 42nd Street area. Many of these adolescents were "throwaways," driven out by their families because they were gay. The girls had often engaged in prostitution, the only way they–and some of the boys–knew to earn a few dollars to sustain themselves. Ritter's Covenant House accepted them in ever-increasing numbers, and social workers rallied to volunteer for the cause, whose need was so obvious. Supported by donations and some assistance from the city, the service acquired new premises in New York and spread to other cities as well. Father Ritter himself maintained the customary façade of asexuality. He conformed to Catholic doctrine in denying his charges access to information on birth control and "safe sex" techniques. On the other hand, he did not discriminate against gay staff members or inmates. He even preached a sermon in which he said that they should be treated with respect. The real peril to the gay youth who took refuge behind the walls of Covenant House was the violent and homophobic subculture of many of the residents, especially the lower-class, Third World "street people" who whenever staff members' backs were turned abused and victimized middle-class or other adolescents who were not tough or "street-wise."

In 1989 a distraught young man emerged with a sensational story. This former resident charged that Ritter had kept him in an apartment in return for sexual favors. At first the priest strongly denied the account, plausibly, since his accuser was known to be unstable, as his own father testified. However, it transpired that another youth had made similar charges earlier, but they had been ignored at the time because of the almost universal esteem for Ritter and his ministry. An investigative reporter for the *New York Post* broke the story, as an insider revealed at a meeting of the Horatio Alger Chapter of NAMBLA, in retribution for the homophobic tone of Ritter's *Sometimes God Has a Kid's Face* (1988). This piece of self-promotion hypocritically excoriated homosexuals, claiming that we prey upon and destroy teenagers forced into prostitution after running away from home or being thrown out by their own parents. To reproach heterosexuals for irresponsibly having children and then neglecting or sadistically mistreating them seldom enters the minds of clerical authors.

Ritter's ultimate doom, however, was the discovery of financial irregularities at Covenant House which were traced to his doorstep. Charitable institutions, like colleges and hospitals, are inherently at risk for such malfeasance because unlike private enterprises whose very survival depends on strict accounting, cost control, efficiency and so forth, their resources are intangibles like public good will and sentimentality and their commodities are imponderables like "child welfare." In any event, the mounting scandal at Covenant House made headlines in New York newspapers day after day. After an inquiry by Catholic authorities Ritter had to step down. With its reputation doubly tarnished, the institution entered on a rocky path. When the friar was later obliged to resign from the Franciscan order, he spent only a few months in a new career as a priest in India, where he presumed few would either know or care about his abnormal proclivities. According to the *New York Post* (December 3 and 4, 1991), the media relentlessly outed him "even in this most remote corner of the world," the Diocese of Allapuzha in Kerala. He found life impossible, frustrated in his hope that he could leave his past behind. So he returned to the United States to begin a new fund-raising campaign. This case shows how in an age of electronic communication, the echoes of an outing can follow even a minor celebrity to the end of the earth.

Particularly embarrassing was a series of scandals involving priests who had abused young children. They exploited the power which the parish clergy hold over the laity in a highly authoritarian institution. Since 1911, in fact, the decree *Quantavis diligentia* had forbidden lay Catholics to bring charges against their clergy in secular courts on pain of excommunication. The glee with which the anticlerical press of that day pilloried the church as a redoubt of the depraved and the abnormal militated for secrecy. It is only fair to state, however, that such individuals, if their conduct came to the attention of superiors within the church, would often be tried in ecclesiastical tribunals–but *in camera* so that nothing would reach the outside world.

A case that achieved wide publicity occurred among the Cajuns of southern Louisiana. The culprit, Father Gilbert Gauthe, received a 20-year prison sentence in October 1985 for molesting at least 37 altar boys plus one girl. By 1987 Lafayette diocese had been obliged to pay parents $12 million in 16 cases. Subsequently insurance companies refused to cover the church for suits of this character. In 1990 the Mount Cashel orphanage for boys in St. Johns, Newfoundland, had to close under pressure. Ten Christian brothers, laymen of the order that ran the orphanage, allegedly abused the boys repeatedly. Moreover, a church inquiry led by a former lieutenant governor found several other priests guilty of similar offenses. The report argued that for several years Catholic leaders ignored, rejected, or failed to deal effectively with the problem. The continuing scandal, and allegations of a coverup, brought about the resignation of Archbishop Alphonsus L. Penney.

Among the most successful of the "televangelists" of the 1980s, the flamboyant team of Jim and Tammy Bakker, ran the PTL (interpreted as the acronym for "Praise the Lord" or "People that Love") Ministries, with an elaborate headquarters and condominium complexes. After a young woman claimed that Bakker and his associates had turned her into a sexual utensil, a male subordinate revealed that Bakker had seduced him with promises of "heaven now." As the effect of these revelations sank in, contributions to PTL fell off drastically. Its properties became bankrupt, amidst disclosures of the lavish lifestyle led by the Bakkers–at the expense of small contributors, many of them pensioners on a limited income. Eventually Bakker was sent to prison for financial irregularities. There he was assigned to clean toilets. Since he could not pay the $500,000 assessed by the court, his creditors moved in July 1990 to attach the 11 cents hourly wages he was receiving.

THE MAKING OF AN AIDS ACTIVIST: LARRY KRAMER

Out of the frustration with indifference and homophobia that the AIDS crisis highlighted, Larry Kramer, writing for the *New York Native,* laid the intellectual groundwork for ACT UP. Of Jewish ancestry, Kramer was raised by, as he relates, "two intelligent parents, both professionals (my father a lawyer and my mother a social worker)." The Yale graduate authored two plays, *The Normal Heart,* about the first phase of the AIDS epidemic, and *Just Say No,* as well as a highly acclaimed screenplay for *Women in Love.* His novel *Faggots* portrayed the uninhibited lifestyle of the euphoric post-Stonewall decade.

Kramer spoke and wrote untiringly to alert people of the plague. Gradually despairing of rational argument, he called for protests. In his article of March 14, 1983, "1,112 and Counting," he referred to the number of AIDS deaths until that time with rage:

> If this article doesn't scare the shit out of you, we're in real trouble. If this article doesn't rouse you to anger, fury, rage, and action, gay men may have no future on this earth. Our continued existence depends on just how angry you can get. . . . I repeat: Our continued existence as gay men upon the face of this earth is at stake. Unless we fight for our lives, we shall die. In all the history of homosexuality we have never before been so close to death and extinction.

Kramer helped inspire the Lavender Hill Mob, a small, close-knit group of New York activists who zapped the uncaring establishment in 1986-87. In its tactics it is often considered the predecessor of ACT UP. In New York City a small band of activists formed the first chapter of AIDS Coalition To Unleash Power (ACT UP) a few days after one of Kramer's more dramatic speeches, which he later published as "The Beginning of ACTing UP":

> So what are we going to do? Time and time again I have said–no one is going to do it for us but ourselves. . . . Did you notice what got the most attention at the recent CDC conference in Atlanta? It was a bunch called the Lavender Hill Mob. They got more attention than anything else at that meeting. They protested. They yelled and screamed and demanded and were blissfully rude to all those arrogant epidemiologists who are ruining our lives.

Kramer particularly deplored the inaction of New York politicians: "Cuomo, D'Amato, Moynihan, Koch. Every single one of them treated me as if I was ungrateful" for all the money that had been allocated for AIDS research. Kramer's howls finally got some result. The dramatic demonstrations and confrontations in New York inspired the formation of smaller but equally committed and daring ACT UP chapters across the country. Many believe that Kramer is vulgar and bombastic as well as self-promoting, that he overestimates his role and influence and that he is unnecessarily and perhaps pathologically rude and abrasive to boot. His style, which often reproaches the gay community for its earlier and current inaction in the face of AIDS, provokes laughter as much as admiration. Nevertheless, the course of the epidemic, much less the gay response to it, could not be discussed without analyzing his role as a founder of both GMHC and ACT UP.

ACT UP

AIDS revived the radical style of political action that had lapsed after the end of American involvement in Vietnam. The official statistics of the Centers for Disease Control in Atlanta showed that by December 31, 1986 23,252 adults had died of AIDS in the United States. ACT UP formed–at Kramer's instigation–in New York City on March 12, 1987 to combat the state and society's inadequate response to the crisis that was striking at the very life of the gay community.

The original New York nucleus found imitators as far away as Des Moines, Iowa and Florence, Italy. By December 1991 ACT UP boasted more than 100 chapters, mostly in the United States. A few have died, while others have split over ideological differences. ACT UP does not have a hierarchy. Members have an equal say, but in most chapters a core of long-term activists preponderate. "Facilitators," periodically elected, chair the weekly meetings, where Treatment Working Group members report. A spirited and informed discussion regularly follows. Activists, for example, may try to induce pharmaceutical companies to permit compassionate use of new drugs, meaning that those who give informed consent are allowed to try untested but potentially efficacious (or toxic) medicines. Members claim that expertise about AIDS and about treatments for its sequelae has become their principal weapon. They hope to halt or retard the epidemic by teaching how the plague spreads and by propaganda for safe sex. Some routinely peruse the scientific and medical press to discover techniques or drugs that might retard the symptoms of AIDS or alleviate the pain and disability that it brings. Others urge pharmaceutical firms to hasten to make new treatments available, while a third group pursues unorthodox and holistic therapies scorned by the medical establishment.

The weekly meeting of ACT UP's founding chapter, in the early days and now once more usually on Monday evening at the Community Services Center at 208 West 13th Street in Manhattan, attracted ever larger numbers of handsome young men. Some 60 percent of them were rumored to be HIV-positive. Others, including some women, were moved simply by the sorrow and tragedy that AIDS had already brought to those near and dear to them.

But facing gruesome death daily, ACT UP effortlessly surpassed the agitprop of the late 1960s by its use of guerrilla theater and rich, imaginative visual symbolism to demonstrate to the media–and through them to the American public–the gravity of AIDS. The truly unique New York chapter has appealing and colorful leaders like the handsome ex-stockbroker Peter Staley, who was diagnosed with ARC in 1985. Depressed at first and feeling that his life was over, he regained his courage to become ACT UP's pinup boy and one of its most tireless activists. The comedian Ron Goldberg has performed with true dramatic flair at ACT UP rallies and facilitated adroitly at meetings. ACT UP excels in street theater, "die-ins," and the hanging of banners on public buildings. Believing in radical and even illegal tactics, they often attack Cardinals Law and O'Connor, and have demonstrated in front of New York's St. Patrick's Cathedral and Boston's Holy Cross, dispersing condoms and sometimes disrupting masses.

Even its critics–and many there are–cannot deny that ACT UP is a small but sharp gadfly prodding the medical establishment and the government to take swifter and more effective steps to save lives and alerting the public to measures needed to combat the plague. It became the cutting edge of the gay movement in the late 1980s even though in principle it remained focused on a single issue.

ACT UP's membership is not clearly defined because it issues no cards and keeps no registration lists. A typical meeting attracts an average of 175 to 200 in New York, 25 to 40 in Boston, and approximately 30 in Washington, D.C., Chicago, and Los Angeles. The San Francisco chapter split into two over differences in ideology and tactics. Many drift in and out: every chapter has leaders and a hard core who volunteer for current projects. Really committed, almost full-time ACT UP activists may not number more than 1,500 to 2,000, although the mailing lists of the New York chapter alone are much larger.

An obscure chapter in Portland, Oregon carried out the first outing of the new type. On February 25, 1989 its members outed Senator Mark Hatfield, who had supported various homophobic initiatives and in October 1987 had even voted for the Helms Amendment. Thereafter ACT UP acquired an intimate connection with outing, and in 1990 spawned Queer Nation, which parallels and supplements rather than rivals its parent body. Endorsing the ideals behind outing, Queer Nation crystallized the principles and justifications for the practice.

CONCLUSION

The 1980s saw the gay movement marking time and on the defensive because of the conservative political climate and AIDS. An assortment of figures of the second rank in various walks of life nevertheless came out, or were brought out in the old-fashioned way by arrests and legal charges–and not always to their detriment. So did many ordinary people from every walk of life. AIDS, however, seized the role of principal outer. For the first time, average Americans became aware that a congressman or movie star, just as much as their next-door neighbor or the woman who worked beside them at the office, could be homosexual.

Most still actively hated and shunned queers. Only a minority truly accepted us. Few, however, could persist in imagining that we were some rare species hardly found outside of bohemian Greenwich Village or San Francisco's Castro. The stereotype of a sleazy or effeminate character haunting parks and restrooms faded with the outing of political leaders and movie stars. Managing one's gay identity could of course still be a problem, as it was sometimes impolitic to offend the mores of a particular subculture even if one could be totally overt in another social setting. Likewise, geographic regions varied: Middle America lagged behind the two coasts, and the Bible Belt retained its fundamentalist intolerance, Baptists gloating along with Roman Catholic moralists that AIDS was God's vengeance for immorality.

In addition to inciting a backlash, AIDS inflicted suffering and death on our community and left gaping holes in the ranks of our male leaders. It also inspired a new wave of organizing and even evoked sympathy from heterosexuals who shared gay friends' and neighbors' grief and loss. AIDS brought some out posthumously, obliquely revealing that figures long in the public eye had private lives that defied convention. The public became more sophisticated if not always more sympathetic. The events of the 1980s, unforeseen though they were, set the stage for the political struggles of the 1990s–in which outing may be cast in an unexpected and even astonishing role.

REFERENCES

Arendt, Hannah. 1951. *The Origins of Totalitarianism.* New York: Harcourt, Brace.

Austen, Roger. 1977. *Playing the Game: The Homosexual Novel in America.* Indianapolis: Bobbs-Merrill.

Bauman, Robert E. 1986. *The Gentleman from Maryland: The Conscience of a Gay Conservative.* New York: Arbor House.

Branch, Taylor. 1982. "Closets of Power." *Harper's,* October, pp. 34-50.

Dawidoff, Nicholas. 1991. "For the Record." *Sports Illustrated,* June 17, p. 98.

Deep Backgrounder. 1982.

Gup, T. 1988. "Identifying homosexuals. What are the rules?" *Washington Journalism Review,* October, p. 32.

Harvard Crimson. 1992. February 20, p. 1; February 21, p. 1.

Harvard Gay & Lesbian Newsletter. 1992. Winter, p. 4.

Higham, Charles, and Roy Moseley. 1989. *Cary Grant: The Lonely Heart.* Sevenoaks, Kent: New English Library.

Hitchens, Christopher. 1987. "It Dare Not Speak Its Name: Fear and Self-Loathing on the Gay Right." *Harper's,* August, pp. 70-72.

Hudson, Rock (with Sara Davidson). 1986. *Rock Hudson: His Story.* New York: Morrow.

King, Billie Jean, and Frank Deford. 1982. *Billie Jean.* New York: Viking.

Kramer, Larry. 1989. *Reports from the Holocaust: The Making of an AIDS Activist.* New York: St. Martin's Press.

Levin, James. 1991. *The Gay Novel in America.* New York: Garland Publishing.

Martin, Robert K. 1979. *The Homosexual Tradition in American Poetry.* Austin: University of Texas Press.

"Martina Navratilova." *Current Biography Yearbook* 1977, pp. 309-312.

"Pact would give Nelson a House." 1991. *The New York Times,* September 20, p. B13.

Pallone, Dave (with Alan Steinberg). 1990. *Behind the Mask: My Double Life in Baseball.* New York: Viking.

Ritter, Bruce. *Sometimes God Has a Kid's Face.* New York: Covenant House.

Thorson, Scott (with Alex Thorleifson). 1988. *Behind the Candelabra: My Life with Liberace.* New York: Dutton.

Chapter VI

Outings by Activists (The 1990s)

Our century's last decade also counts as the last of the second Christian millennium. There are some, of course, who regard this prospect with foreboding: could it be that the apocalypse, which failed to arrive in 1000, was merely rescheduled, and now looms? Others will glimpse in the millennium the glow of a new dawn. Of course different folks will have different hopes. We queer nationals are entitled to ask whether we may at last see the end of 2,000 years of homophobia, so that the new millennium can open a fresh page in our history. This vision is perhaps more utopian than, say, the hope that Americans will have the best schools. Nevertheless, a sense is abroad that now is the time for the queer nation to strive for decisive changes–in life-partner recognition and social benefits, in the right to serve in the military and the clergy, and in putting the record straight on certain prominent denizens of the closet, at least outing hypocrites and traitors. Finally, of course, there is the hope–almost the dream–that the scourge of AIDS may vanish.

Such hopes may seem to fly in the face of political realities–but then our movement has always thrived on going against the odds. Judging from appearances, circumstances may indeed not seem promising. The Republicans' selection of George Bush to succeed Ronald Reagan set the stage for the 1990s. Many felt, however, that Bush's exploitation of the Willie Horton affair, the murderer paroled by the "liberal" Massachusetts governor, was demagogic and boded ill for the future. (Dukakis at least was pro-choice, unlike Bush, but he had alienated gay voters by opposing our right of adoption in his own state.) Once elected, Bush involved himself mainly with foreign policy, his greatest expertise. To his good fortune or credit, depending on how one analyzes it, his first three

years saw the swift and seemingly miraculous fall of Communism–
in the former Soviet satellites in East Central Europe (1989) and
then in the Soviet Union itself (1991). Coauthor Warren Johansson
had foreseen that "the Soviet system is not IBM-compatible," but
never anticipated the haste with which the end came. To almost
everyone's relief, the "red menace" had for all practical purposes
vanished, and both Mikhail Gorbachev and Boris Yeltsin acknowledged a debt to Bush. The collapse of the hard-line military and
Party conservatives' coup in August of 1991 saved the fledgling
Russian gay movement from almost certain extinction. In America
left-leaning leaders of the movement were faced with the need to
rethink their beliefs, but many found it hard to face up to the
consequences of the fact that the party is over. These leadership
cadres have long been at odds with their constituencies, who have
always been more conservative, like the great American public
itself of which lovers of their own sex are, far more than the ethnic
minorities, a cross-section. Even gradualist varieties of socialism
are now losing favor throughout the world. In one of the last out-
posts of Communism, Fidel Castro, whose homophobic policies
now include compulsory isolation for HIV-positives, found himself
more alone than ever. Jerry Brown, who made another unsuccessful
bid for the presidential nomination in 1992, joked that there are
more Communists in Santa Monica or in Cambridge, Massachusetts
than in Managua.

Coming in between Communist collapse in East Central Europe
and the Soviet Union was Desert Storm. Against Saddam Hussein
Bush was able to build an unprecedented international coalition,
including the Soviets. Some movement activists, such as Urvashi
Vaid and John D'Emilio of the National Gay and Lesbian Task
Force, misreading the war, moved their organizations to oppose
American involvement. But to the intense disappointment of aging
radicals who thought that the 1960s had returned, the antiwar movement fizzled before it really got off the ground. Although gay and
lesbian military personnel served in the Gulf war with distinction, the
Defense Department ominously hinted that it might discharge them
once it no longer needed them for cannon fodder. Since most of us
rejected the minority, pacifist, left-leaning line of pseudo-Marxist
"leaders," the perception spread that it was at long last opportune to

end discrimination in our armed forces. Instead of defaming the military as such, as leftists had done during the Vietnam War, gay leaders other than those implacably hostile for ideological reasons to "the state" now insisted that military service be open to all. As will be seen, this interest dovetailed with the most spectacular outing of 1991, that of Pentagon spokesman Pete Williams.

The emergent Soviet gay movement had received the support of the International Lesbian and Gay Organization (ILGA), whose strength had hitherto been largely confined to the advanced capitalist nations. An academic conference at Tallinn, Estonia in May 1990 was followed by an activist one in Moscow in July 1991. In a bold move, the ILGA scheduled its annual meeting for the first time in a Third World country, in Guadalajara, Mexico's second-largest city. When threats of violence from local reactionaries and a decree by its mayor prevented the gathering from being held there in the early summer of 1991 as planned, the meeting was relocated to Acapulco (a beach resort long frequented by American movie stars, who frequently did as they pleased there sexually, and by gay tourists).

On the whole, the 1990s boded well for a gradual reception of the American model and for movement building in developing and former Communist countries. The fall of communism left the United States as the sole superpower and world leader. Almost half our states, however, still retain antisodomy statutes and other homophobic legislation and decisions, rendered constitutional by the Supreme Court's decision in *Bowers* v. *Hardwick* (1986). As Bush's first term, in which foreign events had dominated, neared its close, many felt that he had not done enough on the domestic front. The recession ground on; cities continued to fester; the savings and loan bill mounted; and education and health care deteriorated further. Queer nationals cried, loudly and forcefully, that the AIDS epidemic had not been halted and that the Republican administration neglected the growing number of those afflicted and impoverished by it. Fear of quarantine or other sanctions, vivid for some in the 1980s, had ebbed in the face of pronouncements by officials and responsible professionals. But our souls could not rest. While it may not have been entirely reasonable to blame the country's leadership, mounting frustration gave rise to vigorous new measures. Among these steps was a break in an unwritten rule that had been largely observed up to this point in practice, if questioned in theory: no homosexual should reveal another to heterosexuals without his or her explicit consent.

THE PROGRESS OF AIDS

The plague continued to spread. In America and Europe the highest rates of new cases of HIV-infection and AIDS were now among IV-drug users, passing those among gay men. These marginalized and unorganized sufferers were the hardest to reach. They had no activist groups or media analogous to those which we had created since 1969. The worst peril was that given the new trend the establishment would turn its back on the problem, judging it another misfortune of those for whom life is an unbroken series of misfortunes.

Dire as the epidemic was in the industrialized world, it was soon surpassed in sub-Saharan Africa and in Southeast Asia and India. In Central Africa AIDS has wiped out many extended families, even whole villages. It was predicted that by the year 2000 that region would have 10 to 15 million "AIDS orphans." Thailand, the modern Shangri-la of sexual tolerance, which had inspired the French writer René Guyon's theories of the "legitimacy of sexual acts" and "sexual freedom" set forth in a six-volume work of the 1930s, now began to pay a terrible price. Prostitution, illegal but ubiquitous, is causing the disease to spread there with terrifying speed. A 1990 survey showed 30 percent of Thai prostitutes infected with AIDS. Domestic and international health agencies foresee that by the year 2000 at least three million Thais will be infected. Besides heterosexual contact, the disease is chiefly transmitted by IV-drug users. (On the global scale, AIDS is not a "gay disease," despite our foes' assertions: 75 percent of HIV-infection is heterosexual.) Worst of all, Third World countries lack the resources with which to buy the drugs marketed by American, Swedish, and Swiss pharmaceutical firms at astronomical prices.

The inadequate response of governments, the medical establishment, and private citizens to the crisis continues to spur gay activists. Largely as the result of dissension over whether ACT UP should deal with gay issues having nothing to do with AIDS, in March 1990 another activist group was founded at New York's Community Services Center. Queer Nation, the new splinter organization, took up all gay issues whether they concerned AIDS or not, but kept the élan and the tactics of the earlier group. Rejecting the clumsy formula "lesbian, bisexual, and gay," these new radicals determined to rehabilitate the opprobrious *queer* as a badge of honor.

With the aggressiveness it inherited from its parent, one of whose envious members styled it "ACT UP for HIV-negatives," it asserted our right to have a public presence, even in supposedly straight bars and restaurants. With shouts of "We're here, we're queer, we're fabulous, get used to it!" a working group styled Knights Out in New York and Queer Nights Out in Boston boldly invaded establishments normally frequented only by a straight clientele. The New York group displayed signs in Greenwich Village informing such visitors that "this is queer turf" and "if you do not like gay people, then go elsewhere!" Although lesbians had only auxiliary status in ACT UP chapters, no matter how selflessly they worked against the plague, they attained a greater role as leaders of Queer Nation, in part because so many males sickened and died, but mainly because of Queer Nation's broader agenda. Many older and some younger gay people were, however, repelled by the new group's name–for the adjective "queer" still retains its sting–and by its daringly confrontational style, which some feel alienates outsiders and even moderates in our own community. Responses to outing split along this fundamental divide–between intransigent activism and inveterate caution.

In late September of 1991 riots in all major California cities followed Governor Pete Wilson's veto of AB 101, the gay rights bill. With throngs of new supporters, Queer Nation/Los Angeles, whose meetings had previously dwindled to almost nothing, demonstrated angrily. Just as the victory of Anita Bryant in Dade County in 1977 had inspired the founding of the Coalition for Lesbian and Gay Rights in New York City, this defeat proved a stimulus for reinvigorated activism. On St. Patrick's Day in 1992, queer nationals, sanctioned by a court order, marched through South Boston, a stronghold of Irish Catholic bigotry, but failed in their attempt to force the Ancient Order of Hibernians to let them parade up New York's Fifth Avenue. A group was, however, allowed to march in Cork, the second city of the Irish Republic, where Boston's mayor was visiting. Neither Cardinal Law in Boston nor O'Connor in New York denounced the bigots in their cities–those who insulted and pelted the marchers in Boston and those who barred queer nationals from marching in New York.

In racial matters, unquestioning support for the assimilationist policies that nearly everyone hitherto tacitly accepted as the norm has broken down. In the past second-generation Americans expected and were expected to be raised in the culture of the Anglo-Saxon majority, not the distinctive traditions of their forebears. Now even a growing number of African-Americans whose ancestors were brought here before those of most whites are seeking their African roots. But while racial and ethnic minorities succeeded to a degree in translating their new strength into political and economic gains such as affirmative action policies, homosexuals and bisexuals, as in previous decades, stood to gain no benefit whatsoever from affirmative action in employment because we are not legally recognized as a group deserving that remedy. In part, this omission reflected the fact that we had been invisible in the past; indeed, too many of us remain invisible effectively to assert our claims to such recognition. The opponents of affirmative action for their part cited quotas for homosexuals (or lesbians) as the ultimate absurdity of such policies. In short, we benefitted last and least from the so-called rainbow coalition.

Time *MAGAZINE OUTS OUTING AND* OutWeek

Many roads, it seems, led to outing. Outing had been in the air for months, even perhaps years before word of it reached the mass media in January 1990. New York's *OutWeek* had been practicing it almost from the moment it began to publish in June 1989, but since gay papers have few readers other than their own distinctive audience, the American public remained ignorant of the phenomenon. This obscurity was not to last. When the subject reached the pages of a leading American weekly, it became the talk of readers straight and gay alike.

On January 29, 1990, *Time* carried a story by William A. Henry III entitled "Forcing Gays Out of the Closet." It began: "Gays have long gossiped about which public figures of the past and present might be secret homosexuals. . . .This name dropping is defended as a way of giving the gay community role models and a sense of continuity. When the rumors involve living people, however, discussion about who is in the closet has generally been held to a discreet murmur–partly in deference to libel laws but mostly in defense of privacy. That consensus is fast breaking down with the spread of a phenomenon known as 'outing,' the intentional exposure of secret gays by other gays."

As the article pointed out, the phenomenon grew out of frustration over "the slow pace of gay civil rights legislation" (the movement to repeal the archaic sodomy laws virtually ground to a halt in the 1980s) and what the gay community interpreted as official indifference to AIDS. As a result, activists feel it is their moral right or even duty to force people out of the closet, either to make them support the movement or at least to discredit them as foes, and also to show how many idols of the masses or pillars of the nation are in fact closet queers.

The objects of the initial outings by queer nationals were mainly politicians, but similar action against religious leaders has been threatened. The Roman Catholic Church is in a difficult and ambiguous position. It is reputed to be a cozy nest of the vicious and the abnormal. Surveys indicate that 40 to 60 percent of the priests in the United States today are gay, so hard has it become, since the aborted opening up of the church in the aftermath of Vatican II (the council that undertook to modernize its beliefs and practices but left Catholic sexual morality unaltered), to recruit so-called normal human beings. Yet it has unflinchingly opposed the gay rights movement at every step, and even now shows not the slightest urge to moderate its stand. The implacable and vociferous hostility of O'Connor and Law, regarded by many as the Pope's American mouthpieces, has particularly irked New York and Boston activists. Hence in the long run the clergy are a prime target for outings.

Many people belonging to or sympathetic to our movement, however, deplore outing. The Chicago *Windy City Times* associate editor, Sarah Craig, wrote: "Really, you're only using the same bludgeon used to injure you to injure someone else." For practical purposes, if outing ends someone's career, he (or she) will have, as the *Time* article concluded, little motive for supporting the movement–and often no opportunity to be effective. The Lambda Legal

Defense and Education Fund's executive director, Tom Stoddard, maintained that "The gay movement is actually based upon two principles that collide. One is privacy, and the other is disclosure, the process of coming out."

These ideals clash because of the historical situation in which we find ourselves in the early 1990s. We are oppressed by the anachronistic survival of the infamy inflicted upon us by the Roman Catholic and Eastern Orthodox Churches in the Middle Ages and perpetuated by the Protestant denominations, and by theologically-inspired laws that violate our sexual privacy. But we also must refute the defamation which the churches and synagogues have practiced against us by demonstrating that their teachings are lies, that we are as kind, useful, productive, and patriotic as anybody else, and that now as throughout history, many brilliant, famous, and successful people lead sexually unconventional lives without being any the less worthy of admiration and emulation. Not to be forgotten is the need to refute once and for all the calumny of "mental illness" that persists among civic leaders as well as in the popular mind.

OutWeek, the controversial New York City periodical that did the most outing, began publication in 1989, on the eve of Gay Pride Day, the last Sunday in June. Within weeks of its appearance, under the bold, radical editorship of Gabriel Rotello, it had positioned itself center stage in outing. By taking a journalistic stand against the pious myth that all public figures and celebrities are heterosexual, it aimed to convince members of the young generation that they are not alone. Backed by the publishers, Rotello, a strong advocate of outing, refused to employ a double standard when writing about public figures he knew to be gay. If we do not gloss over celebrities' heterosexuality, he commented, neither are we going to gloss over their homosexuality. We are not going to lie to cover up for them while they flourish hypocritically, making millions while denying their inner nature–their nationality, so to speak. The days of the gentlemen's agreement (or the fairy conspiracy) to keep sexual orientation a secret are over, he declared. Unfortunately, *OutWeek shut down just two years later.* It published its last issue on June 24, 1991, just when it was about to undertake its most sensational outing, that of Pentagon spokesman Pete Williams.

QUEER NATION

Informally associated at the time of its founding with ACT UP, *OutWeek* carried the news of the doings and plans of both ACT UP and its offshoot Queer Nation to the rest of the world. Led by such activists as Robbie Considine, Joe Cooper, Dave Fleck, and Alan Klein, Queer Nation/New York staged a whole range of events meant to promote "queer visibility." Formed in March 1990, this parent chapter in turn cast its seed to the wind, which in a year and a half sprouted some 60 Queer Nation chapters here and abroad.

The phenomenal growth of the parallel sets of activist groups reflected the leadership of the gay movement that the United States had assumed in the wake of Stonewall. If from 1864 to 1933 the homophile movement was German, after 1969 at the latest American activists led the world.

Members are either radical by nature or become so when caught up by the meetings' spirit. They in turn inspire other organizations to which they belong. For example, Queer Nationalists conceived the contingent that dared to march in Boston's St. Patrick's Day parade. Heterosexuals often unduly fear Queer Nation, as when they learned that some of the marchers in South Boston belonged to it. Even other gay activists, especially members of the Log Cabin Club (the gay Republican organization), along with Dignity and similar Christian groups, routinely denounce Queer Nation. Critics of outing–which have included all major movement bodies except ACT UP and Queer Nation, neither of which has ever taken a clear-cut stand–have labeled it an "invasion of privacy" and "fascism." The stand of the radical groups against the Roman Catholic Church and the demonstrations at St. Patrick's Cathedral permanently and completely alienated Dignity and virtually all other Catholic organizations. Many mainstream gay groups, as well as those which voice heterosexual opinion, profess horror at both the goals and the tactics of ACT UP and Queer Nation: proof that they are effective!

MALCOLM FORBES

In February 1990 *USA Today*–correctly described as "not a newspaper, but a television station in print"–published a story about Malcolm Forbes' homosexuality. Its decision may have been motivated by anticipation of the story in *OutWeek*. No issue of *OutWeek* earned more notoriety than the one dated March 18, 1990. Its cover was headlined THE SECRET GAY LIFE OF MALCOLM FORBES, with a photograph of the late multimillionaire socialite and publisher on his motorcycle. Forbes (1919-90), who had died three weeks before, was a flamboyant celebrity, noted for his lavish parties, motorcycles, and well-publicized balloon ascents. *OutWeek* used the revelations about his life to launch a new and startling editorial policy.

The editorial bore the title "Claiming Forbes for the Gay Nation" (a curious halfway house to the emerging idea of a Queer Nation). Because of its electrifying–and polarizing–effect, we must look closely at this editorial. It began:

> The ancient Romans had a time-honored policy that whenever they conquered a nation they would attempt to deprive that nation of its leaders. . . . And the policy worked. Deprived of their native politicians, their philosophers, their literati, artists, thinkers and natural leaders, most nations annexed by Rome sank into centuries of provincial apathy.
>
> Today, 20 years after Stonewall, the Gay Nation is in some way similar to Rome's demoralized provinces. Although we could always count among our ranks some of the greatest Americans in every field, most gay leaders are prematurely and permanently snatched away from us by the dark tyranny of the closet. . . .
>
> The fears of social and professional catastrophe that motivated people like Malcolm Forbes to remain hidden may have been well-founded in 1950 or even 1970; they're wildly exaggerated in 1990. . . .
>
> This is a tragedy for America and it's a tragedy for those who, like Forbes, needlessly cower in the closet. But the greatest losers are gay and lesbian youth. Like subjects of a vanquished Roman province, they seem destined to grow up not ever knowing that wonderful, winning people like Forbes are their soul mates and could be their inspiration in a hostile world. . . .

So we say this to the youth of our tribe. There are idols you aren't allowed to dream of. There are thousands of invisible paragons you aren't allowed to know. . . . They are ours and, like them, Malcolm Forbes was ours. And in your names and for your futures we claim them all.

This editorial was the manifesto of outing. Like nearly all gay political innovations since 1969, when leadership passed from Los Angeles and San Francisco, it came from New York City. The Big Apple has been the starting point of successive waves of activism from the Gay Liberation Front and Gay Activists Alliance (both 1969), to GMHC (1981), ACT UP (1987) and Queer Nation (1990). But New York is also the nation's media capital, where trends are set and reversed. Thus *OutWeek*'s bold move marked a new phase in the struggle to tear down the closet door.

Michelangelo Signorile's article in the same issue, "The Other Side of Malcolm," displayed the caption: "He was the epitome of the fabled American Dream. The guy with the bucks, the brains and the beautiful movie actress by his side. But like so many in the upper echelons of glamour, glitter and glory, Malcolm Forbes was living a senseless lie." Signorile began by noting that many celebrities whose homophobic beliefs and opinions were a matter of public record attended the memorial service for Forbes at St. Bartholomew's Church on Park Avenue. These figures, often nationally known conservative Republicans, had come to pay their last respects to a man whose private life was aggressively and uninhibitedly homosexual. Signorile added: "Actually, *some* of the people present at the memorial service *had* to have known that Malcolm Forbes was gay, no matter what they may actually say. They, after all, were privy to the same information that the rest of us were. But their hypocrisy is easily rationalized."

In conservative circles, it was *de rigueur* to keep quiet about others' private eccentricities. While some may have been shocked by the thought that a pillar of capitalism was a fag, others knew full well what his secret life was and excused it on one ground or another. Although Forbes' marriage to the former Roberta Remsen Laidlaw ended in divorce in 1985, the two had been leading separate lives for years. The marriage served a double purpose: to create a façade and to engender heirs.

But throughout the marriage Forbes never ceased what as the years went by became his predominant, if not exclusive, sexual outlet. Trapped within the confines of an upper-class family life and his business obligations, Forbes found himself trying to fit his homosexual escapades into his daily routine. This meant hiring men as chauffeurs, waiters, and houseboys with whom he could have sex unobtrusively on a daily basis–which led to practices that the resentful partners described as exploitative, coercive, and tantamount, as some felt, to sexual abuse. The current furor over "sexual harassment" had been anticipated in German law, which formally prohibited *"Missbrauch eines Abhängigkeitsverhältnisses,"* "abuse of a relationship of dependency." It should surprise no one that a multimillionaire should engage in such activity. After all, the scandal involving Alfred Krupp, the German industrialist and close friend of Kaiser Wilhelm II, and Italian boys from the resort isle of Capri in the early years of the century brought to light rather similar conduct. A system of justice subject to class pressures exempts those at the very top from laws whose application to the lower strata of society can mean ostracism, economic ruin, public disgrace, and even imprisonment or suicide.

Forbes had a particular employee, a stunning beauty, who worked at his townhouse. His job included being always on the alert for handsome young men who might be induced to have sexual relations with Forbes as part of their duties at the townhouse. "He got Malcolm his boys," said an informant quoted by Signorile. "He was responsible for getting that fresh meat." One can only imagine what went on at his lavish place in Morocco, a country famous for attracting gay tourists.

The position as his chauffeur was linked with sexual services, as it often has been for others such as Dag Hammarskjöld, long-time Secretary General of the United Nations, because it was relatively easy to arrange brief trysts in the car or in garages. It was therefore a "special" position. But rumors and stories inevitably circulated among at least some of Forbes' staff. One of them later told Signorile: "I always wanted to say to him, 'if you would just come out you could be so beneficial to gays instead of being this pathetic, secretive person'."

Forbes rarely enjoyed any long-term relationships because he feared that a prolonged liaison would attract public notice and make his closeted life even more insecure. He steered clear of gay establishments because he could never mingle with the overt and politically conscious types. And besides, he had to keep this side of his life hidden from friends, business associates, and the public. But at times he behaved in a careless way, yearning for forbidden joys and testing the limits of a double life.

Those in his circle heard the rumors, but preferred not to echo them. They would not willingly forego the favor of a powerful and wealthy man. After the outing, Liz Smith, gossip columnist for the New York *Daily News,* claimed to be "too square" to have suspected Forbes' erotic proclivities. "The subject never came up at any time. I never saw any evidence of it. In fact, it never occurred to me," she claimed. Is our society so repressive that even individuals as powerful as Forbes cannot come out of the closet? asked Signorile rhetorically. He went on to reply: "Forbes was the victim of a virulently homophobic society which he too fed into regularly. . . . His own internalized homophobia far outweighed the commanding authority that any amount of dollars could possibly wield." But, he added, "one of the most influential men in America just died, and . . . he was gay. And that must be recorded."

Public response to the outing was ambivalent. Newspapers reporting the disclosures tacitly accepted the legalistic view that the dead cannot be libeled. But what about the unwelcome notoriety for members of his family? Yet to raise that question addresses the whole problem of homosexuality and public opinion. Is it a disgrace by definition? Would outing be the same as calling the deceased a philanderer or an alcoholic? Advocates for the gay movement, who see the matter from their own perspective, accuse the heterosexual world of a built-in bias that distorts its vision. Queer nationals insist on outing at least the dead, if not the living.

The *San Francisco Chronicle* named not only Forbes and the late California publisher Charles K. McClatchy, owner of the McClatchy Newspapers such as the *Sacramento Bee,* who died in April 1989, as "victims" of outing, but also Mayor Edward Koch, whose homosexuality had long been mooted in the Gotham press; Calvin Klein, and Cher's daughter Chastity Bono (the object of exposés in supermarket tabloids). On June 28, 1990 the *Philadelphia Inquirer* intoned: "In the past three months alone, the targets have included: two governors, one lieutenant governor, seven members of Congress, a recording industry mega-mogul, a renowned athlete, a school superintendent from a West Coast city, a married American fashion designer, two male actors who play 'straight' love interests on television and in the movies, the female co-star of a network series, the daughter of a female pop singer, and four Philadelphia TV-news personalities." Despite the attempted blackout, some 40 stories did appear between March and August of 1990 that mentioned Forbes' homosexuality, which thus entered America's folklore. In this fashion one of the most prominent but closeted homosexuals in twentieth-century America underwent outing–after his death. But this was only the beginning. Much, much more was to follow.

MICHELANGELO SIGNORILE, ARCH-OUTER

At the heart of the controversy stands Michelangelo Signorile. This man of the hour makes no bones about where he stands. The 33-year-old writer excoriates gay journalists and editors who toady to queer celebrities in their velvet-lined closets. They act as human shields for the rich and famous who remain smugly indifferent to the mounting violence targeting queers in the streets of our major cities and to the plight of gay prisoners and others victims of blatant discrimination, not to mention AIDS.

For almost a year the New York columnist had been inserting the code words "self-loathing" or "self-hating" before the names of media and entertainment world celebrities. In two issues of *Out-Week* (for instance August 7, 1989) he ran lists of famous people in his Gossip Watch column, under the headline "Peek-A-Boo," but left them without further elaboration. At the same time the San Francisco gay novelist Armistead Maupin was outing prominent homosexuals in the course of speaking engagements on tours to promote his own books. But these trial runs in outing drew little attention save in gay periodicals.

Then Signorile daringly smashed the gentlemen's agreement protecting closeted homosexuals by not merely "naming names" implicitly in his column in *OutWeek*, but outing some explicitly. Suddenly all of New York knew what had been whispered in gay circles for years: that two prominent New York newspaper columnists are queer. Signorile accused them of promoting homophobia by breaking the cardinal rule of honest journalism, Thou Shalt Not Lie to Thy Readers. They were outed for their own hypocrisy and as a warning to others still wearing the mask. But, as we have seen, what grabbed the attention of the mainstream media was the cover story "The Secret Gay Life of Malcolm Forbes."

Signorile personified a new mood in New York's gay subculture. At every meeting of ACT UP/New York, speakers were announcing the deaths from AIDS of one, two, sometimes three activists or supporters of the group. Sensational stories of the murder or attempted murder of gay men–and of police indifference to the crime–were recurring in the newspapers. The activists' admirable new militancy and readily understandable impatience in response to these outrages inspired Signorile's Gossip Watch. It won him myriads of readers–but few friends at first. Mainstream media reacted angrily: the gay writer had violated a taboo of "respectable" journalism. But rules have always set gossip columns apart from ordinary journalism. Honesty is not their overriding criterion: their business is the production, marketing, and image-management of celebrity. Artifice and deception are their stock in trade. To judge this output selectively by the canons of "respectable journalism" is almost farcical. Yet even an avowed leftist like the late Max Lerner could declare, in his column in the *New York Post* in the early 1950s, that "he would not rescue from the burning flames" newspapermen who rushed into print "to tell everyone who is a fag or a swish–knowing that there are few cruelties crueler and that the victim has no recourse."

But by 1990 the political climate has decisively and, we pray, permanently changed. Responses to Signorile's breach of convention ran the full gamut. Militants fervently supported the brave and lonely queer with a skimpy bank account who dared to out those still comfortably ensconced in the closet. The gadfly Larry Kramer, the inspirer though not the founder of ACT UP, dubbed him "one of the greater contemporary gay heroes." Yet Tom Stoddard, whom he had labeled an "Uncle Tom," called Signorile's conduct "revolting" and "infantile" and denounced his "cheap name-calling."

Signorile emerged as the star of *OutWeek* from its first issue. He dedicated his column to attacking the media in general and other gossip columnists in particular. Fearlessly, sometimes crudely, he reproached them for ignoring or downplaying the AIDS crisis and other queer issues, for maintaining the façade of conformity thrown up by public figures whom they know to be "different from the others," and for glorifying the Reagans, Bushes and other political figures who "are keeping us down at best, murdering us at worst." Targets of Signorile's *OutWeek* exposés included, besides Malcolm Forbes, record magnate David Geffen, actress Jodie Foster, gossip maven Liz Smith, Cher's daughter Chastity Bono, actor Richard Chamberlain, and a host of others. He refused to be impressed, intimidated, or made to feel guilty.

Who is this brash young man who moved so suddenly into the spotlight? Signorile was named Michelangelo after his paternal grandfather. His father, who owns a sandwich shop in Brooklyn and two croissant shops on Wall Street, and his mother are both first-generation Italian-Americans whose parents came from the same village in Italy. Raised in Dongan Hills on Staten Island, he remembers having his first homosexual experience at 12 or 13. At Monsignor Farrell High School, where he played left guard on the football team, his uninhibited juvenile sexuality gave him the reputation of being a "fag," leading to constant fights with other boys who called him names. One of these clashes took place in the school library, and as a result he was expelled. He graduated from New Dorp High School on Staten Island, attended Brooklyn College for a year and a half, and then transferred to the Newhouse School of Public Communications at Syracuse University. After graduation he worked for Mike Hall for two years, then left to become a freelance writer. He began his own downtown column for *Nightlife,* and also contributed to *People* and the London magazine *The Face.*

At a club one night late in 1987, he met an ACT UP recruiter. He and his coworker Michael Musto went to their first Monday night meeting at the Community Services Center in Greenwich Village. They were overwhelmed by the spirit and élan of the group and by its message. Signorile began to neglect his journalistic career and to devote himself to the ACT UP media committee.

In the spring of 1989, Signorile got a call from Gabriel Rotello, a keyboard player and musical arranger whom he had met through ACT UP. Saying that he and Kendall Morrison, the owner of Dial Information Services, a phone-sex company, were going to launch a new gay weekly in New York City, Rotello asked Signorile to sign on as a columnist and features editor. Upon going to work for *OutWeek* Signorile came out of the closet to his own family–which at first was unable to accept the fact.

Signorile claimed that he did not at the outset try to force people out of the closet. He conceived the idea of printing a box with people's names in it and calling it "Peek-A-Boo," and letting the readers interpret as they wished. When other gay periodicals reprinted his revelations, he began to realize the political potential of outing. He asserted that before naming a name, he made sure that his source had been sexually intimate with the person, or at least that the source's best friend had been: he did not rely on chance sightings in gay bars on the analogy of "So-and-so was seen last night at the Stork Club with . . . . " He had no hesitation in casually mentioning people in his column if he had the word from others who moved in their social circles or had been intimate with them. Signorile admits that he had not thought much about the issue of press responsibility before he started his columns. He claims that "every newspaper and every reporter has an agenda. . . . I'm attacking the *Daily News* [the New York tabloid] for making believe it's respected journalism when it's not."

Many of the targets of his outings were celebrities from the entertainment world; as George Bernard Shaw once said, there are people to whom "dead prima donnas are more interesting than saints, and extinct tenors than mighty conquerors." But Signorile's aim was more serious than titillation. "Basically, [he outed] people who are famous. I will never think of bringing out a private citizen. . . . People who are rich and famous who are gay almost owe it to humanity to come out of the closet." Forbes was a prime target for outing because he was an attention-craving celebrity, and as publisher of his own magazine, *Forbes,* held considerable control over the flow of news. The most powerful thing such people can do in the face of the AIDS crisis, Signorile asserted, "is to come out of the

closet and address the issue of the crisis in the community." (Kasindorf 1990)

Signorile has partially conceded the argument that a homosexual
who has to be forced out of the closet is a poor role model. People
who remain closeted, said playwright Harvey Fierstein, author of
Torch Song Trilogy, "quite often are filled with shame and have not
accepted themselves." An outed self-hating homosexual can, according to one viewpoint, win the admiration of no one, least of all
heterosexuals. But according to Signorile, "they will provide visibility" and also furnish negative role models. He maintains that
privacy as a basis for gay rights belonged to the 1950s, when outing
meant ruin. At this point in its history our community "should be
making itself as public as possible for visibility." The Queer Nation
must be able to take a census of its citizens!

In his interview Signorile replied to Tom Stoddard's charge that
his behavior was "McCarthyism of the Left": "Joe McCarthy was
pointing out Communists, a thing he perceived to be bad. . . . I am
pointing out gays and lesbians, people I perceive to be good and
normal and natural like me." He expressed doubts as to whether
outing has benefitted his own career, frankly admitting that now no
establishment magazine would hire him. In the eyes of "respectable" journalists, his venture in outing has made him a pariah. The
prime beneficiaries of the "new freedom," according to the editors
of *OutWeek,* were the supermarket tabloids that boosted their sales
by exposing queers (Hartman 1990). In August 1990 Signorile
mentioned receiving "queries from leading newspapers and television news divisions wanting to know if it were true that *OutWeek*
was planning to out U.S. Supreme Court nominee, David Souter."
In the end, all that the public learned from the establishment media
were dutiful reports of Souter's alleged involvements with the opposite sex. The issue remains moot to this day.

In the wake of the demise of *OutWeek,* Signorile was invited to
join the staff of the *Advocate,* which had long condemned outing.
Its issue of November 5, 1991 proudly proclaimed that he would be
writing a column entitled Absolutely Queer that would focus on the
political scene of the entire nation. He has also recently published
a book entitled *Queer in America* (Random House, 1993). It will
be both a personal account of the last five years of activism

and a gay *U.S.A. Confidential,* disclosing how we are placed in the power structures of New York, Los Angeles, and Washington.

MICHAEL PETRELIS–AN AIDS MILITANT

The late spring of 1990 marked a new development: the "privatization" of the practice of outing. Michael Petrelis, a young man of Greek descent, was diagnosed with Kaposi's sarcoma and AIDS in 1985. For a time he was a resident of Bailey House, a hospice for people with AIDS in New York City. After becoming active on their behalf, he joined the newly formed ACT UP. While the organization forged an uneasy détente with its adversaries–although with misgivings on the part of the more militant members–Petrelis advocated escalating the struggle. His inspiration was Stonewall, not Selma: "Civil disobedience has become institutionalized; it's a cliché. We shall *not* overcome by singing 'We Shall Overcome'." Even many ACT UP militants recoil from Petrelis's brash radicalism and maintain that he does not speak for the organization. Larry Kramer, the controversial inspirer of ACT UP, has defended Petrelis as a kindred spirit within the group: "He's turned obnoxiousness into an art form."

In turn Petrelis, who supplied most of this information, as well as other useful points in this book, during his sojourn at coauthor Percy's home in October 1991 and on other visits, sees his role as ACT UP's own ACT UP. On February 23, 1989 he and a few other activists, who had been chewing the fat at a greasy spoon, decided to out Mark Hatfield because the senator was supporting the Helms amendment and other homophobic causes. At a fund-raiser for Hatfield in a small town outside Portland, Oregon they zapped him by outing him. This was a landmark–the first outing ever by activists.

Among his other major feats, Petrelis participated in the massive disruption of the service at St. Patrick's Cathedral on Sunday December 10, 1989 to protest Cardinal O'Connor's obstructionist stance on measures such as the distribution of condoms to prevent the spread of AIDS. Standing on the seat of a pew, he screamed "You're killing us!" until forcibly removed by the police. His personal style of activism provoked conflicts with ACT UP/New York that some believe led him to transfer his residence to Washington,

D. C. There he could better sting the politicos on whose outing he concentrates, in contrast to Signorile, who mainly outs entertainers and media producers. For a time he issued an irregular journal with the piquant title *Piss and Vinegar*. On May 6, 1990 the *San Francisco Examiner* printed a story that began: "There will come a day, in the future that Arthur Evans [author of *Witchcraft and the Gay Counterculture*] envisions, when once a year the names of the famous–the politicians, the preachers, the entertainers–who are secretly gay will be solemnly announced to a gossip-loving public. On this national outing day, closeted public figures who have trampled on the gay community would be exposed as hypocrites and frauds." This prophecy emboldened Petrelis, and at high noon on May 29, 1990 on the steps of the Capitol, he outed a dozen public figures, among them three senators and two governors:

Sen. Mark Hatfield (R., Oreg.)	Rep. Bob Carr (D., Mich.)
Rep. Tom Foley (D., Wash.).	Rep. Roy Dyson (D., Md.)
Sen. Barbara Mikulski (D., Md.)	Rep. Jim McCrery (R., La.)
Rep. Steven Gunderson (R., Wisc.)	Gov. Jim Thompson (R., Il.)
Sen. Herbert Kohl (D., Wisc.)	Gov. William Schaefer (D., Md.)
Comptroller Liz Holtzman (D., NYC)	David Geffen, Geffen Records

The press release that Petrelis distributed on that occasion stated: "I . . . claim these people for the gay and lesbian community. I do this in a positive manner. . . . Some of the elected officials whose names I've read have horrendous voting records" on gay and AIDS-related issues. "Others have great solidarity with our community. In this respect they are just like their heterosexual counterparts. Elected officials in the closet should realize the joy and support that await those who come out of the closet. . . . Even First Lady Barbara Bush recently wrote a letter . . . to say, 'We cannot tolerate discrimination against any individuals or groups in our country'." Petrelis's Washington outings may have only scratched the surface: The Kinsey figure of 4 percent of males that are exclusively homosexual would yield for the United States Congress about 22 with a rating of 6 out of the 439 representatives and 100 senators, not to mention those who would rate 5 or 4 on the Kinsey scale. Barney Frank said as much at a forum in Faneuil Hall in Boston on June 15, 1990 and elsewhere.

The nation's press corps responded with a single voice–silence. No major newspaper, gay or straight, printed the names on Petrelis' list. Like other outings, this one was effectively suppressed by the establishment media. Even most of the gay periodicals that mentioned the event opted not to print the list of 12 names, either for fear of libel action or, more probably, out of unwillingness to be his accomplice in outing. It is true that Petrelis gave a bare list, without any supporting evidence, but the press corps apparently felt no urgency to look for any, a stark contrast with their eagerness to expose the antics of Gary Hart on the yacht "Monkey Business" when he was running for the presidency, or those of Wilbur Mills and the Argentine strip teaser "Firecracker." Petrelis's move nevertheless effectively brought outing to the nation's capital, the center of the political power structure. His press conference touched off a debate within the gay community, where Petrelis was denounced–again–and also led to stories in the establishment press about outing–albeit without naming names. In conversations with Petrelis, representatives of the media invoked the privacy of the outees rather than fear of libel actions; of course, as they well know, many who might sue dread the adverse publicity which such a move would inevitably attract. To be sure, the press is guided less by iron principle than by a certain herd mentality. Peter Prichard, editor in chief of *USA Today,* explained: "There is a phenomenon in our business that everyone decides to withhold something from publication for reasons of taste. But if it slips out elsewhere, everyone tends to use it."

Petrelis himself has excoriated the hypocrisy of the media. They prefer not to tell about gay people in the everyday stream of news stories, but have no objection to lurid accounts such as the affair linking Steve Gobie with Barney Frank. He believes that many prominent media figures are themselves in the closet, together with a goodly number of local anchormen and reporters. Yet the hypocrisy is such that before the new publisher of *The New York Times* took over, according to statements on the floor of Queer Nation/New York, any member of its staff who was openly gay or lesbian was automatically dismissed. Since the summer of 1992, by contrast, the *Times* has been exemplary for its thorough and sympathetic coverage of our concerns. In the 1970s the *Christian Science Monitor* conducted witch-hunts to rid its staff of "perverts." It was only slightly more homophobic than run-of-the-mill newspapers. No mainstream paper employed an openly gay columnist before the *Milwaukee Star* hired one. Women and ethnic minorities now far more often have their voices in print.

The lack of response to his Capitol steps action left Petrelis undaunted. June 23, 1991 was the day of Washington's Gay Pride parade. Captain Greg Greeley, who had been one of the organizers of the event, was scheduled for discharge from the air force the following day. But that Sunday afternoon he opted to lead the parade with a banner that read TOGETHER IN PRIDE '91. The story, appearing in the *Washington Post,* caused a conflict with the air force over his impending discharge. This in turn led to a front-page story in same paper on Tuesday, June 25. Petrelis then seized the occasion to hold a press conference on Friday, June 28, in which he outed a high Defense Department figure, Assistant Secretary Pete Williams. His object was to expose the Pentagon's hypocrisy in harassing Greeley while leaving Williams undisturbed in his closet. In the presence of reporters from an NBC affiliate and the wire services, several of Petrelis's crew told the audience how they had seen Williams frequenting gay bars for years. One even claimed that a friend had had a "brief encounter" with Williams. Petrelis then unrolled a poster labeling the Pentagon spokesman as a CON-SUMMATE QUEER. Although they had noticed Greeley, who came out of his own accord, the mainstream media acted true to form in suppressing the Williams outing. However, this sequence of events, coming just as *OutWeek* was folding, provoked Michelange-lo Signorile to publish the article that he had prepared for it in the *Advocate* of August 27, 1991. This event set a new mark for outing. Petrelis's record was now such that Ann Northrop, a former Boston debutante and now an ACT UP heroine in her own right, said of him at a meeting of the Stonewall 25 Organizing Committee in New York City on December 18, 1991 that "in the last four years he has done more for the movement than whole organizations." We shall interrupt the main drama to discuss various outings in other cities.

OUTINGS IN OTHER CITIES

Outings occurred in places other than Washington or New York. Some have only regional significance. But the outing of a rabbi in Minneapolis compelled Jews there to confront a problem which the celibate Roman Catholic clergy had long faced. The Christian clergy has, through one circumstance or another, felt the scourge of outing on many occasions. Judaism seemed exempt–but no longer. In its issue dated January 7, 1991 the *GLC Voice,* the gay newspaper in Minneapolis, outed the senior rabbi of the largest synagogue in Minnesota. Rabbi Stephen Pinsky admitted that he twice pleaded guilty to charges of sexual misconduct and had an extramarital affair with another man.

In a letter of January 4 to the congregation of more than 2,000, the directors of Temple Israel announced that they had given Pinsky, who is married and has two children, a six-month leave of absence. They acted after Pinsky confessed that he had been romantically involved with a man for several years and had twice pleaded guilty to charges of groping undercover police officers in adult bookstores, in 1982 and in 1983. The *Star Tribune,* a Minneapolis daily, published Pinsky's admissions on January 5. An openly lesbian member of the congregation said: "This is the worst outing I have ever seen. People should be able to make their own choices about whether to come out." Yoel Zahav, the openly gay rabbi of Sha'ar Zahav ("Golden Gate"), a Reform synagogue in San Francisco, said that outing Pinsky will not necessarily help him to resolve his inner conflicts over his sexual orientation but will harm homosexuals in the Jewish community. As he told the *Advocate* (February 12, 1991), Pinsky "is obviously a deeply conflicted individual who has been a public and vocal supporter of the [gay] community."

Boston activists have generally been less spectacular. But in May of 1990 Evelyn Murphy, the Lieutenant Governor of Massachusetts, was unexpectedly outed by author and lecturer Warren Blumenfeld, at the very moment when she was seeking the Democratic nomination for governor. On live television, with no advance warning, Blumenfeld said–to the dismay of the candidate and of her supporters–that everyone in the gay community knew about her. He managed to alienate almost everyone: half of them for outing the lieutenant governor, and half for apologizing to her the very next day for having done so. (She, in any event, refused to receive his call personally.)

David Hamburger, another member of ACT UP/Boston and Queer Nation/Boston, outed a former Democratic Massachusetts state senator by pointedly defacing the closeted legislator's campaign posters on subway cars. The police apprehended him in the act and threatened him with arrest. Hamburger currently leads a working group of Queer Nation/Boston called OutPost, whose posters expose closeted homophobes. The state senator unsuccessfully ran for the nomination to the House of Representatives in the 1992 primary against Studds, who won in November even though his district was in that year gerrymandered, political analysts thought, to his certain detriment.

On a much grander scale, activists in New York have been putting up posters with celebrities' names captioned ABSOLUTELY QUEER. A similar phenomenon hit London in the summer of 1991, to the outrage and disgust of "respectable" journalists. So there is a third method of outing: through direct poster and graffito campaigns that evade the censorship of the ostensibly "free" but in reality tightly controlled establishment media.

The columnist Juan R. Palomo was dismissed from the *Houston Post* on August 30, 1991 after he revealed his sexual orientation in a column that lamented the lack of public concern over a 27-year-old banker, Paul Broussard, murdered by ten suburban youths who chased and attacked him and two companions as they left a gay bar in the Montrose neighborhood. In taking the matter public, Charles Cooper, the senior vice president and editor of the paper, declared that the columnist had acted in a way "detrimental to *The Post*." Hispanic and gay activists criticized the paper, and a protest was planned to demand the rehiring of Palomo.

ILGA CONDEMNS OUTING

At the 12th Annual Conference of the International Lesbian and Gay Association, a network of homosexual rights organizations founded (and still largely based) in Western Europe, in Stockholm on July 1-7, 1990, outing was roundly condemned. Its media workshop reported that according to the Dutch homophile journal *Gay Krant* of June 16, 1990, ACT UP in the United States (presumably ACT UP/New York City) was threatening to publicize the names of

35 closeted gay and lesbian "parliamentarians" (members of Congress) in order to pressure the political establishment to pass laws protecting homosexual rights and dealing with the AIDS crisis. ACT UP had allegedly called on its members around the world to furnish it with the names of closeted politicians so that it could make the list public despite opposition. The workshop proposed a resolution that read: "The ILGA condemns the phenomenon of outing. While encouraging all gay and lesbian persons to come out openly for their sexual orientation, the ILGA recognizes that it is every person's own and indefeasible right to decide himself/herself on this issue. The ILGA considers every interference with this right by others as an unacceptable infringement of a person's right to respect for his/her private life." It further called upon American ACT UP chapters to cease and desist from outing.

END OF OutWeek

The abrupt demise of *OutWeek* in June 1991 left a huge hole in the gay media world. Bravely, the journal had ushered in a new era of queer national activism in the 1990s–but died fighting on the barricades. Much speculation appeared as to the reasons for *OutWeek*'s failure. Some ascribed it to advertisers and subscribers who shied away from outing. Others maintained that advertisers discovered the owners to have overstated circulation figures. Some activists found its pages ever more trivial, dull, and uninteresting, so that they admitted buying it out of sympathy for its politics but barely perusing its contents. To make matters worse, of its leading backers and editors, one was using cocaine, and others were battling AIDS.

There was also a contradiction between its "politically correct" line, proclaimed almost from the first issue, and the interests of its readers and the potential customers for the products and services advertised on its pages: a perpetual dilemma for gay newspapers. The paper had also on occasion been sympathetic to pederasty and the North American Man-Boy Love Association (NAMBLA), an affinity that could hardly have endeared it to much of its readership.

A writer in the French popular weekly *Nouvel Observateur* commented in November 1991:

What the tough gays–25% of the community–have unleashed
within their community is tantamount to civil war, according
to Andrew Sullivan, editor of the Washington *New Republic*.
They have even risked reawakening the dark memories of the
fifties and of McCarthyism, of the time when the American
administration, among other things, organized a hunt for homosexuals and invited every bureaucrat to denounce his colleague. *Outing: la guerre sale* [Outing: The Dirty War] was
the recent title of a publication in Paris of Ornicar, an association for the defense of human rights in the face of sexually-
based discrimination. A dirty war, to be sure, that makes
American society the theatre of a huge psychological show,
but one which despite everything has the merit of forcing both
sides to define their positions. So advertisers have unanimously decided to boycott the weeklies that promoted outing, *Out-
Week* first and foremost: they have since ceased to appear.
(Leibowitz 1991, p. 11)

So this, perhaps the most radical of all gay movement journals,
ended its existence after a mere two years. Its legacy, however, is
enormous, and it must find a successor. Efforts in New York City to
found a replacement created *NYQ*, which in turn became *QW*. It
survived for a time but never really filled the void. The *Advocate*
has moved partially into the brink. Its editor-in-chief, Richard Rouilard, shifted his position on outing, but only with great trepidation,
hesitation and equivocation. In any case, he limited Signorile to 800
words every other week, far less space than he had in *OutWeek*. In
July 1992 Rouilard was removed in the wake of conflicts over the
new, "glossier," but politically even shallower format that the *Advocate* was cultivating (*The New York Times,* August 10, 1992, p.
D6). No other gay publication currently seems enthusiastic about
outing.

THE PENTAGON IS BESIEGED

The revelation of revelations came in August 1991. On the pages
of the *Advocate,* Signorile, fresh from producing the Gossip Watch

for the defunct *OutWeek,* outed a figure who had been in the public eye for months: Assistant Secretary of Defense Pete Williams. Stories had begun to reach his and Petrelis' ears 18 months earlier. A telephone caller had told Signorile: "Pete Williams–the PR guy for the Pentagon–is gay, and they all know it. They have a policy against gays serving in the armed forces, but their spokesman is gay, and it's all right with them."

Signorile was at first reluctant to confront the power of the Pentagon–the nerve center of the "military-industrial complex" against which President Eisenhower had warned the American people in his farewell speech. But the journalist's spine was stiffened by friends and colleagues who stressed the importance of his mission. Brooking no criticism, the government had stubbornly backed the military establishment's policy of excluding us as "incompatible," "security risks," "threats to morale," or simply "undesirable." A Senate subcommittee report of 1950 had praised the armed services for following "a rather uniform and constant pattern in ferreting out and removing these persons from the services." The Pentagon, said Signorile, "relentlessly conducts witchhunts year after year and has netted almost 13,000 queers since 1982, almost all of whom have been discharged. . . . Whether they cooperate or not, the queers are kicked out of the military and branded with a mark on their discharge papers that stigmatizes them forever." He concluded that "while a handful . . . have fought back and gone public with their stories, most slink into obscurity, humiliated and afraid."

In the face of this policy, the retention of a top Pentagon official with the rank of Assistant Secretary of Defense and a top security clearance who is openly homosexual and accepted as such by his superiors represents a classic instance of the double standard, particularly since more than 2,000 servicemen have been discharged for homosexuality just since he was appointed in 1989.

The matter came to a head on June 23, 1991. Scheduled for discharge from the service the day following Washington's Gay Pride parade, Captain Greg Greeley helped to organize it and defiantly led it, granting an interview to reporters. The air force ordered him to appear the next day at the Office for Special Investigations (OSI) in southeast Washington. Refusing to cooperate with the investigators, Greeley turned to the doyen of Capital activists Frank

Kameny. Together they went to the *Washington Post,* which put the story on the front page. At a press conference Petrelis declared: "Pete Williams . . . hypocritically remains silent in his job as Pentagon spokesman while the Department of Defense continues its irrational policy of ejecting thousands" of other homosexuals from the very armed services which he represents. Unsuspected by the public, his orientation was known to his superiors–all enmeshed in a web of hypocrisy and duplicity that has been the norm for centuries.

Of course, the mainstream media chose to suppress the story, even though Petrelis's bold move had capped several months of uninterrupted gossip about Williams' nonconformist sexual life. Most reporters covering the Pentagon had held the story for two years. By late June every commanding figure in the fourth estate had learned from his underlings that "Williams was queer." But the establishment was adhering to its automatic reflex of protecting its own. Signorile asked: "How does a homosexual get to the top in Republican Washington? Actually, the same way any woman-lover does: by possessing a picture-perfect background, making all the right connections, and keeping very quiet regarding those things about oneself that simply can't be discussed in mixed company."

There is even, it seems, an upscale gay bar, J.R.'s, near Dupont Circle, where Congressman Gerry Studds was recently mugged. It is reputed to be the watering place of queer nationals in government jobs, other gay professionals, Georgetown University students, and *openly* gay politicians. Here, even many devotedly Republican and right-wing homosexuals congregate. But others linger in the shadows of private parties. The ultracloseted have only secret liaisons.

An habitué of this fancy dive in the past, Williams stopped coming once the outbreak of the Gulf War made him a media celebrity peering out of the screen of every television set as Americans by the million avidly watched the drama in Saudi Arabia, Kuwait, and Iraq unfold. So many were the gay men in his circle that it is doubtful whether he was ever really in the closet. Williams' situation appears to have been one in which his sexual orientation was not hidden but the knowledge of it was skillfully "managed."

The *Village Voice* considered the story when it became clear that *OutWeek* (just going under) was not to publish it, but its staff vetoed it on July 3. Four weeks later, on Wednesday, July 31, New York's

Channel 11 (WPIX-TV) broadcast a segment using Williams' name and reporting that the *Advocate* was about to out him, airing footage from a late June Queer Nation press conference. This telecast failed to evoke a single echo. Most papers–including the *Washington Post*–refused to print a story by columnist Jack Anderson that was to be syndicated nationwide on Friday, August 2.

So in the issue which appeared that weekend (postdated August 27, 1991), the *Advocate* published Signorile's bombshell together with an editorial that justified the practice in certain circumstances, whereas the magazine had categorically condemned it the year before. The feature bore the heading, "We commit ourselves to this *singular* [our italics] instance of outing in the name of the 12,966 soldiers who have been outed by the military since 1982." The editorial began: "Outing is a weapon of last resort." It concluded a list of grievances by saying: "And the armed forces are booting us out, ruining lives, at the rate of nearly 1,000 per year." The gay community has long known that the right-wing organizations that have made homosexuals and the gay rights movement their target have as many homosexuals in their ranks as do the left-wing organizations that take the opposite stance. If the *Advocate* previously turned a blind eye to those who acquiesced in these right-wing policies, it was because it understood "that all of us have to make some accommodations to a principally heterosexual world and that some progress could, albeit slowly, be made by closeted homosexuals in high places." But what of those in policy-making positions who nevertheless do nothing? In almost all cases we could still suffer their presence, because they were "our people."

But, the editorial continued, "we cannot support the acquiescence of . . . the assistant secretary of defense for public affairs to the policies of the most homophobic department of the U.S. government." Too many of our own people have been harmed, and too egregiously. Williams is clearly involved in policy-making at the highest level, and "his silent complicity in this noxious conspiracy . . . implicitly allows his superiors to continue the blanket exclusion, the hateful investigation, the dishonorable discharges, the ruination of lives." The *Advocate*'s readers, said the editorial, concurred with its new position. A November 1990 survey found that a majority of 1,271 respondents felt that outing was "sometimes a justifiable political action."

The justification in such cases as Williams' could only be strengthened by the news, reported in *The Wall Street Journal* in January and again in July of 1991, that an estimated 700 soldiers who fought in the war were about to be discharged for homosexuality, even though their superiors knew full well that they were homosexual before they were assigned to Operation Desert Shield. The services are quite willing to treat us as expendable–*before, during,* and *after* combat.

Outing is thus justified as retribution for wrongs done to our community by those who bear the double burden of responsibility and hypocrisy. Those who make common cause with obscurantist clergy, the military establishment, and right-wing groups that exploit homophobia to trick the electorate into voting against its economic interests should be publicly exposed and humiliated. Outing in these circumstances is merely an act of self-defense against mortal peril, a weapon of last resort of the belligerent Queer Nation.

While the journal that Signorile chose as the vehicle for his article does not belong to the mainstream, the *Advocate* is the most respected and widely read gay magazine in America with a circulation (August 1992) approaching 120,000, triple its nearest rival's. By adopting, at least in this sole instance, the tactics of outing, its editors signaled that the practice was winning acceptance by centrist media. Moreover, the *Advocate* released advance copies of the story to the regular media. Most editors and columnists remained wary, but some took notice of the outing without naming Williams. What was once a sturdy hull shielding the powerful on the ship of state had now sprung leaks–too many for the upholders of the old policy to plug.

The *Advocate* of September 24, 1991 contained readers' responses. Jim Doust of Chicago wrote: "I have mixed feelings about outing but would support continued outing of destructive, closeted homophobes." In the same vein Richard V. McCune of Los Angeles commented: "I do not support the outing of individuals under most circumstances, especially celebrities in the entertainment industry. There does, however, come a time when it is the morally correct thing to do. In the case of Pete Williams, it was inevitable." Steven Hanson of Coos Bay, Oregon had this to say: "The outing of assistant secretary of defense Pete Williams is to be applauded. . . . Regardless of the fact that outing is simply the telling of the truth, which may hurt but which is never bad, any public figure who hides the truth while persecuting or supporting the persecution of others who share that same truth deserves, at the very least, honest exposure."

Equally explicit were the negative reactions. John Norman of Cañon City, Colorado wrote: "I would like to record a resounding no to outing in general and to the outing of Pete Williams in particular. . . . Williams is the criminal, and, acting as prosecutor, judge, and jury, you have carried out his trial, conviction, and execution. What is his crime? Not something he has done." Tom Scott of San Francisco seconded this view: "The ADVOCATE's attempt to demonize Pete Williams . . . is both cheap and preposterous. You found an easy target, and you grabbed for attention that might, at least temporarily, raise your circulation. . . . You owe Williams an apology, although nothing you might do now could ever repair the unwarranted damage to his career." Randy Curwen of Chicago reasoned: "Yes, the military's position is wrong. . . . But people like Williams (whose bosses, you make it quite clear, have to have known he was gay) have done more to advance our cause by proving that gays can function effectively in any area of employment than, say, someone like Michelangelo Signorile, who can't write an exposé that exposes even one instance in which Williams has done anything reprehensible."

So the outing of Williams divided our community quite as much as previous outings in *OutWeek,* if not more so. It showed that many held the "unwritten law" of silence to be still valid and binding, while others roundly applauded the new tactic and wanted to see even more exposure of closet cases in high places. Honor had yielded to expediency, or a higher cause had triumphed over personal privilege–depending upon one's point of view.

RANDY SHILTS HAS SECOND THOUGHTS

In an op-ed piece in *The New York Times* of April 12, 1990, Randy Shilts endorsed outing. The prominent gay journalist explained why editors routinely lie about the sexuality of public figures, writing that "the refusal of newspapers to reveal a person's homosexuality has less to do with ethical considerations of privacy than with an editor's homophobia. In my experience, many editors really believe that being gay is so distasteful that talk of it should be avoided unless absolutely necessary." He added: "In Hollywood and New York, hundreds of publicists make their living by planting items in entertainment columns about whom this or that celebrity is dating. Many of these items are patently false and intended only to cover up the celebrity's homosexuality."

Homophobia thus continues to closet the living as it has long done the dead. Homosexuals and heterosexuals alike become entangled in the web of deception and falsehood. Obligatory heterosexuality has required that everyone pretend to be heterosexual or be depicted as heterosexual in historical works or literary biographies. As long ago as 1862 Karl Heinrich Ulrichs had written in a private letter that "the Dionaic [heterosexual] majority has no right to construct human society *exclusively* Dionaically [heterosexually]" (Hirschfeld 1914, p. 955). Even those who personally detest homosexuality become accomplices to the monumental dishonesty that permeates public and intellectual life and undermines the self-righteous claims of Christianity to possess a revealed morality that transcends all others.

In a certain respect, outing threatens the established morality far more than does sodomy law repeal. The latter has frequently occurred unobtrusively as part of the revision of an entire penal code, or has only served to make public hypocrisy on the subject more pronounced, since advocates of the changes often justified them solely by abstract philosophical arguments, accompanied them with ringing denunciations of "homosexual conduct," and further extenuated them by assuring the public that there were "better ways to deal with this scourge of society"–which meant that the traditional silence or defamation could, indeed *should*, persist unchanged. *Outing strikes at the very heart of the sodomy delusion: it exposes the dishonesty and hypocrisy of Christian society in regard to this major facet of human sexuality.*

The Kinsey reports amounted, we can now see, to a massive, albeit statistical and anonymous, outing of the gay population of the United States. That is why homophobic psychoanalysts like Abram Kardiner and Edmund Bergler were enraged by Kinsey's finding that most homosexuals were not disturbed individuals who deserved to be on their couches–if not in prison or in an insane asylum–but normal, functioning, purposeful human beings, like most Americans (as Karl Westphal's own disciples had already concluded long before, in 1891). Petrelis and Signorile were merely carrying outing to its next logical step–giving it a political focus and pinpointing celebrities whose hypocrisy had passed the limit of toleration.

It is both rage over the persistence of this hypocrisy and a sense of urgency instilled by the specter of death that has inspired the newest wave of outing. Many of the prominent figures in ACT UP chapters around the country sense that they have only years or months to live, and are indignant that the official response to the AIDS crisis has been so inadequate. Queer Nation is in its turn demanding the loyalty of all who participate in the gay subculture by virtue of their homosexual lives and loves, however private and clandestine they may have been hitherto.

In an interview published in the *Progressive* of May 1991, Shilts commented on the Queer Nation:

> They are a younger generation of people, largely in their early twenties, who are coming out very militant, who are calling the older generation of us 'assimilationists'. . . . They're doing a lot of shock value stuff. It's the most exciting thing to happen to the gay community in twenty years. . . . These younger people grew up at a time when it was much easier being gay, because of the work done by the older people. . . . They're demanding to be called "queers." They're taking back a word that was pejorative.

Shilts told how he came out: "I started by being involved in antiwar marches–the very early gay liberation movements were involved in the antiwar movement, so I was around the gay liberation people more. And once it hit me, a week later I told everybody. It was on May 19, 1972. I told every friend, everybody in my family, that I was gay. And I swore that I'd never live another day of my life in which people didn't know that I was gay."

In the *Los Angeles Times* of August 7, 1991, however, Shilts reversed his earlier opinion and expressed strong disapproval of outing. He reproached the activists who had outed Williams: "Before gloating, however, the outers would do well to consider their own intellectual inconsistencies. The two levels of social change that the gay movement seeks are in conflict. . . . It's doubly hypocritical to seek the right to privacy in courts and then wantonly violate others' rights to privacy in the gay press." Shilts concluded by calling outing "a dirty business that hurts people"–as if the homophobia of American society had not been hurting people since the day the Republic was founded.

John Mitzel at first wrote favorably of outing in his column in the Boston gay monthly *The Guide* of September 1989, then two years later, in September 1991, attacked Michelangelo Signorile in the same periodical. One might suspect an element of professional jealousy to be involved; at all events the sword of outing does have two edges and cuts both ways.

FICTIONALIZED TREATMENTS OF OUTING– TELEVISION, FILM, NOVELS

As Larry Gross noted: "In May 1990, *LA Law,* (NBC) ran an episode featuring the outing of a heroic policeman (largely modeled on Oliver Sipple) by a gay activist editor; the policeman sues but loses in court on First Amendment grounds. In January 1991, *Gabriel's Fire,* (ABC) ran a story that was both unconvincing and homophobic: a divorced pro football quarterback is falsely outed by a gay man who is a member of (the nonexistent) 'Outers of America.' While the football player, who professes to 'have nothing against homosexuals,' wins his lawsuit, the program shows his son choosing to live with his mother, his hopes for endorsements dashed, and his camp for underprivileged children destroyed." While both plays are implicitly homophobic, their plots also argue that outing can be ruinous even to a celebrity, if only through loss of prestige (Gross 1991, p. 383).

The novel by Richard Stevenson, *Third Man Out* (New York: St. Martin's Press, 1992), turns upon the relationship between private investigator Strachey and Queer Nation activist John Rutka–a composite of Petrelis and Signorile. As the story opens, Rutka is outing everyone "out of sight." Not surprisingly snipers take aim at him and his house is firebombed by agents of an exceptionally powerful but frightened closet case dreading that his turn will soon come.

Uneasy at first, Strachey soon grasps that the political stakes are far higher and the ethical issues far more complex than the fate of the celebrity whom Rutka would rashly drag into the limelight.

So long as the Motion Picture Production Code forbade depiction of homosexuality or reference to it, the subject was moot. Even Vito Russo delved far more into Hollywood's imaging of gender and gender stereotypes than into homosexuality proper–because that was all he could find. But when filmmakers gained the freedom to treat gay themes, some produced works which, as it were in a "return of the repressed," simply visualized on the screen the worst stereotypes of the psychoanalytic literature of the 1940s and 1950s, which in turn replicated the paranoid fantasies of the medieval mind. Earlier in this century these baleful interpretations had been confined to the pages of professional journals read only by specialists and to books such as Edmund Bergler's *One Thousand Homosexuals* and Hervey Cleckley's *The Caricature of Love*. *The Silence of the Lambs,* which garnered the chief Academy Awards for 1991, implied that a serial killer was homosexual by giving him stereotypical makeup, lisp, and poodle named Precious. *Basic Instinct* (1992) ascribed the murderous proclivities of its heroines to their lesbianism, implying that their "perversion" is the ultimate antisocial orientation. In Barbra Streisand's *Prince of Tides,* the central trauma is Tom Wingo's rape by a man at the age of 11.

Other scripts virtually eliminated the homoerotic subtext of the original plot, leaving the sexual orientation of the characters in a haze. The screen adaptation of Alice Walker's *The Color Purple* left out the lesbian affair of Whoopi Goldberg's character Celia. The film version of Fannie Flagg's *Fried Green Tomatoes at the Whistle Stop Cafe* suppressed the lesbian bonding between the liquor-loving, pants-wearing Masterson and the demure Parker, illustrating Hollywood's infinite capacity to turn something into nothing.

No film hero or heroine is a Queer National or a positive, admirable homosexual role model. Queers are either murdering villains, self-hating paradigms of psychopathology, or figures of comic relief. Television, though, is ahead of Hollywood. In recent years it has built many screenplays around gay characters. At the same time fundamentalist pressure groups have attempted to force advertisers to withdraw their support of such programs in order to preclude a

positive image of love for one's own sex from reaching the public–
and particularly "impressionable young people." The traditionalists have never abandoned their centuries-old policy: if not defamation, then silence.

Queer Nation, Out in Film, and other activist groups planned a
dual action at the Academy Awards ceremony on March 30, 1992,
both as guests arrived at the Dorothy Chandler Pavilion in Los
Angeles and later during the show, close to the awarding of a major
Oscar. They also announced their intention to out a large number of
closeted stars with maps pinpointing where they live–no doubt to
the trepidation of their press agents. Many appearing on the plat-
form wore the red ribbon, but the threatened outing *no more materialized* than the one announced for Governor Wilson's aides after he
reneged on his promise to support gay rights.

Unsympathetic portrayals have contributed to a rise in queer-
bashing. A survey of by The National Gay and Lesbian Task Force
Policy Institute found that incidents of violence (including harassment, threats, vandalism, arson, police brutality, physical assaults,
and murder) against individuals who were or were perceived to be
homosexual rose 31 percent in five cities during 1991. Kevin Ber-
rill, director of the institute's Anti-Violence Project, declared that
"The wide scope of antigay violence in 1991 should come as no
surprise given the stench of bigotry that routinely emanates from
Hollywood, the halls of Congress, the pulpits of the religious right,
and other venues."

So the problem of appropriate visibility for us in film and television remains. The old attitudes can be insinuated as effectively–and
far more subtly–by the screen portrayal of a homosexual psycho-
path than by a sermon on the doom of Sodom and Gomorrah. Even
more controversial is the issue of how such characters should be
positively depicted, because the community itself is not of one
mind, some preferring conventional types who chance to love their
own sex, others applauding the most flamboyant and uninhibited.

QUEER NATIONALS IN THE MILITARY

Williams ranked as a top official at the Pentagon, with access to
highly classified information. Yet he was never humiliated and

cashiered as were thousands of uniformed homosexual (or bisexual) men and women during his service as spokesman in what was technically wartime. So his outing poses a genuine dilemma for the military. It exposes the blatant hypocrisy of an establishment that goes to great lengths to ferret out homosexuals and expel them from the military, but allows a known homosexual to occupy a high position in the Pentagon itself.

Department of Defense Directive 1332.14 reads:

> Homosexuality is incompatible with military service. The presence in the military environment of persons who engage in homosexual conduct or who, by their statements, demonstrate a propensity to engage in homosexual conduct seriously impairs the accomplishment of the military mission. The presence of such members adversely affects the ability of the Armed Forces to maintain discipline, good order and morale: to foster mutual trust and confidence among service members; to ensure the integrity of the system of rank and command; to facilitate assignment and worldwide deployment of service members who frequently must live and work under close conditions affording minimal privacy; to recruit and retain members of the Armed Forces; to maintain the public acceptability of military service; and to prevent breaches of security. Homosexual acts are crimes under the Uniform Code of Military Justice.
>
> A homosexual act means bodily contact, actively undertaken or passively permitted, between members of the same sex for the purpose of satisfying sexual desires.
>
> Discharge for homosexuality can result from: (1) committing homosexual acts; (2) attempting to commit homosexual acts; (3) stating the desire or intent to commit homosexual acts.

Other countries, it must be admitted, have similar policies. Among those in the common law tradition, or under its influence, which have such a policy are Australia, Canada (reportedly on the verge of reversing it), Cyprus, Great Britain, India, Jamaica, New Zealand, and Trinidad and Tobago. Nations following the civil (Roman) law tradition that bar homosexual service in the military include Argentina, Colombia, Guatemala, Italy, Portugal, and Spain–

in the last three presumably a legacy of fascist regimes in the recent past lingers. So do the Moslem countries of Iraq, Pakistan, and Turkey. Clearly the policy is not peculiar to any single cultural or legal tradition. In most of these jurisdictions homosexual acts are not in themselves criminal when committed by civilians in private. On the other hand, if the United States were to change its policy it would scarcely be alone. A number of countries explicitly *permit* homosexual persons to serve in the armed services–Austria, Belgium, Denmark, the Netherlands, Norway, South Africa, Sweden, Switzerland–and a good many others report no policy one way or the other. Here, in any event, is an opportunity for America to join the ranks of the enlightened.

Unfortunately, the American armed forces did not abandon their policy even during the Gulf crisis, even though they instituted a temporary Stop Loss procedure. This is a wartime device that allows the armed services to defer administrative separations of military personnel who are not involved in actual misconduct.

As reported in the *Advocate*, Donna Lynn Jackson, Reserve Specialist 4 in the U. S. Army's 129th Evacuation Hospital Unit, wrote a letter to her post commander stating: "I am an open lesbian, and I wish to be deployed as such with my unit." Initially this proved no obstacle to her being sent with her unit to Saudi Arabia in preparation for the attack on the Iraqis occupying Kuwait. She alone out of her unit, however, was ultimately left behind in the U.S. to be reassigned to an administrative unit pending an Army investigation. When Jackson was informed that the Department of Defense would resume its antihomosexual policy once the troops returned from the Middle East, the reservist revealed the Pentagon's hypocrisy to the media. After two years of active service and five as a reservist, she faced the possibility of joining the more than 1,000-odd a year whom the military discharges for homosexuality. She was undaunted by her experience, however: "The more who come out, the better the chances of the military changing its policy on homosexuality."

On January 11, 1991 Randy Shilts estimated that 30 percent of women in the armed forces are lesbians: "Lesbians have a much tougher time in the military than gay men. They're kicked out at a rate three times higher than men" (Shilts 1991). His article provoked a Department of Defense denial that the fundamental policy had changed in any way. At the same time Sandra Lowe, an attorney with Lambda Legal Defense, claimed to know a number of service personnel who came out to their superiors but were shipped off to the Gulf anyway.

About the military's antihomosexual policies Shilts made some remarkable revelations in an interview of May 30, 1991 in the *Progressive*:

The military policies are created by the United States Government, and enforced brutally as a matter of policy. . . . The brutality of the policies–they drive people to suicide. Murder is all but condoned in some services. . . . I mean that gay people get murdered, that gay people's lives are routinely threatened in the military, and the military does absolutely nothing about it. If somebody threatens a gay person in an aircraft carrier at sea, and he starts receiving death threats and informs his superiors, the superiors almost always respond by launching an investigation against that person to determine whether he should be kicked out for being gay. They will never respond by launching an investigation of the death threats. I have so many stories of this. . . . For women, lesbians, you're talking as much about women's issues as you are about homophobia. For the first time, you have women being able to go into nontraditional roles. Every time women are allowed into a new job category in the military, they're almost invariably accused of being lesbians. The first women allowed to go onto a ship in the Navy sailed on the *Norton Sound*. Within months, they had their first witchhunt for lesbians. Women who do a good job are women who are good military people, which means they're aggressive and competent. . . . The antigay regulations, as they're used against women, are basically used as a way for men to get women into bed. I've talked to women who have been raped but have not reported it, or have been afraid to report it, because the men said they would accuse them of being lesbians if they reported it. Women who do not submit to the sexual advances of superiors are routinely accused of lesbianism and routinely kicked

out. The level of sexual harassment in the military astounds
me, and is enabled by antigay regulations.

Shilts has devoted his recently published book *Conduct Unbecom-
ing: Gays and Lesbians in the U.S. Military,* to the armed services'
antihomosexual policies and prejudices–a most timely subject.

Openly gay Congressman Gerry Studds of Massachusetts, who
has spearheaded the fight against the exclusionary policy, commented: "It is the lowest form of hypocrisy for the Pentagon to
maintain that gays and lesbians are unfit for military service while it
sends them off to risk their lives in the Gulf. And it is utterly
inconceivable to me that these same men and women, upon the
loyal completion of their tours, will be kicked out of the service
because they are gay."

The issue of outing in the military is complicated by the fact that
in the Korean War and the Vietnam War, revealing one's orientation
was a convenient way of staying out of the armed services–and the
radicals of the Gay Liberation Front wanted nothing more. But
today, as Marxism, "comic book" and other, wanes, some activists
demand for queer nationals the right to serve in the military, either
as career soldiers or in a national emergency as draftees. Miriam
Ben-Shalom, a lesbian who lost her appeal to rejoin the Army
Reserves when the Supreme Court refused to hear her case in February 1990, disclosed that she personally knew 250 homosexual
veterans, many of whom had already endured the rigors of combat,
who would have been willing to *volunteer* for duty–even front-line
service–in the Persian Gulf if the Department of Defense abandoned its policy. Others in contrast called for massive gay support
for the antiwar movement that briefly revived in the winter of
1990-91, with demonstrations in San Francisco, Washington and
elsewhere. So the issue is clouded by fundamental political rifts
within the queer nation itself.

Moreover, activists had long been campaigning for the expulsion
of the Reserve Officers Training Corps (ROTC) from college campuses because of its exclusionary rules and for the banning of military recruiters from campuses. The head of the humanities department, David M. Halperin, persuaded the president of Massachusetts
Institute of Technology to denounce the antihomosexual policy im-

posed by the army, and many colleges, including Dartmouth, are giving notice that they will expel ROTC if the homophobic policies continue. The presidents of more than 60 universities have now denounced the military's ban on homosexual servicemen, which blatantly contradicts the rule against discrimination based on sexual orientation that many colleges have adopted.

THE WILLIAMS OUTING AND THE MILITARY

Events moved swiftly after Williams' outing. Perhaps uninfluenced by it on August 19 the Ninth U.S. Circuit Court of Appeals in San Francisco ruled that the Army had to prove that there is a rational basis for its policy on homosexuals. It would not accept homophobia as a valid reason for exclusion. The decision stemmed from the discharge of Army Reservist Captain Dusty Pruitt after she disclosed during a 1983 interview with the *Los Angeles Times,* in connection with her work for the Metropolitan Community Church, that she was a lesbian. The judges found that past decisions upholding the military's policy were based, in part, on acquiescence to the prejudice of others. That rationale was undermined by a 1984 Supreme Court decision which said that social disapproval of an interracial marriage did not justify denial of child support. "Private biases may be outside the reach of the law, but the law cannot, directly or indirectly, give them effect." The same argument had figured, interestingly, in the dissenting opinion in *Plessy v. Ferguson* (1896), which upheld the right of the southern states to impose racial segregation: the majority cited decisions rendered at a time when the institution of slavery so dominated public opinion that prejudice was the law of the land. In the same way, the courts had tacitly ratified prejudices grounded in medieval intolerance as a valid basis for legal decisions.

Less than two weeks later, on September 1, 1991, in what was clearly at least in part a response to the Williams outing, *The New York Times* carried an editorial headed "Gay Soldiers, Good Soldiers." It began with the questions: "Do homosexual personnel, male and female, threaten the effectiveness of the armed forces? Or is it shortsighted prejudice for the military services to ban homosexuals and to discharge those discovered in its ranks?" The editors explained that in recent weeks the issue had revived, so that Defense Secretary Cheney had been obliged to justify the policy that deemed homosexuality "incompatible with military service." He was not eager to maintain a ban that deprives the armed services of potential talent, brands thousands of individuals with dishonorable discharges that blight their subsequent lives, and costs millions to train their replacements. "Much of the opposition to homosexuals reflects a deep-seated fear that gay personnel would make sexual advances on their heterosexual comrades, provoking fights or starting affairs that would destroy discipline. But that wrongly brands all homosexuals as sexual aggressors."

The editors accused the Defense Department of duplicity, since homosexuals are allowed to serve in civilian jobs, even at the highest and most sensitive levels, under civil service rules outlawing sexual orientation as a criterion for employment. "That is why," it added, "Secretary Cheney has no trouble retaining a trusted aide who was identified as homosexual by a gay magazine"–an obvious allusion to the *Advocate*'s outing. Repeating the arguments advanced in the *Advocate* editorial, the *Times* went on to say that the absurdity of the policy was underscored by a message from Vice Admiral Joseph S. Donnell, the commander of the surface fleet in the Atlantic, in late July of 1990 telling his subordinates that "With the influx of women on our ships and throughout the Navy in general, it is necessary to address the sensitive issue of female homosexuality and ensure equal treatment of male and female homosexuals. There is a perception by many that female homosexuality is somewhat tolerated, while male homosexuality is dealt with swiftly and sternly. [You must] demonstrate equality in the treatment of male and female homosexuals." Investigations of lesbianism must not be "pursued halfheartedly" merely because "experience has . . . shown" that lesbians are generally "hard-working, career-oriented, willing to put in long hours on the job and among the command's top performers." Equality in this instance evidently means the same right to be exposed and punished–a right which the armed services would never deny to anyone.

Rejecting all of the conventional arguments for exclusion of homosexuals, the *Times* cited Gallup Polls that indicate mounting public approval of their admission to the armed forces. It concluded that regulations proscribing sexual harassment could deal with any problems that arise from homosexual propositioning, and that "what consenting adults do on their own time is their business, not the military's," so that there was "no evident justification for discrimination on the basis of sexual orientation." On the heels of this statement, the 99th convention of the American Psychological Association in San Francisco heard attacks on the policy. Speaker after speaker told the professionals that the ban is supported by no data from the social sciences, but that it is brutally enforced and functions in a dehumanizing way. The Department of Defense for its part withdrew the speakers who were assigned to uphold the existing policy.

The prompt response of the foremost establishment newspaper to Signorile's bold move–little more than three weeks had elapsed since the issue of the *Advocate* hit the stands in New York City–vindicated outing and the exposure of hypocrisy. So, just two years after *OutWeek* began its outing of the celebrities in our midst, the practice yielded its first major dividend. Others, it is safe to predict, are on the way.

The New York Times of Friday October 11, 1991 reported that under the pressure of court cases, the Canadian government was about to reverse a policy barring homosexuals from the armed forces. Officials of the Canadian defense establishment had recently informed members of Parliament of the impending change. Nicholas Swales, a member of the staff of the House of Commons Standing Committee on National Defense, called the policy change "inevitable." "It was only a matter of time," he said, "before they came round to this sort of conclusion." Homosexual rights advocates hailed the move as "long overdue." The decisive step was subsequently taken.

Defeats, however, also lay ahead. In December 1991 U.S. District Judge Oliver Gasch rejected the suit of Joseph C. Steffan, a Naval Academy midshipman who, acknowledging his homosexuality, still claimed that the policy was unconstitutional. The judge ruled that the regulations "rationally further legitimate state purposes" and further "a healthy military force, morality, and respect for the privacy interests of both officers and the enlisted." In the wake of this decision the feeling among legal activists was that appeal to the courts is useless because their reasoning runs in a vicious circle, and that only Congress and the president can terminate the policy.

OUTING IN THE UNITED KINGDOM

Britain has the highest age of male homosexual consent in Europe: 21. It is 18 in Germany and Luxembourg, 16 in Belgium, 15 in Denmark, France, and Greece, 14 in Italy, and 12 in the Netherlands, Portugal, and Spain. In Ireland homosexuality is illegal, although the European Court of Human Rights has challenged the validity of the law. In most European Community nations the age of consent for lesbians is the same as for gay men. For British lesbians the age of consent is 16, on a par with that for heterosexuals.

The *Sunday Times of London* reported on December 1, 1991 that Scotland was on the verge of announcing the dropping of criminal charges against consenting homosexual males between 16 and 21 "unless there is evidence of seduction, corruption, or a breach of trust," in the words of Lord Fraser of Carmyllie, the lord advocate. Although British Prime Minister John Major has noted a "changing social attitude towards homosexuality in this country and abroad," he insisted that in England and Wales, where the law differs from Scottish law, the present policy would continue. A Downing Street spokesman declared: "Whatever happens in Scotland has no impact on England and Wales. There has been no change in prosecuting policy. There have always been differences between English and Scottish law," but conceded that more prosecutions were "unlikely." The well-known actor and gay rights activist Sir Ian McKellen went to confer with Major. Another actor, Michael Cashman, chairman of the gay rights organization Stonewall, deplored the inconsistency in the law between Scotland and the rest of the United Kingdom, but thought that "this decision will take enormous pressure off many young gay men. Some have been driven to suicide. It will also allow health education authorities and schools to target young people with safe sex education."

Not surprisingly, the Scottish announcement brought forth a spate of denunciations from Tory right-wingers. Bill Walker, president of Conservatives for the Family, warned that "there is a great danger that people will be left with the impression that it is open house in Scotland and that is not acceptable." Teddy Taylor, a former Scottish minister, vowed to fight the measure: "I have never known such a big decision on a fundamental moral issue being taken in this way. If we cannot overturn this we may as well close Parliament down and turn it into a museum."

In spite of the heat of the ongoing debate about homosexuality in the United Kingdom, there has not yet been a significant outing. In the summer of 1991 activists proclaimed that they were about to out 200, including numerous members of Parliament and other highly-placed people, but whereas in California in the wake of Pete Wilson's veto (discussed later in this chapter) they outed only Mickey Mouse, in Britain the outings did not materialize at all. The chapters of ACT UP and Queer Nation in British cities have not yet successfully outed anyone. Part of the problem there comes from the slander and libel laws, which are much stricter than in the United States. In Great Britain the old common and statutory laws prevail, protecting public officials and politicians as much as private persons, so that anyone resorting to outing there could be sued, while in the United States decisions beginning in the 1960s removed the shield from such celebrities. In Great Britain outers feel obliged to proceed anonymously, as indeed they apparently intended when they threatened to put up posters denouncing the 200.

OUTING REACHES AUSTRALIA

In Australia, where the overt gay community, consisting of those who are out to more than a few friends, sex partners or family members, numbers only in the tens of thousands even at the highest count, outing has provoked tremendous outrage. It is understandable that an outing there might be more detrimental to the outee, who could find few people among whom to take refuge and perhaps nowhere to hide except the outback. But numbers alone cannot explain the extent of the revulsion. One has to speculate whether the continent down under is simply less advanced or less decadent, if one prefers, than Great Britain and Western Europe, where, although there has been little outing, nevertheless the idea has not struck people as so repellent as it seems to the Australians. A single professional outer has shocked and enraged their whole gay establishment.

In the evolution of their gay liberation movement, Australians have followed Americans rather closely, with a time lag of a year or two at most. Hence it is no surprise that outing reached its shores in the summer of 1991, as fast as it made its way to Paris. On the night of Thursday, August 8, a person or persons unknown designed a poster on an Apple computer which bore the headline GUILTY OF DECEIT AND HOMO-HATRED. With the names of two prominent politicians, it was signed "A message from Queer Nation–a nation without borders." This event announced that 17 months after its founding Queer Nation had found citizens in Australia.

A laser printer produced the posters, which were appropriately hung on walls and telephone poles in Sydney. Two were thrust under the door of a clothing store beneath the offices of the gay biweekly *Sydney Star Observer.* At a press conference some hours earlier, State Upper House MP Franca Arena had burst into tears while telling of threats to expose her twin sons Mark and Adrian, 24, as homosexual. Shortly after this event, Melbourne activists disclosed that they had a list containing the names of 40 prominent politicians, including a State governor, two Supreme Court judges, a member of the Hawke cabinet, seven state MPs, two Anglican bishops, four captains of industry, and one captain of a Victorian Football League premiership team. Two former prime ministers, both deceased, were also to be outed from the grave.

In an effort to find the culprits, New South Wales Special Branch police combed the pages of the *Bulletin,* the Australian counterpart of *Newsweek,* which ran an article naming people involved in outing internationally. The state attorney general promised criminal defamation actions. Michael McDougall of ACT UP/Sydney denied that Queer Nation existed in that city "except in the imagination and mind of maybe one person. It holds no meetings, has no office, no address, no agenda. It's a joke." The Australian political establishment and media did not treat the affair as a joke, but reacted with furious indignation. On August 13 the prime minister, Robert Hawke, condemned the outing of prominent homosexuals as "outrageous." He even asserted that he did not care if any of his cabinet members were gay. "I take the view that in these sorts of things people have the right to be what by nature they want to be. And provided they operate within the law, live within the law, then that's their right." He claimed never to have used accusations of homosexuality as a political weapon. Some two years earlier, as it happened, he had confessed on national television that he had been guilty of adultery and besides was too fond of the bottle.

The president of the Australian Federation of AIDS Organizations, Bill Whittaker, warned that outing might result in more homophobia and queer-bashing. He asserted that AIDS and gay organizations were responsible enough to deal with the issue. "This includes the possible strategic outing of someone in an exceptional case where it can be proven that they are homosexual and proven that they are using a position of influence to directly harm the gay and lesbian community or people with HIV/AIDS." He denounced those who "mindlessly follow every American trend" in the name of activism. The secretary of the AIDS Council of New South Wales, David Buchanan, said that "frankly, the action was despicable and childish"–a reproach sometimes addressed to ACT UP/ New York City by those who dub it "GROW UP!" ACT UP/ Sydney issued a statement distancing itself from the outing of Franca Arena's sons. A dozen businesses subscribed to a full-page advertisement in the *Sydney Star Observer* voicing their opposition to outing.

On Thursday, August 15, Donald Horton, 47, a respected judge of the Supreme Court in Brisbane, Queensland, was found dead in his car at his home in suburban St Lucia. Friends confirmed that threats to out him had driven him to suicide. A close friend said that Horton's homosexuality was well known and sensitively accepted among those who worked alongside him. He said: "Don was deeply distressed and was concerned his profession would be demeaned if his persuasion was publicly identified." Another friend added: "It's disgraceful to think the outing issue is moving into Queensland. The concept is cruel and vicious and can only cause unnecessary suffering to many innocent people." The judge, said another colleague, had always carefully kept his homosexuality discreet. Gay activists were quoted to the effect that he should have been the least likely target for an outing campaign, because he had never kept his homosexuality secret from those in his milieu, even from Queensland's former National Party government, which made him a Queen's Counsel and appointed him to the Supreme Court. The president of the Queensland AIDS Council insisted that the judge "simply wasn't in the closet."

Other prominent Australians condemned outing unreservedly. Ron Casey, a radio personality, called the move "despicable" and said (malapropistically) that it had "put the homosexual acceptance cause back light years" (because a light year is a measure of space, not time, it has no relevance to chronology). Another radio commentator, Brian Bury, said: "I think it's disgraceful and cowardly. It's almost a fascist attack on people's private lives." Chris Murphy, a criminal lawyer, was quoted as saying: "Outing homosexuals is a disgraceful abuse of the right that people have to the quiet enjoyment of their private lives." The editor of the *Sydney Star Observer,* Larry Galbraith, called outers "a handful of loose cannons on the deck of the gay community being egged on by certain media people." The *Sun-Herald* labeled outing "dangerous idiocy . . . because the perpetrators have no way of knowing the impact that the revelation will have on the victim, his or her relatives or friends. Put simply, it is sexual McCarthyism."

Early in August it was reported that New South Wales Attorney General Peter Collins would ask the crown solicitor for a detailed legal opinion on possible prosecution of people arrested for putting up outing posters in the streets of Sydney. He said that the government was prepared to bring charges of criminal defamation against such offenders and would not have to pass new legislation to cover the crime; the law already existed, and "the penalty would be left to the judge."

On the other hand, two long-time Melbourne activists held that the issue merited serious consideration by the gay community. Jamie Gardiner, an executive on the Victorian Council for Civil Liberties, told the *Sunday Age* that it was important for gay young people "who often feel they're the only ones–to know there are leaders in every walk of life who are gay." He hastened to add: "We understand that in a society as discriminatory and oppressive as ours people have wanted to stay in the closet. But as time goes on it becomes less excusable to stay in the closet, especially for those who have made it." He also suggested that as a first step, the gay periodicals *OutRage* and the *Sydney Star Observer* could approach successful homosexuals to talk about their experiences and publish such interviews in batches of a dozen, arguing that the community can admire these people.

Tony Westmore, a member of ACT UP/Sydney and Queer Nation/Sydney, justified outing of public figures who, so far from supporting queer political aims, work actively against them in the hope of concealing their true colors. Such people, he said, are to be found in "all sorts of policy debates: employment, planning, health, social services, adoption, defense, immigration and foreign affairs." He added: "Fear of exposure and the concomitant need to fly the flag of conservatism fire their voices. These fires might be damped by the cleansing waters of truth." Such people "in order to protect themselves and their loved ones, legislate against us, make public comments which are lots less than flattering and work in ways to make life dreary. I say let's drag them out of their closets for their families, constituents and audiences to see." In a homophobic society, one Australian wrote, "it is a punishment to be described, against your will, as a homosexual. The disgraceful reality is that it may cost people their jobs and expose them to abuse, ridicule, even violence." So Australians debated the merits of outing as this novel political tactic ruffled public life down under.

MAGIC JOHNSON, FREDDIE MERCURY, AND THE MEDIA

On November 7, 1991 Earvin "Magic" Johnson announced to the world that he was HIV-positive. The basketball superstar carefully insisted that he had contracted the virus from a woman. Since the African variant of AIDS is usually heterosexually transmitted, but the American one is not, the truth of his assertion may be disputed. But the mass media gave this "coming out" more attention than the deaths from AIDS of thousands of people who had contributed infinitely more to society–and might have done far more good had they lived–than the aging player. Activists were infuriated at this distortion of the importance of events: For years their outcries had gone unheeded–including their efforts to warn America that AIDS was spreading among racial minorities, mainly through IV-drug use. Now the media heralded as epoch-making what might otherwise have been filed away in Magic's private medical history.

Richard Rouilard wrote in the *Advocate* of December 17, 1991: "What we have the right to demand from this self-proclaimed spokesman for people with HIV is that he get beyond the divisiveness that he is, knowingly or unknowingly, promoting. We can demand that he cut the heterosexist garbage immediately . . . . Magic's assertions ad nauseam that he's 'not gay' strikes [sic] one of the nastiest chords played out in the AIDS tragedy yet–the notion that there are innocent and guilty victims of this worldwide pandemic." Randy Shilts had commented on the death of Kimberly Bergalis, an "innocent" girl purportedly infected by her dentist, in the same vein in an op-ed piece in *The New York Times,* "Good AIDS, Bad AIDS": "She mentioned how unfair it was that she had to suffer from AIDS even though she 'didn't do anything wrong.' With those words, she seemed to be separating those who don't deserve AIDS from those who do." Unfortunately this distinction is implanted in the popular mind and reinforced by religious traditions. Early in the epidemic medical personnel had dubbed the condition WOG (Wrath of God) by allusion to Romans 1:18: "The wrath of God is revealed from heaven against all unrighteousness of men." In this view homosexuals and IV-drug users are being punished for immoral behavior, while heterosexuals, hemophiliacs and others who acquire the disease through blood transfusions or in the womb are the "innocent victims" of others' wrongdoing.

A few weeks after Magic's disclosure, Freddie Mercury, the lead singer of the rock band Queen, became Britain's most famous casualty. A star of international renown, he died of AIDS-related pneumonia at the age of 45, only a day after he confessed that he too had the disease. AIDS groups declared that Mercury's case will make it easier for others to publicize that they are HIV-positive. Born Frederick Bulsara, a name which he long kept hidden, the scrawny musician with greasy hair studied music-hall kitsch and developed his own grand style. Because of his flamboyance with his Bechstein grand piano, Mercury has been dubbed "the Liberace of heavy metal." Having made it to the big time in England with the song "Keep Yourself Alive," his band first swept American audiences with "Killer Queen." Writing in the *Boston Phoenix* (December 6, 1991), the critic Michael Bloom pointed out that "by their name alone, suggesting either royalty or homophilia, Queen alerted you that they trafficked in ambiguities, embraced disparities, and reconciled contradictions in their art and their very being." He noted that each of Queen's most famous songs, "We are the Champions" and "We Will Rock You" "became both an anthem for gay solidarity and something to holler at sporting events–another contradiction they bridged with ease."

PETE WILSON'S BETRAYAL OF THE QUEER NATION

The veto by Governor Pete Wilson of the gay rights bill on September 29, 1991 triggered riots and demonstrations unparalleled in California since the assassination of Harvey Milk. It provoked not only violence but a reassessment of gay politics. And rightly so!

The former real estate salesman, who apparently had no principles or scruples beyond achieving success in sales and in elections, had deceived gay Republicans. As a gubernatorial candidate Wilson had promised the Log Cabin Club, the gay Republican group that had formed in California and was strongest there, that he would sign the measure into law. When the legislature did pass the bill, the religious right–well organized in the state–and other conservative homophobes generated a tremendous backlash. Although the gay lobby and liberals pressured the governor, he caved in to the other side and to caveats from Washington and vetoed it, in callous disregard of his solemn campaign promises.

When confronted by activists at Stanford, who were protesting his speech at the university, he had the temerity to call them fascists. The unscrupulous tactics of right-wing Republicans in California have been notorious since "Tricky Dick" Nixon first rose to fame by smearing Representatives Jerry Voorhis (1901-84) and Helen Gahagan Douglas (1900-80) as "fellow travelers." Ronald Reagan had also gained his political start by attacking Communists in the Actors' Guild, Hollywood's left-leaning union. Although Governor and then Chief Justice Earl Warren proved that there were liberal Republicans in California, the thrust of California Republicanism has been arch-conservative and homophobic. Republican Congressman Dannemeyer of California was the homophobe in the House of Representatives matching Jesse Helms in the Senate. Thus Wilson's betrayal shook Republicans' credibility among queer national voters across the nation, even in Massachusetts, whose Republican governor, William Weld, is the most sympathetic to gay rights the nation has yet seen.

The reaction propelled people into Queer Nation. As long-time activist Jim Kepner told us, its Los Angeles chapter was limping along until the veto, when its membership suddenly soared into the hundreds, and a similar reaction occurred the length and breadth of the state. There were nightly actions for weeks. The word "queer" had never been so popular among Californians. It was equally popular at the academic conference held at Rutgers in November 1991, as Wayne Dynes himself noted with some chagrin. If the group in Chicago is still languishing, as Paul Varnell reported to us, unlike the two coasts the midwestern heartland has never been in the forefront of the gay movement, even if it can thank the survival of the populist-progressive tradition of the early twentieth century for some firsts in practical achievement–enactment of desired legislation.

On May 15, 1992 the District of Columbia's Queer Nation chapter outed Anne-Imelda Radice, the new chair of the National Endowment for the Arts. The *Washington Post* on May 28 threatened to publicize the outing if she did anything "noteworthy," such as deny funding to a gay artist. In the meantime the *Advocate* was readying an article calling her "George Bush['s] new doormat homosexual" and quoting lesbian leader Vivian Shapiro who termed Radice "a lesbian from hell." Queer Nation's Margaret Cantrell said that Radice's lesbianism "is widespread knowledge. Mainstream reporters have confirmed it to me but they won't print it because of what they call 'the privacy issue'." Radice's lover, identified as Noel Brennan, is in the telephone book at the same address but under a different number. Radice is thus another queer national whom the Bush Administration allows to remain in office, presumably for obediently carrying out its conservative, homophobic policies (Wockner 1992).

CONCLUSION

The exposure of Pete Williams was spectacular. It may well be commemorated as having been overwhelmingly beneficial in its results. The episode took Signorile's career onto a new plateau, though he has not done much outing in the *Advocate*. It justified the long-term, strenuous efforts of Petrelis, who dogged the footsteps of the shrinking number of candidates in the 1992 primaries, even though Jerry Brown told him at a rally at Boston University when Petrelis asked him whether he practiced safe sex that he did not discuss his sexual life in public. If outing persists, as it undoubtedly will, the place of Signorile and Petrelis in the history of gay liberation is assured. Less visible but even more important benefits impend for millions of men and women in the American military, today and in the future. More than ever, a revision of the discriminatory policy seems inevitable, though a Democratic administration in Washington will probably be needed. The Williams outing may well prove to be the catalyst that brought to fruition this long-needed change, which Frank and Studds, the only openly gay members of the House, have been urging for several years. The coming out of "Magic" Johnson as HIV-positive and the death of a rock music star attracted even more attention among the masses.

Of course sharp differences of opinion on the merits of outing persist. Inasmuch as ours is a pluralistic society, no one reasonably expects unanimity on such a thorny issue among those most likely to be affected–or even among the least likely. Even queer nationalists debate whether to favor assimilation into existing society or defiance of its conventions on sex and gender. At all events, the socialist/communist option of the late 1960s no longer exists for the younger generation. For many heterosexuals the whole subject of attraction to one's own sex is still charged with negative feelings and beliefs. The path to full legal toleration and social acceptance remains a steep and challenging one. Perhaps we shall have to go our own way. As on other issues, political differences extend to both means and ends. Yet we can and must approach ours with as much finesse and sound judgment as we can muster. Long live Queer Nation!

REFERENCES

Advocate (Los Angeles).
Body Politic (Toronto).
Boston Phoenix.

Bronski, Michael. 1990. "The Power of the Closet." *Gay Community News,* no. 45, June 3-9, centerfold.

"Claiming Forbes for the Gay Nation" [Editorial]. 1990. *OutWeek,* no. 38, March 18, p. 5.

Cockburn, Alexander. 1991. "Gay Abandon." *New Statesman & Society,* August 23, p. 11.

Gay Community News (Boston).

Gelman, David. 1990. "'Outing': An Unexpected Assault on Sexual Privacy. Gay Activists Are Forcing Others Out of the Closet." *Newsweek,* April 30, p. 66.

Gross, Larry. 1991. "The Contested Closet: The Ethics and Politics of Outing." *Critical Studies in Mass Communication* 8: 352-388.

The Guide (Boston).

Guyon, René. 1929-38. *Etudes d'éthique sexuelle,* vols. 1-6. Saint-Denis: Dardaillon.

Hartman, Mitchell. 1990. "When to Say Someone Is Gay." *The Quill,* November-December, p. 6.

Henry, William A. III. 1991. "To 'Out' or Not to 'Out'." *Time,* August 19, p. 17.

Henry, William A. III. 1990. "Forcing Gays Out of the Closet." *Time,* January 29, p. 67.

Hirschfeld, Magnus. 1914. *Die Homosexualität des Mannes und des Weibes.* Berlin: Louis Marcus Verlagsbuchhandlung.

IN (Boston).

Kasindorf, Jeanie. 1990. "Mr. Out: A Gay Journalist's Campaign to Expose Famous Homosexuals Prompts Charges of McCarthyism." *New York,* May 14, pp. 84ff.

Kent, Chris. 1991. "Most of Press Declines to 'Out' DOD Official." *Washington Journalism Review,* October, pp. 13-14.

Leibowitz, Nicole. 1991. "Quand les gays se dénoncent entre eux." *Nouvel Observateur,* November 7-13, pp. 10-11.

Mills, Kim I. 1990. "Gays Crying 'Gay'." *Washington Journalism Review,* October, pp. 22-25.

Monroe, Bill. 1991. "The Press Respected Privacy–Twice." *Washington Journalism Review,* October, p. 6

OutWeek (New York).

Safire, William. 1990. "On Language: Outing." *New York Times Magazine,* May 6, p. 20.

Schafer, Jack. 1991. "Going on an Outing." *City Paper* (Washington, DC), July 12, p. 12.

Shilts, Randy. 1991. "Military May Defer Discharge of Gays." *San Francisco Chronicle,* January 11, p. A19.

Shilts, Randy. 1990. "Is 'Outing' Gays Ethical?" *New York Times,* April 12.

Signorile, Michelangelo. 1991. "The Outing of Assistant Secretary of Defense Pete Williams." *Advocate,* August 27.

Signorile, Michelangelo. 1990. "The Other Side of Malcolm." *OutWeek,* no. 38, March 18, pp. 40-45.

Sullivan, Andrew. 1991. "Sleeping with the Enemy." *New Republic,* September 9, p. 43.

Sydney Star Observer.

Udesky, Laurie. 1991. "Randy Shilts: 'For me, coming out was very political'." *Progressive,* May, pp. 30-32, 34.

Willrich, Michael. 1990. "Uncivil Disobedience." *Mother Jones,* November-December, p. 16.

Wockner, Rex. 1992. *"Washington Post* Prepared to 'Out' NEA Chair." *IN* (Boston), Issue 40, June 2-8, pp. 1, 20.

Chapter VII

To Out or Not to Out–
That Is the Question

THE CASE FOR OUTING

Activists could not out those still "in the closet" until they themselves were fully and unashamedly out. A critical mass began to form only after Stonewall. In the 1980s, activists began to argue that persons who have come out to themselves but not to the general public can have a negative impact on the welfare of other queer nationals.

This claim brings us to the heart of the matter. Are we merely individual "sinners" or "deviates," or do we form a community or even a "nation within a nation" with legitimate interests that the rest of society should recognize and respect? Are our sexual orientations superficial to the extent that they might be considered merely matters of taste or preference in a less prejudiced society or are they essential and fundamental? Would such differences, whether innate or acquired, remain the basis for a sort of ethnicity, even in a society that was not homophobic?

Clerics and rabbis and their medical, legal, and academic allies cling to the view that we are sinners, deviants, criminals or, at the very least, if not ill, immature and irresponsible. From this standpoint, those who practice outing are only sinners exposing other sinners to society's just reprobation. At this stage, gay liberationists might affirm the collective identity of their constituents and refuse to compromise with any person or institution that will not concede to us the rights of a legitimate community that is an enduring part of humanity. On the other hand, we might argue that we merely form a temporary group because of homophobia. If so, we must nevertheless not imagine that homophobia will disappear in the foreseeable future. The acknowledgement of such a common interest, even if it be only a result of intolerance, then imposes a duty on every member to work toward the goal of converting our pariah community into a prestigious one. Persecution doubtless strengthens collective identity.

Intolerance sought to blot homosexuals off the face of the earth, or at least to erase our names and memories from history. Such is the capacity of the religious mind for self-deception that some of the persecutors imagined that they had succeeded when they had only made us outcast and unseen. What then was their rage and disgust when they discovered to their horror that we still existed in huge numbers and had no intention of disappearing, and that we were even organizing to promote our rights and interests! The battle that commenced with the declaration of independence of the gay community, or more forcibly of the Queer Nation, from heterosexual society and its norms and values is ongoing, and will last far beyond the lives of the authors of this book—and indeed of its first readers. We of the Queer Nation are staging a two-front war against AIDS and against homophobia. Outing is a weapon in our struggle. The struggle began 129 years ago in Germany, was quenched in Hitler's death camps, was born anew in California, and took on a powerful and angry visibility in front of the Stonewall Inn. It is now being waged, in spite of the scourge of AIDS, or rather with greater urgency because of it, in every city and town where queer nationals courageously proclaim our identity and fight for our collective rights and dignity as well as for our lives.

According to Randy Shilts, a "truism to people active in the gay movement [is] that the greatest impediments to homosexuals' progress often [are] not heterosexuals, but closeted homosexuals":

> By definition, the homosexual in the closet [has] surrendered his integrity. This makes closeted people very useful to the establishment: once empowered, such people are guaranteed to support the most subtle nuances of anti-gay prejudice. A closeted homosexual has the keenest understanding of these nuances, having chosen to live under the subjugation of prejudice ... [and] is far less likely to demand fair or just treatment for his kind, because to do so would call attention to himself.

Thus gay activists should out closeted judges, politicians, journalists, and other movers and shakers. A hypothetical situation that might well legitimize or at least provoke an outing would be one in which a Supreme Court justice or any other judge who was gay, especially if still active or known to have been active before elevation to the bench, or who even merely enjoyed gay pornography, worked against gay interests. Such a judge voting to uphold the ban on homosexuals in the military, the ban on admitting HIV-positive aliens into the country, or the right of states to outlaw sodomy between consenting adults in private as in *Bowers* v. *Hardwick*, would be a hypocrite. Of course we should have to be sure that there was not some overriding legal technicality that would tie the judge's hand. But otherwise, such hypocrisy should not be tolerated to the extent of allowing it to perpetuate injustices to others of us. Such a character, especially one with life tenure, which most American judges have, should be outed as soon as possible, even if he (or she) is presently deciding *for* queer national interests, or does so occasionally, if only because it is time to make up for historians' failure thus far to identify even one gay Supreme Court justice.

In this regard the outing of any prominent or powerful closet case, even one who has never voted, worked, written, or spoken against gay interests, might be advisable. For example, if he had long been holding a top secret clearance or performing admirably some critical job for which queer nationals were normally deemed ineligible or morally unfit, we might out him merely to prove how wrong such suppositions are. Conscious acquiescence in homophobic policies or actions would make the case for outing such types even clearer. Bureaucrats have often hidden behind their gray flannel suits or colorful military uniforms, perjuring their sexual identity while routinely doing vast harm to others of their ilk, if only by dutifully administering or implementing homophobic policies. Examples of this might be Pete Williams, who was outed, or FBI Director J. Edgar Hoover, whose homosexuality is still denied by right-wing admirers. A homosexual in the military establishment who allows discrimination against other homosexuals to continue, is complicitous by his silence. Williams seems not to have instigated any such moves or policies, but Hoover did. Nevertheless, both merited outing.

Elected, as opposed to appointed or tenured homosexuals may have thought that they could do more good by staying in the closet. Candidates, it is true, often have to wear a mask (and not just over their sexuality) to win and retain office. Exposing them may well lead to their unseating in the next election, if not to their precipitate resignation or even suicide. Congressmen Frank and Studds are the only two who were outed (or in Frank's case, who came out to avoid being outed) yet were reelected to Congress–if we do not count Senators Mark Hatfield and Claiborne Pell and a number of representatives whose outings by Petrelis, our chief outer, were muted by lack of media coverage. And no one self-acknowledged as gay has ever been elected for the first time to a federal office or to a governorship or lieutenant governorship. Known homosexuals have recently been elected to state legislatures in increasing numbers, of whom Elaine Noble of Massachusetts and Alan Spear of Minnesota were the first. Winthrop Rockefeller of Arkansas, Jim Thompson of Illinois, and Evelyn Murphy, lieutenant governor of Massachusetts, were outed while in office. But many outed officials denied the charges, which in any case received little attention.

THE GAMUT OF OPTIONS

Virtually all who have taken a position on outing have qualified their approval or disapproval to some degree. At their opposing poles, the theoretical views might be formulated as follows: "No one should be outed against his or her own wishes, not even the dead. I would not out my worst enemies, even as a last-ditch action to prevent them from scoring a decisive victory over me"; or "Everyone should be outed, whether he or she wishes to be or not. I would out my best friends, even if this action threatened their careers and brought them to the brink of suicide." Very few have in fact seriously championed either extreme.

In fact, our community today holds four principal viewpoints on the advisability of outing: (1) *hypocrites* only, and then solely when they actively oppose gay rights and interests; (2) these last plus *passive accomplices* who support a homophobic institution, like Father Ritter or Jim Bakker the Catholic or Baptist churches, or Pete

Williams the Pentagon; (3) *prominent individuals*–well-known and influential authors, professors, lawyers, physicians, businessmen, and sports and media figures whose outing would shatter stereotypes and compel the public to reconsider its attitude because their being in the closet allows prejudice to flourish; or (4) solely *the dead*.

These four and the further nuances that lie between the hypothetical antipodes of opinion reflect differing perceptions of the responsibility of the individual and the consequences of the outing. Is outing a violation of journalistic ethics and of the privacy of the individuals so exposed, or is it a weapon that the spokesmen for a still largely invisible minority must use in order to end its oppression and defamation? Will the act irreparably harm the outee's income, career, family, lover, health, or very life? Will it make him or her more glamorous? Will it hinder the aims of our movement or further them? What are the motives of the outer: envy, jealousy, spite–or altruism, duty, and queer nationalism? What of the problem that friends of those outed because their views are deemed "politically incorrect" may out others on the opposite side of the political spectrum in a never-ending cycle of bitter recriminations?

Outing No One

Counting the two extremes and four basic intermediate positions, there are thus six hypothetical positions in regard to outing, which we shall now explore in further detail.

The first–which few now actually suggest in earnest, although some Christian authors who would obliterate even our memory uphold this principle–indeed, practice it–is to out no one: to hide homosexuals from history (Duberman 1989). This would mean denying or ignoring the evidence for the homosexuality even of those who died ages ago. Such a policy is unthinkable to the authors of this book. Yet this deliberate obliteration of the past, which may well have begun in Hellenistic Judaism, as suggested by omissions in the book of Chronicles (Dion 1981, pp. 47-48), is still perpetuated by many scholars, including closeted ones, who lock the subject of their studies into the closet with themselves, so traducing the Queer Nation.

In the spring of 1990 a forum of long-time homophile activists in Los Angeles discussed outing. They included Harry Hay, one of the founders of the Mattachine Society, Morris Kight, a member of the board of Christopher Street West, which stages the annual Gay Pride parade, and Don Slater, keeper of one of the biggest gay archives. Among their principal conclusions, even the generally unsympathetic old-timers had to concede, was that an outee was in far less jeopardy in the United States today than he (or she) would have been 30 years ago, when with greater reason the code of silence went unchallenged. So outing conforms more to the mood and the political arsenal of the new generation of activists ("Symposium on Outing," 1990). The founders of the movement, had they so much as attempted in 1951 what Queer Nation blithely did in 1991, would have been jailed, physically assaulted, or even murdered in cold blood on the street—with the indifference or collusion of the police. So the controversy sets the older, more cautious age cohort in opposition to the bolder, far more self-assured queer nationals of the 1990s, just as it highlights the conflict between privacy and gay nationhood.

Outing Only the Dead

The second position is that only the dead should be outed, since they cannot personally suffer from the revelation or sue for libel or slander (that the dead cannot be libeled is a legal maxim). Outing the dead would seem at first glance to be harmless and unthreatening. But those whom they have left behind—spouses, children and grandchildren, siblings, nieces and nephews, business associates, and perhaps most of all, lovers or even casual partners—could be harmed. How long after an individual's demise may the outing most legitimately be done? Can it be in the obituary published the day after in the local newspaper? Or should one wait months, years, even decades before outing the deceased? The problem there is that the subject's fame and importance may have so faded that he might as well never have lived at all—so that the outing is otiose. On the other hand, someone little known when alive may gain in renown and attention, so that the outing will cause history and literary biography to be rewritten.

The question was in fact posed by the outing of Malcolm Forbes in *OutWeek* the week after his death–violating as it were the principle *de mortuis nil nisi bonum* (of the dead [say] nothing but good). On the other hand, the opposite maxim holds: *On doit des égards aux vivants; aux morts on ne doit que la vérité* (one owes respect to the living; to the dead one owes only the truth). Of course, outing the dead is essential to the progress of gay studies, as the old-timers know, busily searching as they have been for decades as far back as David and Jonathan and Achilles and Patroclus. There may well be cases where it might be more admirable to wait until their families and companions would suffer less. At a large public meeting in June of 1990 at Faneuil Hall in Boston, Barney Frank rashly opposed outing even the dead. But when queried by Percy, he said: "I guess the dead have fewer rights than the living." Trying desperately to put the genie that he had helped escape back into the bottle, Barney had not thought this issue through. Earlier, however, he had threatened to out gay Republican congressmen if the Republicans did not stop the gossip that Tom Foley, the new Democratic Speaker in the House, was gay–which Frank denied, though Petrelis maintains that he is. The congressman repeated the old saw that one does not truly believe in a right (privacy) unless others are allowed to exercise it in a manner that runs contrary to one's own convictions. Therefore he opposed outing all except the most arrant hypocrites–a viewpoint that is steadily winning gay adherents and may now have a majority behind it, although it hardly satisfies the demands of Queer Nation.

Lacking outings of the dead, of course, we should have little basis for the study of our own past, and the writing of gay history would become impossible. Remote as their deeds may be from the immediate concerns of the living, outing the dead has a significance of its own. The theologically motivated campaign against homosexuality has entailed a far-reaching suppression of the historic role of individuals more attracted to their own sex than to the other. The importance of *paiderasteia* in Hellenic civilization was blacked out in works other than those printed for classicists in editions of 600 copies–often in Latin! Biographies were rewritten and falsified to deny the sexual interests of their subjects and to involve them in imaginary heterosexual relationships. Major figures in political or cultural history, from Sappho, Alexander the Great, and Julius Caesar to Melville, Whitman, and Emily Dickinson, were portrayed as exclusively heterosexual, asexual, or having "sublimated" their sexual urges. Heroes that every schoolchild was taught to admire had the homoerotic side of their lives suppressed. Textbooks and standard reference works–too numerous to mention here–will all have to be revised to erase this Orwellian falsification and bring them into harmony with the truth. This task alone will provide work for at least a generation of historians and literary critics.

It has been claimed that even long-deceased persons should not be outed inasmuch as they have no way of defending themselves by "setting the record straight" in case the ascription is wrong. At a certain point, however, as the individual recedes into the past and his (or her) associates vanish, does it not then become proper to suggest the awful truth, even if the evidence for it is equivocal–as it often is, given the customary efforts to destroy and deny it–before that evidence is lost without a trace?

Almost every major book ever written on homosexuality has had its lists of the great and near-great. There have been biographical compendia, ranging from Albert Moll's *Berühmte Homosexuelle* (1910) to Noel I. Garde's (pseudonym) *Jonathan to Gide* (1964) and A. L. Rowse's *Homosexuals in History* (1987), that celebrated, in not always critical or insightful fashion, the great figures of history whose lives included homosexual episodes. Such lists are not easily compiled. It is extremely difficult to prove that historical figures of the Western world were homosexual or bisexual; almost all, except the pagan Greeks and Romans, hid their proclivities and actions in every possible way. Thus it is imperative to out as many as we can who died in recent decades, where the evidence is fresh and, because of the waning of intolerance and persecution, not so carefully hidden. No one can legitimately object in any convincing fashion to outing the dead after an appropriate lapse of time. This interval may last for decades if, for example, publicity would greatly harm the deceased's life companions.

Outing someone whose career had been wholly undistinguished– the neighborhood mailman or the corner grocer–would be pointless. The only characters really worth outing would be ones that had achieved at least fleeting celebrity or left their mark in some note-worthy endeavor. The most desirable targets of all would be the great and memorable. Mere celebrities of the hour, for whom press agents conjured up romances to fill the gossip columns, will in the long run pale beside those who "had one hand in heaven to write their names in leaves of stars." It is the outing of these above all that can provoke a still intolerant society to rage and intervention.

John Addington Symonds (1840-93), under the influence of Karl Heinrich Ulrichs, was perhaps the first in the English-speaking world to become almost what would later be styled a "gay activist." He came out in the older manner–and to his own detriment, resulting in his failure to secure a chair at Oxford–in his *Studies in the Greek Poets* (1875), and then posthumously in the German translation of the book which he coauthored with the pioneer British sexologist Havelock Ellis, *Das konträre Geschlechtsgefühl* (1896). But his heirs put the corpse back into the closet by forcing Ellis to remove the name of the deceased from the title page of *Sexual Inversion* (1897). Symonds' *Problem in Greek Ethics* and *Problem in Modern Ethics* were privately printed volumes that pleaded for toleration.

The late southern novelist and philosopher Walker Percy in 1989 and 1990 attempted to put his first cousin once removed and adoptive father William Alexander Percy (1885-1942), who had come out in the old way, in the subtle allusions in his poetry and in his best-selling autobiography, *Lanterns on the Levee* (1941), back into the closet. Walker Percy and his brothers withheld pertinent data from Bertrand Wyatt-Brown, who is doing a book on the family for Oxford University Press and trying to discover hereditary or at least intergenerational family traits. Of these homosexuality is one of the most striking in the Percy clan. Lest homophobic family members retaliate by withdrawing permission to use private papers, Wyatt-Brown seems reluctant to publish the truth which had been supplied him, among others, by Shelby Foote, one of "Uncle Will's" protégés, and by William A. Percy, III, coauthor of this book, who is as closely related by blood to "Uncle Will" as were Walker and his brother.

One of the topics still taboo is the homosexuality of American presidents. Charley Shively has just outed George Washington and his circle (Shively, forthcoming) and Abraham Lincoln (Shively 1989). Earlier, Ernest Hemingway and Carl Sandberg had both intimated that Lincoln had homosexual involvements as a young man. Buchanan, the only president who never married, is the most common candidate. While in the White House, which he decorated lavishly with Second Empire furniture, he was openly ridiculed as "Miss Nancy" for associating too much with another middle-aged man. Recently Robert I. Cottom (1975) found evidence that James Garfield may have had a prolonged affair with a male. When Percy and Shively discussed these four ostensibly queer presidents at the American Historical Association meeting in New York in December 1990, a great-great nephew of Buchanan's disclosed to the gathering that the family had told him that the President was attracted to other males.

Jim Kepner, who was present, stated that he has material in the International Gay and Lesbian Archives that may in one way or another implicate 12 to 14 presidents. The lesbian affair of Eleanor Roosevelt, perhaps the most politically active and influential of all first ladies, was brought to light (Cook 1992) with as hysterical an opposition as the outings of presidents have provoked. The newest revelation is Gore Vidal's outing of Franklin Pierce.

The tenacity of homophobia is shown by the insistence with which those still under its spell deny or ridicule the evidence for the homosexuality of great or significant figures of the past. And families, even generations later, will deliberately put obstacles in the path of those seeking the truth. This is, to be sure, just another form of the monumental dishonesty and hypocrisy which the Christian tradition imposed not just on homosexuals, but on the whole of society. The crime of darkening and destroying the lives of those who loved their own sex it compounded by a crime against the truth: plunging the entire social order into a morass of lies and falsehoods in regard to sexuality.

While the dead cannot sue for libel, their homophobic, hypocritical friends, relatives, and admirers bent on preserving their (allegedly) tarnished reputations can put obstacles in the outer's path. But as time passes, all who linger in the closet will have the mounting reproach of cowardice to face, even after their deaths. They will not be able to say to the court of public opinion, like the veterans of ACT UP and Queer

Nation: "In the moment of crisis we proved ourselves equal to the challenge that confronted us; in the hour of trial we were weighed in the balance and not found wanting. Through ages after ages our spiritual descendants will rise up, will remember our deeds, and bless our memory. But those who shirked the call of duty and self-affirmation will escape the scorn of posterity only if they find refuge in a merciful oblivion."

Outing Only Hypocrites

The third position, which has found much favor, is that of outing only hypocrites–closet cases who defame and persecute other queer nationals while secretly indulging–in order to destroy their influence and perhaps also to punish them for their insolence. They, it is felt, have violated their claim to personal privacy by their public, political activity. As Barney Frank has said: "There's a right to privacy but not to hypocrisy." Many believe that one should out only those who publicly and by using their influence oppose queer rights or interests–arch-hypocrites. Such persons forfeit their privacy when their clandestine conduct invalidates their public utterances: for example, Robert E. Bauman (R., Maryland), who routinely voted against measures favored by the gay lobby in Washington; or, more prominently, Roy F. Cohn, Senator Joseph R. McCarthy's aide, who furthered his career by outing others who then lost their jobs and were branded as "security risks." This principle would presumably exempt such figures as press magnate Malcolm Forbes, whose publications never intentionally defamed or harmed other homosexuals, or Pete Williams who, so far as we know, never personally did or said anything against others of his kind.

In a phone conversation with William A. Percy in November 1991, Frank Kameny stated this position eloquently. He claimed that three conditions should be met before a person was outed. First, the outee should have a clear and well-established pattern of homophobic pronouncements and/or actions. Second, the evidence should not be mere gossip but should be well substantiated and convincing. Third, the person should be warned in advance and allowed the opportunity to cease the offensive conduct and *if possible* to repent past errors and come out voluntarily. Kameny's thoughtful conditions will seem very reasonable to many, but too lenient and perhaps too gradualist to others, especially because his third requirement might allow a reformed closet case to stay *in camera*.

To expose a hypocrite is to remove a needless obstacle from the path of the queer nation. The criteria for outing the living are therefore overwhelmingly utilitarian rather than vindictive. If you are one of us, you must further our interests or we will out you. If you belong to the freemasonry of homoeroticism, you are bound by its discipline. If you violate and betray it, you can expect to be outed. But who is to judge and what will be the court's criteria? Moreover, unlike members of the Masonic Order or the Third International, queer nationals have not taken an oath to loyalty to any mythical "Homintern." We are therefore under no obligation to adhere to restrictions that others deem wise. Perhaps the most conclusive argument against the attempt to ban outing is the old cry of the French revolutionaries: "*Ça ira,*" it will go on. Only the media can frustrate outings by blacking them out in turn.

Outing Collaborationists

The fourth position, which provokes a great deal of ambivalence, is that of outing those who function as passive accomplices of homophobic institutions and oppose gay rights. Although they are no better than quislings, a case of this sort raises grave problems. Such an institution is likely to fire an outee or pressure him into resigning. Although judges and professors who work for what might be deemed homophobic institutions usually have tenure, and bureaucrats generally have civil service protection, the average employee in a law firm, brokerage house, bank, newspaper or other business does not have such protection unless it be written into a union contract, local ordinance or state statute. Most are thus unprotected from retaliation.

Signorile did not know that Williams would be able to retain his job when he outed him, yet he felt that it was more important to demonstrate the hypocrisy and stupidity of the military's policies than to protect Williams' privacy and career. A great many activists likewise maintain that no matter what the consequences to the outee, those working for homophobic institutions are ipso facto collaborationists and should therefore be outed, regardless of the consequences to them, for the good of the queer nation. Others hold that one should not out those whose careers or positions the revelation would destroy–Southern Baptist preachers, Catholic clergy, military careerists, certain politicians, or any others in sensitive posts–*if* they adroitly support us without identifying themselves to their constituents, if they operate as a fifth column within these institutions. To end their effectiveness would, it is held, deprive our community of an invaluable corps of clandestine activists.

Outing Prominent Individuals

The case for outing those who in no positive way are damaging the gay nation, either by attacking other queers from the closet or by working for homophobic institutions, may be stronger than it appears at first sight. A respected author or professional, a matinee idol or athlete, a rock star or a popular talk show host, in other words anyone at all who might serve as a role model or shatter a long-standing stereotype might be outed regardless of how cooperative the person has been, unless, of course, outing would destroy the subject's proven effectiveness in furthering our cause.

On first glance, one might consider that an individual's right to privacy might outweigh the advantages derived from his or her outing. But the reluctance of truly prominent individuals from each and every walk of life to come out may prevent the ordinary queer national from gaining toleration, much less acceptance. If the most prominent, respected, and venerable homosexuals and bisexuals insist on remaining in the closet, as indeed almost all do, we can never point to a sufficient number of live role models, especially for today's historically illiterate, celebrity-minded, sports- and entertainment-oriented youth, and thereby also disprove the demeaning stereotypes that continue to circulate about us, even among the educated. For example, stockbrokers often brag that no gay stockbrokers exist, as others do about their groups or professions. Though their ranks are often rife with invisible queers, they insist that we only become hairdressers, nurses, interior decorators, fashion designers, or perhaps organists. Many still believe that most female construction workers, truck drivers, gym teachers, and military personnel are lesbians. If people whose coming out would shatter the stereotype refuse to do so and hence are disloyal to our common interest, they must be outed for the sake of the queer nation, especially if they are given a warning and some time to come out on their own.

It has been objected that closeted celebrities who lead "private" lives are not harming anyone. But they benefit from the movement that they scorn, simply because they can live much fuller, far less anxiety-ridden lives while we fight daily against intolerance. Their indifference provokes the ressentiment of activists who take on all the risks and disadvantages of participation in the movement.

There are some who remain in the closet but quietly do whatever they can to further the gay cause without becoming too conspicuous. An example would be a police officer who warned gay patrons about forthcoming bar raids or other roundups or entrapments. To out them would be foolish because at this stage they might be fired or at the very least hindered in the performance of their clandestine mission.

Outing Everyone

The sixth option is to out all identifiable lovers of their own sex. This is hardly practical, given the problem of defining who is homosexual (or bisexual) and securing the necessary evidence. Such a vision has been cherished at times by activists who fantasied that if only everyone could be involuntarily outed–perhaps by a sudden change of skin color to violet or deep purple, according to the degree of their homosexuality on the Kinsey scale–then a hitherto intolerant society would be dumbfounded by the sheer numbers and perceive the futility of its present beliefs and practices. But such an event will remain forever in the realm of the Arabian Nights. A few radicals might wish to out everyone–no exceptions!–in order to shock heterosexuals with the revelation of how many everyday people as well as idols of the masses are queer nationals. However, if AIDS continues unabated and the death toll in the United States rises to 200,000, the possibility might arise of outing every identifiable person with a peremptory demand to aid the Queer Nation's life-and-death struggle, like the *levée en masse* (national draft of every able-bodied male) of 1792 that saved the French Revolution.

If queer nationals were in such massive evidence, every city, town, and hamlet would have to face the fact that we are everywhere.

Much of the strength of our nation arguably lies in its very invisibility, with nine-tenths submerged like an iceberg: its ability to influence events unobtrusively, to sit on both sides of the table in crucial negotiations, to be seemingly absent yet omnipresent. To out the influential among us who, working behind the scenes, are benevolent toward their fellows could diminish their usefulness and their ability to further collective interests. Nevertheless visibility is crucial. Outing must continue, even if with discretion.

CLAIM TO PRIVACY

A great many, if a dwindling number, of activists still maintain that because our movement has raised the claim of privacy–and tried, albeit unsuccessfully, to extend it from birth control to homosexuality, as in *Bowers* v. *Hardwick*–it is wrong to out any living person. In this connection, the French theoretician of sexual freedom René Guyon stressed in the 1930s that everyone is entitled to have a rigorous veil of secrecy drawn over his sexual conduct. Gossip and talebearing are reprehensible. Everyone should be answerable solely to his own conscience on the issue of coming out, which always impacts others, many of whom, even though heterosexual, will be at least obliquely affected.

Professor Richard D. Mohr discussed the sexual aspect of privacy in *Gays/Justice*:

> The sexual realm is inherently private. The sex act creates its own sanctuary which in turn is necessary for its success. The whole process and nature of sex is interrupted and destroyed if penetrated by the glance of an intruder–unless that glance itself becomes incorporated in the process just described. The gazes of non-participants in sex are not the harmless matrix of intersecting looks of the marketplace or town meeting, which, by virtue of their very complexity, cancel each other out like randomly intersecting waves. Rather, being viewed by an uninvited other is as intrusive in sex as the telephone ringing. (Mohr 1988, p. 103)

An issue troubling many is: if the privacy claimed by the gay movement is an absolute right, what justification can there be for overriding it, even for the good of the group? The Supreme Court in *Griswold* v. *Connecticut* (1965) established a right of sexual privacy which created the possibility that homosexual conduct might be included under the cloak which the court extended to heterosexual behavior within marriage. However precious in its own right, privacy clashes with the call from queer nationals not only to punish traitors and passive fellow travelers but for greater visibility in order to overcome and discredit defamatory stereotypes.

Privacy, as it relates to homosexual activity, has two distinct strata and five historical oppositions. It originated in the fundamental opposition made by the ancient Greeks and Romans between the private and the public person (*idiōtikos/dēmosios, privātus/publicus*). Not accidentally, the word *privātus* is cognate with *privilēgium,* "a law enacted to the detriment or for the benefit of a private person, a special right, prerogative or privilege"(*Oxford Latin Dictionary,* p. 1461). Whoever enters public life forfeits a significant element of his privacy, in fact relishes and craves the attention of *society* if not of the *state*. The ancient distinction was exactly between the citizen who minded only his private affairs and the one who participated in the political life of the city-state.

A primary notion rooted in the deep structure of Western *society* is that sexual behavior should be hidden from all except the participants. Its corollary is that sexual activity is obscene and unmentionable in society. Reinforcing and yet contradicting this imperative are the infamy which the Western church caused society to attach to homosexual activity, even in private, and the right of the *state* to enforce sexual morality even by violating the privacy of the participants (recently confirmed by the Supreme Court in *Bowers* v. *Hardwick*).

All these factors caused lovers of their own sex to conceal their sexual identity and activity from a condemnatory society and state, falsifying our public image in self-defense against intolerance.

Another stratum involves the concept of privacy as a right interposed between the state and its citizens. This secondary form of sexual privacy was a recent innovation in criminal law in opposition to the state's supposed right or duty to enforce sexual morality.

At the same time, two new oppositions to privacy and its derivatives have emerged: the political belief that homosexuals (queer nationals), particularly celebrities, should reveal our identity to society; and the right or duty of the scholar to reveal to society the truth about the sexual lives of historical figures (to out the dead).

Thus there are five oppositions:

"*primary* sexual privacy (as custom)"	vs.	"the right of the state to enforce sexual morality"
"being in the closet"	vs.	"infamy"
"*secondary* sexual privacy (as right)"	vs.	"the right of the state to enforce sexual morality"
"being in the closet"	vs.	"coming out"
"unmentionability"	vs.	"the right to tell the truth"

Hence in sexual life the private/public distinction is not a hard and fast line of demarcation, but has evolved around multiple and incongruous contradictions in the political, legal and academic realms.

Privacy is a more complex subject than previous authors (Mohr 1988, pp. 71-76, 94-126) have assumed. "The sociology of knowledge has in no way merely the sociology of the knowledge of truth, but also the sociology of social delusion, of superstition, sociologically determined errors and forms of deception as its object" (Scheler 1960, p. 63). Privacy in fact results from the superimposing of a formal-semantic concept upon a notion latent in social psychology. The term *privacy* is unique to the English language: the major languages of the Continent have no equivalent. Where international agreements have the English word *privacy,* the corresponding French term is *vie privée.* This fact is all the more striking as the word itself, though of classical origin, did *not* exist in Greek or Latin. The semantic range of *privatus* is not identical with the later English meaning of *privacy,* or even *in private* as contrasted with *in public.* All these expressions first appear only in Renaissance England, in the Early Modern English of the Elizabethan era (*OED2* 12, 515-19). This late origin means that these concepts are not to be found in law texts of the Angevin or Plantagenet periods and did not immediately enter the common law. Privacy as a designation of the sphere of life that is closed to the public and hidden from it, as a

sense of being in a space where one is unseen and therefore uncon-
strained by others' notice or censure, is culture-specific and peculiar to the English language. "The related concepts of private and
public are rich in emotional associations of a complicated and contradictory kind, and are used in connection with a wide range of
social referents" (Madge 1950, p. 191). Only in the eighteenth
century did privacy enter British law, and then in a limited civil
application.

The definition of privacy is elusive, multidimensional and not
easily reducible to a single opposition. All privacy is tantamount to
a right of concealment by socially sanctioned mechanisms (Jourard
1966, p. 307; Lundsgaarde 1971, pp. 872-73). Privacy amounts to a
"zero relationship" between two persons or between a person and a
group. It is constituted by the denial of interaction, communication,
or perception in contexts where such an interface can be and is
accorded to others (Shils 1966, p. 282). Privacy is the outcome of
the wish to withhold from others knowledge of one's past and
present experience, status, and actions and one's intentions for the
future (Jourard 1966, p. 307) and to retain the option of communi-
cating such information to others. It fulfills a genuine psychological
need for a locus where the self is inaccessible to others except at
one's own invitation, a place for solitude or for communion solely
with others who share one's innermost values and feelings (Jourard
1966, p. 310). Privacy thus furnishes an "offstage" area where one
is relieved of the burden of playing the role scripted by society. Just
as the actor or actress must rest during the day in order to perform
convincingly on the stage in the evening, so the role player in a
social scene must be able to retreat into a space where he can both
recover from the tension that he endures in public and assume the
role dictated by his own inner consciousness (Freund 1971, p. 195;
Jourard 1966, pp. 310-11, 316). Differing from one culture to another, rules governing privacy amount to a tacitly accepted code for
interrupting or suspending a relationship, for lowering the curtain on
one social performance and raising it on another.

In all societies one discloses one's private self to those whom one
perceives as trustworthy, as capable of an intimate liaison, and as
willing to reveal themselves in equal depth and breadth (Jourard
1966, p. 311). Withdrawal into privacy often is "a means of making

life with an unbearable (or sporadically unbearable) person" or group possible. The ability to "close the door" on others, even members of one's immediate family, is a technique for avoiding confrontation and conflict (Schwartz 1968, p. 741).

The physical symbol of privacy is the inner door, in contrast to the outer door meant to keep out intruders and protect life and property. It must have originated among those who already possessed such a sense of individuation from kith and kin that they could feel oppression by the presence of others and the need for isolation from them. The very act of closing a door that cannot be opened except by the leave of those behind it grants release from a role and the identity which others impose upon the role player (Schwartz 1968, p. 747). Private life has three aspects: (1) privacy in regard to relationships with other people such as neighbors, (2) privacy within the home, and (3) privacy in the physical sense of not being under others' watchful or chance observation (Willis 1963, p. 1138). Even within a household there are "gradations of privacy, both in relation to neighbours and as between members of the family" (Madge 1950, p. 197) and rather explicit rules as to what doors may be opened and at what hours. The parent reserves the right to enter the child's room and examine the contents of drawers, but the child may not similarly infringe the privacy of the parents' bedroom, office, or safe (Schwartz 1968, pp. 748-749). Parental recognition of the adolescent's right to engage in sexual activity often takes the form of allowing the youngster to spend the night with a partner behind the locked door of his (or her) bedroom or to have drawers and closets that no other family member can enter or search.

Society requires that the role of lover, of sexual actor, be assumed only "behind closed doors," outdoors but hidden in woods, or "under cover of darkness," where there can be no audience. The voyeur experiences a pathological, compulsive desire to see, by stealth, others in some stage of undress or in the sexual act, a craving so intense that it surpasses in importance the sexual act itself (Yalom 1960, p. 305). The voyeur's victim is outraged at having been viewed in a role in which one ordinarily desires no spectator. In the past individuals engaging in homosexual activity usually opted to disclose the fact solely to others equally compromised in the eyes of society–and certainly not to the authorities of the church or the state whose duty it was to ferret out and punish such activity. Only in privacy could one drop the heterosexual role demanded by society and give vent to one's true feelings. The governing principle was *bene vixit qui bene latuit*, "he lived well who hid well" (Middleton 1935, p. 329). Each time one person revealed homosexual desires to another, a secret society was born (Jourard 1966, p. 313). The need to have other homosexuals in one's social environment was prompted by the measure of relief that the "glass closet" (a situation in which the homoerotic procliv- ities of others are tacitly assumed but rarely if ever mentioned) at least afforded from the burden of constantly projecting a false image in order to deceive potentially hostile others. The network of members of those secret conclaves, the freemasonry of forbidden love, was compelled to maintain a "zero relationship" with hetero- sexual society because of the latter's undisguised hatred and merci- less intolerance. The coercive practices of the one imposed clandes- tinity on the other, and forced the homosexual and bisexual to become accomplices in perpetuating the illusion of a nonhomo- sexual universe. The resistance to politicization of the crypto-ho- mosexual subculture stemmed in large part from the unwillingness of its denizens to make a public issue of what they deemed an entirely private affair. Even today, those who question the need for statutory safeguards against invasion of privacy tacitly assume that such intru- sion is objectively impossible without the active collusion "of those willing to make public disclosure of private facts" (Lundsgaarde 1971, p. 875).

A stable social order must have guarantees of privacy, that is, rules about who may and who may not observe or reveal informa- tion about whom. Lacking these norms, every withdrawal from visibility may be accompanied by a measure of attempted surveil- lance. Where privacy is denied, its attainment becomes a matter of stealth and deception (Schwartz 1968, p. 742). Islands of privacy exist in all institutions and even in the most intimate households. Such islands are protected by an intricate set of rules, and when these rules are violated, the denizens seek and discover secret places where they can engage in covert activity (Schwartz 1968, p. 750). No society can, even if it wishes, obliterate all privacy. Walls, fences and doors create private, inaccessible spaces reinforced by social norms that deny access to the unwanted–with the exception of the secret police or the vice squad. Save in George Orwell's fantasy world of *1984,* the authorities cannot gain access to everyone's life at every moment; they cannot saturate the territory of the state with hidden cameras and listening devices so that not one act or utterance goes unmonitored and unrecorded. Even the political elites of the most inquisitorial, totalitarian regimes understood that complete surveillance lay beyond their grasp (Shils 1966, p. 288), though they went so far as to encourage children to denounce their parents as "enemies of the people." However, the network of spies and informers through whom the absolute rulers of antiquity kept a watchful eye on their subjects inspired the belief in a God who is–a philosophical impossibility–both omniscient (Zechariah 4:10) and omnipotent.

A derivative of privacy is discretion, a quality which the private person has a right to demand of others who are privileged to invade his or her seclusion (Schwartz 1968, p. 748 and n. 33). This has been a crucial aspect of homosexual existence: if one was to survive in heterosexual society, knowledge of one's true orientation had to be kept within the invisible community of one's peers. One was forbidden to approach other members of it openly and tactlessly, as such indiscrete acts could expose one's own as well as their masquerade and deception. Likewise a homosexual affair had to be conducted far more unobtrusively, indeed, secretly, than a heterosexual one. Partners who had spent the night in bed together might interact as virtual strangers the next day at work or at an office party.

Privacy is not a psychological given: it is rather a privilege that society accords to different individuals in varying degrees (Schwartz 1968, p. 744). It is always conditioned by the technological possibilities of inquiry and surveillance. The privacy of the upper social strata is ensured by structural arrangements. They not only live and work apart from others, but often can be reached only through subordinates–secretaries, assistants, orderlies and the like (Schwartz 1968, pp. 742-43). Lower-class residences are often characterized not only by crowding and enforced intimacy but even by lack of doors. In such an environment privacy is virtually impossible (Madge 1950, p. 190). The ability to invade privacy also reflects status. The provision of the

Hippocratic Oath that forbids the physician sexual commerce with "free persons or slaves, female or male" limits his right to ignore boundaries of privacy in observing and examining the bodies of complete strangers of either sex in the exercise of his calling (Schwartz 1968, p. 743).

Modern technology has radically redefined the privacy of public records. It is one thing to travel to a distant city to leaf through files of yellowing documents taken from the locked archives of a court or a bank and quite another to press the right buttons and instantly "access" a bank account, credit rating, or arrest record. High-powered camera lenses and minuscule listening devices can render seeming privacy illusory. Almost 25 years ago laboratory models showed the feasibility of storing on one 4800-foot reel of one-inch material the equivalent of a 20-page dossier on every one of the 200 million people in this country (Freund 1971, pp. 188, 193-94 and n. 14). The new computer chip to be developed by IBM, Toshiba, and Siemens will no doubt be able to "do more with less."

Inmates of total institutions–ones that attempt to control every aspect of their inmates' lives, such as prisons, mental hospitals, military bases–characteristically have little or no privacy, and therefore are forbidden to engage in sexual activity of any kind. In a prison, ironically enough, the only locus of privacy is solitary confinement–which incarcerated pederasts and pedophiles often request for self-protection. The superiors or keepers of such institutions have a right to maintain a relentless surveillance over their charges at all times. It is curious that Jeremy Bentham, the pioneer advocate of tolerance of homosexual expression in the English-speaking world, also invented the Panoptikon, a prison in which the staff could at every moment observe the inmates from a convenient vantage point. Those who have the least privacy of all are celebrities who run afoul of the law (such as Nixon's accomplices in Watergate) and are sent to total institutions where they suffer not only the usual deprivation of personal invisibility but also exposure to hundreds of millions of eyes by hostile media gloating over their downfall. The run-of-the-mill convict is not so publicly humiliated because he is little more than a number in the prison records.

Bourgeois individualism and the limitations which liberalism imposed on the state reinforced privacy as a cultural norm. It was the negation of it by the printing press, and the modern concept of the celebrity, that first reactivated the notion of privacy in civil law. The term *célébrité* in the modern sense first appears in French about 1829 (*Trésor de la Langue Française* 5, p. 359), the English equivalent some twenty years later (*OED2* 2, p. 1019). Another 40 years and the invention of instantaneous photography saw the article by Brandeis and Warren in the first volume of *Harvard Law Review* (1890) in which privacy, defined in overly general but meaningful terms as "the right to be let alone," was invoked against the yellow press of that day (Lusky 1972, pp. 192, 195). All these decisions and arguments pertained to civil law, not to criminal. Subsequently, and in the other direction, legal decisions virtually stripped celebrities of their privacy by reasoning that the individual who enters the public arena and courts the attention of the masses is thereby renouncing privacy and all claim to be ignored and unnoticed. Those at the center of society are legitimate objects of curiosity to those on the periphery.

Celebrities voluntarily renounce privacy by courting public attention. At the same time, however, they either interpose physical barriers (such as estates with high walls and armed guards) between themselves and the prying media, or create a façade of private life by means of press agents and cleverly arranged public appearances, interviews, and biographical articles. The courts have affirmed this loss of privacy by severely limiting their recourse in cases of libel and slander.

In a democratic society, the more exalted or sensitive a public office, the more closely will the holders be scrutinized by the media (Freund 1971, p. 187), and the more deeply will their private selves be encapsulated in the impenetrable armor of their public personae. Increased leisure and idle hedonism on the part of those without sufficient education or intelligence "to expand the radius of their interest or imagination beyond their neighbors, beyond the personal onto a more transcendent level" (Shils 1966, p. 302), or to find gratification in reading fictional accounts of private lives, created a demand for allegedly real accounts of the private lives of the talented and influential. Whether out of desire for wider conviviality or the envious wish to degrade and humiliate others, intrusion–on one's own or others' initiative–into the private affairs of others is a

stable phenomenon of human society. But since those at the political epicenter of society feel a need to know at least certain aspects
of the lives of those on the periphery, in Europe the modern state
also began to develop techniques of information-gathering and surveillance that culminated in the police apparatus of twentieth-century totalitarian regimes. Armed with such data, the authorities could
then take the necessary coercive or punitive measures to enforce
their policies and frustrate hostile countermoves (Jourard 1966,
p. 312). The American "loyalty-security" programs of the 1940s
and 1950s, with investigators prying into the sexual lives of those
under scrutiny, were their counterpart on this side of the Atlantic.

Privacy entered criminal law, one may justly say, by the back
door. Late medieval governments enacted drastic penalties for all
sexual activity that violated the tenets of Christian moral theology.
They claimed the right and indeed the duty to punish all acts that
contravened a supposedly revealed morality. Enlightenment legal
theory led to the abolition of medieval laws against fornication,
adultery, and sodomy. The new codes retained the exception that
sexual behavior "in public or in a place of public resort" should
remain criminal in deference to the more fundamental norm resid-
ing in the deep structure of society that forbids sexual behavior of
any kind in places open to the presence and observation of nonparticipants. Otherwise it would cause scandal and outrage. It is not
that privacy is a positive attribute. Rather publicity is the "marked,"
negative, taboo-violating component of sexual behavior that persistently warrants intervention by the state power. In the past, homosexual behavior was not legal when it took place in the utmost privacy.
A "reckless disregard" in offending others can still lead to conviction,
even in jurisdictions where the same conduct is legal in private. This
prohibition stems from the inability of nonparticipant witnesses to a
sexual act to experience the pleasure which the tactile sense affords
the actors. The visual and auditory stimuli seem to most either ridiculous or disgusting, seldom a neutral, biological event.

For this reason the psychiatric discovery of sexual inversion
prompted a hostile society to classify homosexuals among the mentally ill. The proclivity to derive pleasure from acts that inspired
aversion and disgust in heterosexuals was defined by psychiatrists
as a "perversion of the sexual instinct." The person with homo-

sexual tendencies was dehumanized into a mental patient. We could even be deprived of our physical liberty. We could be confined to a mental institution and there subjected to electric shocks, injections of insulin, administration of tranquilizing drugs, and interrogations by a professional psychiatrist or psychologist. This last practice was labeled psychotherapy, as if the mind of the homosexual (or bisexual) were being treated for a pathological disorder (Jourard 1966, p. 308). The entire procedure was an intolerant society's invasion of the privacy of those who loved their own sex.

If one legal text may be identified as the starting point for the current discussion, it is the British Criminal Law Amendment Act of 1885 (48 & 49 Victoria c. 69). Its eleventh clause provided a term of imprisonment not exceeding two years, with or without hard labor, for any male person guilty of an act of gross indecency with another male person "in public or in private." This opposition of *public* and *private* space as loci of sexual activity then generated the belated claim that the individual possesses a right of privacy which the state is infringing by seeking to intrude the police power. It is only one aspect of the legal right to be free from intrusion into one's personal life: protection against eavesdropping, searches and seizures, electronic and other surveillance, intrusive questioning by employers, insurance companies, government agencies, and the like. The scope of the right, however, remains clearly delimited by the relative importance and exigency of society's countervailing interest (Freund 1971, pp. 191-92).

The right of privacy in the sexual domain entered American criminal law only in *Griswold* v. *Connecticut* (1965). There a majority of the Supreme Court found that various emanations and radiations from the Bill of Rights gave the citizen a right of privacy against government. On that basis it invalidated a Connecticut birth control law that penalized the giving of birth control advice to married couples (Freund 1971, p. 192). If the right of privacy can be said to inhere in the United States Constitution at all, it is solely thanks to decisions of the Supreme Court (Lundsgaarde 1971, p. 863). But gay rights advocates voiced a similar argument unsuccessfully in *Bowers* v. *Hardwick* (1986), in which the majority reaffirmed the religious precedents that underlay the sodomy statute of the state of Georgia (Hunter, Michaelson, and Stoddard 1992, pp. 121-22).

The breakdown of traditional taboos on the public discussion of forbidden sexual conduct in itself prompted a redefinition of the boundaries of private and public. What was once prurience and voyeurism is now draped in the mantle of "scientific curiosity" or "candid journalism." In the trial of William Kennedy Smith the whole world gazed at the television screen and the front pages of tabloids exposing the intimate details of the alleged rape. What formerly amounted to "exhibitionism" has become participation in "scientific inquiry." Activity once confined to "blue films" and "circuses" now falls into the definition of a "research situation" (Shils 1966, p. 299). And last but not least, the open proclamation of one's homosexual tendencies and liaisons is no longer a "shameless confession of depravity," but a "political act" (Hunter, Michaelson, and Stoddard 1992, p. 9).

In its newest version, the claim of privacy seeks to interpose a concept more archaic than the medieval one between the actors and the state. It holds that society has long assigned consensual sexual activity to a realm in which the participants should be immune to the presence and gaze of nonparticipants–and therefore *even* the state. Sodomy laws "can be enforced only through inquiry into (or eavesdropping upon) what happens in bedrooms" or parked cars at night. If public opinion deems such interference by the police "intolerable, the statutes should be taken off the books" (Lusky 1972, pp. 200-201).

This is the central paradox of the privacy issue. The social convention of privacy allows members of a society to violate its moral norms without threatening or undermining the operation of those norms. In fact, privacy functioned to maintain Christian sexual taboos by reinforcing the assumption that departure from the norms was statistically insignificant, indeed rare, and that only "abandoned sinners" dared to defy the "law of God and this country." The young were traditionally kept in ignorance of the "facts of life" and especially of the mysteries of homosexual union (Moore and Tumin 1949, p. 791). Stephen Wayne Foster even uncovered a nineteenth-century tract in which a Protestant minister assured his readers that there is no way to gratify the sexual urge without reproductive consequences. Ignorance created by the veil of privacy particularly inhibited homosexual activity. The strong tendency to cross the boundary of sexual intimacy was repressed in part out of the belief that potential partners were few or simply unavailable.

Privacy also upheld the stereotype of the "obvious" homosexual. Thus, the vast majority of those who "passed" as heterosexual while clandestinely engaging in the forbidden sexual practices "could not be queer" in the eyes of the unsuspecting (Moore and Tumin 1949, p. 793). On the other hand, awareness that affect-laden norms were being violated with impunity might lead to vigorous repressive measures that would otherwise lapse owing to sheer indifference. One by-product of the Kinsey Reports was that widespread knowledge of homosexual practices materially stimulated further, and certainly less inhibited and guilt-ridden, enjoyment of them (Moore and Tumin 1949, p. 791). It was Kinsey's collective outing of the extent and ubiquitousness of American homosexual behavior that set the stage both for the persecution of "sex perverts" in the loyalty-security campaigns of the 1950s, and for the emergence in 1969 of a gay community with a political consciousness of its own. We acquired a conviction that the stigma attached to our private sexual conduct conferred a set of common interests and grievances that alienated us from the rest of society.

But for the individual who has deeply internalized the image of a God who watches and judges his every thought and deed *there is no privacy*. There is no place on earth, however remote, hidden, or shrouded in darkness, to which the sexually depraved can flee to commit their shameless crime unseen. "We do not have a right not to be observed by God," declares a contemporary philosopher, "for it is unreasonable to believe that (assuming God exists) we are not observed by God" (Taliaferro 1989, p. 192). The implicit visibility of all homosexual acts to a deity whose "wrath is revealed from heaven" (Romans 1:18) is integral to the paranoid belief system which coauthor Warren Johansson has labeled the "sodomy delusion." As far back as the intertestamental period Jewish teachers had proclaimed that God is long-suffering with all sins except fornication. Wherever sexual immorality occurs God is promptly offended and outraged, and will exact a dreadful vengeance on any community that tolerates such wickedness in its midst. The state, in deference to medieval Christian belief, is only enforcing a morality revealed by an omniscient deity.

The new affirmation of privacy is therefore part and parcel of the movement to exclude the lingering influence of canon law on civil law in the sexual domain. Thus it is one aspect of the secularization of Western society. In the absence of the *Code Napoléon* as a model and of a viable sexual reform movement, all common law jurisdictions continued to reenact the sixteenth-century laws punishing the "crime against nature" into the mid-twentieth century, and many keep them on the books to this day.

However deeply ingrained the notion of "privacy" may be in the human psyche, its invocation in contemporary legal philosophy must be seen not as a timeless verity but as an innovative weapon in the struggle against the persistence of the ascetic morality in the Christian tradition. So far from being a self-evident, neutral concept, it is a flanking attack on Christian moral theology as entrenched in the criminal law (Bowman 1949, pp. 632-33). It is part of a dialectical reordering of private and public, of allowed and forbidden, as a counterpoise to the ambition of political and cultural elites to govern, to manipulate or to please vast collectivities–the gay community or queer nation among them (Lusky 1972, pp. 198-99; Shils 1966, p. 305).

Last of all, homosexual expression deserves to be subsumed under the legitimate "play activity" with which the coming generation should be taught to utilize its leisure time. In stark contrast to the Christian rejection of sexuality as an evil that must be kept to the irreducible minimum, within marriage and then solely for the purpose of procreation, the enlightened society of the future will enhance the pleasures of private life by cultivating the erotic in its most refined and unorthodox forms. Safe sex, a by-product of the AIDS crisis, encourages such practices. The legal guarantee of privacy could open new paths of sensual experimentation that will ultimately enrich the aesthetic experience of all, even of those who encounter it only obliquely in literature and art (Jourard 1966, pp. 317-18).

For the purpose of our argument, suffice it to say that since the interests of the Queer Nation are manifestly opposed to the perpetuation of Christian morality, it must hold that personal privacy entitles its members only to gratify their aberrant sexual urges, not to act against its collective well-being. The professional or economic segment of society to which they individually belong would surely take sanctions against them if they publicly and deliberately contravened its interests. Since the sexual activity in which they–as morally responsible human beings–engage includes them in the Queer Nation, it has the right to make the same demands of them. The shield of privacy in this case would be a weapon used against one's own side to stymie its political gains–and ultimately against one's own interests. Activists leading the struggle against the obscurantist and reactionary clergy and their pawns and followers have the right to strip disloyal members of the Queer Nation of that covering and expose them as hypocrites and traitors.

On this issue Richard Mohr writes in *Gay Ideas: Outing and Other Controversies*: "It is sexual acts, and derivatively talk of them, not sexual orientations that are protected by privacy. The reporting of sexual orientation does not violate any of the senses of privacy that are legitimately invoked in sexual matters" (1992, p. 17). He opts for a distinction between privacy and secrecy. "Privacy, taken in a moral sense and put broadly, is control over the access that others have to one. Secrecy, broadly, is the intentional concealment of something, usually information. Control of access is the core of privacy; hiding is the core of secrecy" (1992, p. 12). Insightfully he points out that "normally one's private life, one's own affairs, are not a secret. They cannot be intruded on, but they are usually known and acknowledged." His corollary is that "no legitimate gay privacy interest is violated by making public the secret of someone's sexual orientation" (1992, pp. 14-15).

Sexual orientation, however, is an intrinsically and unalterably private matter just because it cannot be observed, but only experienced. Only the subject can know his own sexual feelings and desires, no one else can fathom them. Even a computer printout of a complete sexual history (itself unrealizable) would not record unfulfilled urges and longings. Moreover, sexual orientation can change independent of the subject's will over time; it is not unalterably fixed in all human beings. By contrast sexual acts–other than solitary masturbation–always involve a partner, an accomplice to the secret who may later reveal all to an amused or horrified world.

Mohr states the truth that hypocrisy, so far from being the exception, is rather the norm in liberal democracies, where "politicians with their competing constituencies will be particularly subject to this process of selling out . . . and of professing beliefs they do not hold. . . . Hypocrisy is chiefly a sin of the intellect, a sin against reason, not a moral sin" (1992, p. 24).

Our comment on this analysis is that until quite recently such hypocrisy was mandatory for lovers of their own sex who aspired to public office, in fact as late as the 1960s only those not personally compromised could argue for the rights of homosexuals and gain a hearing from anyone. But since then much has changed: the election of 1992 was a turning point in the political history of the Queer Nation. From being an outcast, pariah community, an embarrassment to those whom it claimed as allies, a group on the outer margin of political life, it has gravitated far–if not all the way–toward the status of one interest group among many within the establishment. Those whose own sexual lives make them citizens of the Queer Nation now have an obligation to that interest group, not an absolute one, but tempered always by enlightened self-interest. To revile, betray, and consciously harm that constituency or any significant part of it is intolerable behavior even for a politician.

Mohr disposes of another argument against outing, namely that "outing someone prevents him or her from achieving the dignity that attaches to the coming-out process," by asking "Does the outed person retain the possibility of having a robust, positive, dignifying relation to his sexual orientation?" This question he answers in the affirmative, citing the case of congressman Gerry Studds, who has retained his House seat by forthrightly admitting and justifying his sexual orientation (Mohr 1992, pp. 40-42).

Elsewhere in the same essay, he declares: "We ought to stick to the vision of the Declaration of Independence and believe that communities exist to guarantee rights of individuals and we should be very wary when the concept of community is used to generate obligations. For the tyranny of the majority will almost always be found there working in finely sinuous, deeply insidious ways" (Mohr 1992, p. 21). David Greenberg in a private communication noted that Bentham's "principle of the greatest good for the greatest number came in for major criticism 20 years ago from the neo-Kantian John Rawls on the grounds that it would allow all the interests of a minority to be sacrificed if the majority were to benefit sufficiently. Rawls argues on those grounds for a social contract theory that would not permit such a sacrifice."

The critique of this argument resumes the point made in our analysis of the 1969-73 period. During the past 75 years, the American Left has been the sorry example of a house divided against itself–a contradiction that spelled its historic failure. Even though it donned the program and the rhetoric of European collectivist movements, its authentic belief system was anarcho-individualistic. It could never have achieved its ostensible goal of a Socialist or Communist regime, least of all on the Soviet model, because then it would have found itself farther than ever from its real one. Strictly speaking it stems not from the nineteenth-century tradition of collectivism, but from the last, decadent phase of the Enlightenment–its hypertrophy of the doctrine of the freedom of the individual at the expense of the collective. Carried to its logical conclusion it would abrogate membership in a community or nation of any kind. In that respect the concept of a Queer Nation, whatever the current politics of its members, is implicitly collectivist. It is a nation at war that by definition insists upon communal responsibility and communal obligations on the part of lovers of their own sex at least *until the legal oppression and pariah status from which we all now suffer are ended forever.*

At the close of his article Mohr reasons excellently that "the normal-appearing person being out is a major threat and source of cultural anxiety. For that the normal can be queer means that anyone–father, brother, even you–may be gay." It is the refusal of gay people to pass for straight that is "the perceived threat to and imagined betrayal of society. . . . So gay progress requires both being publicly out and living in the truth, a necessary concomitant of which is that closet cases will be outed" (1992, pp. 46-47).

Celebrities will in this context of struggle have to find more purposeful techniques for projecting and managing their public images. Columnists have contributed to keeping celebrities closeted, first by not reporting gossip about their homosexual escapades that crosses their desks, and second, by circulating press agent-concocted tales that maintain their heterosexual façade. With such collusion many stars have led double "private" lives for decades, carefully hiding their homosexuality behind a sequence of press agent-arranged and lavishly publicized marriages, infidelities, and sensational divorces with which the purveyors of gossip titillated the readers of tabloids and fan magazines. But departing as they ostentatiously did from the norm of "lifelong, indissoluble monogamy," indirectly they made divorce respectable even in upper-middle- and upper-class American society. It is hardly by chance that a former movie star, Ronald Reagan, conservative though he was, became the first divorced candidate ever elected president (1980).

In addition, certain mass media even without a political motive have profited from scandalous revelations about celebrities. Sensational accounts of the vices and amours of the rich and famous are guaranteed to increase circulation of such scandal-mongering media. Fortunes are to be reaped even from posthumous exposés.

Outing is thus a revelation that affects the personality's reputation. The criteria for it must be formulated within the framework of the ethics of public life. To publish a list of noncelebrities–farmers, factory workers, or stenographers, invisible to all but their families and the few others who deal with them in everyday life–and identify them as queer would not be outing in the sense now current.

Much depends on the nature of what is deemed to be deviant and guilty: in this case homosexual activity or orientation. In the last analysis privacy is not an absolute right, and cannot be invoked to shield the closeted hypocrite from public exposure. Christian morality effectively violated and abrogated the privacy of those discovered to belong to the pariah community. Hence the queer nation, in its struggle against the burden of infamy, is not obliged to respect privacy if this serves to perpetuate its own defamation and outlawry.

THE CASE AGAINST QUEER NATION

Wayne R. Dynes, who originally planned to author this work with us, withdrew in consequence of disagreements over the concept of a queer nation. The following is a summary of his argument, often in his own words.

The idea of a nation (queer or otherwise) appears unbuttressed by any sustained argument. Queer Nation is evoked as if the concept had a self-evident validity. Apart from the merits of the case, the assumption that the reader will readily accept an idea that is new to him or her is not valid. Just to utter an expression, whether in capital letters or not, does not ipso facto convince others of the necessity of adopting the idea it connotes.

Moreover, this putative nationhood is not in any way essential as a foundation for the continuation of the practice of outing–which will continue. The *Advocate* did not endorse the Queer Nation concept when it outed Pete Williams; it was under no obligation to do so, as the information it provided speaks for itself. Thus the notion of gay/queer nationhood has no enabling character with respect to the continued practice of outing. If some outer has the goods on someone and outs him, no one is entitled to conclude that the action is somehow invalid or ineffectual simply because the outer does not subscribe to the orthodox ideology. Such an exclusion would be a kind of neo-Donatism, the early Christian heresy that maintained that only morally pure priests could work the miracle of the mass. The efficacy of the act of outing is independent of the belief system entertained by the outer. Jesse Helms can out as effectively as Michael Petrelis. Thus the purported theoretical underpinning of some sort of nationhood for the process of outing may be deemed otiose; it constitutes neither a necessary nor a sufficient condition for its continuance.

From the standpoint of the rights of the individual, the point raised by Richard Mohr could be conclusive: few if any gay or lesbian persons have *contracted,* by oath, by written agreement, or by any other binding instrument, to membership or to citizenship in a "nation" or any other corporate entity of this kind. Absent such binding agreement, lovers of their own sex owe no allegiance to any posited Queer Nation; consequently, we cannot be expected to abide by its norms, rules, or laws as defined by the tiniest of minorities within a minority. What if the leaders of Queer Nation were to decree Marxism as its official ideology? Would we have to go along? Obviously we would not. It may be argued that *none of us in fact belongs to any Queer Nation,* so that we are not bound by any statutes that may be propounded for it. To haul people before an inquisitorial body (the "Council" proposed in Chapter VIII) for disregarding obligations that they have never incurred defies both law and common sense. No one can be expected to acknowledge allegiance to something that does not exist.

Some may say in response to this point that while the Queer Nation (in its full sense, as distinct from the organization of that name) does not yet exist, it will exist at some future date. But, with all due respect, no one has provided a model of what such nationhood would mean once it came into being. Details on this are lacking in materials so far provided. The analogy with the Jews is imperfect since one can become a Jew only by birth, in effect by socialization within the family, or voluntary conversion. Moreover, the Jews now do have their territory *de jure* and always have had it in aspiration ("Next year in Jerusalem!"). Where is our Jerusalem? Where even is our Sodom? The comparison with Soviet nationalities, which except for the Jews are all territorial [Dynes might have added Tatars and Gypsies], sends shivers down everyone's spine in this country: The almost limitless possibilities of divisiveness inherent in such a Soviet-style nationality concept is one of the numerous arguments against extreme forms of multiculturalism. Moreover, the idea of erecting a separate, quasi-national entity on American soil–like the Québecois separatist movement in Canada– is deeply repugnant. Today few if any African-Americans or Hispanics are asking for such status. We should consider what they may know that the authors of this book apparently do not. In the considerable literature on nation-building by Benedict Anderson, Eric Hobsbawm, and others, I have detected no patterns that would be useful to our cause. In any event, a reasoned discussion of this question cannot afford to neglect this literature.

What does nationhood mean? Could one, like the Cherokee, register one's membership in Queer Nation? Would we have separate courts? Representatives in Congress elected solely by us? Designated residential areas in which non-queer nationals could not live? If none of these things, what could it mean? The whole notion is deeply alien to the cultural temper of this country, and could enjoy no constitutional standing. Even if such a status were possible, we would be among the last to obtain it, since prejudice against gay people still far exceeds that against ethnic minorities. We shall only add to the hatred that is deployed against us if it is perceived that our loyalty to the country is less than that of other citizens. In our case, a demand for differentiation in treatment might quickly turn into a rationale for discrimination.

An additional problem is posed by the insistence on the epithet *queer*. After several decades of gay and lesbian liberation, we now have a certain number of people who acknowledge a gay, lesbian, or bisexual identity. Insofar as identity is one of the components–though only one–of nation-building, there is something to work with there–in terms of *gay* or *lesbian* identity. Yet how many claim a *queer* identity? How many ever will? Another difficulty with the Queer Nation slogan is its capacity for double offense: Those (like many participants in the Rutgers gay academic conference held in November of 1991) who have adopted the label *queer* may not subscribe to the idea of nation; and vice versa. By continuing to yoke these two together, you queer nationalists further narrow your circle of adherents.

Sadly, the notion of a Queer Nation is a group fantasy shared by only a few hundred individuals. The support of these enthusiasts was not enough to keep *OutWeek* afloat. They will also not suffice to support a significant movement or indeed even this book. It is perhaps understandable that in our frustration we should grasp at the straw of a utopian proposal. But this one, like so many other "revolutionary" dreams of the tiny band of individuals who have appointed themselves to speak for the gay community, is destined to pass leaving scarcely a trace. A mirage, it will go the way of our purported "national home" in Alpine County, California. In effect advocates concede this fate in advance, since nowhere in this book or elsewhere does anyone offer a reasoned discussion and defense of the idea of gay nationhood. It looks to some very much as if it is not defended because it is indefensible.

In 1973 Jill Johnston published a book called *Lesbian Nation*. She later acknowledged that she was in a state of mental agitation when she wrote it. Others have stated the lesbian separatist case more calmly, but even so it has not taken hold. A discussion of the vagaries of this separatist thesis, as it unfolded in the last two decades, should form part of a reasoned account of assertions about a "Queer Nation."

In summation, the Queer Nation proposal, in any version, must elicit rejection and derision on the part of the overwhelming majority of the Kinseyan masses who practice homosexuality; they have never contracted for anything remotely resembling it. No historical parallels have emerged that are persuasive in the context of American society as it has historically evolved. No one has addressed the question of feasibility–how we might get from here to there–nor provided any ultimate model of what is to be accomplished. It is just talk that makes gay/queer people feel better. And not many of these, either. The idea floats in the air, with no modalities whereby it might be implemented. To invoke it as if it self-evidently possessed such properties is to adhere to a chimera, one that offers no benefits to gay people and may even prove, through its very siring, counter-productive.

A solid book would provide a range of historical examples and arguments about outing. Tacitly to assume the cogency, as is often done by way of repeated unsupported references, of a controversial utopian proposal, does not, in the opinion of many, befit a serious work. This book offers immense stores of valuable information; it should not advocate chimerical theories.

THE CASE FOR QUEER NATION

The term Queer Nation, which came into use only recently, bothers a great many people because they remember clearly the time when *queer* was a term of opprobrium. But it is not unheard of to take a pejorative term and make it one of pride, as some did in the 1790s with *democracy* (previously meaning mob-rule), and as Proudhon did early in the next century with *anarchism*. The essential problem is not with the word *queer* but with the word *nation*. The choice of this word represents an attempt to embody a concept stronger than the loose collectivist notion of "community" that has been popular since 1969 or the legalistic (homosexual) "minority" which had predominated since the 1950s. While it may be argued whether we are *born* gay or not (*nation* is derived from Latin *natus,* born), hardly anyone would now deny that once a person becomes gay, no "treatment" will make him or her straight. One cannot simply quit the gay nation in the same way that one moves out of a neighborhood or renounces one's extended family or resigns from the staff of some institution to end one's affiliation with a *Gemeinschaft* or *Gesellschaft,* as pioneer German sociologists distinguished groups with a fundamental community of interests from those with more artificial and slight ones such as a corporation.

On the other hand, belonging to Queer Nation does not diminish one's loyalty to the United States. Dual citizenship is an old concept. One can still be a Queer-American, a member of the newest hyphenated minority. Just as John D'Emilio subtitled his book *The Making of a Homosexual Minority in the United States, 1940-1970,* what is emerging is not merely a legal "minority" or a subjective "community," but a vibrant nation within a nation. But this is a *new,* not an old nation such as the Jews were on the eve of the French Revolution. Hannah Arendt argued in *The Origins of Totalitarianism* (1951) that "the breakdown of the feudal order had given rise to the new revolutionary concept of equality, according to which a 'nation within the nation' could no longer be tolerated. Jewish restrictions and privileges had to be abolished together with all other special rights and liberties." In this respect the queer nation stands diametrically opposed to the assimilationist strivings of post-Enlightenment Jewry: its goal is separatist; even if it cannot aspire to an independent state, it can claim namely the right to its own institutions, its own media, its own representatives in positions of power. But since Israel seems unlikely to cede the city of Sodom and its environs to Queer Nation at any foreseeable conference on Middle Eastern boundaries, the closest thing we can achieve is the set of gay ghettos that have developed in all major cities throughout the world and to which we may in the coming decades annex a ring of gay suburbs.

Nations customarily reproduce by the heterosexual mating of their members, but we do not ordinarily reproduce from our own numbers. Nature reproduces us by allotting us a certain, if variable, percentage of breeders' children in each generation, so that our community/nation is constantly renewed with no effort on our part. A nation in the strictest sense, of course, we are not; but in the loyalty that we might inspire or require, we are comparable. Closer still is our resemblance to a religious community, whose adherents need no geographical or ethnic tie to the place where or the people among whom their faith was first propagated. They belong to that community by virtue of the identity which they have acquired as part of their socialization and which they deem integral to their personalities. What is more, on account of common enemies, homophobia, and more recently AIDS, we of necessity are more closely and irrevocably bound together than most communities. Oppression and peril are forging our minority, our far-flung "communities," into a nation at war.

The concept of a Queer Nation, like that of a gay community, emphasizes mutual responsibility, but is more militant. In our struggle against plague and the homophobes who obstruct measures to combat it, those who put their private affairs and interests above those of the nation are not just cowards but traitors. Those who actively resist the demands of the Nation are collaborationists and quislings. As such they at least have to be outed, if not punished more severely as those refusing in wartime to fight! What grounds are there for conscientious objectors in this war of ours?

The question then becomes: without the concept of a Queer Nation–or some such collective entity, whatever its name might be, that resembles a nation in demands of fealty and patriotism–could outing in its current sense be justified at all? It would make no sense to out someone as a member of a garden club or the Audubon Society. A loosely federated community from which one can withdraw at will is not a nation. A nation is something intrinsic to the individual, far more significant to his or her identity. Until Stonewall, it seemed sufficient to most homosexuals to consider ourselves part of a culture or subculture or of a minority seeking toleration. Afterwards, when gay pride burst forth, those who came out of the closet demanded acceptance and spoke of ourselves as a "gay community." Now we aspire to the loftier status of nationality.

The AIDS crisis intensified the feeling of brotherhood and sisterhood that the notion of community expresses. Out of this unparalleled situation, in which we are stalked by a vicious killer which the heterosexual majority seems to ignore, rejecting our frantic cries for help, was born the idea of a Queer Nation. Outing of hypocrites is justified by the belief that those whom it targets are disloyal to their nation at a moment of great peril and distress. The homophile movement has gone through three stages: from obsequious *homosexual* to assertive *gay* to confrontational *queer*. Only a few have fully grasped the implications of this semantic change. Doubters should remember that the establishment media resisted the use of *gay* for many years just as they are now resisting the use of *queer.*

"Queer Nation" is no more misleading, perhaps less so, than "gay community." The concept of a community implies a locality where people who identify as gay live or congregate. In fact we are scattered horizontally and vertically, throughout the world and from the top to the bottom of society, exactly like the adherents of a major religion. We are divided, it is true, into countless local ghettos, gay resorts, or other isolated groups that might be considered communities. Community, however, implies intimacy and contemporaneity, whereas homosexuals, especially pederasts, and bisexuals are found throughout history as well as across the entire surface of the earth. Community, at least as interpreted by the radicals of the 1960s who popularized the phrase "gay community" or "lesbian and gay community," had a deliberate sense of class interest which ignores the vertical dimension, replete with class antagonisms, of queer nationalism. The notion has now grown to the awkward "lesbian/bisexual/gay male community," to which some would even add transvestite and/or transsexual. Our ranks, however, are too diverse as well as too widespread to form a community in the traditional sense. We include individuals from the commanding heights of industry and finance as well as from the poorest and most destitute in the shelters. Many in our nation, which if we are 10 percent of the world's population, may comprise 500 million individuals, share nothing positive except unchosen sexual orientation. We have no *community* ethos; but common dangers and enemies are fostering a political will to resist. Proposals are occasionally heard for a gay political party. For the first time in history we are building a world-wide movement with our own media and conferences, and a mounting sense of our cohesiveness.

The vast majority are not organized or "activist," in fact not even out of the closet. Even in metropolises such as New York or Los Angeles, London or Berlin, Rio or New Delhi, Lagos or Cairo, we do not exactly constitute a close-knit body with a broad range of common interests that could properly be defined as a community:

> The body of those having common or equal rights or rank, or distinguished from the privileged class; the body of commons;

> the commonality; a body of people organized into a political, municipal, or social unity; a state or commonwealth; a body of men living in the same locality; often applied to those members of a civil community, who have certain circumstances of nativity, religion, or pursuit, common to them, but not shared by those among whom they live; *the community,* the people of a country (or district) as a whole; the general body to which all alike belong; the public. (*OED*)

We have no common ownership, character, or agreement, often not even a common self-identity, and we share no common social intercourse or communion. The gay world is a microcosm of the larger one, with all its diversity and heterogeneity. One could speak perhaps of the gay community of Cincinnati, or better still of Baton Rouge or Boise, where the small body of threatened, isolated queers may all more or less know one another or at least about one another and huddle together for strength and protection from the hostile authorities and environment. It would be far less appropriate to speak of a gay community in Moscow, Paris, or Tokyo. To designate all lovers of their own sex worldwide as a community defies logic. Queer Nation seems less unsustainable than the currently still more popular gay community.

There may indeed be a worldwide gay culture, or subculture, if you prefer, dominated at this time by the American prototype, but if so, most who merely interact with their own sex do not participate in it (Altman 1982). Those terms "culture" and "subculture," too, are limited in their applicability and controversial in their definition.

Another, older term is "the homosexual minority," forged after the Second World War from *homosexual* (1869) and, by analogy with the ethnic meaning, *minority* (1918). Universal persecution and ostracism forged a homosexual minority in America between 1940 and 1970. If the backdrop for such condemnation was the Judeo-Christian tradition, the West transmitted this through imperialism and Marxism to the non-Western world. Like Jews and Gypsies, we who inhabit the lands of others (in our case, those of the hostile and persecuting heterosexuals) feel a unity born of intolerance, persecution, and suffering.

Only after 1969 did gay liberationists adopt the notion of a community. This change in attitude came about in part because the visibility of the constituents, our social contact through meetings, demonstrations, fund-raising activities, and celebrations gave us the shared experience that we needed to internalize an identity. Inspired by the various National Liberation Fronts, the younger leaders who took to the streets, loudly repudiating "experts" and the older ultra-gradualist types, tended to mouth a pseudo-Marxist rather than liberal (in the post-New Deal sense) line and scorned patriotism and nationalism.

But it took AIDS to catalyze our minority or community into a nation, just as the Holocaust, the *shō'āh*, was needed to transmute the Zionist movement and the Yishuv into the state of Israel, although the idea had been germinated long before by the pogroms in Tsarist Russia and the Dreyfus affair. As late as 1893 Anatole Leroy-Beaulieu had predicted that the reestablishment of an independent Jewish state within its ancient boundaries would recede into the realm of the metaphysical, like the Second Coming of Christ, to be realized not by human agency but only by divine intervention at the end of time. But just three years later Theodor Herzl declared: "*Wir sind ein Volk,* **ein** *Volk*" (We are a people, *one* people). Then at the First Zionist Congress in Basel, Switzerland in 1897, one of the Jewish leaders said: "*Wenn ihr wollt, es ist kein Märchen*" (If you will, this is no fairy tale). Utopian and absurd as the project of such a state seemed then, in 51 years it became a reality when the United Nations partitioned Mandate Palestine to create a homeland for the victims of National Socialist persecution and genocide. It took the First and Second World Wars and the Holocaust to persuade the majority of Jews to abandon the liberal dream of assimilation into Gentile society and to favor the integral-nationalist state of Israel. What event will be needed to make a Queer Nation?

We may be less than a nation but we are more than a leftist community and more than a minority as defined in American law. As long as the Judeo-Christian tradition prevails, we shall remain social outcasts if not pariahs. We include individuals having little in common in wealth, social status, politics or ideology. The sole common positive factor is that some unseen element in our personalities, or in our genes and hormones, impels us to have sexual intimacy with others of our own sex or at least to feel an erotic yearning for such partners. There is that inner selfhood, there is homophobia, and there is AIDS.

Whether we are the product of biology or of society, we cannot leave our group or escape from it or be "cured." Our condition is permanent, unalterable, so that William F. Buckley's plan to brand us on the buttocks has a certain reality behind it. Our stigma cannot be removed like a pink triangle from a concentration camp uniform. Experience and history teach us that we are inextricably bound together for as long as anyone can now foresee and have been ever since the Christians began to persecute those guilty of the "sin of Sodom." Bills of toleration and gay rights laws cannot abolish the loathing and aversion which affluent and impoverished, high and low alike will continue to suffer.

NATION BUILDING

Outing by homophobes for either personal or religio-political reasons has been all too prevalent over the centuries. In view of the noxious, sometimes fatal effects, queers have until recently demanded the shield of "privacy." Evidently the more enlightened heterosexuals now entertain serious reservations regarding outing, recognizing the past harm that the hostile variant has wrought. They sometimes express puzzlement that we are increasingly employing a new version of the practice for our own ends.

This sequence–virulent outing by homophobes, then a decline of the practice, and finally revival by queer nationals–suggests that some cyclical process is at work. Earlier we hazarded the suggestion that outing has a "historic mission." Some may feel that, in the present stage of deployment of outing in its new form, such a claim is premature. Yet it seems certain that the present crescendo of outing has more than casual significance. What is this significance?

For many the rationale for outing is that the target has been hypocritical or has acted to harm us, that he has betrayed our nation. One could even say that such a morally dubious character has failed to respond to the allegiance he owes not only to his community, but to truth itself. More than community bonds, national allegiances are binding. They must not be betrayed for personal gain. In America today, hypocrisy is acquiescence in oppression.

Outing thus needs to be considered within the larger framework of the evolution of the even more politicized Queer Nation. The radical activists of the 1970s, opposed as they were to America's involvement in the Vietnam War, preferred "gay and lesbian community." In the age of AIDS, we aspire to nationhood so that we can war against AIDS and homophobia, allied as they are. Outing may play a formative role in our nation-building.

Queer nationals feel a stronger allegiance to our nation than gay people to a community and infinitely greater identity than homosexuals as a minority. To this some might reply that there is an inescapable problem with the very concept of a queer nation to which all lovers of their own sex putatively belong, whether they will or no. Some of us have joined homophile activist, service, and scholarly organizations. By doing so, we affirm our adhesion to their specific goals. But it takes a nation to go to war.

One might say that we implicitly agree to a contract that we will not harm our common interests and will work actively to end discrimination, injustice, and untimely deaths. But the majority who engage in homosexual acts do not wish to belong to such an association. Indeed, some of them actively disapprove of such organizations and of the spotlight which these have focused on homosexuality. When interviewed they even deny such experiences and loudly condemn "perverts" (Humphreys 1970). They have consented to no contract that entails anything beyond their chosen behavior. One could say–and we do–that opting out in this way is outrageous; these individuals who would ignore or scorn their benefactors while profiting from the advantages secured by them with such effort are simply "free riders."

After all, free riders are recognized as such and justly criticized in many other situations. If the Sierra Club achieves a reduction of pollution from which I gain cleaner air to breathe, while the members acknowledge that they cannot *compel* me to contribute, they nonetheless judge their cause important enough to pursue, and relentlessly out polluters.

We referred to the notion of a contract, or some other device, possibly an informal one, which would clarify this question of the allegiance owed to the Queer Nation. The idea of such contracts has a long history in Western political thought. The political fiction of the social contract that Hobbes and Locke created is in crucial ways no fiction at all. The need for publicly supported fire and police protection and the like is generally recognized. According to this widely accepted theory, one is a party to the social contract simply by virtue of being born and raised in the society. No formalities or signatures are required. What holds for the citizens of the nation-state, however, does not apply to voluntary bodies subsisting within it. Western democracies foster myriads of volunteer organizations, which one joins by paying a fee, signing an application blank, taking an oath, or performing some other act of formal adhesion.

As things stand today, most of us queer nationals fall into neither of these categories–the involuntary one of state citizenship nor the voluntary one of the circumscribed organization. A small, if grow-ing, number would be so idealistic (or dogmatic) as to say that we form a nation transcending all other boundaries, to which we must belong whether we wish it or not. But most people who have rela-tions with others of their own sex do not acknowledge that doing so makes them members of a community, let alone a nation. Nor can we activists "join" for them. Even if such a community existed in some sense, or could be expected to arise in the future, how would one determine membership? Only a small portion of those who engage in homosexual acts are exclusives (ranking 6 on the Kinsey scale). The overwhelming majority–the Kinsey 1-5 groups–have varying amounts of heterosexual experience. What degree of homo-sexuality would qualify one for full queer nationality? How much heterosexual dalliance would compromise one's queer citizenship? Then there is the vexing question of whether there might be one nation for all queers or two, one for gay men and one for lesbians.

Some years ago Benedict Anderson made a study of "invented communities," showing how countries such as Indonesia, Pakistan, Nigeria, and Zaire did not simply emerge when "natural" countries were freed from subjection to colonial rule, but were in large mea-sure created by political geniuses who evoked a national conscious-ness where none existed before. Is it possible that some such pro-cess of consensus building is at work today for those who love their own sex, and that outing is a step towards this goal? Unfortunately, some communities cannot be raised to the status of full, unambiguous nationhood. We cannot hope to acquire, nor would most of us want, an independent nation-state of our own. Despite our chafing under discrimination, much of it sanctioned by our respective governments, we remain citizens of our conventional nation-states first and queer nationals second.

But it is possible to proceed some way along this road, so as to create a more cohesive and caring entity to supersede the often divided and contentious community that we have now, a strong nation to fight our wars against homophobes and AIDS. Outing can assist in this process. Participation in it, requiring toil and often courage, may prepare us to act collectively in other worthwhile pursuits. Also, outing enlarges the "pool" of visible citizens, and increased visibility is a prerequisite for the enhanced community that we hope will come into being. On the other hand, as a nonconsensual process which many believe violates privacy, outing sparks animosity. The target, and others dreading the same fate or merely disapproving the tactic, may vehemently object. So it is likely that, for a considerable period at least, outing will increase tensions in our midst.

But what must take precedence over this is the implicit demand for *recognition by heterosexuals that homosexuals form a minority, gay people a community, and queers a nation possessing legitimate interests* that in many spheres of life set us apart from them. This recognition is not a reversion to the status quo that existed before Christianity; *it is qualitatively new and without precedent.* For centuries Western society had classed sodomites and buggers as the lowest of the low. We were denizens of criminal subcultures subject to chronic police repression and relentless social ostracism. The legitimacy of our lifestyle, of our community, of our Nation and its representatives–all these are radical innovations. But they flow inexorably from the political consciousness of belonging to a stable segment of society with an enduring character. None of this means that queers are less loyal than ethnic "minorities" to the nations in which we reside, indeed we are far more so because we have never constituted an ethnic or racial group distinct from the one to which our heterosexual ancestors and relatives belong. Hence we demand full citizenship, including the right that has so often been denied us to serve in the military and intelligence establishments. Only we insist that the obligations which apply to one and all not submerge our legitimate wish to associate freely with one another and to defend our rights with force if necessary.

Be this as it may, the prospect of a unified nation or a harmonious community remains problematic, even apart from the question of outing. The question of whether participation in erotic acts with members of one's own sex reflects a contractual engagement is crucial. Without the leverage that such a commitment would give, the organizing potential of those who would seek to move towards queer nationalism is crippled. Even today the leaders are more inclined to aggressive or radical tactics than are the rank and file.

Leaders might find stronger support by leaning less toward the left. The National Gay and Lesbian Task Force decided to oppose Desert Storm, even though the overwhelming majority of queer nationals supported the action. In their efforts at lobbying and coalition-building, many leaders joined the "liberal" establishment–which gay Republicans and other conservatives find distasteful–or, worse even in the eyes of many Democrats, the Rainbow Coalition. A great number became pseudo-Marxists or supported coalitions led by them, even though their real ideology inclined toward anarcho-individualism. Many liberals perceive outing as an impermissible radical tactic. Queer nationalism, like other forms of nationalism, contradicts Marxism, because it is grounded in social divisions not based on conflicts of economic interest. Hence it may drive a new, deeper wedge between its advocates and those whom they would represent. The prime mover of our nationalism is the persistence of persecution–made more unbearable by the plague–not agreement on a collectivist agenda.

Even members of such "front-line" groups as ACT UP and Queer Nation do not agree on outing. Given their anarchistic tendencies, most still believe that coming out should be by personal choice. On the other hand, most would agree that even those most deeply in the closet should do *nothing* to harm other queer nationals, and when the opportunity presents itself, should act–however quietly or invisibly–to further the cause.

We feel that the majority of activists believe that closet cases who oppose and attack them should be exposed as traitors and hypocrites. When *OutLook* readers were queried, 69 percent favored outing "elected or appointed officials who obstruct the fight against AIDS," 73 percent would out government officials who perpetuate homophobic policies and obstruct the cause of gay rights, while only 22 percent would out "well-known individuals (not politicians)" who by their invisibility are depriving us of needed role models. Respondents identifying themselves as HIV-positive gave figures of 83, 88, and 45 percent respectively.

We are left with a series of questions. Is the enhanced gay community which some would call queer nationhood realizable? If so, will this goal require a major shift in tactics? Will outing help or hinder progress towards it? How will outing effect the reshaping of the movement, and our collective self-awareness in general, over both the short run and the long run? How will it impact society's attitude toward us?

COMPARISONS WITH OTHER MINORITY GROUPS

Our situation historically parallels that of certain religious minorities whose members, like us, were not physically identifiable as such. Driven underground by savage intolerance, they pretended to observe the state religion. They were found in many countries: the Marranos, Spanish and Portuguese Jews forcibly baptized into Roman Catholicism after 1391; the Moriscos, Spanish Muslims; the Recusants in Elizabethan England; the Nicodemites, secret Protestants in Bohemia and Moravia, Jesuit-dominated after the battle of White Mountain (1620); the crypto-Christians in the Ottoman Empire; and secret Catholics in Japan between 1630 and 1865. In cases like these, a simple decree of toleration could change their status almost overnight. By contrast the French Constituent Assembly's repeal of the sodomy laws in 1791 ended our legal plight but did not ameliorate the social one. We remained subject to ostracism, economic boycott, sporadic violence, and blackmail. All this was even more true in jurisdictions that failed to abolish such laws. Those that have kept them on the statute books to the present day include 23 of our own states.

Larry Gross has written (1991, p. 377): "But the analogy to Jews and concentration camps is also used by the proponents of outing, who see powerful closeted gays as analogous to the assimilated Jews who never believed that they would be touched by the crude anti-Semitism directed at the ghetto dwellers." Writing on the response of the Orthodox Jewish communities to the Holocaust, Menachem Friedman (1990) concluded that they chiefly fell victim because for religious reasons they first ignored the nationalistic appeals of the early Zionists, then owing to their visibility they could not escape the German authorities bent on deporting and exterminating them. By contrast the assimilated Jews, if carrying false identity papers, were able to disappear into the general population and, with the collusion of righteous or merely venal Gentiles, survive the Holocaust. But AIDS has not looked at identity cards: it has struck down even the minimalists, even those who imagined themselves wholly invisible to the outside world while they were leading secret (and often uninhibited) homosexual or bisexual lives. Outing thus amounts to a demand for solidarity with the Queer Nation by the legion of celebrities who crave the public eye while cravenly hiding in the closet.

Emancipation and then Zionism divided the Jewish communities of central and eastern Europe into three categories: (1) those who remained attached to traditional Judaism and therefore ignored the Zionist appeals, (2) those who successfully assimilated into the ethnic groups on whose territory they lived and therefore felt no need to emigrate to become part of an exclusively Jewish state, and (3) those who renounced traditional Judaism but failed to assimilate and perforce had to adopt a Jewish national identity. The third group–those who identified as Jews by reason of their origin rather than of any religious commitment–became the pioneers of settlement and nation-building. In a sense our current antagonism is between the second and third types: those who have successfully assimilated into the heterosexual majority, to whom we might add those who suppress their homosexuality out of religious conviction and therefore scorn identity with sinners like us, and those who have opted for a queer national identity.

A queer equivalent of the first group scarcely existed, apart from certain "obvious" types in the bohemian quarters of the large cities (or the scorned but tolerated village queers). Yet it was this small, marginalized band that was in great measure responsible for Stonewall. However, the plight of all three groups stems from a contra-diction which Western society has failed to resolve: its persistence in pre-Enlightenment attitudes toward homosexuality long after it had enshrined the principles of universal human rights and freedom of conscience and in their wake disowned most other forms of medieval superstition and intolerance.

By a curious paradox, the condemnation of homosexuality in all the Abrahamic religions stems from biblical Judaism, yet since 1897 individuals of Jewish ancestry, if not religious belief, have been in the forefront of the gay rights movement–from Magnus Hirschfeld and Kurt Hiller in Germany (Haeberle 1981) to Edward Sagarin ("Donald Webster Cory") and Frank Kameny in the United States. More recently Martin Duberman and Larry Kramer have played leading roles in creating organizations like NGTF, CLAGS, GMHC, and ACT UP. In the gay movement, as in modern intel-lectual life in general, Jews have contributed disproportionately. Given the intensity and ubiquitousness of the taboo, none of the Abrahamic religions will ever be able to find a *modus vivendi* with homosexuality. The issue will continue to provoke endless, unre-solvable conflict.

Inquisitorial and municipal records demonstrate that homosexual subcultures, like clandestine religious sects and other invisible groups and "undergrounds," have existed since the Middle Ages. Peter Damian in his *Liber Gomorrhianus* (1982) thought he de-tected one in the monasteries of eleventh-century Italy, and numer-ous chroniclers described one among the Anglo-Norman nobility in the eleventh and twelfth centuries. Warren Johansson (1984) un-earthed the London subculture of the late twelfth century, H. A. Mason (1992) has suggested that Brunetto Latini had a "retinue" in thirteenth-century Italy, and Iwan Bloch (1908) found evidence for clandestine rendezvous at Cologne in the fifteenth century. Guido Ruggiero (1985) analyzed the Venetian subculture of the Renais-sance, and Michael J. Rocke (1988) the Florentine one. The "molly houses" of early eighteenth-century London, which catered to a new type of androphilia, perhaps centered more on oral sex than was traditional, were well described by Randolph Trumbach. It was the natural and inevitable consequence of the intolerance that forced those who engaged in the forbidden behavior to lead secret lives and to hide their true identities while consorting with one another. Although it preceded the rise of industrialization and mass urbanization, it became politicized only from the end of the nineteenth century. In America resistance to the new political consciousness frustrated the effort to create a viable homosexual rights organization until the beginning of the 1950s, and the movement could not really "go public" until 1969.

This general matter of concealment has been incisively analyzed by the sociologist Erving Goffman, who couched it in terms of the "management of spoiled identity." Other groups which confront this problem of limiting the information that others have about them are ex-cons, who will find it hard to hold jobs or retain friends if their prison past becomes known, and people who have spent time in psychiatric hospitals and asylums. It is now recognized that the casual "outing" of such individuals can be cruel and runs counter to society's proclaimed aim of rehabilitation. Such groups, however, also need role models and examples to break the derogatory stereotypes.

PROSPECTS OF OUTING

What is the significance of outing for gay history and for the future? As it progresses it will contribute mightily to the final liquidation of the "infamy of fact" from which we have suffered so long. It will strike a blow at this, the most pertinacious survival of medieval intolerance in the Western world–and at a means of social control by which the Roman Catholic Church, followed or even enhanced by its Protestant critics, had imposed outward conformity to ascetic morality even on those who inwardly scorned it. Such a challenge to the established order must have far-reaching consequences, not all of which can be foreseen today.

Outing marks a further stage in the march of the gay community or the Queer Nation toward social acceptance, as distinct from mere legal toleration. This is a concession which the pious would even less readily grant than the formal repeal of the sodomy laws. But queer visibility also contributes to liquidating all the fantasies with which the medieval imagination had enveloped the "sodomite" as an object of loathing and horror. These paranoid beliefs, repeated in works of edification for the laity over the centuries, have largely vanished from public discourse, but survive as an unconscious substratum of fear and aversion subsumed under "respectability" and exploited by homophobes. No longer monsters of depravity or repellent stereotypes, we shall be just "folks next door." The wall of separation between them and us will collapse of its own falsehood and absurdity, and the militant Queer Nation will no longer have to wage war on many fronts. The ghetto, spiritual as well as physical, in which we have been forced to live will disappear as completely as the one in which Christian intolerance once immured the Jews.

Moreover, the trend set by *OutWeek* and now the *Advocate* and perhaps *QW* and by professional "outers" will sooner or later reach the gay organizations that now flourish in droves. Local groups that can be expected to copy the big cities' vanguard model know the closet cases in their ambiance. They are often exasperated by the obstinate refusal of such people, who bask in the approval of the local elite, to act on behalf of their community's rights and interests. When outing gains popularity in the smaller cities and in corporations and other major institutions, many will be forcibly brought out of the closet by exasperated activists–with resulting dilemmas for their own identities, not to speak of careers and status.

Those outed in the 1990s in advanced countries are not liable to find the police at their doors, to be arrested and tried for their "unnatural" offenses. They could suffer loss of prestigious positions, lucrative contracts, political opportunities, and career prospects, even spouses or offers of marriage. The attitude of society on such an affect-laden issue changes but slowly.

So outing has a historic mission. It has emerged as a necessary part of the emancipation of queer nationals from the deception and hypocrisy forced upon us by the Old Regime in Europe. Moreover, it marks a new stage, the queer national one, in homosexual self-awareness. Finally, it may presage a new era for sexuality freed from the shackles of ascetic reprobation in which lovers of their own sex can be fully appreciated and can contribute to society and culture without inhibition or hindrance. Heterosexuals have suffered as much from Christian sexual morality as have we: trapped in arranged, loveless marriages with incompatible partners which they could not dissolve because divorce was impossible, or forbidden all sexual gratification outside of marriage, they too were doomed to lives of unalloyed frustration and misery (Blumenfeld 1992, pp. 8-13).

Only when an entire generation has been raised in the belief that homosexual is as natural and legitimate as heterosexual will our movement have attained its goal. We know well that such a radical shift in public morality will not occur in the 1990s, probably not in the following decade either. Before the AIDS crisis set our movement back, ending lives and consuming time and money, some optimists believed that the sodomy laws of the 50 states would be repealed before the end of the century. Now such a happy event, and a climate in which one's sexual orientation will be as irrelevant as the color of one's hair, seems remote. The efforts in the current decade must aim at laying the groundwork for a transformation of sexual mores on which our spiritual heirs and descendants can build.

REFERENCES

Altman, Dennis. 1982. *The Homosexualization of America, the Americanization of the Homosexual*. New York: St. Martin's Press.

Bloch, Iwan. 1908. "Die Homosexualität in Köln am Ende des 15. Jahrhunderts," *Zeitschrift für Sexualwissenschaft* 1: 528-535.

Blumenfeld, Warren J. (ed.). 1992. *Homophobia: How We All Pay the Price*. Boston: Beacon Press.

Bowman, Claude C. 1949. "Cultural Ideology and Heterosexual Reality: A Preface to Sociological Research." *American Sociological Review* 14: 624-633.

Cook, Blanche Wiesen. 1992. *Eleanor Roosevelt*. New York: Viking.

Damian, Peter. 1982. *The Book of Gomorrah: An Eleventh Century Treatise against Clerical Homosexual Practices*, ed. and trans. by Pierre J. Payer. Waterloo, Ontario: Wilfrid Laurier University Press.

Dion, Paul E., O. P. 1981. "Did Cultic Prostitution Fall into Oblivion during the Postexilic Era? Some Evidence from Chronicles and the Septuagint." *Catholic Biblical Quarterly* 43: 41-48.

Duberman, Martin (ed.). 1989. *Hidden from History: Reclaiming the Gay and Lesbian Past*. New York: Meridian.

Freund, Paul A. 1971. "Privacy: One Concept or Many." In *Privacy*, edited by J. Roland Pennock and John W. Chapman, New York: Atherton Press, pp. 182-198.

Friedman, Menachem. 1990. "The Haredim and the Holocaust." *Jerusalem Quarterly* 53 (Winter): 86-114.

Haeberle, Erwin J. 1981. "Swastika, Pink Triangle, and Yellow Star: The Destruction of Sexology and the Persecution of Homosexuals in Nazi Germany." *Journal of Sex Research* 17: 270-287.

Herzl, Theodor. 1896. *Der Judenstaat. Versuch einer modernen Lösung der Judenfrage.* Leipzig and Vienna: Breitenstein.

Humphreys, Laud. 1970. *Tearoom Trade: Impersonal Sex in Public Places.* Chicago: Aldine.

Hunter, Nan D., Sherryl E. Michaelson and Thomas R. Stoddard. 1992. *The Rights of Lesbians and Gay Men.* Carbondale, IL: Southern Illinois University Press.

Johansson, Warren. 1984. "London's Medieval Sodomites." *Cabirion* 10: 6-7, 34.

Johnston, Jill. 1973. *Lesbian Nation: The Feminist Solution.* New York: Simon & Schuster.

Jourard, Sidney M. 1966. "Some Psychological Aspects of Privacy." *Law and Contemporary Problems* 31: 307-318

Lundsgaarde, Henry P. 1971. "Privacy: An Anthropological Perspective on the Right to Be Let Alone." *Houston Law Review* 8: 858-875.

Lusky, Louis. 1972. "Invasion of Privacy: A Clarification of Concepts." *Political Science Quarterly* 87: 192-209.

Madge, Charles. 1950. "Private and Public Spaces." *Human Relations* 3: 187-199.

Mason, H. A. 1992. "A Journey through Hell: Dante's Inferno Re-visited." *Cambridge Quarterly* 21: 150-169.

Middleton, Warren E. 1935. "The Propensity of Genius to Solitude." *Journal of Abnormal and Social Psychology* 30: 325-332.

Mohr, Richard D. 1992. "The Outing Controversy: Privacy and Dignity in Gay Ethics." In, *Gay Ideas: Outing and Other Controversies.* Boston: Beacon Press, pp. 11-48.

Mohr, Richard D. 1988. *Gays/Justice: A Study of Ethics, Society, and Law.* New York: Columbia University Press.

Moore, Wilbert E., and Melvin E. Tumin. 1949. "Some Social Functions of Ignorance." *American Sociological Review* 14: 787-795.

Nickel, Jeff. 1992. "The Ethics of Outing." *IN*, no. 40, June 2, pp. 5, 30.

Oxford Latin Dictionary, ed. P. G. W. Glare. 1982. New York: Oxford University Press.

Rocke, Michael J. 1988. "Sodomites in Fifteenth-Century Tuscany: The Views of Bernardino of Siena." *Journal of Homosexuality* 16/1-2: 7-31.

Ruggiero, Guido. 1985. *The Boundaries of Eros: Sex Crime and Sexuality in Renaissance Venice.* New York: Oxford University Press.

Samar, Vincent J. 1991. *The Right to Privacy: Gays, Lesbians, and the Constitution.* Philadelphia: Temple University Press.

Scheler, Max. 1960. *Die Wissensformen und die Gesellschaft.* Bern and Munich: Francke Verlag.

Schwartz, Barry. 1968. "The Social Psychology of Privacy." *American Journal of Psychology* 73: 741-752.

Shils, Edward. 1966. "Privacy: Its Constitution and Its Vicissitudes." *Law and Contemporary Problems* 31: 281-306.

"A Symposium on Outing." 1990. Homosexual Information Center (Bossier City, LA). *Newsletter*, Number 41, Spring.

Taliaferro, Charles. 1989. "Does God Violate Your Right to Privacy?" *Theology* 92: 190-196.

Willis, Margaret. 1963. "Designing for Privacy. 1. What Is Privacy?" *Architects' Journal* 137: 1137-1141.

Yalom, Irvin D. 1960. "Aggression and Forbiddenness in Voyeurism." *Archives of General Psychiatry* 3: 305-319.

Chapter VIII

Tactical Guide to Outing

Tactical aspects of outing include ethical considerations and practical techniques. Dilemmas confront journalists or activists who undertake outing: Charges of irresponsibility or inhumanity are bound to be directed against them.

INCOME AND CAREER OF OUTEE

The character and circumstances of the outee matter. Outing is not likely to cause financial distress to an individual living on unearned income, or in a safely tenured position. But for those liable to be fired and even blacklisted so that they can never again work in their trade or profession, then outing might be cruel and destructive. If the outee is an entertainer dependent upon fans, or dependent upon sales or business from customers, or a professional dependent upon clients, he or she could suffer drastic loss of income. This is undoubtedly one reason why so very few, and those only in certain categories, have ever dared to come out, except perhaps to friends, families, and other intimates. The homophobic public would cease to patronize them, they fear–probably correctly–and consequently they would suffer economic ruin and failed careers. Some of the young and poor, it is true, incline little to sympathy for the rich and elderly. They would not feel sorry, they say, if a person making $1,000,000 beforehand would be making $100,000 after being outed. Similarly, if a person who had been in the closet for a number of years had accumulated a fortune of, say, several million dollars, the typical outer would hardly worry about the outee's financial security.

By the same token, a singer or actor who had made his or her career as a sex object, like Rock Hudson, would, when outed, at the very least have difficulty maintaining his or her persona and would undoubtedly have to play a different role–that is, if he or she were able to continue as a star. One can imagine the harassment that an outed athlete would have to endure. Few politicians when outed would be able to win reelection as Studds and Frank did, in what is probably the most liberal state in the nation. Never has an open queer national been appointed to a high position in the federal or state bureaucracy. Bureaucrats rightly fear for their careers if they came out or were outed. Although diminishing prejudice and increasing legal protection are now reducing such risks, they still effectively intimidate most government employees and public servants.

PLACE OF RESIDENCE

For similar reasons, the outee's social environment and location must be considered. A closet case living in a small town in the South largely inhabited by fundamentalists might be assaulted and even murdered. On the other hand, the resident of a sophisticated suburb or, better still, of a gay ghetto would have far less to fear from neighbors. Anonymity often sufficiently protects from vindictive homophobes.

Certain suburbs try to prevent gay or lesbian couples from buying or even renting houses within their jurisdictions. Condominium associations' and cooperatives' assent is necessary in order to buy there or at least to stay comfortably. Fellow tenants can harass gay dwellers out of an apartment building and landlords are often more homophobic still.

Outees can therefore often lose not only their jobs but their dwellings, even if they live with parents, spouse, or children. One has therefore to consider the consequences for an outee, depending on the section of the country, the size and attitude of the city or town, the nature of the neighborhood, and even of the building in which he or she resides, because today, ejection will often be the result.

NATURE OF SEXUAL LIFE

The real facts of the sexual life of the subject–and the degree of detail about it which the outing reveals–must also be weighed. The mere fact that someone is "homosexual," due allowance being made for the paranoid fantasies and absurd stereotypes that still flourish on this topic, may tell very little about him or her. On the other hand, an exposé complete with photographs of the outee in all-too-compromising positions could have the effect of making him the butt of endless ridicule and abuse. Then too, should a distinction be drawn between an individual in a stable monogamous relationship and one who seeks only casual sex in bathhouses and movie theaters or one-time partners along lonely roads in the dead of night? What about pederasts and pedophiles, sadomasochists, pimps and prostitutes? Mohr thought that the orientation should be public, acts private; but orientation alone, abstracted from acts, is ultimately private and unprovable.

The hearings on the nomination of Clarence Thomas to the Supreme Court, apart from making the United States a laughing stock, have raised the issue of the quantum and nature of evidence needed to validate an outing. The uncorroborated testimony of an accomplice can always be vigorously denied, so that it becomes a question of who is telling the truth. And if the full details of a subject's sex life must be made public to confirm an outing, what will they do to his or her reputation and legal standing, partners, or social life? An outee who indulged in sordid forms of sexual gratification might be prosecuted by authorities and insulted and abused by associates. Such an outee would scarcely be able to wield influence on behalf of the queer nation, or to be a role model. Hence there are constraints on outing.

Larry Gross asked (1991, p. 384): "What constitutes proof of someone's sexual identity (especially when evidence is likely to have been suppressed or destroyed), and what ethical considerations should influence the decision to reveal a person's previously hidden homosexuality? Are historians the 'outers' of the past, or are outers the historians of the present?" Perhaps the criterion of potential targets is that while they engage in homosexual activity, they refuse to acknowledge their citizenship in the queer nation. So far from having a positive identity and sense of belonging to the movement, they are indifferent and often hostile to its demands and aspirations. This discrepancy between action and belief, between behavior and identity, justifies our determination to expose their double lives.

The hypocrisy and exploitation of boys by pedophile priests may justify their outing, but because they will hardly provide role models or shatter stereotypes, such outings should be left to police or other authorities. Queer nationals as such have no motive for outing them, unless we plan a full-scale attack on the church. Groups like the North American Man-Boy Love Association (NAMBLA) have argued for inclusion of pedophiles in the "gay community" with little success. Even pederasts have become a marginal category of homosexuals in modern industrialized societies. Those who prefer adolescents under the age of consent pose a problem somewhat like that of the pedophiles. Strictly speaking they are "homosexual," but they have little social interaction with the "gay" community. Holland lowered the age of consent to 12 in 1990, virtually removing the stigma of criminality from the pederast. In Spain and Portugal it is 12 for both male and female homosexuality, in Italy it is 14 for both, while in the United Kingdom it is 21 for male homosexuals and 16 for lesbians. On the other hand, only since 1911, even in American jurisdictions, was the age of consent to heterosexual acts raised from 11 or 14 and only since 1961 has a differential been created between heterosexual and homosexual ages of consent in those jurisdictions that repealed laws against sodomy between consenting adults.

Should one out a "good" boy-lover–one who, in the positive image propagated by J. Z. Eglinton in *Greek Love* (1964), is truly concerned with the best interests and the intellectual and moral growth of his boy? A New York welfare officer said that her agency often looks the other way when a stable relationship is established between an older man and a boy–understood as in his teens–since this is probably better for the boy than either returning to an abusive family or becoming a street hustler–usually the only other options. If the boy-lover falls into one of the categories judged suitable for outing–an individual who is in some way harming us–then he should be outed. But what about the consequences to the boy? Should a pederast's boy be stigmatized for the rest of his days? And, whatever his shortcomings, what about the fate of the boy-lover himself?

Even the staunchest advocates of outing today concede that in Nazi Germany or in McCarthyite America the practice would have so endangered the outee as to fall out of consideration. Yet Kurt

Hiller outed living members of the National Socialist hierarchy in his obituary of Magnus Hirschfeld in the German weekly *Wahrheit* in Prague in 1935! But are the dangers not comparable for boy-lovers in the United States even today? In jail, stigmatized as "short eyes," they might be mutilated or even killed. During the Boston-Boise scandal, the lesbian state representative Elaine Noble even advocated a hot line by which callers could denounce pederasts and pedophiles to the police. But this move to separate the good from the bad reflects an internal problem of the queer nation: the wish of some androphile homosexuals and gynecophile lesbians to condemn intergenerational relationships in order to win the approval of "respectable" society. There is no unanimity on where the line between the good and the bad should be drawn and who should draw it. In any case, many consider pedophiles, that is, those attracted to prepubescent children, no more gay than those who engage in sex with animals or corpses homosexual or heterosexual. Pedophiles in turn do not think of themselves as part of the "gay subculture" and make little or no contact with it.

Individuals engaging in extreme forms of sadomasochistic practice form another special category, but not as small as most assume. Outing would certainly stigmatize them and might even subject them to police investigations and to extralegal recriminations and violence. Yet unlike the pedophiles they usually identify with the gay community and frequent its bars and social centers.

INTIMATES, FAMILY, AND FRIENDS

The family circumstances of the subject must be evaluated with the aim of sparing needless suffering to those who are personally without blame. A man with a wife, children, and a façade of respectability should not be outed unless his behavior is so treacherous to the queer nation as to warrant the likely penalty. On the other hand, a subject living alone, with no family or dependents, is less likely to drag others down in his personal exposure. Conventional media attention will often send family members not trained to face the limelight into a state of shock (McBride 1992, p. 19). But what if the revelation is precisely that the family's flesh and blood is "one of those" hated, subhuman "perverts"? If such an individual's family members would be stunned and abashed, should their feelings, however homophobic, be considered? The case of Oliver Sipple (related in Chapter IV) is a classic example. Is it right to expose close associates who would almost certainly be doomed to anguish, contumely, ostracism, even the ruin of their careers? What if the deceased had been the life partner of a U.S. Army general or of a Catholic bishop? Activists might well deem the effects on lovers or ex-lovers to be a more important consideration than family members, especially homophobic ones.

Recent publications indicate that the problems of parents voluntarily coming out to their children are now being addressed. Heterosexuals do not realize how many homosexually oriented individuals have had children. If the parent controls the coming out process, the potential for emotional distress can be reduced. If outing occurs through circumstances beyond the elder's control it may unnecessarily stress the child. At school the child may be subjected to ridicule or even violence by peers who learn that the parent is a "lezzie" or a "fag." Separated and divorced spouses may try to take the child away from the queer parent on grounds that he or she is "morally unfit," as evidenced by the trauma that the child is undergoing.

Is it fair, then, to out parents whose children do not yet know of, or do not yet fully understand, their mother's or father's sexual orientation? This move would make the "innocent suffer with the guilty." On the other hand, is it fair to exempt parents from outing? Should a Pete Williams be let off the hook on the grounds of being a parent? What should the decision be if the marriage and family form the façade erected by a particularly self-hating and vicious closet case–a pillar of the church and of political conservatism?

FAME OR EVIL REPUTATION

Another matter to be judged is the existing fame or reputation of the individual. Activists clearly should not out a notorious criminal or mass murderer as they would a famed medical missionary or celebrated inventor. Then there are debatable cases, such as that of Roger Casement, the Irish patriot whose treason to England long cast a shadow over his life's work.

A very real case in point was that of prominent figures in the National Socialist regime. While émigrés, particularly certain Jewish ones, claimed that the hypervirility of the Nazis and even their sadomasochism was owing to their homosexuality or, in psychoanalytical terms, "latent" homosexuality, a viewpoint later popularized in Luchino Visconti's film *The Damned,* apologists generally preferred to deny that homosexuality was widespread among Nazi leaders after the purge of Roehm and his associates on the night of June 30, 1934. Massimo Consoli has reversed this tendency by dwelling at length on the homosexuality of the early followers of the NSDAP (National Socialist party). One gay scholar, Richard Dey, for years has with others collected data computerized into what he dubs the *Encyclopedia Homophilica.* Recent publicity about Deputy Führer Rudolf Hess's homosexuality has led him to conclude that the tragically unsuccessful plot to assassinate Hitler in 1944 carried out by Colonel Count von Stauffenberg was masterminded by Admiral Canaris and backed by a network of other conspirators, like them rightist homosexuals (one outed by Hiller in *Wahrheit* in 1935) who were trying to save Germany from destruction. In general, it seems best for scholars to admit the facts and publicize the homosexuality of all who have earned fame, whether we deem them good or bad, Nazis or Mafiosi, heroes or traitors, "politically correct" or "hopelessly incorrect." It would be as untruthful to claim that all queer nationals were models of propriety as that they were all fiends of one sort or another. No one would be convinced. In any case, clergy, police, and the medical establishment have over the years concentrated largely on outing unworthy or simply unfortunate lovers of their own sex; the principal task left to us is to out the admirable, successful ones.

Now let us turn from the nature and character of the outee to those of the outer.

MOTIVES OF OUTER

As is abundantly clear from what has been said above, outing stems from a complex of motives. Neither in Germany after 1897 nor in the United States since Stonewall did those who already enjoyed wealth, power, and fame feel any need to sacrifice their own prestige for the less privileged of their ilk. It was the silence that answered such appeals that led to the demand for the outing of "closet cases in high places." One may conclude that it is the pressure of middle-class, activist queer nationals on the prestigious but closeted ones that underlies this political ultimatum.

Early in this century a few realized that if everyone with homosexual feelings or activities were suddenly to become visible, the long-standing taboo would collapse overnight because the prejudices and falsehoods that maintain it would be refuted at one stroke. Outing is thus a selective spotlighting of those who have the potential for ending the pariah status of the community–in fact converting it into a prestigious one. It implicitly overrides the convention, born of helplessness, that members of the clandestine subculture or underground community should not betray one another, on the principle that hypocrisy and disavowal are the greater betrayals.

The character of the outer merits scrutiny. The motive should be solely to advance the cause–not envy, ressentiment, or personal vindictiveness. Should one engage in a practice the merits of which sharply divide our community and which may lead to bitter recriminations, not just from those outed but from movement leaders who consider the tactic indefensible? An editor or journalist may profit enormously from the audience gained by outing someone in a scandal-provoking fashion; but does such an act necessarily benefit the cause? *OutWeek*'s outings did not keep it solvent. The long-term resonances and aftereffects of the outing have to be taken into consideration, if the practice is to be a responsible tactic.

Circumstances are now vastly different from what they were 40 years ago, when Senator McCarthy launched his demagogic campaign against "sex perverts in government." An argument can even be made that progressive social evolution requires that outing be widely practiced, since the elite persist in refusing to come out even now when prejudice has abated and so many punitive laws have been repealed. Nevertheless, perhaps each case should be considered individually on its own merits. If outings by activists resulted in suicide, as outing by police or other authorities so often did in the past, they could hardly be considered propitious. But then, who is to decide? If everyone is free to out everyone else, as is now the case, the media will decide what to publicize–and what not to. They cannot be forced to headline even the most important cases.

At its most elementary level, outing is a form of gossip. And gossip is a practice of which homosexuals have been as fond as any other group–perhaps more so. Unless the media can be muzzled, which does not seem likely, there is little way to stop the tabloids and late-night television from picking up gossip and spreading it. And as we have recently seen in several prominent heterosexual cases, this publicity then "authorizes" the respectable media to mention the allegations in the guise of "reporting the news." The story imparts the information that so-and-so has been *discussed* in such-and-such a way in another, perhaps less fastidious organ of the media. In the long run, of course, the remedy is to make sexual orientation no more critical than left-handedness or right-handedness. But this utopia is not visible on the immediate horizon. In 1893 Otto de Joux posed as a precondition for coming out *en masse* an "international Uranide amnesty" (Joux, p. 244). But as John Alan Lee concluded 84 years later, society, "having given homosexuals masks to wear, is not about to agree readily to their abandonment by those who, at whatever personal cost, decline to wear their masks any longer" (1977, p. 76).

Historical and social conditions supply a framework which needs be taken into account in applying these arguments. At the same time, the truism must be acknowledged that each of us is "human, all too human"–that is to say, moved by irrational factors rooted in psychological quirks. Let us begin by examining some irrational factors that promote outing, and then turn to those factors that inhibit it. First is exhibitionism. Many people crave the limelight, but their modest station in life does not afford them the notoriety that they seek. Even if personally unremarkable, they may be able to attract attention by loudly proclaiming the secrets of others. And they may seek the additional satisfaction of having done something meritorious. In the old days the exhibitionist, homophobic outer could smugly claim to have helped to rid society of a "moral pest." Today the queer national outer congratulates himself for having deflated hypocrisy or curbed the malice of some self-hating closet case in public office.

Another factor, regrettably enough, is spitefulness. Deny it though we will, sad to say many of us retain homophobic residues in our mentality which in some instances could contribute to the motives for outing. Such self-hatred may blend into motives of mere personal spite or even add a tone of vindictiveness to them. By revealing the secret failings of someone you dislike or envy, you may place obstacles in his path, and remind him of his limitations. Of course, motives such as these could be mingled with good reasons for outing, which would not thereby be invalidated. But there may also be petty motives. Although outwardly projected self-contempt was formerly much more common, unfortunately the likes of Quentin Crisp persist in believing that straight people are better than we, so that to "reduce" someone to our status is to demean the person.

Yet another factor is the desire to be "more radical than thou," evidenced by some members of Queer Nation and by grandstanding writers in the gay press. Since the policy of letting people remain in the closet is interpreted as conservative, it is possible to "gain points" or one-up others by advocating outing *en masse*. In this way "vanguard" outers show how "advanced" they are by comparison with the timid stick-in-the-mud types who–in their view–only want to get by through protecting the assimilationist and appeasing the oppressor. There are probably other dubious motives that make a certain sense for the outer but not for anyone else.

Andrew Miller, news editor of *OutWeek,* found it appalling that so many of his colleagues were tripping over each other to justify the longest media coverup ever: hiding the homosexuality of the rich and famous. He also confessed the envy that he, as an openly gay journalist, felt for closeted journalists in well-paying, high-level jobs that will be forever denied him. This certainly is a potential if not common motive for outing: the envy that the separatist cannot repress for the assimilationist, who magically passes through the barriers. This conflict may not last. For the marginalized, open individual puts his pampered colleagues on notice that their defenses are not impregnable.

Now let us examine the opposite side of the coin: irrational factors that work to inhibit outing. Many closet cases intensely fear the possible consequences of being outed. They respond with empathy when another is outed, since the event triggers these fears–even though they may be groundless. In this way excessive fear of one's own outing contributes to an overall dread of the process. A more general theme is the desire to "let sleeping dogs lie." It is felt that society already must cope with too much inner conflict over the "gay issue"; one should not add more fuel to the fire. Besides, outing is not "nice"–Miss Manners would not recommend it.

Finally, just as in the opposite situation, self-contempt may play a role in inhibiting outing just as we have seen that it can in prompting it. Some who feel that to be queer is a disgrace think that society had better be as little reminded of such loathsome intruders as possible. The fewer who are out, the less reason, they hope, society will have for inflicting its justly merited sanctions on those that it can track down. It is back into the woodwork for everyone!

Needless to say, the authors do not believe that we belong in the woodwork–or any other place of concealment or confinement. But only when our civilization has been so profoundly transformed that the shame of love for one's own sex is banished forever will all and sundry be exempt from such curious perversions of the truth.

LIBEL AND SLANDER

Outers should possess sufficient information to support their revelations if need be in a court of law (without revealing more details to the media than they demand in order to cooperate). They should not publicize any trivial gossip that comes their way. They should carefully examine the reliability of their informants and the probability that these possess correct data on the most intimate aspects of the subject's life. Merely having espied the subject in a gay bar or even at a gay resort is not enough.

Ultimately we may hope for the dawn of a toleration such that the statement that someone is gay will no longer constitute grounds for a libel action, because well-informed, right-thinking people will only say: Who cares? Just a few decades ago, one could sue if falsely called a Jew, but by 1950 an American court held that this attribute was no longer sufficient grounds for libel because society had renounced most of its prejudices against Jews. When courts recognize that it is no longer slander or libel to call a person gay, they will have confirmed that the reasonable majority is no longer homophobic.

How far off is that day? Signorile is quoted as optimistic: "The only way to get acceptance of homosexuality is to show people the image of gay sex, to let them see as many of us as possible. On some warped level, the tabloids do breed acceptance. After five years of this, it won't be a story anymore" (Hartman 1990).

Of course, just as to call someone a ———— dike, to call one a ——— queer or a dirty c—ks——r in a tough bar can be illegal under the "fighting words" doctrine because it might provoke civil disorder. Such an utterance might be construed, depending on tone, volume, and other circumstances, as a provocation rather than as slander, even if true.

But the ultimate defense against a charge of slander or libel is truth, not intent, for the intent of the slanderer or libeler is assumed to be malicious. Civil slander entails monetary compensation carefully measured with respect to loss of employment, business, and the like–not mental pain, anguish, or loss of social acceptability. Criminal libel can result in fine or imprisonment. But criminal cases, which must involve criminal intent, are rare and seldom pursued unless one party is trying to harass another so as to silence him or drive him out of town, into an asylum, or to suicide. Alongside such a criminal prosecution, a civil suit can also seek monetary compensation. Incidentally, it is no bar to conviction if the defendant alleges that he was quoting a third party, but it may mitigate his guilt and lessen the award against him. Finally, a prompt and full apology if possible, published within a week or two where the original appeared, is likely to mitigate the offense.

PUBLICITY

Publicizing an outing may be difficult because media often try to suppress or ignore the inconvenient revelation. A story carried in the gay press is as often as not blacked out by the establishment media. This can both discourage outings and nullify their effect. But the multiplication and circulation growth of gay periodicals has been enormous since 1969. While only the *Advocate*, *Fag Rag*, and *Gay Community News* (which just ceased to appear) have a continuous record of publication since the early 1970s, every major city now has at least one gay paper.

In the last few decades, the major newspapers that maintain national and international reporting staffs have shrunk from nearly 20 to a mere five: *The New York Times, Washington Post, Los Angeles Times, Boston Globe,* and *Chicago Tribune.* These have usually ignored comings out and outings, whether reported in gay newspapers or viva voce. In fact, most have not yet used the term "outing," almost as if it were taboo. Of course, such papers have also refused to repeat or investigate stories broken by the *National Enquirer,* the *Star,* and other supermarket tabloids. The weeklies *Time,* which introduced the concept of "outing" to the general public early in 1990, and *Newsweek* have been more forthright.

Today the danger from public figures suing for libel is generally past. But as yet editors have apparently not been able or willing to comprehend that outing has become largely political–not one opponent trying to crush another, but a valid movement tactic and therefore clearly relevant and not in bad taste. It is not as though they are obliged to publish exactly who did what to whom and how often (however novel or entertaining the sex play between a pair of queers might be to many readers). The details, such as who was active or passive and what orifices of the body were involved, hardly matter. The respectable newspapers squeezed juicy details out of the Barney Frank and Gerry Studds cases, as well as from the straight ones of Wilbur Mills and Gary Hart, without going into the physical details. (The trial for rape of William Kennedy Smith was an exception.) Were the Forbes and Williams exposés less newsworthy? Why should the straight press not at least trail outings by activists? It apparently cannot grasp the altruistic motives or appreciate the significant purposes of the new outings. At the very least its editors are insensitive and unsupportive. Perhaps their lack of cooperation is more from ignorance of the theory, which it is one of the principal aims of this book to explain and justify. In any event, until we have regular columnists–as African Americans, Native Americans, Asian Americans, Hispanics, women, Jews, and others have–our viewpoint will be scanted in mainstream publications and outing will remain a difficult, prolonged, and only partially effective procedure.

It might be argued that the straight media suppress outings because their decision makers think that the gay leadership is in favor of them. In fact, most of the gay leaders have themselves opposed outing except perhaps in extreme cases where they saw hypocrites repeatedly using their positions of influence to oppress other lovers of their own sex or to deny us our rights. So far gay leaders have done their best to keep the closet doors closed for politicians with whom they frequently deal. The gay press, too, has often decided not to publicize outings.

Outers can circumvent the blackout imposed by the establishment media in several ways: (1) printing and hanging leaflets or posters with information about closet cases (illegal solely if placed without permission on others' property), (2) spray painting slogans on walls or pavements, (3) defacing existing (publicity, campaign) posters of the outee, and (4) defacing existing billboards. However, all four tactics yield publicity limited only to small geographical areas, and often face systematic efforts to remove and obliterate the messages in a matter of days or even hours.

COUNCIL ON OUTING

"Ripple effects" of the kind adumbrated above, whereby closeted figures–or gay politicians–become active or passive accomplices of homophobia in varying degrees, present highly ambiguous cases which nonetheless need to be considered. But just saying that in turn poses a complex question. It is one thing to ponder them in the abstract, within the covers of this book, another to proceed to seek redress. What about gay classicists, like certain ones known to the authors, who persist in writing about ancient Greece and Rome as if pederasty had never existed there, or English or history professors who never mention the subject when lecturing on Whitman or Frederick the Great? Are they homophobic fellow travelers who deserve to be outed? Assuming legitimate discord on such questions, what body would be competent to deliberate them? This raises the question of the possibility of "gay courts" to decide a transgressor's fate. Have some queer nationals the right to adopt such procedures to judge others? And if so, why, and what sort of credentials should they have?

The authors suggest a Council on Outing that would process applications, review information, evaluate each case, and give the object of the intended outing time to reply or to mend his sinful ways by coming out or at least stopping his homophobic words and deeds. (Anyone whom the council decided to out or even whose case it decided to study should probably be notified so that the person could have time to come out, to prepare himself or herself for outing, or to try to persuade the council that he or she should *not* be outed.) Such a body might gain a modicum of control over the flow of compromising data and be a partial safeguard against outings inspired base motives such as by personal animosity or the failure of an attempt at blackmail.

A Council on Outing might be composed of successful outers such as Petrelis and Signorile, editors of movement periodicals that have not taken a stand against outing, scholars, lawyers, journalists, politicians, and other queer rights activists. Such a committee, if carefully composed, could lend weight to outings and facilitate their gaining credence. Its endorsements might well induce the press to take up outing stories.

In addition to a central body, councils could be constituted for various geographical areas or professions. And of course, the formation of such a body would not infringe the rights or obligations of individuals or other groups to do their own outings. Certain outings will always be primarily a local concern. Others might be organized and carried out by peers or coworkers within a particular business or profession, perhaps in the meetings or newsletters of their professional organizations. Each university might form a local group for outings; each business (for example, Macy's, which has been discussed by Queer Nation/New York); even each church.

Nevertheless, the organization of a central committee would remain essential to support crucial outings and overcome media resistance. Our youth is not only impatient, especially because of AIDS, but also self-confidently free of the fear and timidity ingrained in their elders by the all-pervasive homophobia of pre-Stonewall America. Our aim would be to reinforce these brave young outers, who have largely run up against a blank wall. With so many gay celebrities reluctant to leave the closet, so many prelates, military officers, capitalists, bureaucrats and administrators, the movement remains thwarted from its goal of proving that many of the most prestigious members of America's political and cultural elites are secret citizens of our still largely pariah nation. (One might quibble about whether sports and entertainment figures merit outing as urgently, especially as they seem to have somewhat more recourse at law than the other sorts of figures named.)

No one could be naive enough to imagine that the formation of such a self-appointed, self-perpetuating committee or council would not cause enormous controversy and dissent. But the overarching importance of its goal would induce enough volunteers to serve even in the face of the severest risk of personal attack and abuse. It must be supposed that such a council or councils could convince some of the mainstream media not only of the credibility of the outings but of their desirability. Claiming for ourselves and proclaiming to the public the names of closeted members of the elite would help our cause, even if there were some grief and a few minor setbacks caused thereby. The failure of ensconced, comfortably prestigious queer nationals to come out to help their less fortunate, often impoverished, and still manifestly oppressed brethren may not indeed be treason, if there be no Queer Nation for them to betray, but it is hardly socially responsible or morally unreprehensible. If some might complain that such a self-appointed tribunal was interfering with rights of privacy, careers, marriages and long-time partnerships, one could reply that cowardice, selfishness, and greed should not be rewarded by a cloak of invisibility while many are dying of AIDS and others suffering ostracism, persecution, and financial loss because they are out of the closet. Bentham's collectivist principle of the greatest good for the greatest number must be weighed against the individualistic notion of privacy and other rights when deciding what is ethical.

Just as no one can (or should) stop outings by individuals or local groups, certainly no one can stop outings by police or other authorities, indeed by heterosexuals in every walk of life. No closeted queer is safe from such outings, especially unofficial but no less devastating ones effected by gossip and innuendo. The very act of remaining in the closet not only makes one invisible in the ranks of our cause, even unable to appear at our rallies, but leaves one prey to fear, blackmail, or other kinds of pressure. Arguably, in many cases outing such persons may be for their own good. At any rate, the authors do not as of this writing know anyone who has been hurt by being outed by an activist. What, for example, did Pete Williams lose by being outed? He is in fact now in a much stronger position than before and may well be happier and more secure. It would be wonderful to hear from Pete himself just how he feels about it.

Most activists will denounce the idea of such a council and anyone who volunteers to serve on it. But even the leaders of major gay organizations cannot suppress outing, however much they may deplore it. They should, if they think about it carefully, prefer that a committee having the best credentials be selected from those willing to volunteer. Thus outings would be more carefully planned and coordinated and better documented than if left to random actions. Institutionalization of outing would likely prove more effective than the current anarchy, where only a few have heroically succeeded against overwhelming odds.

The main rational objection to outing (other than apodictic *pronunciamentos* for privacy over and against all social responsibility and intellectual honesty) can come only from the belief that the rich and famous will come out voluntarily and in time. By now, however, that pious hope, so dear to the hearts of activists in the early 1970s as well as in Wilhelmine Germany, has been bitterly frustrated. Only the naive still cherish such an illusion. The growing disenchantment, which had already begun before the onset of the plague, diminished what glamour gayness had gained after Stonewall; but on the other hand the gravity of the situation makes HIV-positives especially unwilling to be patient with those who turn their backs on the plight of the ill and dying. It is highly significant that the newest phase of outing began a little more than two years after the founding of ACT UP on March 12, 1987.

It is immoral for the privileged few to hide their gayness while so many others suffer and die. If they do not find the courage to come out, they must be outed–and the sooner the better!

OUTING LESBIANS

With women more than ever in the political, sports, and entertainment spotlight, activists have outed the politicians Barbara Mikulski, Liz Holtzman, and Evelyn Murphy; tennis stars Billie Jean King and Martina Navratilova were both outed in palimony suits; and the sexualities of Jodie Foster, Chastity Bono, and Madonna too are now common knowledge. Before 1940 police and other authorities hardly outed lesbians at all–far less frequently than gay men. Afterwards lesbians became much more visible, partly because of women's service in the military and the freedom and opportunities they obtained during wartime to take jobs normally reserved for men, and to congregate together when millions of men were away on military duty. Traditionally, women were outed far less because the worst sexual offense with which women could be charged was adultery, entailing the moral offenses of cuckolding their husbands and casting the shadow of illegitimacy on their children. Lesbian relationships implied neither of these twin sins. It was prostitutes and at times cross-dressers rather than typical lesbians whom the police harassed. In addition, as Havelock Ellis pointed out as late as 1927, society long regarded the single mother as virtually a criminal. The "scarlet letter" retained its vivid hue. A pregnancy or child out of wedlock outed the poor woman as "unchaste," dooming her in many cases to marginality with little if any prospect of marriage. The adulteress, the single mother, and the prostitute thus bore the brunt of society's intolerance in the sexual realm. The lesbian ran a poor fourth because her sexual failings eluded interaction with men. Although the male was at least half responsible for their sins, society hypocritically stigmatized the female half of the guilty pair. The lesbian activity of the single or married woman, by contrast, could have no reproductive consequences and directly infringed the rights of no male, except when it led to alienation of affection.

When women did not generally play a public role, their private, heterosexual "misconduct" was nonetheless enough to justify stigmatizing them for the reasons mentioned above–cuckolding their husbands and/or risking conception and thus illegitimacy or bastardy. On the other hand, the heterosexual adventures of a boy or man in private life were usually tolerated and even tacitly encouraged as a sign of masculinity or red-bloodedness. Only when he entered the public arena might a man's heterosexual dalliances be exposed to scorn and vituperation by his individual or institutional enemies, for political reasons. Of course, *homo*sexual behavior by any man, even one in private life, could have disastrous consequences. The travails of growing up queer in the American South, for example, have been amply documented by Sears (1991). It is notable, however, that Sears does not mention a single case of a lesbian outed there.

OUTING AND THE CLERGY

Religious denominations are a problem unto themselves. One of the central paradoxes of history is how many who loved their own sex served churches that formally rejected them and defamed their sexual orientation. Some doubtless felt a calling which stemmed from their innermost selves and could not renounce it, even if Christianity unreservedly condemned homosexual expression and glorified lifelong abstinence; others in churches that demanded celibacy may have wished to escape pressures to marry. Outwardly they confessed Christ Jesus and made themselves "eunuchs for the kingdom of heaven's sake," but inwardly they worshipped only the goddess of love. Doomed to lead a double life within their religious communities, they found solace only in the awareness that many of their fellow religious shared their sinful proclivities. If we out many of them, can institutional Christianity do without these personnel, or must it tolerate their mode of sexual gratification as a "necessary evil"? Can theologians admit that they have been wrong for the past 1900 years, as they repudiated their fulminations against witches during the Enlightenment and against Jews after Hitler, without shaking the pillars of the institutions they profess to lead? These are painful questions, and the outing of prominent clerics and lay leaders will demand answers to them.

Clergy, whether Roman Catholic, Protestant, Jewish, or Muslim, continue serving institutions that denounce homosexuality and formally prohibit active homosexuals from serving in their ranks. Even those who do not preach against homosexuality, even if they fail or refuse personally to endorse their institution's homophobic utterances or policies, may nevertheless be outed in the way Pentagon officials should be. Outing them would show their superiors, fellows, and congregations that people whom they believed to be straight are gay. Richard Sipe, a priest turned psychologist, projected from his sample of 1,500 priests interviewed between 1960 and 1985 that 20 percent of the 57,000 Catholic priests in the United States are homosexual and that half of them are sexually active (*Newsweek,* February 23, 1987). Many, even some Roman Catholic sources, conjecture that up to 40 or maybe 50 percent of their priests, monks, and nuns, in the United States at least, are oriented toward their own sex and may often engage in sacrilegious acts. If they or the large number of ministers or rabbis oriented toward their own sex were outed, these religious groups could scarcely maintain the homophobic stance which their hypocrisy currently allows. We are truly everywhere, but until this fact is acknowledged, it is unlikely that we shall gain full acceptance rather than grudging toleration. Hence outing the clergy, whose mean hypocrisy is inordinately blatant and galling, is a special need.

So far the only clergy outed are those accused of child molestation, charges which are rapidly increasing in number and in the vindictiveness of the accusers or those caught in the net. Not one cleric has yet been outed on ideological grounds. Earlier in this century, in Massachusetts Cardinals O'Connell and Wright were known by insiders to be attracted to their own sex. Even the arch-hypocrite Francis Cardinal Spellman managed to escape outing while he was alive. The outing of a living American cardinal might be as beneficial to the queer nation as the outing of a Supreme Court Justice, and it can scarcely be believed that there are none.

IN THE WAKE OF FORBES' OUTING

Two months after the initial bombshell, the *OutWeek* of May 16, 1990 was headlined SMASHING THE CLOSET, THE PROS AND CONS OF OUTING. An introductory comment by Signorile was headed "Outing Seizes America!" It began: "Not too long ago, some of us at *OutWeek* decided that we could no longer participate in helping rich and famous gays . . . stay in the closet. We felt an obligation to tell the truth. In one such case–that of Malcolm Forbes– all of the editors of *OutWeek* decided that we would frankly discuss his homosexuality in the magazine. That cover story hit the stands three weeks after the famous multimillionaire died and sent shock waves throughout the media."

"Telling such truths is now called 'outing,' named, of course, by heterosexuals. . . . It's a term that suggests something negative; something active, aggressive and evil. And it makes a silly metaphor seem only more real. Lest we forget, there is no closet, no door, no hinges. There are just individuals who've told a lot of people that they're queer [The new term had 'arrived'], and individuals who've told fewer people that they're queer."

The magazine denied having an official position on outing, and even its editors professed widely divergent views. Hunter Madsen, coauthor of *After the Ball: How America Will Conquer Its Fear and Hatred of Gays in the 90s* (1990), wrote that the San Francisco gay novelist Armistead Maupin had posed the question: If he possessed a big, thick computer list naming every gay person in America, would he be willing to *publish* that list for the heterosexual world to see? Despite positive urges of his conscience, he replied: No, he simply could not publish the "homo-files."

This hypothetical question raises some issues of fact. Madsen's chief objection to outing was that "being flushed into the open before one is ready–before one has overcome shame and guilt, before one has constructed a solid personal alternative to society's mores–can crush a person. . . . And, of course, when you take upon yourself to force others out of the closet you may wreak havoc in unintended ways. . . . Your highhanded intervention might expose them to real hardships and discrimination that they should have had a chance to weigh for themselves."

Victoria A. Brownworth, a former editor of *Philadelphia Gay News,* described her experience as a featured speaker at the Gay Pride Week celebration at Haverford and Bryn Mawr colleges. She told the students that she no longer had patience for anyone in the closet. "Every gay man . . . who 'passes' (and tries to) oppresses me further and reaps the benefits of my activism while hiding the strength of our numbers from the people to whom those numbers would make a difference. . . . What are we really talking about? We're talking about exposing the collaborationists." When a student asked if outing did not represent a threat to the privacy of the individual, she answered that "in one sense it does . . . yet if we look at the history of oppression, the most virulent backlash has been directed toward those groups who were able to 'pass' as members of the majority group–like the majority of Jews in Germany in the final days of the Weimar Republic." As a woman, Brownworth perceived that the patriarchal old-boy network ensured "closet rights" for the rich and famous by enlisting male journalists as junior members (Beery et al. 1990, pp. 48-49).

Thus the issues raised by Brownworth far exceed the limits of outing. She questioned the legitimacy of an assimilationist policy that seeks to minimize the differences between the in-group and the out-group, but in so doing challenges a basic assumption of American life. The social politics of the United States have always been assimilationist. While immigrant groups were allowed their own community life and their own organizations and media, the fundamental premise was always that the second generation would be raised with the new land as its horizon, speaking the English language, and steeped in American values and traditions. The demand for "multiculturalism" that underlies the position taken by Brownworth marks a failure of assimilation and a threat to the continued viability of that policy. To be sure, we are not and have never been a religious or ethnic group distinct from all others; rather, like women, we cut across all conventional lines of religious and ethnic identity. Our separatism must always be imperfect separatism, since homosexual males, like lesbian separatists, cannot attain state power. A Queer Nation in the geographical sense of an independent state would, to put it bluntly, have a rather gloomy demographic future, unless it functioned as an asylum for the persecuted queer offspring of "breeders." The most that we can hope to achieve is a social space that we can call our own within the territory of the state on which we reside. Ours is a nation without a state!

VARIETY OF OPINIONS WITHIN OutWeek *AND ELSEWHERE*

After outing Forbes, Rotello offered his own considerations. He saw the outing debate as a reappraisal of basic assumptions about the movement, as a declaration that powerful closeted homosexuals, and by extension, all of us, have an inherent obligation to our community (or nation). Such an assertion presupposes that we constitute a genuine, inescapable minority into which we are born or compelled by personality to join, from which we derive advantages and disadvantages, and to which we owe inherent allegiance. "Such an unexpected definition of gayness is being bitterly resisted by both straights who fear and loathe the concept of gays as a legitimate minority, and by gays who are unprepared for the implications of such a redefinition."

Lindsy Van Gelder, a lesbian freelance writer, mentioned (1990) that the heterosexual editor of a small southern newspaper told her he would never run a profile of someone in a happy, committed gay relationship. This was part of his editorial mission to protect vulnerable teenage readers from finding gay life "too appealing." This is but one facet of how the media defame us and our supporters. As this editor made clear, the protection of privacy was not the concern. By and large, public figures and their families effectively have none. In 1973-74, when the media were staging a bloodless coup d'état against Richard Nixon (far less analyzed ever since than the violent one against John F. Kennedy), they exposed details of his private life that in past generations would, if committed to writing at all, have lain in manuscripts sealed until 75 years after the authors' deaths. Now that the rules have changed, they should be the same for one and all.

However, the journalist should proceed from the recognition that we now form a Queer Nation, even if it remains in social and legal limbo. But it is a nation with a public image and political interests of its own. A companion ethical problem to outing is "inning"– keeping gay people in the closet even when they have no desire to be there. The classic example is the refusal of many newspaper obituaries to name surviving lovers or life partners. Van Gelder mentioned that most reporters would not write a story about a lesbian hunting for her life partner presumed buried under debris in the 1989 Bay Area earthquake.

Behind much media obfuscation is the feeling that homosexuality is such a "marked" characteristic–so suspect, so bizarre, and so overwhelming–that any mention of it automatically makes it the focus of the story. The neutralization of the stigma is therefore a precondition for journalistic objectivity.

CONCLUSION

Outing represents a pressure brought by the visible and vocal portion of the Queer Nation on the invisible, silent, prestigious minority, as it were a demand that the elite of our community recognize their allegiance and act to further the collective interests of our nation to which–by birth, socialization, or choice–they belong. This practice stems from the growth of a political consciousness that sees all of us as sharing a common fate and as responsible for one another. If it succeeds, it will magnify our symbolic presence at the upper levels of society and make the public aware of how many prominent individuals prefer tabooed sexual pleasures. But at the same time it can engender a sense of the rift within society caused by sexual orientation, and perhaps recriminations against a community that is still feared and shunned by traditionalists.

Members of the 50+ generation would still have to face peer pressure of such intensity that voluntary coming out would be exceedingly difficult. For the young activists who boldly take to the streets in ACT UP and Queer Nation the intolerance of the pre-Stonewall era is ancient history. They embody a self-assurance and a self-confidence that no previous generation, crushed as it was by all-pervasive homophobia, could have felt. And so they can demand, perhaps oblivious of the trauma and anguish that their elders suffered in their own teens and twenties, that the older, rich-and-famous cohort cotton to the new standard of behavior.

As intolerance diminishes through the irreversible passing of generations and increased insight into homosexuality, the need for concealment and deception will correspondingly lessen. The hypocrisy in sexual matters that has poisoned Western civilization for centuries will ebb. The burden of secrecy and falsehood will then more easily be discarded, and the truth will rather be welcomed. In turn the anxiety felt by many heterosexuals uncertain of the sexual identity of others will abate, just because a frank admission will be almost a matter of courtesy in dealings with friends and acquaintances. Of course, there have always been heterosexuals who subtly intimated to their gay associates that they knew of their orientation but preferred not to have it mentioned–but in this new era the unease and pain associated with such knowledge will be minimized.

Candor about sexual orientation may have broader effects. Social psychologists have investigated a phenomenon called disclosure. In daily life, one observes that some individuals will freely convey personal information–about their job, spouse, political views, and the like–while others will remain guarded. The closeted by definition are reluctant to discuss their sexuality or anything related to it, such as home arrangements, vacation plans, and the like. In this way they develop an overall pattern of self-censorship, denying others any bits of information which may be assembled to uncover the secret pattern of their lives. Once homosexuality is out in the open, this motive for hiding knowledge about oneself will disappear. No longer fearful of disclosure, homosexuals will bond more easily with other self-revealing individuals.

Outing, like coming out, is part of the process whereby the homosexual culture or subculture, driven underground by religious intolerance, is regaining or asserting its public identity and image. This process now seems irreversible. The AIDS crisis could not stop it; instead it served to strengthen our resolve to resume our forward march and to assert our nationalism. This is not to say that vestigial attitudes toward the "crime against nature" will not make this process a protracted and painful one. The task presents a supreme and exciting challenge: it is not for everyone.

It is courageous for individuals to risk personal advantage to further the interests of the erotic minority to which they belong. Others guilty of injuring their own kind or even actively persecuting them should be unmasked as hypocrites. But outing must, in the last analysis, be seen in the context of the cowardice and hypocrisy forced upon us by our fanatical persecutors. The ending of obligatory heterosexuality is essential for the resolution of this dilemma. Homosexual behavior is entitled to the same respect and privacy as heterosexual, no more and no less. The German Romantic poet August von Platen wrote in 1823: "Those who feast on virtue leave to us the sin alone." The heterosexual claim to a monopoly on virtue must be dislodged. This dislodgement is the precondition for freedom of conscience in the sexual sphere and the emancipation of those who love their own sex from this last major relic of the Middle Ages.

As Charley Shively said at the Gay Pride Rally in Boston on June 9, 1990, the greatest obstacle confronting the gay movement is the dogma of obligatory heterosexuality imposed upon homosexuals in Western civilization by the religious intolerance of the late Middle Ages. Whatever its source, nothing positive or beneficial to society rests upon the ideology of obligatory heterosexuality. Once it is abandoned, the question of outing will cease, as no stigma will attach to departures from the norm. Everyone will be free to sound the depths of his or her sexual orientation and to act upon it, even to declare it or boast of it. While the citizen's right to privacy in sexual matters–despite the Supreme Court–should be recognized and honored by the *state* (even if only as a legal fiction), the principle that one should be forthright about one's sexual feelings should prevail in *society*. Obligatory heterosexuality is as useless to America as the Berlin Wall was to Germany, and tearing down the artificial barriers that separate American queer nationals from their fellow-citizens, even while recognizing their dual citizenship, will at long last end the postmedieval anachronism of conformity and unanimity in sexual life. It will relegate the need for outing to the dustbin of history.

REFERENCES

Beery, Steve; Victoria Brownsworth; Ayofemi Folayan; Hunter Madsen; Andrew Miller; Sarah Pettit; and Gabriel Rotello. 1990. "Smashing the Closet: The Pros and Cons of Outing." *OutWeek*, no. 45, May 16, pp. 41-53.

Eglinton, J. Z. 1964. *Greek Love*. New York: Oliver Layton Press.

Gross, Larry. 1991. "The Contested Closet: The Ethics and Politics of Outing." *Critical Studies in Mass Communication* 8: 352-388.

Hartman, Mitchell. 1990. "When to Say Someone Is Gay." *The Quill*, November-December, p. 6.

Joux, Otto de. 1893. *Die Enterbten des Liebesglückes. Ein Beitrag zur Seelenkunde*. Leipzig: Max Spohr.

Lee, John Alan. 1977. "Going Public: A Study in the Sociology of Homosexual Liberation." *Journal of Homosexuality* 3: 49-78.

McBride, Donald L. 1992. "What Do You Say to Those in the Spotlight of the News Media?" *Journal of Pastoral Care* 46: 19-21.

Mohr, Richard D. 1992. *Gay Ideas: Outing and Other Controversies*. Boston: Beacon Press.

Sears, James T. 1991. *Growing Up Gay in the South: Race, Gender, and Journeys of the Spirit*. Binghamton, New York: Haworth Press.

Signorile, Michelangelo. 1990. "Outing Seizes America!" *OutWeek*, no. 45, May 16, p. 40.

Van Gelder, Lindsy. 1990. "Straight or Gay, Stick to the Facts." *Columbia Journalism Review*, November-December, pp. 52-53.

Appendix
The Legal Side of Outing

In 1991-1992 law journals published four articles on the novel subject of outing. Each seeks to establish the grounds upon which actions can be brought against a potential outer for violation of the outee's right to privacy as that has been defined in American law over the past century.

More precisely, the great expert William Prosser, "distilled the tort of invasion of privacy into four distinct causes of action, one of which is the public disclosure of private facts. Today, thirty-eight states and the District of Columbia recognize the public disclosure of private facts tort. The most common form of the tort sets forth four requirements of cause of action. . . : (1) public disclosure; (2) of private facts; (3) concerning a matter which would be highly offensive and objectionable to a reasonable person; and (4) which is not of legitimate concern to the public. Unlike the tort of defamation, truth is no defense" (Elwood 1992, pp. 753-54).

Elwood maintained that "even celebrities should be considered private figures with regard to their sexuality." The precedent for this proposal is the Supreme Court's ruling in the defamation case *Tine, Inc.* v. *Firestone* (424 U.S. 448 [1976]), which "held that the former wife of a wealthy industrialist, manifestly a 'celebrity,' had not forfeited her status as a private figure with regard to her divorce." He concluded that "under the *Firestone* analysis, a gay celebrity would thus retain privacy rights regarding his sexuality unless he made a full, knowing and voluntary waiver of them, or unless his sexuality somehow became relevant to some larger controversy" (pp. 771-72). But what if the celebrity is publicly voicing the opinion that homosexual behavior is despicable, immoral, and criminal? Is he not perpetuating the belief that his own clandestine acts are not a private concern at all, but ones which the state has a legitimate interest in preventing and punishing? Given the status of acts between members of the same sex in American criminal law, how can the same individual invoke a right of privacy in civil law that he would expressly deny himself and others in criminal law? As the old saying runs, you cannot eat your cake and have it too.

Pollack and Wick asked "Is outing highly offensive to a reasonable person of ordinary sensibilities?" or does it unearth "knowledge that will offend the community mores"? (Pollack 1992, pp. 724-31; Wick 1991, pp. 423-24, 429-30). Opinion on homosexuality now ranges from the belief that those who engage in unnatural vice should be prosecuted and punished to the intention of adding as many outees' names as possible to the honor role of the queer nation. To be sure, in the not too remote past the very mention of homosexuality in a mass circulation journal did give offense. When in January of 1955 the London *Spectator* (the conservative counterpart of the *New Statesman & Nation*) published an article under the pseudonym "Biological Homosexual," its readers could scarcely contain their outrage that a "self-confessed pervert" should have been allowed to plead his case on its pages. One indignantly declared homosexuality a subject "which I have always thought is talked about with bated breath as a thing unspeakable, and rightly so, but nowadays there is nothing too shameful to be discussed, and explained and apologized for int he pages of the public Press." Another warned the editor that "sodomy is not only an offence against the law of God and this country, but the natural law itself," and that "if you continue to espouse this wickedness I shall not be the only one of your regular readers to recoil from your paper with disgust" (Birch *et al.* 1955). Today such cries of offended modesty would scarcely reach the office of a journal with a readership of any sophistication, and if they did, would be promptly filed in the waste-basket. But the exact mean of public opinion in 1993 would likely be uncertainty if not sheer bewilderment–scarcely an appropriate starting point for sound legal doctrine. One cannot derive a known from an unknown, nor wisely erect an edifice on shifting sands.

Elwood cited (pp. 758-59) a most interesting case, *Diaz* v. *Oakland Tribune, Inc.* (188 Cal. Rptr. 762 [Ct. App. 1983]). It "involved a newspaper columnist's revelation that Toni Diaz, the first female student body president of a California college, was a transsexual. Diaz contended that, as a result of the publication, she became depressed and suffered insomnia, nightmares, and memory lapses." The court held that because Diaz had kept the operation "secret from all but her immediate family and closest friends," her sexual identity belonged in the private realm. "Though Diaz was involved in a public controversy (she had charged the college administration with misuse of student funds), the court found the disclosure of Diaz's transsexuality to be irrelevant to this matter and thus unnewsworthy." The "tenor of the article" made it clear that its motive was pure sensationalism. Apart from the fact that for better or worse, the transsexualizing operation is not criminal, and to boot there now also exists a transsexual community concerned with its public image, political outings have no such motive: they cannot be dismissed as mere yellow journalism, even if articles in supermarket tabloids do sadly merit that label.

All four articles cited the first outing case to go to trial, *Sipple* v. *Chronicle Publishing Co.* (201 Cal. Rptr. 665 [Ct. App. 19984]), which we have discussed earlier (pp. 127-128). The San Francisco County Superior Court's summary judgment for the newspaper was upheld by the appellate court on two grounds. Sipple's sexual proclivities were well known to "hundreds of people in a variety of cities." The facts disclosed were newsworthy in that the "legitimate political consideration" for publicizing them was to destroy the stereotype of the "timid, weak and unheroic" homosexual (shades of the Old Norse *argr* and Anglo-Saxon *bædling*) and to highlight the president's own political biases–his refusal to invite Sipple to the White House because the ex-Marine was gay. Last of all, the publication of such a story in San Francisco, the "gay capital" of the nation, was not "so offensive . . . as to shock the community notions of decency." Pollack observed rightly that "such unwarranted intrusion into the details of a person's private life may well have a chilling effect on the willingness of citizens to involve themselves in community activities . . . to speak to the media, or attend political rallies," but this inhibition applies in some degree to all who lead double lives. Wick concluded that "the facts in *Sipple* . . . were so unfavorable to the plaintiff that it is hardly dispositive as to whether other plaintiffs could maintain a cause of action for outing . . . . Few other plaintiffs . . . will be celebrities by an act of physical bravery so blatantly adverse to heterosexist stereotypes." In fact, a presumptive case will rather turn on the outee's blatant moral cowardice and hypocrisy (Elwood 1992, pp. 757-58; Grant 1991, pp. 128-29; Pollack 992, pp. 741-43; Wick 1991, pp. 420-21).

Seeking to resolve the problem of outing, the legal mind loses its way in the maze of contradictions created by the criss-crossing of traditional norms with an ideological impasse for which the common law world knows no precedent. Th e legal and social situation of lovers of their own sex had in the past scarcely any better parallel than that of the Recusants"-secret Catholics in Elizabethan England, a matter long ago relegated to the archives. As argued earlier (p. 251), the theological reasoning that stigmatizes sodomy as a sin and a crime admits of no privacy. From this standpoint, the "protection of privacy rights" cannot be "a compelling state interest"'-in fact it is no interest at all. In strict logic, the private person cannot invoke the claim of privacy because "the Supreme Court decided whether the right of privacy extended to homosexuality in *Bowers* v. *Hardwick*, a case challenging the Georgia state statute criminalizing sodomy. Though recognizing the right to privacy, the majority held that homosexual activities did not fall within the purview of protected private, intimate relations. . . . Since the Court did not differentiate sexual orientation from homosexual activities, when faced with an 'outed' plaintiff, the court might have difficulty defining the contours of the private self that the press allegedly invaded" (Grant 1991, pp. 127-28).

The public figure or public official, on the other hand, cannot ask for the privilege of being protected in this one area where the banal fraud and deception by which he maintains his public image are compounded by the ciminality and infamy of his clandestine behavior. That image is always a persona maintained by consciously deceiving the outside world; any exposure of the figure's true self threatens and may in fact undermine it. Evidently the wearer of such a fictitious persona has a vested interest in upholding its credibility. But while a trade secret, let us say, a manufacturing process, withholds certain information from the public which is still able to buy the product so manufactured and derive whatever use or benefit it accords, what benefit do others derive from not knowing the homoerotic tendencies of a public figure? Leaving aside imaginary romances with movie stars, spurious heterosexuality confers no good whatever, unless society be held to have a legitimate interest in underpinning such a fiction. The bearer of the persona might claim that to perjure his sexual orientation is mandatory (and an obligation shared with accidental public persons and private persons), while his other forms of deception are, so to speak, professional and optional. But a juridical condemnation of outing would merely guarantee the right to practice both. The legal dilemma amounts therefore to a "conflict of fiction."

In proposing legal remedies for outing, our four lawyers are obliged to ignore crucial aspects of the phenomenon. "Courts may wish to dispense with the truth/falsity standard altogether and instead return to the older common-law notion of reputation. By only requiring a showing that the publication damaged the plaintiff's reputation, without questioning the publication's truthfulness, the plaintiff could succeed in a defamation suit, yet avoid the seemingly endless proof problems" (Grant 1991, p. 136). However, outing involves not just the subject's sexual orientation and behavior, but the discrepancy between that private behavior and his public acts or utterances that affect others having the same orientation. In other words, there is the charge of hypocrisy manifestly not present in the cases cited as precedents, which mainly concern unauthorized revelation of the names of sexual assault victims, with the further insinuation that the press disclosed them for their sensational "market value"'-in striking contrast to the political aims of the outer. Even if the plaintiff won his case against the outer, he would both magnify the public attention aroused by the revelations and compound his political hypocrisy and treachery.

Instructively enough, none of the legal theorists cites cases from the loyalty-security program of the 1950s, even though the charge of McCarthyism has been publicly leveled at Michelangelo Signorile and his imitators. But the junior senator from Wisconsin'-with the collusion of the media quoting his privileged utterances on the floor of the Senate–was allegedly exposing individuals who not merely sympathized with Communism but were actively "aiding and abetting the international Communist conspiracy." Outing is aimed at closeted homosexuals who turn their backs on the queer national cause or are actively betraying it. Once again, the political and cultural experiences of the Anglo-American world offers no precedent for the paradoxes that have shaped the current confrontation.

Not one of our legal authors is able to conceptualize the problem unique to outing: its challenge to the norm of obligatory heterosexuality. So long as this mandate was absolute, for both public figures and private persons an outward persona of exclusive heterosexuality was a virtual necessity. Self-disclosure would have incurred infamy of fact if not actual prosecution, would have led to a civil death. It is a significant fact that while Jews, heretics, prostitutes, lepers and other marginalized elements of late medieval society had their distinctive "signs of infamy" (Robert 1891), sodomites had none. They were not simply forced to the periphery of the sacral community of Christendom, they were utterly and irrevocably banished from it. Such a marking would in fact have defeated its own purpose. The Jew badge was instituted precisely in order to keep its wearers from having sexual intercourse with Christians, but a similar badge for sodomites would only have signaled their availability to one another– as the pink triangle and like symbols do today. The revelation of Oscar Wilde's departure from conventional morality, however ruinous it may have been to him, set in motion political processes that contributed to the homosexual rights movement: it gave lovers of their own sex the consciousness that they were not isolated sinners, but a persecuted minority in Western society. The pink triangle now worn as a badge of pride by gay activists stemmed not from the Middle Ages, but from the concentration camps of Nazi Germany. Not one of our four theorists is able or willing to argue that the moral order of society has a vested interest in the fiction of universal heterosexuality. Otherwise a court decision that held outing tortious would be tantamount to recognizing a public figure's right to maintain a heterosexual image by consciously and deliberately deceiving the public. To boot, the debate over outing echoes the clash between separtist and assimilationist tendencies within the queer nation, and this conflict is and remains a political one: no ruling of a court of law can hope to resolve it. To a certain extent the antagonism polarizes as well the differing ability of homosexual subjects to don a heterosexual persona.

In face of the dilemma posed by outing the common law tradition is helpless, stemming as it does from a centuries-long cumulative practice of balancing rights and obligations, of weighing personal freedom against public interest. "The First Amendment . . . has caused the Court to define the scope of privacy as a balance between the private attributes of an individual and whether those facts are of any public concern" (Grant 1991, p. 130). But no fine balance can be struck between the "right to privacy" of lovers of their own sex and the "public concern" spurred by the religious taboo on homosexual behavior. The secular concept of "homosexuality" is the dialectical negation of the sacral notion of "sodomy." The one is not a variant of the other, but its irreconcilable antithesis. No golden mean between the two can ever be reached, and by no feat of Hegelian reasoning can the two be "merged in a higher synthesis." The dictum that the sexual life of all persons—public figures, involuntary public figures, and private persons—is a private matter not to be revealed without express authorization fatally contradicts the Supreme Court's ruling in *Bowers* v. *Hardwick* that gives the states power not merely to intrude upon their private lives but even to prosecute all and sundry for consensual sodomy.

The solution is not to straddle the issue by manipulating legal definitions and precedents, not to accord a qualified license to fraud and hypocrisy, but to end the absurd pretense of universal heterosexuality for good and for all. When Western society acknowledges that bisexuality and homosexuality are biological and psychological realities, when it accepts that a certain percentage of all human beings love members of their own sex, when it abandons the paranoid beliefs instilled by "millennia of religious teaching," then outing will have no rime nor reason. The Supreme Court would be well advised to pursue that enlightened goal by ruling, in Elwood's formulation (p. 776), that in both criminal and civil law "all persons, famous and obscure, are private persons for purposes of their sexuality." Such a decision would let the legal problem escape from the maze of contradictions and vanish into the light of truth.

REFERENCES

"Biological Homosexual." 1955. "Homosexuality." *Spectator* 194: 37-38.

Birch, A. N. B., W. J., and C. Paxman Tiptaft. 1955. Letters to the Editor. *Spectator* 194: 68-69

Elwood, John P. 1992. "Outing, Privacy, and the First Amendment." *Yale Law Journal* 102: 747-776.

Grant, Jon E. 1991. " 'Outing,' Privacy, and Freedom of the Press: Sexual Orientation's Challenge to the Supreme Court's Categorical Jurisprudence." *Cornell Law Review* 77: 103-141.

Pollack, David, H. 1992. "Forced out of the Closet: Sexual Orientation and the Legal Dilemma of 'Outing'." *University of Miami Law Review* 46: 711-750.

Robert, Ulysse. 1891. *Les signes d'infamie au Moyen âge: Juifs, Sarrasins, hérétiques, lépreux, Cagots et filles publiques.* Paris: Honoré Champion.

Wick, Ronald F. 1991. "Out of the Closet and Into the Headlines: 'Outing' and the Private Facts Tort." *Georgetown Law Journal* 80: 413-433.

Index

AIDS Memorial Quilt, 85
Alcibiade fanciullo a scola, 44
Aletrino, Arnold, 57
Alexander the Great, 232
Alegro, John and Adele, 4
Aloisia Sigea (Chorier), 44
American Bar Association Model
    Penal Code, 72
American Civil Liberties Union,
    76,108,129
American Gay Arts Festival, First,
    151
American left
    J. Edgar Hoover opinion of, 86
    self-deception of, 112-113,255,270
American Psychiatric Association,
    15,116
American Psychological Association,
    15,211
American right, homophobia as
    unifying theme of, 67-68
American Speech, 4
"amour socratique", 12
And the Band Played On (Shilts),
    138
Anderson, Benedict, 268
Anderson, Jack, 197
Anderson, Sumner E., 159
androphilia, first writings on, 50
Anne, Queen of Great Britain and
    Ireland, 63
Anselm, Saint, 42
archives, homosexual, 230. *See also*
    International Gay and
    Lesbian Archives
Arena, Franca, and sons, 214,215
Arendt, Hannah, 141,261
Argentina, military policies, 205
Aristophanes myth in Plato's
    Symposium, source of, 35
Aristotle, 33-34
    opinion falsified by Thomas
    Aquinas, 39
Arvin, Newton, 100
asceticism. *See* sexual asceticism

assimilation
    forced, of homosexuals, 27-29,39,
    77,261,272,300
    rejection of, 174,300
    of Jews, 261,265
      comparisons with homosexuals,
      271-272
Atlanta Constitution, 4
Augustine, Saint, 37,42
Australia
    AIDS organizations, 215,216,217
    military policies, 205
    outing in, and condemnations of,
    213-215
Austria, military policies, 206
Autobiography (Cellini), 44

Bacchus, Saint, 42
Baden-Powell, Sir Robert, 64
baedling, 12
Bailey, Derrick Sherwin, 72,102-103
Bakker, Jim and Tammy, 162
Baldwin, James, 150
Baptists, 166
    Southern, 28
Barber, Samuel, 147
bardache, 12
Barnett, Marilyn, 151-152
Bartel, Paul, 149-150
Basic Instinct (film), 203
Bauman, Robert E., 154-156,235
Bayle, Pierre, 45-46
Bazzi, Giovanni Antonio Il Sodoma,
    44
Belgium
    age-of-consent laws, 212
    military policy, 206
Ben-Shalom, Miriam, 208
Benkert, Karl Maria. *See* Kertbeny,
    Károly Mária
Bentham, Jeremy, principles of, 46,
    47,246,294
    criticisms of, 254-255
Berg, Vernon "Copy" III, 123